The **Princeton** Review®

Cracking the

SAT

Subject Test™

in Math 1

2nd Edition

The Staff of The Princeton Review

PrincetonReview.com

Penguin
Random
House

The Princeton Review
555 W. 18th Street
New York, NY 10011
Email: editorialsupport@review.com

Published in the United States by Penguin Random House LLC, New York, and in Canada by Random House of Canada, a division of Penguin Random House Ltd., Toronto.

Terms of Service: The Princeton Review Online Companion Tools ("Student Tools") for retail books are available for only the two most recent editions of that book. Student Tools may be activated only twice per eligible book purchased for two consecutive 12-month periods, for a total of 24 months of access. Activation of Student Tools more than twice per book is in direct violation of these Terms of Service and may result in discontinuation of access to Student Tools Services.

ISBN: 978-1-5247-1079-8
eBook ISBN: 978-1-5247-1095-8
ISSN: 2374-1236

SAT Subject Tests is a trademark of the College Board, which is not affiliated with The Princeton Review.

The Princeton Review is not affiliated with Princeton University.

Editor: Aaron Riccio
Production Artist: Deborah A. Silvestrini
Production Editors: Liz Rutzel and Harmony Quiroz

Printed in the United States of America on partially recycled paper.

10 9 8 7 6 5 4 3 2

2nd Edition

Editorial
Rob Franek, Editor-in-Chief
Casey Cornelius, VP Content Development
Mary Beth Garrick, Director of Production
Selena Coppock, Managing Editor
Meave Shelton, Senior Editor
Colleen Day, Editor
Sarah Litt, Editor
Aaron Riccio, Editor
Orion McBean, Associate Editor

Penguin Random House Publishing Team
Tom Russell, VP, Publisher
Alison Stoltzfus, Publishing Director
Jake Eldred, Associate Managing Editor
Ellen Reed, Production Manager
Suzanne Lee, Designer

Acknowledgments

Special thanks to Christina Becker for her tremendous effort to develop the new content in this edition. Thanks also to Jonathan Chiu, National ACT & SAT Content Director, for his contributions to this title, and to those who have worked on this book in the past. Our gratitude as well to the stellar production team of Deborah A. Silvestrini, Liz Rutzel, and Harmony Quiroz: they literally make this book look good.

Special thanks to Adam Robinson, who conceived of and perfected the Joe Bloggs approach to standardized tests, and many other techniques in the book.

Contents

Get More (Free) Content

1   Go to **PrincetonReview.com/cracking.**

2   Enter the following ISBN for your book: 9781524710798.

3   Answer a few simple questions to set up an exclusive Princeton Review account. (If you already have one, you can just log in.)

4   Click the "Student Tools" button, also found under "My Account" from the top toolbar. You're all set to access your bonus content!

Need to report a potential **content** issue?

Contact **EditorialSupport@review.com**.
Include:

- full title of the book
- ISBN number
- page number

Need to report a **technical** issue?

Contact **TPRStudentTech@review.com** and provide:

- your full name
- email address used to register the book
- full book title and ISBN
- computer OS (Mac/PC) and browser (Firefox, Safari, etc.)

Once you've registered, you can...

- Access a third Math 1 practice test

- Take a full-length practice SAT, and/or ACT

- Get valuable advice about the college application process, including tips for writing a great essay and where to apply for financial aid

- If you're still choosing between colleges, use our searchable rankings of *The Best 382 Colleges* to find out more information about your dream school

- Access comprehensive study guides and a variety of printable resources, including bubble sheets, score conversion tables, and chapter summary pages

- Check to see if there have been any corrections or updates to this edition

- Get our take on any recent or pending updates to the SAT Subject Test in Math 1

Look For These Icons Throughout The Book

- ONLINE ARTICLES
- ONLINE PRACTICE TESTS
- PROVEN TECHNIQUES
- APPLIED STRATEGIES
- STUDY BREAK
- MORE GREAT BOOKS

Part I
Orientation

Chapter 1
Introduction

Welcome to the world of the SAT Subject Test in Math 1! This chapter will help you get familiar with this book and show you how to use it most effectively. We will also talk about when to take a Math Subject Test and which level is right for you. If you're sitting in the bookstore right now trying to decide whether to take Math Level 1 or Level 2, skip to the section titled "Which Test Should I Take?" on page 5). Let's get started!

WHAT ARE THE MATH SUBJECT TESTS?

The Math Subject Tests are standardized tests in mathematics. Colleges use these tests to assist in admissions decisions and to place incoming students in classes at the right level. The Subject Tests are written by ETS, a company in the business of writing tests like these. ETS makes money by charging students to take the SAT and SAT Subject Tests, and charging again to send the scores to colleges. You'll also run into ETS exams if you ever apply to graduate school.

Each SAT Subject Test in Math, whether it's Level 1 or Level 2, has 50 multiple-choice questions and is one hour long. The tests are scored from 200 to 800 points. Math Level 1 and Math Level 2 test a range of mathematical topics, from basic algebra to trigonometry to statistics. There is substantial overlap between the subjects of the two tests, but they are nevertheless very different.

Many colleges require some SAT Subject Tests (frequently two, but occasionally one or three). The subjects available are varied: two in mathematics, three in science, two in history, one in English, and twelve in foreign languages. Different schools have different preferences and requirements for which tests to take, too. For example, an engineering program may want to see the Math Level 2 and a science. Check each school's website to determine how many tests you must take and which ones (if any) are preferred.

What's on These Tests?

The content of each Mathematics test is approximately as follows:

Topic	Math Level 1	Math Level 2
Functions	6 questions	12 questions
Trigonometry	4 questions	10 questions
Algebra	15 questions	9 questions
Plane Geometry	10 questions	0 questions
Coordinate Geometry	5 questions	6 questions
Solid Geometry	3 questions	3 questions
Statistics	4 questions	4 questions
Miscellaneous	3 questions	6 questions
TOTAL	50 questions	50 questions

The Math Level 1 focuses on Algebra I, Geometry, and Algebra II, while the Math Level 2 focuses on Geometry, Algebra II, and Precalculus. The tests overlap, but the Math Level 2 tests more advanced material, and it tests basic material in greater depth.

For example, while both tests cover trigonometry, the SAT Subject Test in Math 2 has more than twice as many questions on trigonometry, so it asks about many more different trigonometry topics than the SAT Subject Test in Math 1 does. Similarly, Math 2 rarely tests geometry except in the coordinate plane or in three dimensions, so that it can combine a geometry question (say, about triangles) with a *xy*-plane question (say, about slope).

Don't worry if you don't recognize some of the topic headings. Students taking the SAT Subject Tests in Math are not expected to have spent time on every one of these topics in school. What's more, you can do quite well on these tests even if you haven't studied *everything* on them.

Which Test Should I Take?

Taking the SAT Subject Test in Math 1 is a fine idea for most students applying to more selective schools. You should base that decision on the admission requirements of the schools that interest you. The SAT Subject Test in Math 2, on the other hand, is not for just anyone—it's a much harder test. The great majority of students who take one of these tests choose to take Math 1.

Math 2 is appropriate for high school students who have had a year of trigonometry or precalculus and have done well in the class. You should also be comfortable using a scientific or graphing calculator. If you hate math, do poorly on math tests, or have not yet studied Trigonometry or Precalculus, Math 2 is probably not for you. It's worth noting, however, that while this test is difficult, the test is scored on a comparatively generous curve. If you find yourself making random (or "silly") mistakes more than anything else, this test's scoring grid may work in your favor.

Colleges also receive your percentile (comparing you to other test takers), as well as your scaled (200–800) score. For the most part, they pay attention to the scaled score and ignore the percentile. However, to the small extent that percentiles matter, Math 1 has considerably more forgiving percentiles. People who take Math 2 are generally really good at math; about 13% of them get a perfect score! Fewer than 1% of Math 1 test-takers get a perfect score, though. As a result, a 790 in Math 2 is only in the 85th percentile (about 13% get an 800 and 2% get a 790), while a 790 in Math 1 is still in the 99th percentile. This disparity between the percentiles continues down the entire score range.

If you are very unsure about which test to take, even after working practice questions and taking practice tests, you can take both tests.

WHEN SHOULD I TAKE A MATH SUBJECT TEST?

The right time to take the SAT Subject Test in Math 1 varies from person to person. Many students take this test at the end of a Precalculus class in school. (Precalculus also goes by many other names, such as Trigonometry, Advanced Functions, or other, less recognizable names.) A few students take Math 1 immediately after taking Algebra II, especially if they will not take another math class in high school. Such timing must be chosen with caution, however, because students who have not taken Precalculus may not yet have been exposed to all of the topics that can appear on the test.

The SAT Subject Test in Math 1 is offered six times a year. The six dates are always the same dates as the SAT Reasoning test, so you CANNOT take both the "regular" SAT and the SAT Subject Test in Math 1 on the same day. This means that if you plan on taking the SAT, you need to plan ahead in order to meet application deadlines. You can, however, take up to three subject tests (or up to 2 if you take a foreign language with listening test in November) in one day. For most subject tests, the most popular test dates are in May and June, because they are at the end of the school year and the material is freshest in the student's mind. Whenever you choose to take the test, make sure you have time to do some practice beforehand, so you can do your best (and not have to take the thing again!).

The Calculator

The SAT Subject Test in Math 1 is designed to be taken with the aid of a calculator. Students taking this test should have a scientific or graphing calculator and know how to use it. A "scientific" calculator is one that has keys for the following functions:

- the values of π and e
- square roots
- exponents (beyond squaring)
- sine, cosine, and tangent
- logarithms (base-10 and natural)

Calculators without these functions will not be as useful. Graphing calculators are allowed on the SAT Subject Test in Math 1. The graphing features on a graphing calculator are helpful on a fairly small number of questions on the SAT Subject Test in Math 1, and they are necessary for at most one question per test. If you're going to take a graphing calculator to the test, make sure you know how to use it. Fumbling over your calculator trying to figure something out during the test is just not a productive use of your time!

This book is going to focus on the TI-84. If you have another family member of the TI-80 series, know that these comments still apply to you with minor adjustments. Check with your manual for specific key stroke changes. If you have a scientific calculator, we'll be showing you your key stroke changes in the sidebars throughout the manual.

The ETS Predictor
ETS says that for the SAT Subject Test in Math 1, a calculator is useful or necessary for about 40–50 percent of the questions.

Certain kinds of calculators are not allowed. For example, a calculator with a QWERTY keyboard (like a computer keyboard) is not allowed. Your calculator must not require a wall outlet for power and must not make noise or produce paper printouts. There will be no replacements at the test center for malfunctioning or forgotten calculators, though you're welcome to take a spare, as well as spare batteries. Laptops, tablets, and cell phones are also not allowed to be used as calculators. To ensure that your calculator is allowed, visit collegeboard.org and read the day-of-test information for the Subject Tests.

Bottom line: You need a calculator for this test, but it doesn't have to be fancy. A $10 scientific calculator is certainly good enough.

HOW TO USE THIS BOOK

It's best to work through the chapters of this book in sequence, since the later chapters build on the techniques introduced in earlier chapters. If you want an overall review of the material on the SAT Subject Test in Math 1 just start at the beginning and cruise through to the end. If you feel a little shaky in certain areas of math and want to review specific topics, the chapter headings and subheadings will also allow you to zero in on your own problem topics. As with any subject, pay particular attention to the math topics you don't like—otherwise, those are the ones that will burn you on the real test.

If you really want to get the most out of this book and nail the test, you'll follow this study plan:

- Take the diagnostic full-length practice test that appears in Part II.
- Score your test and review it to see where your strengths and weaknesses lie.
- Focus on the chapters associated with the questions that you got wrong or didn't understand.
- Read through each lesson carefully until you feel that you understand it.
- Try the questions on your own before moving on to the "Here's How to Crack It" explanations that follow.
- Complete the drill at the end of the section.
- Check your answers and review any questions you got wrong until you understand your mistakes.

Study Guide
In your free online student tools, you'll find a printable copy of two different study guides that you can use to plot out your progress through this book.

- Complete the comprehensive drill at the end of the chapter. As with the in-chapter drills, check your answers and review the explanations. If you're still struggling, review the relevant section of the chapter.
- Take the final in-book full-length practice test. Score and review it.

This book focuses on what you need to know in order to succeed on the SAT Subject Test in Math 1. Many of these topics are far deeper than what you'll see here, but that's because ETS only wants you to know so much. If you understand the practice questions you'll find in this book, you'll be ready to succeed on the day of the test!

Need More?
You can visit CollegeBoard.org for more information and some practice questions. You can also go to PrincetonReview.com and find out more about Subject Tests, the SAT and ACT, and applying to college! Also, don't forget to register your book online for access to a third full-length practice test!

Chapter 2
Strategy

It's easy to get the impression that the only way to do well on the SAT Subject Test in Math 1 is to become a master of a huge number of math topics. However, there are many effective strategies that you can use. From Pacing and Process of Elimination to how to use your calculator, this chapter takes you through the most important general strategies, so you can start practicing them right away.

CRACKING THE SAT SUBJECT TEST IN MATH 1

While it's true that you have to know some math to do well on the SAT Subject Test in Math 1, there's a great deal you can do to improve your score without staring into math books until you go blind.

Several important strategies will help you increase your scoring power.

- The questions on the SAT Subject Test in Math 1 are arranged in order of difficulty. You can think of a test as being divided roughly into thirds, containing easy, medium, and difficult questions, in that order.
- The SAT Subject Test in Math 1 is a multiple-choice test. That means that every time you look at a question on the test, the correct answer is on the paper right in front of you.
- ETS writes incorrect answers on the SAT Subject Test in Math 1 by studying errors commonly made by students. These are common errors that you can learn to recognize.

The next few pages will introduce you to test-taking techniques that use these features of the SAT Subject Test in Math 1 to your advantage, which may help to increase your score. These strategies come in two basic types: Section strategies, which help you determine which questions to do and how much time to spend on them, and question strategies, which help you solve an individual question once you've chosen to do it.

SECTION STRATEGY

The following is a sample scoring grid for the SAT Subject Test in Math 1. The scoring grids vary somewhat from test to test, so this is just a general guide.

Raw Score	Scaled Score	Percentile	Raw Score	Scaled Score	Percentile
50	800	99	25	560	31
49	790	99	24	550	29
47–48	780	99	23	540	27
46	770	98	22	530	24
45	750	95	21	520	22
43–44	740	97	20	510	20
42	730	93	19	500	18
41	720	86	18	490	16
39–40	710	83	17	480	14
38	700	80	16	470	13
37	690	76	14–15	460	11
36	680	72	13	450	10
35	670	69	12	440	8
34	660	66	11	430	7
33	650	62	9–10	420	6
32	640	59	8	410	5
31	630	55	7	400	4
30	620	51	6	390	4
29	600	43	4–5	380	2
28	590	40	3	370	2
27	580	37	2	360	1
26	570	34	1	350	1

A few points to note:

- While it is theoretically possible to score less than a 350 on the test, to do so usually requires a negative raw score (getting more than 4 times as many questions wrong as right). In practice, the scale is from 350–800.
- On some test dates, some scores are not possible, such as 610 in the above grid.

Pacing

The first step to improving your performance on the SAT Subject Test in Math 1 is *slowing down.* That's right: You'll score better if you do fewer questions. It may sound strange, but it works. That's because the test-taking habits you've developed in high school are poorly suited to the SAT Subject Test in Math 1. It's a different kind of test.

Think about a free-response math test. If you work a question and get the wrong answer, but you do most of the question right, show your work, and make a mistake that lots of other students in the class make (so the grader can easily recognize it), you'll probably get partial credit. If you do the same thing on the SAT Subject Test in Math 1, you get one of the four wrong answers. But you don't get partial credit for choosing one of the listed wrong answers; you lose a quarter-point. That's the *opposite* of partial credit! Because this test gives the opposite of partial credit, accuracy is vitally important!

How Many Questions Should I Do?

Use the following chart to determine how many questions to attempt on your next SAT Subject Test in Math 1 Practice test.

On your last test, you scored:	On your next test, attempt:	If you get this many raw points...	You'll get a score near:
200–500	30	24	550
510–550	35	29	600
560–600	40	33	650
610–650	45	38	700
660–700	49	45	750
710–800	50	50	800

As you improve, your pacing goals will also get more aggressive. Once you take your next practice test and score it, come back to this chart and adjust your pacing accordingly. For example, if you initially scored a 550, but on your second test you scored a 610, then use the 610–650 line for your third test, and you may score a 700 (or even higher!).

Personal Order of Difficulty (POOD)

You probably noticed that the previous chart doesn't tell you *which* questions to do on the SAT Subject Test in Math 1, only how many. That's because students aren't all the same. Even if a certain question is easy for most students, if you don't know how to do it, it's hard for you. Conversely, if a question is hard for most students, but you know how to do it, it's easy for you. Analyzing your practice tests after you score them can help you determine what your strengths and weaknesses are. That being said, most of the time, you'll find lower-numbered questions easier and higher-numbered questions harder, but not always, so you should always listen to your POOD.

Develop a Pacing Plan

The following is an example of an aggressive pacing plan designed to maximize your score. You should begin by trying this plan, and then you should adapt it to your own needs.

First, do questions 1–20 in 20 minutes. They are mostly easy, and you should be able to do each one in about a minute. (As noted before, though, you must not go so quickly that you sacrifice accuracy.) If there is a question that looks more time-consuming, but you know how to do it, mark it so that you can come back to it later, but move on.

Second, pick and choose among questions 21–50. Do only questions that you are sure you can get right quickly. Mark questions that are more time-consuming (but you still know how to do them!) so that you can come back to them later. Cross out questions that you do not know how to do; there's no point wasting time on a question that you're likely to get wrong anyway.

Third, once you've seen every question on the test at least once and have gotten all the quick points that you can get, go back to the more time-consuming questions. Make good choices about which questions to do; at this point, you will be low on time and need to make realistic decisions about which questions you will be able to finish and which questions you should give up for lost.

This pacing plan takes advantage of the test's built-in order of difficulty and your POOD. You should move at a brisk but not breakneck pace through the easy questions so that you have enough time to get them right but not waste time. You should make sure that you get to the end of the test and evaluate every question, because you never know if you happen to know how to do question 50; it may be harder for most students than question 30, but it just may test a math topic that you remember very well from class (or this book).

Delaying more time-consuming questions until after you've gotten the quick and easy points maximizes your score and gives you a better sense of how much time you have left to spend on those longer questions. After some practice, it will take only a few seconds to recognize time-consuming questions.

QUESTION STRATEGY

It's true that the math on the SAT Subject Test in Math 1 gets difficult. But what exactly does that mean? Well, it *doesn't* mean that you'll be doing 20-step calculations, or huge, crazy exponential expansions that your calculator can't handle. Difficult questions on the SAT Subject Test in Math 1 require you to understand some slippery mathematical *concepts*, and sometimes to apply familiar math rules to unfamiliar situations.

This means that if you find yourself doing a long series of calculations, stop. There's a shortcut, and it probably involves using one of our techniques. In other words, your job is to recognize the opportunity to use one of The Princeton Review techniques to quickly and accurately solve the problem.

Process of Elimination (POE)

It's helpful that the SAT Subject Test in Math 1 contains only multiple-choice questions. After all, this means that eliminating four answers that cannot possibly be right is just as good as knowing the right answer. And on many questions, it's much easier to eliminate four wrong answers than it is to prove the right answer. Eliminating four answers and choosing the fifth is called the Process of Elimination (POE).

POE can also be helpful even when you can't get down to a single answer. Because of the way the test is scored (one raw point for a correct answer and minus a quarter point for an incorrect answer), if you can eliminate at least one answer, it may be to your advantage to guess.

When deciding whether to guess on a question, consider two things. First, consider whether you need this question to reach your pacing goal. Second, consider whether you are able to eliminate at least one incorrect answer. If you both need the question to meet your pacing goal and you are able to eliminate something, then it's to your advantage to guess. The more answers you can eliminate, the more likely your guess will pay off.

So, the bottom line:

> To increase your score on the SAT Subject Test in Math 1, eliminate wrong answers whenever possible, and guess aggressively when you need to answer a question to meet your pacing goals AND you are able to eliminate at least one answer.

There is a major elimination technique you should rely on as you move through the test: ballparking.

Ballparking

Sometimes, you can approximate an answer:

> You can eliminate answer choices by ballparking whenever you have a general idea of the correct answer. Answer choices that aren't even in the right ballpark can be crossed out.

Take a look at the following three questions. In each question, at least one answer choice can be eliminated by Ballparking. See whether you can make eliminations yourself. For now, don't worry about how to do these questions—just concentrate on eliminating answer choices.

21. If $x^{\frac{3}{5}} = 1.84$, then $x^2 =$

(A) -10.40
(B) -3.74
(C) 7.63
(D) 10.40
(E) 21.15

Here's How to Crack It

You may not have been sure how to work with that ugly fractional exponent. But if you realized that x^2 can't be negative, no matter what x is, then you could eliminate (A) and (B)—the negative answers, and then guess from the remaining answer choices. (In case you're curious the answer to this question is (C); we'll cover a couple of approaches to this question in Chapter 5.)

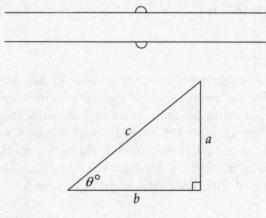

Figure 1

28. In Figure 1, if $c = 7$ and $\theta = 42°$, what is the value of a ?

(A) 0.3
(B) 1.2
(C) 4.7
(D) 5.2
(E) 6.0

Can I Trust The Figure?
To throw you off, sometimes ETS inserts figures that are deliberately inaccurate and misleading. When the figure is wrong, ETS will print underneath, "<u>Note</u>: Figure not drawn to scale." When you see this note, trust the text of the problem, but don't believe the figure, because the figure is just there to trick you.

Here's How to Crack It

Unless you're told otherwise, the figures that the SAT Subject Test in Math 1 gives you are drawn accurately, and you can use them to ballpark. In this example, even if you weren't sure how to apply trigonometric functions to the triangle, you could still ballpark based on the diagram provided. If *c* is 7, then *a* looks like, say, 5. That's not specific enough to let you decide between (C), (D), and (E), but you can eliminate (A) and (B) since they're not even close to 5. At the very least you're down to a 1-in-3 chance, which are much better odds! (The correct answer here is (C); check out Chapter 10 for more on Trigonometry.)

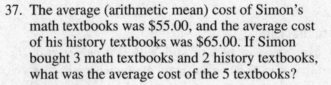

37. The average (arithmetic mean) cost of Simon's math textbooks was $55.00, and the average cost of his history textbooks was $65.00. If Simon bought 3 math textbooks and 2 history textbooks, what was the average cost of the 5 textbooks?

    (A) $57.00
    (B) $59.00
    (C) $60.00
    (D) $63.50
    (E) $67.00

Here's How to Crack It

Here, once again, you might not be sure how to relate all those averages. However, you could realize that the average value of a group can't be bigger than the value of the biggest member of the group, so you could eliminate (E). You might also realize that, since there are more $55 books than $65 books, the average must be closer to $55.00 than to $65.00, so you could eliminate (C) and (D). That gets you down to only two answer choices, a 50/50 chance. Those are excellent odds. (The correct answer here is (B). We'll discuss averages in Chapter 5.)

These are all fairly straightforward questions. By the time you've finished this book, you won't need to rely on Ballparking to answer them. However, Ballparking will work well when you're looking for the answer to a question you can't figure out using math.

"Better" Than Average

What makes a question hard? Sometimes a hard question tests more advanced material. For example, on the SAT Subject Test in Math 1, trigonometry questions are relatively rare before question 20, because ETS considers trigonometry to be an advanced topic. Sometimes a hard question simply requires more steps—four or five rather than one or two. Given the time constraints on the test, this can be an issue. More often, however, a hard question has trickier wording and better trap answers than an easy question.

ETS designs its test around certain trends and traps, looking to catch the average student with the sort of tricks and problems that have tripped test-takers up in the past. While this does mean that you'll have to be alert, it also means that many of these questions have predictable wrong answers, and you can use this knowledge to "beat" the curve. For example, when ETS writes a question that mentions "a number," ETS counts on students to think of numbers like 2 or 3, not numbers like −44.76 or 4π. Don't be led astray by these instincts; use them to your advantage.

The SAT Subject Test in Math 1 revolves around math that students have already learned, so to make sure that students get wrong answers, they offer traps: answers that are too good to be true. Whenever you see tempting oversimplifications, obvious answers to subtle questions, and all sorts of other answers that seem comforting and familiar, take a step back. Try eliminating these choices, and check or pick another one instead.

> ### Stop and Think
> Anytime you find an answer choice immediately appealing on a hard question, stop and think again. ETS collects data from thousands of students in trial tests before making a question a scored part of the SAT Subject Test in Math 1. If it looks that good to you, it probably looked good to many of the students taking the trial tests. That attractive answer choice is almost certainly a trap answer. The right answer won't be the answer most people would pick. On hard questions, obvious answers are wrong. Eliminate them.

---

43. Ramona cycles from her house to school at 15 miles per hour. Upon arriving, she realizes that it is Saturday and immediately cycles home at 25 miles per hour. If the entire round-trip takes her 32 minutes, then what is her average speed, in miles per hour, for the entire round-trip?

    (A) 17.0
    (B) 18.75
    (C) 20.0
    (D) 21.25
    (E) 22.0

Here's How to Crack It

This is a tricky problem, and you may not be sure how to solve it. You can, however, see that there's a very tempting answer among the answer choices. If someone goes somewhere at 15 mph and returns at 25 mph, then it seems reasonable that the average speed for the trip should be 20 mph. For question 43, however, that's far too obvious to be the correct answer. Eliminate (C).

You can use Ballparking to keep eliminating answers. Ramona is going to spend more time cycling to school than she spends cycling home, because she's going slower. Because she's spending more time cycling at 15 miles per hour than at 25 miles per hour, her average is going to be closer to 15 than 25; eliminate (D) and (E). Now you're down to two choices on a question 43 without doing much real math!

(Note: the answer is (B). Chapter 5 will cover how to do average speed problems.)

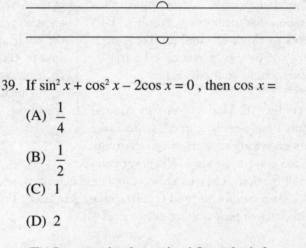

39. If $\sin^2 x + \cos^2 x - 2\cos x = 0$, then $\cos x =$

   (A) $\dfrac{1}{4}$

   (B) $\dfrac{1}{2}$

   (C) 1

   (D) 2

   (E) It cannot be determined from the information given

Here's How to Crack It

On a question like this one, you might have no idea how to go about finding the answer. That "It cannot be determined" answer choice may look awfully tempting. You can be sure, however, that (E) will look tempting to *many* students. It's too tempting to be right on a question this hard. You can eliminate (E). (The correct answer is (B). We'll cover trigonometric identities in Chapter 10.)

> Always look for traps whenever you're looking to eliminate answer choices, especially on hard questions!

SO DO I HAVE TO KNOW MATH AT ALL?

The techniques in this book will go a long way toward increasing your score, but there's a certain minimum amount of mathematical knowledge you'll need in order to do well on the SAT Subject Test in Math 1. We've collected the most important rules and formulas into lists. As you move through the book, you'll find these lists in the summaries at the end of each chapter.

The strategies in this chapter, and the techniques in the rest of this book, are powerful tools. They will make you a better test taker and improve your performance. Nevertheless, memorizing the formulas on our lists is as important as learning techniques. Memorize those rules and formulas, and make sure you understand them.

Using That Calculator

> Your calculator is only as smart as you are.

It's worth remembering. Some test takers have a dangerous tendency to rely too much on their calculators. They try to use them on every question and start punching numbers in even before they've finished reading a question. That's a good way to make a question take twice as long as it should.

The most important part of problem solving is done in your head. You need to read a question, decide which techniques will be helpful in answering it, and set up the question. Using a calculator before you really need to do so will keep you from seeing the shortcut solution to a problem.

Scientific or Graphing?
ETS says that the SAT Subject Test in Math 1 is designed with the assumption that most test takers have graphing calculators. ETS also says that a graphing calculator may give you an advantage on a handful of questions. If you have access to a graphing calculator and know how to use it, you may want to choose it instead of a scientific calculator. Remember, however, that at most one question on the test will require the use of the graphing capabilities of a graphing calculator.

When you do use your calculator, follow these simple procedures to avoid the most common calculator errors.

Set It Up!
Some questions on the SAT Subject Test in Math 1 can be answered without much calculation—the setup itself makes the answer clear. Remember: Figure out *how* to do the problem with your brain; then *do* the problem with your calculator.

- Check your calculator's operating manual to make sure that you know how to use *all* of your calculator's scientific functions (such as the exponent and trigonometric functions).
- Clear the calculator at the beginning of each problem to make sure it's not still holding information from a previous calculation.
- Whenever possible, do long calculations one step at a time. It makes errors easier to catch.
- Write out your work in your text booklet! ETS provides you with plenty of space, so do everything on the page. Label everything, and write down the steps in your solution after each calculation. That way, if you get stuck, you won't need to do the entire problem over again. Writing things down will also prevent you from making careless errors.
- Keep an eye on the answer choices to see if ETS has included a partial answer designed to tempt you away from the final answer. Eliminate it!

Above all, remember that your brain is your main problem-solving tool. Your calculator is useful only when you've figured out exactly what you need to do in order to solve a problem.

Part II
Diagnostic
Practice Test

Chapter 3
Practice Test 1

MATHEMATICS LEVEL 1

For each of the following problems, decide which is the BEST of the choices given. If the exact numerical value is not one of the choices, select the choice that best approximates this value. Then fill in the corresponding oval on the answer sheet.

Notes: (1) A scientific or graphing calculator will be necessary for answering some (but not all) of the questions on this test. For each question, you will have to decide whether or not you should use a calculator.

(2) The only angle measure used on this test is degree measure. Make sure that your calculator is in degree mode.

(3) Figures that accompany problems on this test are intended to provide information useful in solving the problems. They are drawn as accurately as possible EXCEPT when it is stated in a specific problem that its figure is not drawn to scale. All figures lie in a plane unless otherwise indicated.

(4) Unless otherwise specified, the domain of any function f is assumed to be the set of all real numbers x for which $f(x)$ is a real number. The range of f is assumed to be the set of all real numbers $f(x)$, where x is in the domain of f.

(5) Reference information that may be useful in answering the questions on this test can be found below.

THE FOLLOWING INFORMATION IS FOR YOUR REFERENCE IN ANSWERING SOME OF THE QUESTIONS ON THIS TEST.

Volume of a right circular cone with radius r and height h:

$$V = \frac{1}{3}\pi r^2 h$$

Volume of a sphere with radius r: $V = \frac{4}{3}\pi r^3$

Surface area of a sphere with radius r: $S = 4\pi r^2$

Volume of a pyramid with base area B and height h:

$$V = \frac{1}{3}Bh$$

---

1. If $9a - ab = 108$ and $9 - b = 4$, what is the value of a ?

    (A)   5
    (B)   12
    (C)   27
    (D)   36
    (E)   104

USE THIS SPACE FOR SCRATCHWORK.

2. Two distinct integers, a and b, are divided and the quotient $\dfrac{a}{b}$ is an even integer. Which of the following must be true?

    (A) Both integers are odd.
    (B) a is odd, b is even.
    (C) One of the integers is 2.
    (D) At least one of the integers is even.
    (E) Both integers are even.

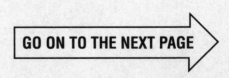
GO ON TO THE NEXT PAGE

3. If $x + y = 6$ and $2xy = 16$, then $x^2 + y^2 =$

(A) 12
(B) 20
(C) 22
(D) 36
(E) 64

USE THIS SPACE FOR SCRATCHWORK.

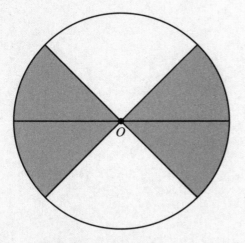

Note: Figure not drawn to scale.

4. In the figure above, the four shaded sectors of the circle with center O each have a central angle of 60 degrees. What fraction of the circle remains unshaded?

(A) $\dfrac{1}{6}$

(B) $\dfrac{1}{4}$

(C) $\dfrac{1}{3}$

(D) $\dfrac{2}{5}$

(E) $\dfrac{2}{3}$

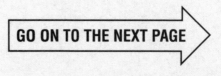
GO ON TO THE NEXT PAGE

MATHEMATICS LEVEL 1—*Continued*

5. Which of the following graphs shows a line with both a positive slope and a positive *x*-intercept?

USE THIS SPACE FOR SCRATCHWORK.

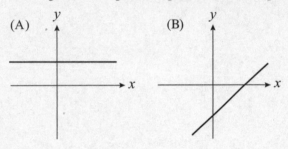

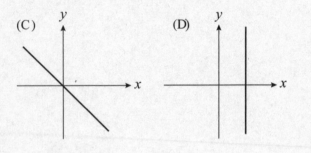

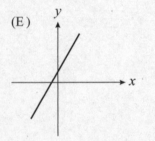

6. If $2y^2 + 16 = 25 + y^2$, what are all possible values of y ?

(A) 1 only
(B) 3 only
(C) −3 only
(D) −3 and 3 only
(E) 1, 3, and −3

7. If $k^{7x-6} = k^{9x+2}$ for all values of k where $k \neq 0$, what is the value of x ?

   (A) –4

   (B) –2

   (C) $\dfrac{1}{2}$

   (D) 2

   (E) 4

USE THIS SPACE FOR SCRATCHWORK.

8. Orders for coffee at the Foggy London Cafe have been dropping by 80 cups per week, and orders for tea have been rising by 120 cups per week. This week's receipts show 4,800 coffee orders and 1,200 tea orders. Which of the following equations could be used to calculate the number of weeks w until tea orders are equal to coffee orders at the Foggy London Cafe?

   (A) $1,200 - 80w = 4,800 + 120w$
   (B) $1,200 + 120w = 4,800 - 80w$
   (C) $4,800 - 120w = 1,200 - 80w$
   (D) $120 (w - 1,200) = 80 (w - 4,800)$
   (E) $12w + 8 = 48w - 12$

9. If $y = 10.2 - \sqrt[3]{x}$, for what value of x does $y = 9$?

   (A) –0.69
   (B) 1.06
   (C) 1.73
   (D) 2.08
   (E) 2.17

GO ON TO THE NEXT PAGE

10. A rectangular flower bed has an area of 81 square feet, and is 9 times as wide as it is long. What is the perimeter of the flower bed?

   (A) 27 ft
   (B) 30 ft
   (C) 36 ft
   (D) 60 ft
   (E) 108 ft

USE THIS SPACE FOR SCRATCHWORK.

11. The function S, where $S(t) = 63.158t + 200$, represents the correlation between likely test score $S(t)$ and the number of hours t that Astrid sleeps the night before her test. Based on this function, approximately how many hours did Astrid sleep the night before she scored a 720 ?

   (A) 1.1
   (B) 4.6
   (C) 8.2
   (D) 9.5
   (E) 14.6

12. Which of the following is equivalent to
$x^3 - 3x^2 - 2x + 9 = -2x^3 + 3x^2 - 1$?

   (A) $-x^3 - 2x + 8 = 0$
   (B) $3x^3 - 6x^2 - 2x + 10 = 0$
   (C) $3x^3 - 2x + 10 = 0$
   (D) $3x^6 - 6x^4 - 2x + 10 = 0$
   (E) $-x^6 - 2x + 8 = 0$

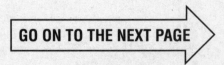

USE THIS SPACE FOR SCRATCHWORK.

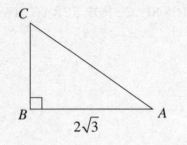

13. In right triangle *ABC* shown above, side

$AB = 2\sqrt{3}$ and $\cos A = \dfrac{\sqrt{3}}{2}$. What is the length

of side *AC* ?

(A) 1
(B) $\sqrt{3}$
(C) 2
(D) 4
(E) $4\sqrt{3}$

14. Which of the following numbers serves to
DISPROVE the statement "Every number which
is a factor of a prime number is itself a prime
number" ?

(A) 1
(B) 2
(C) 4
(D) 7
(E) 25

15. If $f(x) = \dfrac{x^2}{4 - 3x}$, what is the value of $f(-\dfrac{1}{2})$?

(A) $-\dfrac{2}{11}$

(B) $-\dfrac{1}{10}$

(C) $-\dfrac{1}{22}$

(D) $\dfrac{1}{22}$

(E) $\dfrac{1}{10}$

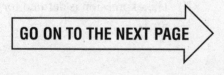

GO ON TO THE NEXT PAGE

16. Oakland is located 8.36 miles from San Francisco. On a scale map of the Bay Area, this distance is represented as 5.73 inches. If, on the same map, the distance from Menlo Park to Berkeley is represented as 20.07 inches, what is the actual distance in miles between Menlo Park and Berkeley?

    (A) 2.39
    (B) 13.76
    (C) 22.70
    (D) 27.83
    (E) 29.28

USE THIS SPACE FOR SCRATCHWORK.

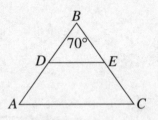

17. In triangle *ABC* shown above, $m\angle ABC = 70$, $AB \cong BC$, and points *D* and *E* are the midpoints of sides *AB* and *BC*, respectively. What is the sum of the degree measures of $\angle ADE$ and $\angle DEC$?

    (A)   55
    (B) 110
    (C) 140
    (D) 220
    (E) 250

18. For what value of *x*, if any, is $\dfrac{(3 + 2x)(x - 3)}{(3 + 2x)}$ undefined?

    (A) $-\dfrac{3}{2}$

    (B) $\dfrac{2}{3}$

    (C) $\dfrac{3}{2}$

    (D) 3

    (E) The expression is defined for all values of *x*.

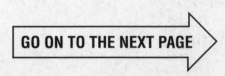

GO ON TO THE NEXT PAGE

19. A conservation team wishes to plant 600 new trees this year in local parks. With 6 months remaining in the year, the team is planning to raise the average number of trees planted per month to 72. After reviewing the plan, it is discovered that, even with the increase, the team will still fall short of its goal by 6 trees. What was the team's average number of trees planted per month during the first 6 months of the year?

(A) 22
(B) 27
(C) 28
(D) 162
(E) 432

USE THIS SPACE FOR SCRATCHWORK.

20. At what value of x does the graph of the linear equation $7y - 6x = -5$ cross the x-axis ?

(A) -5

(B) $-\dfrac{5}{6}$

(C) $-\dfrac{5}{7}$

(D) $\dfrac{5}{6}$

(E) $\dfrac{6}{7}$

GO ON TO THE NEXT PAGE

USE THIS SPACE FOR SCRATCHWORK.

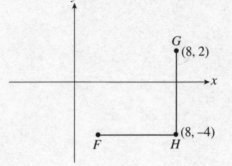

21. In the figure above, line segment *GH* is perpendicular to line segment *FH*. If points *F* and *G* are equidistant from point *H*, what is the approximate distance from point *F* to point *G* ?

    (A) 4.24
    (B) 6
    (C) 7.21
    (D) 8.49
    (E) 12

22. Six friends are playing a board game in which they each select one of six pieces: a rabbit, a clock, a dragon, a horse, a telephone, or a train. If Casey ALWAYS picks the dragon, in how many different arrangements can the pieces be selected by the six friends?

    (A) 5
    (B) 25
    (C) 36
    (D) 120
    (E) 720

23. In triangles *ABC* and *RST*, the measure of ∠*B* is equal to the measure of ∠*S*, and the measure of ∠*C* is equal to the measure of ∠*T*. If side *AC* = 5.7 and side *RT* = 17.1, what is the ratio of the perimeter of triangle *ABC* to the perimeter of triangle *RST* ?

(A) 1:27
(B) 1:9
(C) 1:3
(D) 1:2
(E) 3:1

USE THIS SPACE FOR SCRATCHWORK.

24. The graph of $3x - 5y = 15$ will be perpendicular to the graph of which of the following?

(A) $y = -\dfrac{5}{3}x + 10$

(B) $y = -\dfrac{3}{5}x - 3$

(C) $y = 3x - 5$

(D) $y = \dfrac{5}{3}x - 3$

(E) $y = \dfrac{3}{5}x + 15$

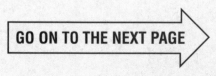
GO ON TO THE NEXT PAGE

USE THIS SPACE FOR SCRATCHWORK.

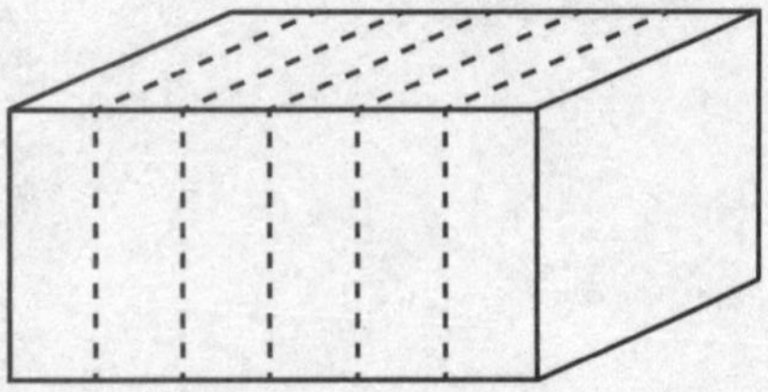

25. The rectangular prism shown above has all of its faces painted green, and is then cut vertically along the dotted lines into six congruent rectangular prisms. The new faces created by the cuts remain unpainted. What fraction of the faces of the six rectangular prisms are NOT painted green?

(A) $\dfrac{1}{6}$

(B) $\dfrac{5}{18}$

(C) $\dfrac{1}{3}$

(D) $\dfrac{2}{3}$

(E) $\dfrac{13}{18}$

GO ON TO THE NEXT PAGE

MATHEMATICS LEVEL 1—*Continued*

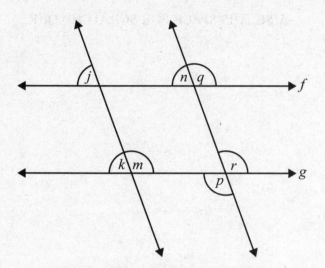

Note: Figure not drawn to scale

26. In the figure above, line *f* is parallel to line *g*. Which of the following must be true?

    (A) $\angle n \cong \angle k$
    (B) $m\angle n + m\angle r = 180$
    (C) $\angle j \cong \angle m$
    (D) $\angle m \cong \angle r$
    (E) $m\angle p + m\angle q = 180$

27. Maria is building a 45 foot long fence and has been completing approximately 4 feet of the fence every 12 hours. If Maria is able to increase her rate by 25 percent, approximately how many hours will it take her to build the remaining 29 feet of the fence?

    (A) 108
    (B) 69.6
    (C) 65.3
    (D) 49.7
    (E) 12.1

28. If $|m| - |n| < 0$, which of the following must be true?

    (A) $n^2 > m^2$
    (B) n is positive.
    (C) Both m and n are negative.
    (D) $n^3 > m^3$
    (E) $|m - n| < 0$

GO ON TO THE NEXT PAGE

29. In triangle *RST*, the measures of $\angle R$ and $\angle S$ sum to 90 degrees. Which of the following is equal to tan *R* ?

USE THIS SPACE FOR SCRATCHWORK.

(A) $\dfrac{RT}{RS}$

(B) $\dfrac{RT}{ST}$

(C) $\dfrac{ST}{RS}$

(D) $\dfrac{ST}{RT}$

(E) $\dfrac{RS}{ST}$

30. A magazine publisher has a fixed amount of monthly production costs. If, each month, he sells 600 copies of the magazine, his monthly profit is $4,800, and if he sells 450 copies, his monthly profit is $2,550. What are the publisher's monthly production costs?

(A) $2.33
(B) $15
(C) $2,250
(D) $4,200
(E) $9,000

31. A line segment in the *xy*-plane with endpoints (*x*, 4) and (2*x*, 10) has a midpoint located at (12, *x* – 1). What is the value of 2*x* ?

(A) 4
(B) 7
(C) 8
(D) 14
(E) 16

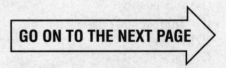
GO ON TO THE NEXT PAGE

USE THIS SPACE FOR SCRATCHWORK.

32. If $\frac{1}{2}$ of $\frac{1}{5}$ of a certain number is $\frac{2}{3}$ of $\frac{3}{5}$, what is the number?

(A) $\frac{1}{25}$

(B) $\frac{1}{15}$

(C) 1

(D) $\frac{9}{4}$

(E) 4

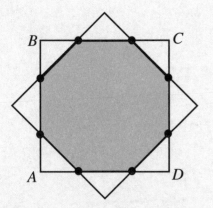

33. In the figure above, the sides of square *ABCD* are intersected by the sides of a second square, such that the intersection points divide the sides of square *ABCD* into equal thirds. What is the ratio of the shaded area to the area of square *ABCD* ?

(A) 2:9
(B) 7:9
(C) 9:7
(D) 7:4
(E) 7:2

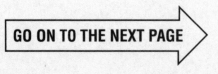

GO ON TO THE NEXT PAGE

34. Which of the following represents the domain of the function $f(x) = \dfrac{\sqrt{x+4}}{x-12}$?

    (A) $x > -4, x \neq 12$
    (B) $x < -4, x = 12$
    (C) $x > 12, x \neq 4$
    (D) $x > 0, x \neq 12$
    (E) $x > 4, x = -12$

USE THIS SPACE FOR SCRATCHWORK.

35. Which of the following is the graph of the solutions to the inequality $|m| + 3 \geq 5$?

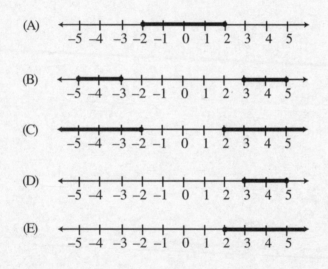

(A)

(B)

(C)

(D)

(E)

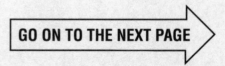

GO ON TO THE NEXT PAGE

USE THIS SPACE FOR SCRATCHWORK.

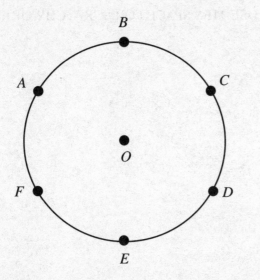

36. In the figure above, points A, B, C, D, E, and F are placed on Circle O such that the arcs between adjacent points are each equal to one-sixth of the circumference, and point O is the center of the circle. How many line segments can be drawn connecting any two labeled points such that the length of the segment is equal to the radius?

(A) 3
(B) 6
(C) 7
(D) 12
(E) 14

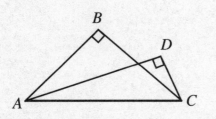

37. In the figure above, right triangle ABC has legs measuring 15 and x, and right triangle ADC has legs measuring 7 and $x + 4$. What is the length of segment AC?

(A) 20
(B) 22
(C) 24
(D) 25
(E) 30

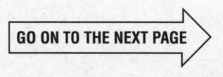

USE THIS SPACE FOR SCRATCHWORK.

Second Choice

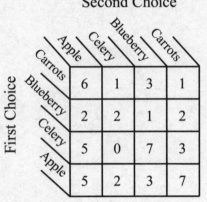

First Choice

	Apple	Celery	Blueberry	Carrots
Carrots	6	1	3	1
Blueberry	2	2	1	2
Celery	5	0	7	3
Apple	5	2	3	7

38. At snack time, students in a school can choose any 2 of 4 options: an apple, carrots, celery sticks, or blueberries. They may also choose the same item twice. The table above shows the results of 50 first grader's choices. If one of these students were selected at random, what is the probability that the student's second choice was fruit?

(A) $\frac{1}{10}$

(B) $\frac{11}{50}$

(C) $\frac{21}{50}$

(D) $\frac{12}{25}$

(E) $\frac{16}{25}$

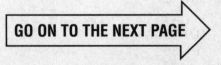

GO ON TO THE NEXT PAGE

USE THIS SPACE FOR SCRATCHWORK.

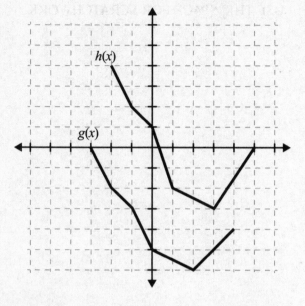

39. According to the graph above, for which of the following values of x does $g(h(x)) = 0$?

(A) –2
(B) –1
(C) 0
(D) 1
(E) 3

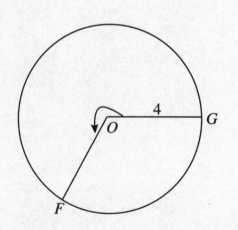

40. In Circle O shown above, major arc FG has length 16.76. What is the measure, in degrees, of the indicated angle?

(A) 120
(B) 135
(C) 240
(D) 270
(E) 300

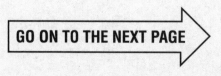
GO ON TO THE NEXT PAGE

$$(x + 3)^2 + (y + 1)^2 = 9$$
$$(x - 3)^2 + (y + 1)^2 = 9$$
$$(x)^2 + (y + 4)^2 = 9$$

USE THIS SPACE FOR SCRATCHWORK.

41. The system of equations above, when graphed in the xy-coordinate plane, yields three congruent circles. Which of the following is the solution set to this system of equations?

   (A) $(-3, -1), (3, 1), (0, -4)$
   (B) $(0, -1)$ only
   (C) $(0, -1), (-3, -4), (3, -4)$
   (D) $(3, 1), (-3, 1), (0, 1)$
   (E) $(0, 1), (3, 4), (-3, 4)$

42. A cube-shaped fish tank has a volume of m. If the tank is placed on a table, which of the following is an expression for the area of the table surface that the tank will occupy?

   (A) $\sqrt[3]{m^2}$

   (B) $2\sqrt[3]{m}$

   (C) $\dfrac{m^2}{9}$

   (D) $\dfrac{2m}{3}$

   (E) $4\sqrt{m}$

43. If a and b are integers, for how many values of a could the equation $y = (x + a)(x + b)$ have a y-intercept of 24 ?

   (A) 1
   (B) 4
   (C) 8
   (D) 16
   (E) 24

MATHEMATICS LEVEL 1—*Continued*

44. What is the sum of the hundreds, tens, and units digits of 5^{57} ?

    (A) 7
    (B) 8
    (C) 10
    (D) 13
    (E) 17

USE THIS SPACE FOR SCRATCHWORK.

45. Which of the following is an interval on which $f(x) = x^3 - 2x^2 - 5x + 2$ is decreasing?

    (A) $-1.68 < x < 0.36$
    (B) $-0.79 < x < 2.12$
    (C) $0.36 < x < 3.32$
    (D) $-1.68 < x < 3.32$
    (E) $2.12 < x < 3.32$

46. How many sides does a regular convex polygon have if the sum of any two of its exterior angles is 72 degrees?

    (A) 5
    (B) 8
    (C) 10
    (D) 12
    (E) 14

47. If the graph of $y = mx^2 + mx$ is shifted upward 2 units, it will yield a graph whose equation has exactly one real double root. What is the value of m ?

    (A) -8
    (B) -4
    (C) 4
    (D) 6
    (E) 8

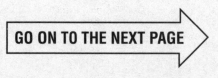

GO ON TO THE NEXT PAGE

48. If $1 - \cos^2 B = \sin B$, which of the following could be the value of $\sin B$?

    (A) -1
    (B) 0.707
    (C) 0.866
    (D) 1
    (E) 2

USE THIS SPACE FOR SCRATCHWORK.

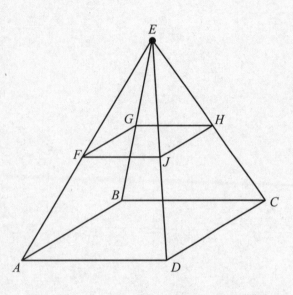

49. In the figure above, square pyramid *ABCDE* has a volume of 256 and a height of 12, and is similar to square pyramid *EFGHJ*, which has a volume of 32 and a height of 6. What is the approximate distance between the midpoint of *AF* and the midpoint of *CH* ?

    (A)   4.90
    (B)   6.00
    (C)   6.29
    (D)   8.49
    (E) 10.39

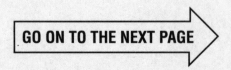

GO ON TO THE NEXT PAGE

50. If $f(x) = 2x^2 - 6x + 5$ and $g(x) = -x - 2$, which of the following is equal to $-f(-g(-x))$?

    (A) $2x^2 - 2x + 1$
    (B) $-2x^2 - 14x - 25$
    (C) $-2x^2 + 2x - 1$
    (D) $2x^2 + 14x + 25$
    (E) $2x^2 + 6x + 25$

USE THIS SPACE FOR SCRATCHWORK.

STOP

IF YOU FINISH BEFORE TIME IS CALLED, YOU MAY CHECK YOUR WORK ON THIS TEST ONLY.
DO NOT WORK ON ANY OTHER TEST IN THIS BOOK.

Chapter 4
Practice Test 1:
Answers and
Explanations

PRACTICE TEST 1 ANSWER KEY

Question Number	Correct Answer	Right	Wrong	Question Number	Correct Answer	Right	Wrong
1	C	——	——	26	B	——	——
2	D	——	——	27	B	——	——
3	B	——	——	28	A	——	——
4	C	——	——	29	D	——	——
5	B	——	——	30	D	——	——
6	D	——	——	31	E	——	——
7	A	——	——	32	E	——	——
8	B	——	——	33	B	——	——
9	C	——	——	34	A	——	——
10	D	——	——	35	C	——	——
11	C	——	——	36	D	——	——
12	B	——	——	37	D	——	——
13	D	——	——	38	E	——	——
14	A	——	——	39	E	——	——
15	D	——	——	40	C	——	——
16	E	——	——	41	B	——	——
17	E	——	——	42	A	——	——
18	A	——	——	43	D	——	——
19	B	——	——	44	B	——	——
20	D	——	——	45	B	——	——
21	D	——	——	46	C	——	——
22	D	——	——	47	E	——	——
23	C	——	——	48	D	——	——
24	A	——	——	49	D	——	——
25	B	——	——	50	C	——	——

PRACTICE TEST 1 EXPLANATIONS

1. **C** The question is asking for the value of a. Begin with the second equation and solve for b: $9 - b = 4$, $b = 5$. Next, plug the value of b into the first equation to solve for a: $9a - a(5) = 108$. Simplifying further yields $9a - 5a = 108$, $4a = 108$, and $a = 27$. The correct answer is (C).

2. **D** The question is asking which answer must be true. Since the question involves variables, Plugging In will aid in effective POE. Must Be questions usually involve plugging in multiple times, so be prepared to choose numbers that will help eliminate answers efficiently. Start with easy numbers for a and b that satisfy the restrictions: a and b are distinct and the quotient $\frac{a}{b}$ is an even integer. If $a = 4$ and $b = 2$, then the quotient is $\frac{4}{2} = 2$, an even integer, so all restrictions are satisfied. Check the answers and use POE. Both integers used are even, so (A) and (B) can be eliminated this round. Plugging in different numbers like $a = 6$ and $b = 3$ will help to test the descriptions in the remaining answers. In that case, the quotient is $\frac{6}{3} = 2$, so the restriction is met and (C) and (E) can be eliminated. Alternatively, knowing the properties associated with even and odd integers can help to tackle this question: even × (even or odd) = even, and odd × odd = odd. The correct answer is (D).

3. **B** The question is asking for the value of $x^2 + y^2$. Start by squaring both sides of the equation $x + y = 6$. This results in $x^2 + 2xy + y^2 = 36$. Use the provided equation of $2xy = 16$ to rewrite the quadratic as $x^2 + 16 + y^2 = 36$. Subtract 16 from both sides to arrive at the solution: $x^2 + y^2 = 20$. The correct answer is (B).

4. **C** The question is asking what fraction of the degrees in the circle are unshaded. A circle has 360° total. The provided circle is divided into six equal sectors, each measuring 60° at the central angle. There are two unshaded portions for a total degree measure of 60° + 60° = 120°. Divide this total by 360° to determine the final fraction: $\frac{120°}{360°} = \frac{1}{3}$. The correct answer is (C).

5. **B** The question is asking for the graph that contains a line with both a positive slope and a positive x-intercept. Use Bite-Sized Pieces to help with POE. Choices (A), (C), and (D) can be eliminated since the slopes are not positive. Choice (E) can be eliminated because the x-intercept is negative. The correct answer is (B).

6. **D** The question is asking for all possible values of y. Since the answer choices contain numbers, PITA is an effective technique. Let $y = 1$: $2(1)^2 + 16 = 25 + (1)^2$. Perform the arithmetic to arrive at $18 = 26$. This is untrue, so (A) and (E) can be eliminated. Let $y = 3$: $2(3)^2 + 16 = 25 + (3)^2$.

Simplifying both sides yields 18 + 16 = 25 + 9, or 34 = 34. This is a true statement, so (C) can be eliminated. Finally, let $y = -3$: $2(-3)^2 + 16 = 25 + (-3)^2$. Simplifying both sides yields 18 + 16 = 25 + 9, or 34 = 34. Eliminate (B). Alternatively, perform the algebra by combining like terms to solve for y: $2y^2 + 16 = 25 + y^2$, $y^2 = 9$, and $y = \pm3$. The correct answer is (D).

7. **A** The question is asking for the value of x. To solve an expression with bases raised to exponents containing variables, the bases need to be the same. Since both bases equal k, the exponents can be set equal: $7x - 6 = 9x + 2$. Combine like terms to solve for x: $-8 = 2x$, and $-4 = x$. Alternatively, PITA can be used since the answers are all possible values for x. The correct answer is (A).

8. **B** This question is asking for the equation that can be used to determine the number of weeks until tea orders are equal to coffee orders. Use Bite-Sized Pieces to translate statements in the word problem. For coffee orders, they have been dropping by 80 cups per week, and this week had 4,800 total orders. This can be set up as the equation $4{,}800 - 80w$. Choices (A), (C), (D), and (E) can all be eliminated. Alternatively, the answers contain the variable w, so Plugging In for the number of weeks is also an option. The correct answer is (B).

9. **C** The question is asking for the value of x when $y = 9$. Plug 9 in for y and solve for x: $9 = 10.2 - \sqrt[3]{x}$, $-1.2 = -\sqrt[3]{x}$, and $1.2 = \sqrt[3]{x}$. Solve for x by raising both sides to the third power: $(1.2)^3 = \left(\sqrt[3]{x}\right)^3$, and $1.728 = x$. Alternatively, PITA is an option since the answers are all possible values for x. The correct answer is (C).

10. **D** The question is asking for the perimeter of the rectangular flower bed. Begin with the area. The formula for area of a rectangle is $A = l \times w$. The width is nine times the length, so the width can equal $9x$ and the length can equal x. Plugging this into the formula, along with the provided area of 81 square feet, yields $81 = (x) \times (9x)$. Simplify to solve for x: $81 = 9x^2$, $9 = x^2$, and $3 = x$. Since the length is equal to 3, the width can be calculated as $9 \times 3 = 27$. The formula for perimeter of a rectangle is $P = 2l + 2w$, so plug in the values for length and width to answer the question: $P = 2(3) + 2(27) = 6 + 54 = 60$. The correct answer is (D).

11. **C** The question is asking for the number of hours slept to score a 720. Utilize the formula provided $S(t) = 63.158t + 200$, where $S(t)$ is the likely test score and t is the number of hours. The final score provided is 720, so plug this in for $S(t)$ to solve for t: $720 = 63.158t + 200$, $520 = 63.158t$, and $8.2 \approx t$. Alternatively, PITA is an option since the answers are all possible values for t. The correct answer is (C).

12. **B** The question is asking for the simplified form of the provided equation. Begin using Bite-Sized Pieces to combine like terms. Start with the terms raised to the third power: $x^3 + 2x^3 = 3x^3$. Choices (A), (D), and (E) can be eliminated. Next, $-3x^2 - 3x^2 = -6x^2$, and (C) can be eliminated. Alternatively, since the question and answers contain variables, Plugging In could be used. The correct answer is (B).

13. **D** The question is asking for the length of $\overline{AC}$. Since cosine = $\dfrac{adjacent}{hypotenuse}$, and $\cos A = \dfrac{\sqrt{3}}{2}$, it follows that the ratio of $\overline{AB}$ to $\overline{AC}$ must be $\sqrt{3}$ to 2 for all values. Given $\overline{AB} = 2\sqrt{3}$, set up a proportion to solve for $\overline{AC}$: $\dfrac{\sqrt{3}}{2} = \dfrac{2\sqrt{3}}{\overline{AC}}$. Cross-multiply to solve for $\overline{AC}$, or recognize that the numerators differ by a factor of 2: $(\sqrt{3})\,\overline{AC} = 4\sqrt{3}$, and $\overline{AC} = 4$. The correct answer is (D).

14. **A** The question is asking which number serves to disprove the statement *every number which is a factor of a prime number is itself a prime number*. Choices (C) and (E) can be eliminated, as 4 and 25 are not prime numbers. Out of the remaining answers, (B) and (D) are prime, but actually prove the statement correct since they themselves are prime numbers. 1 is a factor of all prime numbers, but since it only has one factor, not the required two factors to be prime, it is not a prime number and disproves the statement. The correct answer is (A).

15. **D** The question is asking for the value of $f\left(-\dfrac{1}{2}\right)$. To evaluate the function, plug $-\dfrac{1}{2}$ in for x and solve: $\dfrac{\left(-\dfrac{1}{2}\right)^2}{4 - 3\left(-\dfrac{1}{2}\right)} = \dfrac{\dfrac{1}{4}}{4 + \dfrac{3}{2}} = \dfrac{\dfrac{1}{4}}{\dfrac{11}{2}} = \dfrac{1}{4} \times \dfrac{2}{11} = \dfrac{2}{44} = \dfrac{1}{22}$. The correct answer is (D).

16. **E** The question is asking for the actual distance in miles between Menlo Park and Berkeley. The question provides the relationship that 8.36 miles is represented by 5.73 inches. Set up a proportion to determine the miles for 20.07 inches being sure to keep the same units on top and bottom: $\dfrac{8.36 \text{ miles}}{5.73 \text{ inches}} = \dfrac{x \text{ miles}}{20.07 \text{ inches}}$. Cross-multiply and solve for x: $(8.36)(20.07) = (5.73)(x)$, $167.7852 = 5.73x$, and 29.28188482 miles $= x$. The correct answer is (E).

17. **E** The question is asking for the sum of $\angle ADE$ and $\angle DEC$. Provided that $\overline{AB} \cong \overline{BC}$, it can be concluded that $\angle BAC$ and $\angle BCA$ are equal. Since there are 180° in a triangle, and $\angle ABC = 70°$, an equation can be set up to solve for the bottom two identical angles: $70° + \angle BAC + \angle BCA = 180°$, or $70° + x° + x° = 180°$. Combine like terms to solve for x: $70° + 2x = 180°$, $2x = 110°$, and $x = 55°$. Since points D and E are the midpoints of $\overline{AB}$ and $\overline{BC}$, respectively, it follows that $\angle BDE$ and $\angle BED$ must also equal 55°. To determine the measures of $\angle ADE$ and $\angle DEC$, utilize the property of a straight line having 180°: $55° + \angle ADE = 180°$, and $\angle ADE = 125°$. Solving in the exact same way for $\angle DEC$ yields $\angle DEC = 125°$. $\angle ADE + \angle DEC = 125° + 125° = 250°$. The correct answer is (E).

18. **A** The question is asking for which value of x the provided function is undefined. For a rational function to be undefined, a value of zero must occur in the denominator. It may be tempting to cancel out the common factor of $(3 + 2x)$ from both the numerator and denominator, but be sure to set the denominator equal to zero and solve for x first: $3 + 2x = 0$, $2x = -3$, and $x = -\dfrac{3}{2}$. The correct answer is (A).

19. **B** The question is asking for the team's average number of trees planted per month during the first 6 months of the year. The first thing to realize is the result, even with the increase of average number of trees planted, will fall short by 6 trees for an overall yield of $600 - 6 = 594$ trees planted. Since average $= \dfrac{total}{number\ of\ things}$, focus on the period of which more information is provided. In this case, the last six months. The average is planned to be 72 trees planted over the 6 months. Multiplying these two values together will provide the total number of trees to be planted of $72 \times 6 = 432$ trees. Knowing the total for the entire 12-month period and the total for the 6 months remaining in the year, the total for the 6 months that have passed, x, can now be determined: $594 = 432 + x$, and $x = 162$. Knowing the total for the 6 months means that the average can now be calculated: $\dfrac{162}{6} = 27$. The correct answer is (B).

20. **D** The question is asking for the x-coordinate of the x-intercept. Recall that the x-intercept occurs at the point $(x, 0)$. In the provided equation, let $y = 0$ and solve for x: $7(0) - 6x = -5$, $-6x = -5$, and $x = \dfrac{5}{6}$. Alternatively, PITA is an option given that $y = 0$ and the answers represent possible values for x. The correct answer is (D).

21. **D** The question is asking for the approximate distance from point F to point G. First, utilize the information provided in the figure to determine more information. In this case, points G and H are located at $(8, 2)$ and $(8, -4)$. Since point G lies directly above point H, the vertical distance can be calculated by subtracting the y-coordinates: $2 - (-4) = 6$. Since $\overline{GH}$ is equal to 6, and points F and G are equidistant from point H, it follows that $\overline{FH}$ must equal 6. The question states that $\overline{GH}$ is perpendicular to $\overline{FH}$, so it can be concluded that ΔFGH is an isosceles right triangle. From this point, either Pythagorean Theorem or properties of 45: 45: 90 right triangles can be utilized to determine the length of $\overline{FG}$. Using the ratio of side lengths for a 45: 45: 90 right triangle, $s: s: s\sqrt{2}$, the ratio becomes 6: 6: $6\sqrt{2}$, and the length of is $6\sqrt{2}$. The correct answer is (D).

22. **D** The question is asking for how many different arrangements, or orderings, that the pieces can be selected by the six friends. This is a permutation, that can be tackled either using the formula, or creating placeholders and assigning the total options to each place. Usually the latter tends to be the friendlier option, so create six places. The question states that *Casey always picks the dragon*. This restriction means that the first place can be Casey, and there is only one outcome that gets assigned to that placeholder. Moving to the second placeholder, this space could be any of the five remaining friends to select any of the five remaining pieces, so assign a 5. In the third place, one fewer piece is available for selection, so assign a 4. Repeating this process yields a 3 in the fourth place, a 2 in the fifth place, and a 1 in the sixth place. Multiply the possibilities together to find the total arrangements: $\underline{1} \times \underline{5} \times \underline{4} \times \underline{3} \times \underline{2} \times \underline{1} = 120$. The correct answer is (D).

23. **C** The question is asking for the ratio of the perimeter of $\triangle ABC$ to the perimeter of $\triangle RST$. Since the triangles are similar (same angle measurements), the side lengths of the two triangles are proportional to each other. To determine the value of the proportion, calculate $\dfrac{\overline{RT}}{\overline{AC}} : \dfrac{17.1}{5.7} = 3$. Knowing this, each side of $\triangle RST$ will be three times the corresponding side of $\triangle ABC$. It can be concluded that the perimeter of $\triangle RST$ will be three times the perimeter of $\triangle ABC$, resulting in a ratio of 1:3. Alternatively, values could be plugged in for the unknown side lengths to determine perimeter values, then arrive at the ratio. The correct answer is (C).

24. **A** The question is asking which equation would provide a graph perpendicular to $3x - 5y = 15$. To determine if two lines are perpendicular, the slopes need to be compared with the perpendicular line having a slope that is the negative reciprocal of the other line. To calculate the slope of a line in the form $Ax + By = C$, calculate $\dfrac{-A}{B}$. In the provided line, $A = 3$ and $B = -5$ and the slope is $\dfrac{-(3)}{(-5)} = \dfrac{3}{5}$. Get the perpendicular slope by taking the reciprocal and making it negative, $-\dfrac{5}{3}$. The answers are provided in the slope-intercept form of $y = mx + b$, where m represents the slope. Only one option has $-\dfrac{5}{3}$ as a slope. The correct answer is (A).

25. **B** The question is asking for the fraction of the faces of the six rectangular prisms that are NOT painted green. To determine the total number of faces, take the six faces on a rectangular prism and multiply that by the six total rectangular prisms: 6 faces × 6 prisms = 36 total faces. When the big rectangular prism is cut, the inner rectangular prisms will each have four painted faces and two larger unpainted faces. Each of the end prisms will have five painted sides and just one unpainted side. Add those values together to get the total number of unpainted sides: 1 + 2 + 2 + 2 + 2 + 1 = 10. Place 10 over the 36 total faces and reduce to get the answer: $\dfrac{10}{36} = \dfrac{5}{18}$. The correct answer is (B).

26. **B** The question is asking for the answer that must be true. Pay attention to the figure. Since it is NOT drawn to scale, rely on the facts provided by the question. In this case, line f is parallel to line g. When two parallel lines are cut by a diagonal, sets of equal angles are created. The only angles that will share a relationship will be grouped along the same diagonal line, so compare the answers to see what can be proven. Choice (A) says $\angle n \cong \angle k$, but as nothing is known about the respective diagonal lines, it cannot be proven that these two angles are equal. Eliminate (A). For (B), $m\angle n + m\angle r = 180°$, find the angles on the figure. They are both grouped along the same diagonal line, and n is a small angle, while r is a big angle. With parallel lines cut by a diagonal, any

big angle plus any small angle is equal to 180°, so keep (B) for now. Choices (C) and (D) can be eliminated for the same reasoning as (A). Choice (E), $m\angle p + m\angle q = 180°$, may look tempting at first, but both angles are big angles and do not sum up to 180°. Choice (E) can be eliminated. The correct answer is (B).

27. **B** The question is asking how many hours it will take Maria to build the remaining 29 feet of the fence. Begin by figuring out Maria's rate for the completed fence. She completes 4 feet of the fence every 12 hours, or $\dfrac{4}{12} = \dfrac{1}{3}$ = fence/hour. She increases her rate by 25%, or $\dfrac{1}{3} \times \dfrac{1}{4} = \dfrac{1}{12}$. Her new rate becomes $\dfrac{1}{3} + \dfrac{1}{12} = \dfrac{15}{36}$ fence/hour. Use the rate equation *distance* (or *work*) = *rate × time* to determine the number of hours it will take to complete the remaining 29 feet of fencing at the new rate of $\dfrac{15}{36}$ fence/hour: $29 = \dfrac{15}{36} \times time$. Solving for time yields $29 \times \dfrac{36}{15} = 69.6$ hours. The correct answer is (B).

28. **A** The question is asking for the answer that must be true based on the provided restriction. Since variables are contained in both the question and answer choices, Plugging In is an effective approach that will aid in POE. Be prepared to plug in more than once and choose numbers that will help to disprove answer choices. Start simple with $m = 2$ and $n = 3$: $|2| - |3| < 0$, so the restriction is met. Checking the answers with these numbers reveals that (C) and (E) can be eliminated this round. Two positive numbers were selected the first round, so this time try a positive and a negative, like $m = 1$ and $n = -2$. $|1| - |2| < 0$ qualifies the restriction so proceed to the answers. Choices (B) and (D) can now be eliminated. The correct answer is (A).

29. **D** The question is asking what is equal to tan R. Since $\angle R$ and $\angle S$ add up to 90°, and there are 180° in a triangle, it can be concluded that $\angle T$ must be a right angle, and RST is a right triangle. Draw the picture to label the sides:

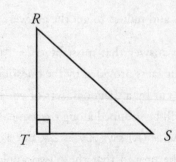

Since tangent = $\dfrac{opposite}{adjacent}$, it can be concluded that $R = \dfrac{\overline{ST}}{\overline{RT}}$. The correct answer is (D).

30. **D** The question is asking for the publisher's monthly production costs. Use Bite-Sized Pieces to create equations from the provided information. If the publisher sells 600 copies of the magazine, the monthly profit is $4,800. Since *profit = sales − costs*, an equation can be created as $4,800 = 600x − y$, where x represents the cost of each magazine and y represents the production costs. Using similar methodology yields a second equation of $2,550 = 450x − y$. Subtracting the second equation away from the first yields a result of $2,250 = 150x$, and $x = 15$. Plug this value for x into either equation to determine the production cost: $4,800 = 600(15) − y$, $4,800 = $9,000 − y$, and $y = $4,200$. The correct answer is (D).

31. **E** The question is asking for the value of $2x$. The midpoint of a line segment containing the points (x_1, y_1) and (x_2, y_2) is defined as $\left(\dfrac{x_1 + x_2}{2}, \dfrac{y_1 + y_2}{2}\right)$. Choose one set of coordinates and plug them into the formula to answer the question. Checking the x-coordinates yields $\dfrac{x + 2x}{2} = 12$. Multiply both sides by 2 then solve for x: $x + 2x = 24$, $3x = 24$, and $x = 8$. *Be careful!* The question is asking for $2x$: $2 \times 8 = 16$. The correct answer is (E).

32. **E** The question is asking for the number that satisfies the restriction. Translate using Bite-Sized Pieces to solve for the number. *If* $\dfrac{1}{2}$ *of* $\dfrac{1}{5}$ *of a certain number* translates to $\dfrac{1}{2} \times \dfrac{1}{5} \times n$ or $\dfrac{1}{10}n$. Next, *is* $\dfrac{2}{3}$ *of* $\dfrac{3}{5}$ translates to equals (=) $\dfrac{2}{3} \times \dfrac{3}{5}$, or $\dfrac{2}{5}$. Set the two translations equal to solve for n: $n = \dfrac{1}{10}n = \dfrac{2}{5}$. Multiply both sides by 10 to solve: $n = \dfrac{2}{5} \times 10$, and $n = 4$. The correct answer is (E).

33. **B** The question is asking for the ratio of the shaded area to the area of square *ABCD*. Ballparking can be a powerful tool for geometry questions in which the provided figure is drawn to scale. Looking at the square that contains the shaded portion, almost all of it is shaded except for the four triangular portions at the corners. Since the question mentions the square cuts the other into equal thirds, make each side 3, making each segment 1. Combining the unshaded portions yields two squares of dimensions 1 × 1 and there would be seven shaded squares of dimensions 1 × 1, resulting in a ratio of 7:9. Alternatively, plug in a length for the sides of square *ABCD* to make the math easy, like 3. The overlapping "diamond" creates congruent segments of 1 each. The area of square *ABCD* is *side*^{2} or $3^2 = 9$. Cut the "diamond" up into a rectangle in the middle with dimensions 3 × 1, resulting in an area of 3, then a square on top and bottom with four right triangles. The area of the square would be $1^2 = 1$, but since there are two, the total shaded area would be 1 × 2 = 2. The area of the right triangle can be calculated as $\dfrac{1}{2}bh$, or $\dfrac{1}{2}(1)(1) = \dfrac{1}{2}$. Since there are four right triangles, find

the total shaded area to be $\frac{1}{2} \times 4 = 2$. Add the calculated shaded areas to arrive at $3 + 2 + 2 = 7$.

The resulting ratio of shaded area to area of *ABCD* is 7:9. The correct answer is (B).

34. **A** The question is asking which choice expresses the domain of the provided function. Since the function provided is a rational function, check to see if the denominator equals zero for a value of x by setting the denominator equal to zero and solving: $x - 12 = 0$, and $x = 12$. Since $x = 12$ produces a zero in the denominator, $x \neq 12$, and (B), (C), and (E) can be eliminated. To figure out the domain restriction in the numerator, set the function under the radical greater than or equal to zero and isolate x: $x + 4 \geq 0$, and $x \geq -4$. The correct answer is (A).

35. **C** The question is asking for the number line representation of the provided inequality. Plugging in can be a powerful tool to help with POE on questions like these. If $m = 0$, then the inequality results in $3 \geq 5$, which is an untrue statement. Choice (A) can be eliminated, as it contains $m = 0$. Try another value like $m = -3$. This results in an inequality of $6 \geq 5$, which is a true statement. Choices (D) and (E) can be eliminated because they do not contain $m = -3$ in the shaded number lines. Choose $m = -2$ to distinguish between (B) and (C). This results in an inequality of $5 \geq 5$, which is true, and (B) can be eliminated for not including it. Alternatively, solving the absolute value inequality can provide the solution: $|m| + 3 \geq 5$, and $|m| \geq 2$. To solve this, apply both the negative and positive results remembering to flip the sign producing the two ranges of $m \geq 2$ and $m \leq -2$. The correct answer is (C).

36. **D** The question is asking for the total number of line segments able to be drawn that equate in length to that of the radius. Since the answer options are all small, starting at a point and counting may be the safest plan of attack, keeping in mind not to repeat line segments when counting. Start at point *A*. The lines that can be drawn to produce the same length as the radius would be segments $\overline{AF}$, $\overline{AO}$, and $\overline{AB}$, for a total of 3. Moving next to point *B*, the same approach would be taken, but do not count $\overline{AB}$ again. $\overline{BO}$ and $\overline{BC}$ yield 2 more line segments, as will points *C*, *D*, and *E* with the same process. Arriving at point *F*, remember that $\overline{AF}$ and $\overline{FE}$ were already counted, so only one more line segment, $\overline{FO}$, is created. Sum the line segments together to arrive at the total: $3 + 2 + 2 + 2 + 2 + 1 = 12$. The correct answer is (D).

37. **D** The question is asking for the length of line segment $\overline{AC}$. Find $\overline{AC}$ in the provided figure and recognize that it is the hypotenuse of both right triangles *ABC* and *ADC*. Since the right triangles share the same hypotenuse, use the provided side lengths in conjunction with the Pythagorean Theorem, $a^2 + b^2 = c^2$, to solve for a value of x by setting the two expressions equal to each other: $(15)^2 + (x)^2 = (7)^2 + (x + 4)^2$. Simplifying both sides yields $225 + x^2 = 49 + x^2 + 8x + 16$. Combine like terms to arrive at $160 = 8x$, and $20 = x$. *Be careful!* the question is asking for the length of the hypotenuse, so eliminate (A). Either triangle will produce the required result, so using *ABC* yields sides of 15, 20, and $\overline{AC}$. Either use Pythagorean Theorem again or recognize this is a multiple of the 3: 4: 5 Pythagorean triple and arrive at $\overline{AC} = 25$. The correct answer is (D).

38.   **E**   The question is asking for the probability that the student's second choice was a fruit option. Probability is defined as $\dfrac{favorable\ outcomes}{total\ outcomes}$, and since the question provides the overall total of 50 students, the denominator will be 50. To calculate the numerator, utilize the provided table of values and focus on the second choice. There are two fruit outcomes (apple and blueberry), so find the relevant values associated with the second choice being either of those. If the first choice was carrots, then there are 6 students who chose apple and 3 who chose blueberries, for a total of 9 students in the first row. Using the same approach, find the remaining favorable outcomes in the remaining rows: Blueberry first means 2 apple + 1 blueberry = 3 total, Celery first means 5 apple + 7 blueberry = 12 total, and Apple first means 5 apple + 3 blueberry = 8 total. Sum the individual totals found per row to get the numerator: 9 + 3 + 12 + 8 = 32. Since more than half of the students chose fruit for the second option, (A), (B), (C), and (D) could safely be eliminated now. Alternatively, plug the total of favorable outcomes and total into the probability formula and reduce, if necessary: $\dfrac{32}{50} = \dfrac{16}{25}$. The correct answer is (E).

39.   **E**   The question is asking which value of x results in the provided composite function producing a result of zero. Since the answers provided are numbers and represent possible values of x, PITA is a solid approach to help tackle this. Start with (C), $x = 0$. This results in $g(h(0))$. With composite functions, start from the inside and work outwards. Find $h(0)$ by referencing the provided graph. According to the graph, $h(0) = 1$. Next plug 1 into $g(x)$ and refer to the graph of g to find that $g(1) \approx -6.5$. This does not match the provided target of 0, so (C) can be eliminated. It may not be clear which direction to travel, so just move to an answer and repeat the process. In (D), $x = 1$. Repeating the process yields $h(1) = -2$, and $g(-2) = -2$. Eliminate (D) and check (E), $x = 3$. This yields $h(3) = -3$, and $g(-3) = 0$, which matches the target. Alternatively, visual inspection can also be utilized to tackle the question. Find where $g(x) = 0$. This occurs when $x = -3$. Next, find where $h(x) = -3$. This occurs where $x = 3$. The correct answer is (E).

40.   **C**   The question is asking for the degree measure of the angle that creates major arc $\overset{\frown}{FG}$. In circles, the interior angle is proportional to the arc length that is created. The property required here is $\dfrac{interior\ angle}{total\ degrees} = \dfrac{arc\ length}{circumference}$. Using the provided information, the proportion becomes $\dfrac{x°}{360°} = \dfrac{16.76}{2\pi(4)}$. Cross-multiply and simplify using a calculator to solve for x: $8\pi \times x = 360 \times 16.76$, and $x = \dfrac{360 \times 16.76}{8\pi} = 240.0693162$, which is closest to 240°. The correct answer is (C).

41. **B** The question is asking for the solution set to the system of equations provided. Since expanding and solving looks to be time-consuming and tedious, this question would be an ideal candidate for PITA since the answers contain the possible solutions. There's no order to the points provided, so just pick an ordered pair and check it in the equations. Start with (A) and use the point (3, 1). The first equation produces $((3) + 3)^2 + ((1) + 1)^2 = 9$. Simplify the left side to arrive at $36 + 4 = 9$, an untrue statement. Choices (A) and (D) can be eliminated, as they both contain this coordinate. In (B), plug (0, −1) in the first equation to see if it works: $((0) + 3)^2 + ((-1) + 1)^2 = 9$, which can be simplified to $9 + 0 = 9$, a true statement. Move to the second equation: $((0) - 3)^2 + ((-1) + 1)^2 = 9$, and $9 + 0 = 9$, also true. Finally, check the final equation: $(0)^2 + ((-1) + 4)^2 = 9$, and $0 + 9 = 9$, also true. Since (0, −1) works for all three equations, (E) can be eliminated because it does not contain this point as an option. Pick any of the points in (C) to see if they work. Plugging (−3, −4) into the second equation yields $((-3) - 3)^2 + ((-4) + 1)^2 = 9$, and $36 + 9 = 9$, an untrue statement, and (C) can be eliminated. The correct answer is (B).

42. **A** The question is asking for an expression representing the area of the table surface that the fish tank will occupy. Given a variable in both the question and the answer choices, plugging in is a solid technique to use. The volume formula for a cube is $V = s^3$, where s represents the length of one of the edges. Plug in a number for m that is a perfect cube, like $m = 27$. Plug this into the volume formula to solve for the side length: $27 = s^3$, and $3 = s$. To calculate the area, use the area formula for a square, $A = s^2$: $A = (3)^2 = 9$. Circle this as the target answer and proceed to the checking the answer choices using $m = 27$. Choice (A) becomes $\sqrt[3]{(27)^2} = 3^2 = 9$. Keep (A) for now and check the remaining choices. Choice (B) becomes $2\sqrt[3]{(27)^2} = 2(3) = 6$. Eliminate (B). Choice (C) becomes $\frac{(27)^2}{9} = 81$, and it can be eliminated. Choice (D) becomes $\frac{2(27)}{3} = 18$, and it can be eliminated. Choice (E) becomes $4\sqrt{27} \approx 20.785$, and it can be eliminated. Alternatively, this can be solved using m and doing the algebra: $V = s^3$, $m = s^3$, and $\sqrt[3]{m} = s$. Next, $A = s^2$, so $A = \left(\sqrt[3]{m}\right)^2 = \sqrt[3]{m^2}$. The correct answer is (A).

43. **D** The question is asking for the total number of values that a can take on to have a y-intercept of 24. For a quadratic provided in the factored form, the y-intercept will occur when $x = 0$, and the y-coordinate will be the product of the last terms in the factors. In this case, $a \times b = 24$. List out the various factors of 24, being sure to account for both the positive and negative possibilities as a negative times a negative yields a positive: ±1, ±2, ±3, ±4, ±6, ±8, ±12, and ±24 for a total of 16 possible values that a can take on. The correct answer is (D).

44. **B** The question is asking for the sum of the hundreds, tens, and units digits of 5^{57}. Proceeding to the calculator will yield some number either ridiculously large that can't be determined, or an error of some sort. To tackle bases raised to large exponents, start listing out the powers to establish a pattern. Begin with $5^1 = 5$, and continue up until a pattern is recognized: $5^2 = 25$, $5^3 = 125$, $5^4 = 625$, $5^5 = 3,125$, $5^6 = 15,625$, $5^7 = 78,125$, $5^8 = 390,625$, and so on. The pattern, as higher powers of 5 are encountered, appears to be that the last three digits of odd powers are 1, 2, and 5, and the last three digits of even powers are 6, 2, and 5. Since the question is requiring an odd power of 57, use the digits found for odd powers and add them together to arrive at the answer of $1 + 2 + 5 = 8$. The correct answer is (B).

45. **B** The question is asking for the interval on which the provided function is decreasing. This question is a prime candidate for the graphing calculator. In the $y =$ menu, type the function $x^3 - 2x^2 - 5x + 2$ and hit graph. Press "2nd TRACE" and select "maximum." On the graph, move the cursor to the left of the first "peak" and hit enter, then move the cursor over to the right of the peak and press enter twice to arrive at an x-value of -0.7862981. Choices (A), (C), (D), and (E) can be eliminated since the graph starts decreasing at the calculated x-value and to the right. If a graphing calculator is not available, simply plug in values for x from the provided range of values to compare the results and determine the behavior of the graph. The correct answer is (B).

46. **C** The question is asking for the number of sides a regular convex polygon has provided the sum of any two exterior angles is 72°. Since the question is asking for a specific value, and the answers are the possibilities of the specific value, this question is a prime candidate for PITA. Start with (C), 10 sides. Calculate the total number of degrees in a 10-sided figure using the formula $180°(n - 2)$, where n represents the number of sides. This results in $180°(10 - 2) = 180°(8) = 1440°$. To figure out the value of the interior angles of this regular 10-sided polygon, divide the total degrees by 10 to get $\dfrac{1440°}{10} = 144°$. To determine the degree measure of the exterior angle, take the interior angle, 144°, and subtract it from the total degrees in a straight line, 180°. The exterior angle will be $180° - 144° = 36°$. Check to see if adding two exterior angles produces the required target of 72°: $36° + 36° = 72°$. The correct answer is (C).

47. **E** The question is asking for the value of m given the provided restrictions. Begin by applying the provided vertical shift to the function: $y = mx^2 + mx + 2$. Since the question is asking for a specific value of m, and the answers provide the possible values, this question is a prime candidate for PITA. Start with (C), $m = 4$. This yields $y = 4x^2 + 4x + 2$. To determine the number of roots of a quadratic in the form $y = ax^2 + bx + c$, study the behavior of the discriminant, $b^2 - 4ac$. The discriminant in (C) is $(4)^2 - 4(4)(2) = 16 - 32 = -16$. Since the discriminant is less than zero, the quadratic will have two imaginary roots and does not qualify the requirement posed in the question of one real root.

Eliminate (C). It may be unclear which direction to travel, so just select an answer and continue checking. In (D), $m = 6$, the equation becomes $6x^2 + 6x + 2$, and the discriminant is $(6)^2 - 4(6)(2)$ $= 36 - 48 = -12$. This is the same instance as in (C), so (D) can be eliminated. Move to (E), $m = 8$. The equation becomes $8x^2 + 8x + 2$, and the discriminant is $(8)^2 - 4(8)(2) = 64 - 64 = 0$. When the discriminant is equal to zero, this means that the quadratic has exactly one real root. If the discriminant were greater than zero, then there would be two real roots. The correct answer is (E).

48. **D** The question is asking for a possible value of sin B given the provided equation. Use the identity $\sin^2 \theta + \cos^2 \theta = 1$ and solve for $\sin^2 \theta$: $\sin^2 \theta = 1 - \cos^2 \theta$. Use the solved expression, replacing θ with B, to rewrite the provided equation: $1 - \cos^2 B = \sin B$ becomes $\sin^2 B = \sin B$. Begin solving by getting both terms on one side of the equal sign and then factor the expression. This becomes $\sin^2 B - \sin B = 0$, and $\sin B(\sin B - 1) = 0$. Set each factor equal to zero and solve for B. This yields $\sin B = 0$ and $\sin B - 1 = 0$, or $\sin B = 1$. Since 0 is not an option, sin B must equal 1. The correct answer is (D).

49. **D** The question is asking for the approximate distance between the midpoint of $\overline{AF}$ and $\overline{CH}$. Begin by labeling the height of square pyramid $ABCDE$ as 12. Since the volume is provided, write down the volume formula for a pyramid: $V = \dfrac{1}{3} Bh$, where B represents the area of the base and h represents the height. The base of the pyramid is a square which has an area of s^2, so the volume formula becomes $V = s^2h$. Plug the volume of 256 and the height of 12 into the formula to determine the length of the side, s: $256 = \dfrac{1}{3} s^2(12)$, $256 = 4s^2$, $64 = s^2$, and $8 = s$. Repeat this process for pyramid $EFGHJ$: $32 = \dfrac{1}{3} s^2(6)$, $32 = 2s^2$, $16 = s^2$, and $4 = s$. To calculate the distance between the respective midpoints of $\overline{AF}$ and $\overline{CH}$, create a right triangle with the hypotenuse representing the required distance, and the base and height running along triangular faces AED and DEC, respectively. The base and height of the created right triangle are equal, and as they are half way between 4 and 8, they each have a length of 6.

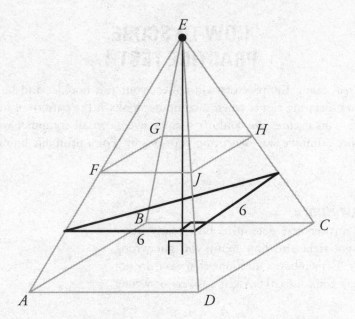

Use either the property of the 45:45:90 isosceles right triangle or the Pythagorean Theorem to arrive at the required length. The ratio of side lengths in a 45:45:90 right triangle are $s:s:s\sqrt{2}$, which yields $6:6:6\sqrt{2}$. Type $6\sqrt{2}$ in the calculator to get 8.4852, which is closest to 8.49. The correct answer is (D).

50. **C** The question is asking for the expression that is equal to $-f(-g(-x))$. Since the question and answers contain a variable, plugging in is a great technique to aid with POE. Start by letting $x = 2$, and work using Bite-Sized Pieces from the inside out. The first step is to deal with $g(-x)$. Plugging in 2 for x becomes $g(-2)$ and can be evaluated as $g(-2) = -(-2) - 2 = 2 - 2 = 0$. Next, apply the negative sign to $g(x)$ to arrive at $-g(-2) = -(0) = 0$. The next step is to use $f(x)$ and determine $f(0)$: $f(0) = 2(0)^2 - 6(0) + 5 = 0 - 0 + 5 = 5$. Apply the negative sign to $f(0)$ to arrive at $-f(0) = -5$. Circle this as the target and proceed to checking the answers using $x = 2$. Choice (A) becomes $2(2)^2 - 2(2) + 1 = 8 - 4 + 1 = 5$, which does not match the target and can be eliminated. Choice (B) becomes $-2(2)^2 - 14(2) - 25 = -8 - 28 - 25 = -61$, which does not match the target and can be eliminated. Choice (C) becomes $-2(2)^2 + 2(2) - 1 = -8 + 4 - 1 = -5$. Keep (C), but check the remaining choices just in case. Choice (D) becomes $2(2)^2 + 14(2) + 25 = 8 + 24 + 25 = 61$, which does not match the target and can be eliminated. Choice (E) becomes $2(2)^2 + 6(2) + 25 = 8 + 12 + 25 = 45$, which does not match the target and can be eliminated. Alternatively, let x equal $-x$ in each function and apply the appropriate negative signs to each function to arrive at the answer: $-[g(x)] = -[(-x) - 2] = 2 - x$, then $-[f(-g(-x))] = -[f(2 - x)] = -[2(2 - x)^2 - 6(2 - x) + 5] = -[2(4 - 4x + x^2) - 12 + 6x + 5] = -[8 - 8x + 2x^2 - 12 + 6x + 5] = -[2x^2 - 2x + 1] = -2x^2 + 2x - 1$. The correct answer is (C).

HOW TO SCORE
PRACTICE TEST 1

When you take the real exam, the proctors will collect your test booklet and bubble sheet and send your bubble sheet to a processing center where a computer looks at the pattern of filled-in ovals on your bubble sheet and gives you a score. We couldn't include even a small computer with this book, so we are providing this more primitive way of scoring your exam. (For a printable bubble sheet, check your online student tools.)

Determining Your Score

STEP 1 Using the answer key, determine how many questions you got right and how many you got wrong on the test. Remember: Questions that you do not answer don't count as either right answers or wrong answers.

STEP 2 List the number of right answers here.

(A) _____

STEP 3 List the number of wrong answers here. Now divide that number by 4. (Use a calculator if you're feeling particularly lazy.)

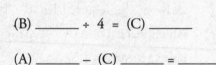

(B) _____ ÷ 4 = (C) _____

(A) _____ − (C) _____ = _____

STEP 4 Subtract the number of wrong answers divided by 4 from the number of correct answers. Round this score to the nearest whole number. This is your raw score.

STEP 5 To determine your real score, take the number from Step 4 and look it up in the left column of the Score Conversion Table on the next page; the corresponding score on the right is your score on the exam.

PRACTICE TEST 1
SCORE CONVERSION TABLE

Raw Score	Scaled Score	Raw Score	Scaled Score	Raw Score	Scaled Score
50	800	25	560	0	350
49	800	24	550	−1	340
48	790	23	540	−2	330
47	780	22	530	−3	330
46	770	21	520	−4	320
45	760	20	510	−5	310
44	750	19	500	−6	300
43	740	18	490	−7	290
42	730	17	490	−8	280
41	720	16	480	−9	270
40	720	15	470	−10	260
39	710	14	460	−11	260
38	700	13	450	−12	250
37	690	12	440		
36	680	11	440		
35	670	10	430		
34	660	9	420		
33	650	8	410		
32	640	7	400		
31	630	6	390		
30	620	5	390		
29	610	4	380		
28	600	3	370		
27	580	2	360		
26	570	1	360		

Part III
Content Review

Chapter 5
Arithmetic

You've been doing arithmetic as long as you've been studying math. This chapter will review basic arithmetic used on the SAT Subject Test in Math 1, such as factors, multiples, fractions, percents, and exponents. It will also give you some techniques to better assist you in tackling certain arithmetic questions. A calculator can be especially useful on arithmetic questions, so don't forget to use one when appropriate.

DEFINITIONS

There are a number of mathematical terms that will be thrown around freely on the test, and you'll want to recognize and understand them. Here are some of the most common terms:

Integers	Positive and negative whole numbers, and zero; NOT fractions or decimals.
Prime Number	An integer that has exactly two distinct factors: itself and 1. All prime numbers are positive; the smallest prime number is 2. Two is also the only even prime number. One is not a prime number.
Rational Numbers	All positive and negative integers, fractions, and decimal numbers; technically, any number that can be expressed as a fraction of two integers—which means everything except numbers containing weird radicals (such as $\sqrt{2}$), π, or e.
Irrational Numbers	Any number that does not end or repeat (in other words, any number that isn't rational). This includes all numbers with radicals that can't be simplified, such as $\sqrt{2}$ (perfect squares with radicals, such as $\sqrt{16}$, don't count because they can be simplified to integers, such as 4). Also, all numbers containing π or e. Note that repeating decimals like 0.33333... are rational (they're equivalent to fractions, such as $\frac{1}{3}$).
Real Numbers	Any number on the number line; everything except imaginary numbers.
Imaginary Numbers	The square roots of negative numbers, that is, any numbers containing i, which represents $\sqrt{-1}$.
Consecutive Numbers	The members of a set listed in order, without skipping any; consecutive integers: –3, –2, –1, 0, 1, 2; consecutive positive multiples of 3: 3, 6, 9, 12.
Distinct Numbers	Numbers that are different from each other.
Sum	The result of adding numbers.
Difference	The result of subtracting numbers.
Product	The result of multiplying numbers.
Quotient	The result of dividing numbers.

Remainder	The integer left over after dividing two numbers. For example, when 17 is divided by 2, the remainder is 1. Remember that on the SAT Subject Test in Math 1, a remainder is ALWAYS an integer.
Reciprocal	The result when 1 is divided by a number. For example, the reciprocal of 2 is $\frac{1}{2}$, the reciprocal of $\frac{3}{4}$ is $\frac{4}{3}$, and the reciprocal of $\frac{1}{16}$ is 16.
Positive Difference	The number you get by subtracting the smaller of two numbers from the bigger one. You can also think of it as the distance between two numbers on the number line.
Absolute Value	The positive version of a number. You just strike the negative sign if there is one. You can also think of it as the distance on the number line between a number and zero.
Arithmetic Mean	The average of a list of values; also simply referred to as the "mean."
Median	The middle value in a list when arranged in increasing order; in a list with an even number of members, the average of the *two* middle values.
Mode	The value that occurs most often in a list. If no value appears more often than all the others in a list, then that list has no mode.

At the beginning of each chapter in this book, you may see additional definitions that pertain to the material in that chapter. Every time you see such definitions listed, be sure that you know them well. One way to memorize the definitions is to make flash cards for them.

FACTORS AND MULTIPLES

The "factors" of a number are all of the numbers by which it can be divided evenly. ETS sometimes refers to factors as "divisors." Some questions on the SAT Subject Test in Math 1 will specifically require you to identify the factors of a given number. You may find factorizations useful for solving other questions, even if they don't specifically talk about factorizations. There is also a special kind of factorization called prime factorization.

Factors

The factorization of a number is a complete list of its factors. The best way to compile a list of all of a number's factors is to write them in pairs, beginning with 1 and the number itself. Then count upward through the integers from 1, checking at each integer to see whether the number you're factoring is divisible by that integer. If it is, add that integer to the list of factors, and complete the pair.

Here is the factorization of 60:

1	60
2	30
3	20
4	15
5	12
6	10

Start with 1 and the original number as your first pair and move up (2, 3, 4, etc.) to ensure that you won't miss any. You'll know your list is complete when the two columns of factors meet or pass each other. Here, the next integer after 6 that goes into 60 is 10, so you can be sure that the factorization is complete. This is the most efficient way to get a complete list of a number's factors.

Prime Factors

Prime factorization is a special kind of factorization. The prime factorization of a number is the unique group of prime numbers that can be multiplied together to produce that number. For example, the prime factorization of 8 is $2 \times 2 \times 2$. The prime factorization of 30 is $2 \times 3 \times 5$.

Prime factorizations are found by pulling a prime number out of a number again and again until you can't anymore. The prime factorization of 75, for example, would be found as follows:

$$75 =$$

$$3 \times 25 =$$

$$3 \times 5 \times 5$$

Notice that it doesn't matter which prime number you see first as a factor of the original. When you've got nothing but prime numbers left, you're done. Here's the prime factorization of 78.

$$78 =$$

$$2 \times 39 =$$

$$2 \times 3 \times 13$$

A Note About Factors
Remember that the largest factor of a number is that number!

Because they're often useful on the SAT Subject Test in Math 1, you should be able to take prime factorizations quickly.

DRILL 1: PRIME FACTORS

Find the prime factorizations of the following numbers. Answers can be found in Part IV.

1. 64 = _____
2. 70 = _____
3. 18 = _____
4. 98 = _____
5. 68 = _____
6. 51 = _____

Prime factorizations are useful in many questions dealing with divisibility. For example:

> What is the smallest number divisible by both 14 and 12 ?

To find the smallest number that both numbers will go into, look at the prime factorizations of 12 and 14: $12 = 2 \times 2 \times 3$, and $14 = 2 \times 7$, so it's easy to build the factorization of the smallest number divisible by both 12 and 14. It must contain at least two 2s, a 3, and a 7. That's $2 \times 2 \times 3 \times 7$, or 84. That's the smallest number you can divide evenly by 12 ($2 \times 2 \times 3$) and 14 (2×7).

Multiples

ETS also expects you to know the definition of a "multiple." The multiples of a number are simply all the numbers that are evenly divisible by your original number. An easy way to think of multiples is to recite the times tables for a number. For example, the "positive integer multiples of 6" are simply 6×1, 6×2, 6×3, and so forth, that is, 6, 12, 18…. If ETS asks you for the "fifth positive integer multiple of 6," that just means 6×5, or 30. It's easy to confuse factors and multiples (ETS hopes you will), so here's a way to keep the two straight. If you look back at the factorization of 60, you'll see that there are only 12 factors of 60, which is few. But 60 has as many multiples as you like. So think "factors are few, multiples are many."

Also notice that factors are smaller than or equal to your original number, whereas multiples are larger than or equal to your original number.

> What is the largest factor of 180 that is NOT a multiple of 15 ?

A Note About Multiples
Remember that the smallest multiple of a number is that number!

To answer the question, just make the biggest number you can, using the prime factors of 180. The prime factorization of 180 is $2 \times 2 \times 3 \times 3 \times 5$. Since 15 is the same as 3×5, just make sure your number doesn't have 3 *and* 5 as factors. The factor $2 \times 2 \times 5$ may look tempting, but the largest number that fits the bill is $2 \times 2 \times 3 \times 3$, or 36.

DRILL 2: FACTORS

Try the following practice questions. The answers can be found in Part IV.

3. What is the smallest integer divisible by both 21 and 18 ?

   (A) 42
   (B) 126
   (C) 189
   (D) 252
   (E) 378

7. If ¥x is defined as the largest prime factor of x, then for which of the following values of x would ¥x have the greatest value?

   (A) 170
   (B) 117
   (C)   88
   (D)   62
   (E)   53

9. If $x \, \Omega \, y$ is defined as the smallest integer of which both x and y are factors, then $10 \, \Omega \, 32$ is how much greater than $6 \, \Omega \, 20$?

   (A)   0
   (B)   70
   (C) 100
   (D) 160
   (E) 200

EVEN AND ODD, POSITIVE AND NEGATIVE

Some questions on the SAT Subject Test in Math 1 deal with the way numbers change when they're combined by addition and subtraction, or multiplication and division. The questions usually focus on changes in even and odd numbers, and positive and negative numbers.

Even and Odd Numbers

Even and odd numbers are governed by the following rules:

Addition and Subtraction
even + even = even
even − even = even
odd + odd = even
odd − odd = even
even + odd = odd
even − odd = odd

Multiplication
even × even = even
even × odd = even
odd × odd = odd

Division does not have neat rules. For example, 8 divided by 4 is 2 (an even divided by an even can be an even), but 8 divided by 8 is 1 (an even divided by an even can be an odd), and 8 divided by 16 is 0.5 (an even divided by an even may not be an integer). Only integers can be even or odd; fractions and decimals are neither even nor odd.

Positive and Negative Numbers

There are fewer firm rules for positive and negative numbers. Only the rules for multiplication and division are easily stated.

Multiplication and Division
positive × positive = positive
positive ÷ positive = positive
negative × negative = positive
negative ÷ negative = positive
positive × negative = negative
positive ÷ negative = negative

These rules are true for all numbers, because all real numbers except zero—including fractions, decimals, and even irrational numbers—are either positive or negative. Addition and subtraction for positive and negative numbers are a little more complicated—it's best simply to use common sense.

The one important rule to remember is that subtracting a negative is the same as adding a positive. So,

$$x - (-5) = x + 5$$
$$9 - (-6) = 9 + 6 = 15$$

If you remember this rule, adding and subtracting negative numbers should be simple.

Your understanding of these rules will be tested in questions that show you simple mathematical operations and ask you about the answers they'll produce. In the next chapter, we'll talk about another way to solve these problems in case you forgot a particular rule.

DRILL 3: POSITIVE AND NEGATIVE NUMBERS

Try the following practice questions. The answers can be found in Part IV.

15. If n and m are odd integers, then which of the following must also be an odd integer?

    I. mn

    II. $\dfrac{m}{n}$

    III. $(mn + 1)^2$

(A) I only
(B) III only
(C) I and II only
(D) I and III only
(E) I, II, and III

18. If c and d are integers and $cd < 0$, then which of the following statements must be true?

(A) $\dfrac{cd}{d} > 0$

(B) $c + d = 0$

(C) $c^2 d > 0$

(D) $3cd^2 \neq 0$

(E) $cd(3 + cd) < 0$

20. If x is a positive even integer and y is a negative odd integer, then which of the following must be a positive odd integer?

(A) x^3y^2

(B) $(xy + 2)^2$

(C) $xy^2 - 1$

(D) $x + y$

(E) $\dfrac{x + y}{xy}$

DOING ARITHMETIC

This chapter deals with the basic manipulations of numbers: averages, word problems, exponents, and so on. Most of these operations can be greatly simplified by the use of a calculator, so you should practice them with your calculator in order to increase your speed and efficiency. Remember the points about calculator use from Chapter 1, however. If you use your calculator incorrectly, you'll get questions wrong. If you use it on every question without thinking, it will slow you down. Keep your calculator near at hand, but think before you use it.

The Order of Operations

The Order of Operations or PEMDAS (Please Excuse My Dear Aunt Sally) is the order you must use to correctly solve an arithmetic problem. PEMDAS stands for Parentheses, Exponents (and roots), Multiplication and Division, Addition and Subtraction.

When using PEMDAS, it's important to remember that exponents and roots should be calculated from left to right, just as multiplication, division, addition and subtraction should be. You can think of PEMDAS in the following way:

> **PEMDAS**
> Parentheses
> Exponents and roots
> Multiplication and Division
> Addition and Subtraction

PEMDAS and Your Calculator

The safest way to do multistep problems like this on a calculator is one step at a time.

Pretty Print
Some calculators can display calculations the way that they would be written by hand (for example, using a horizontal bar with a numerator above and a denominator below to represent a fraction). This feature is called Pretty Print, and if you don't have a calculator, it may be worth buying a calculator that has this feature. It may also be possible to install an add-on or change the settings in your calculator to add this feature. It's makes it easier to check if you've made a mistake, which is valuable!.

On scientific and graphing calculators, it's possible to type complex expressions into your calculator all at once and let your calculator do the work of grinding out a number. But in order for your calculator to produce the right answer, the expression must be entered in exactly the right way—and that takes an understanding of the order of operations.

For example, the expression $\dfrac{2\sqrt{3^3-2}}{5}$ would have to be typed into some calculators this way:

$$(2 \times \sqrt{(3 \wedge 3 - 2)}) \div 5 =$$

On other calculators, it would have to look like the following:

$$(2(3\wedge3 - 2)\wedge(1/2))/5 =$$

Any mistake in either pattern would produce an incorrect answer. On other calculators, the equation might have to be typed in in still another way. If you intend to make your calculator do your work for you, check your calculator's operating manual, and practice. In general, use lots of parentheses to make sure the calculator does the arithmetic in the right order. If you use too many parentheses, the calculator will still give you the right answer, but if you don't use enough, you may get the wrong answer. And remember, the safest way to use your calculator is one step at a time.

DRILL 4: PEMDAS AND YOUR CALCULATOR

Check your PEMDAS skills by working through the following complex calculations with your calculator. The answers can be found in Part IV.

1. $0.2 \times \left[\dfrac{15^2 - 75}{6} \right] =$

2. $\dfrac{5\sqrt{6^3 - 20}}{2} =$

3. $\sqrt{\dfrac{(7^2 - 9)(0.375 \times 16)^2}{10}} =$

4. $\sqrt{5\left[(13 \times 18) + \sqrt{121} \right]} =$

5. $\sqrt{\dfrac{2025^{0.5}}{0.2}} - \dfrac{5}{\frac{1}{3}} =$

FRACTIONS, DECIMALS, AND PERCENTAGES

On arithmetic questions, you will often be called upon to change fractions to decimal numbers, or decimal numbers to percentages, and so on. Be careful whenever you change the form of a number.

You turn fractions into decimals by doing the division represented by the fraction bar.

$$\frac{1}{8} = 1 \div 8 = 0.125$$

To turn a decimal number into a fraction, count the number of decimal places (digits to the right of the decimal point) in the number. Then place the number over a 1 with the same number of zeros, get rid of the decimal point, and reduce.

$$0.125 = \frac{125}{1000} = \frac{25}{200} = \frac{1}{8}$$

Decimals and percentages are essentially the same. The difference is the percent sign (%), which means "÷ 100." To turn a decimal into a percentage, just move the decimal point two places to the right and add the percent sign.

$$0.125 = 12.5\%$$

To turn percentages into decimals, do the reverse; get rid of the percent sign and move the decimal point two places to the left.

$$0.3\% = 0.003$$

It's important to understand these conversions, and to be able to do them in your head as much as possible. Don't rely on the percent key on your calculator; it's far too easy to become confused and use it when converting in the wrong direction.

Watch out for conversions between percentages and decimals—especially ones involving percentages with decimal points already in them (like 0.15%). Converting these numbers is simple, but this step is still the source of many careless errors.

Word-Problem Translation

Most of the common careless errors made in answering math questions are made in the very first step: reading the question. All your skill in arithmetic does you no good if you're not solving the right problem, and all the power of your calculator can't help you if you've entered the wrong equation. Reading errors are particularly common in word problems.

The safest way to extract equations from long-winded word problems is to translate, word for word, from English to math. All of the following words have direct math equivalents:

English	Math
what what fraction how many	x, y (a variable)
a, an	1 (one)
percent	÷ 100
of	• (multiplied by)
is, are, was, were	=
per (creates a ratio), out of	÷ (divided by)
x is how much more than y	$x - y$
x is how many times (more than) y	$x ÷ y$
x is how much less than y	$y - x$

Don't Get Tripped Up
Start writing your multiplication sign as a dot, not an ×, if you haven't already. Using an × can get very confusing, especially if your variable is an *x*. Make it easy and don't trip yourself up!

Using this table as a guide, you can translate any English sentence in a word problem into an equation. For example:

3. If the bar of a barbell weighs 15 pounds, and the entire barbell weighs 75 pounds, then the weight of the bar is what percent of the weight of the entire barbell?

All this question is really asking is what percent of 75 is 15 ? The question can be translated into:

$$15 = \frac{x}{100} \bullet 75$$

Solve this equation, and the question is answered. You'll find that x is equal to 20 and that 20% is the correct answer.

Fractions and Your Calculator

Raising a number to a power is shown in two different ways on your calculator, depending on the type of calculator you have. A scientific calculator will use the y^x button. You'll have to type in your base number first, then hit the y^x key, then type the exponent. So 4^3 will be typed in as "4 y^x 3 =" and you'll get 64. If you have a calculator from the TI-80 series, your button will be a ^ sign. You'll enter the same problem as "4^3 [ENTER]." Think of these two keys as the "to the" button, because you say "4 to the 3rd power."

Fractions and Your Calculator

You can also use your calculator to solve fraction problems. When you do, AL-WAYS put each of your fractions in a set of parentheses. This will ensure that your calculator knows that they are fractions. Otherwise, the order of operations will get confused. On a scientific calculator, you can write the fraction in two different ways:

- You will have a fraction key, which looks similar to "$a\frac{b}{c}$." If you wanted to write $\frac{5}{6}$, you'd type "5 $a\frac{b}{c}$ 6."

- You can also use the division key, because a fraction bar is the same as "divided by." Be aware that your answer will be a decimal for this second way, so we recommend the first.

On a graphing calculator, you'll use the division bar to create fractions. Keep in mind that, whatever calculator you are using, you can always turn your fractions into decimals before you perform calculations with them. Just be aware that the answer won't always be exact.

DRILL 5: WORD PROBLEMS AND TRANSLATION

For each of the following exercises, translate the information in English into an equation and solve. The answers can be found in Part IV.

1. 6.5 is what percent of 260 ?
2. If there are 20 honors students at Pittman High and 180 students at the school in all, then the number of honors students at Pittman High is what percentage of the total number of students?
3. Thirty percent of 40 percent of 25 marbles is how many marbles?
4. What is the square root of one-third of 48 ?
5. The square root of what positive number is equal to one-eighth of that number?

Word for Word
Use the English to math conversion chart to translate each word into math.

Percent Change

"Percent change" is a way of talking about increasing or decreasing a number. The percent change is just the amount of the increase or decrease, expressed as a percentage of the starting amount.

For example, if you took a $100.00 item and increased its price by $2.00, that would be a 2% change, because the amount of the increase, $2.00, is 2% of the original amount, $100.00. On the other hand, if you increased the price of a $5.00 item by the same $2.00, that would be a 40% increase—because $2.00 is 40% of $5.00. Use the following formula when computing a percent change:

$$\%\,\text{Change} = \frac{\text{Amount Change}}{\text{Original}} \times 100\%$$

Whenever you work with percent change, be careful not to confuse the *amount of the change* with the total *after* you've worked out the percent change. Just concern yourself with the original amount and the amount of the increase or decrease. The new total doesn't matter.

DRILL 6: PERCENT CHANGE

Test your understanding of percent change with the following practice questions. The answers can be found in Part IV.

2. A 25-gallon addition to a pond containing 150 gallons constitutes an increase of approximately what percent?

(A) 14.29%
(B) 16.67%
(C) 17.25%
(D) 20.00%
(E) 25.00%

5. The percent decrease from 5 to 4 is how much less than the percent increase from 4 to 5 ?

(A) 0%
(B) 5%
(C) 15%
(D) 20%
(E) 25%

Your Calculator Is Your Friend

Here's a great place to test out how you're putting equations in your calculator.

12. Nicoletta deposits $150.00 in her savings account. If this deposit represents a 12 percent increase in Nicoletta's savings, then how much does her savings account contain after the deposit?

   (A) $1,100.00
   (B) $1,250.00
   (C) $1,400.00
   (D) $1,680.00
   (E) $1,800.00

Percent change shows up in many different problem types on the SAT Subject Test in Math 1—it can be brought into almost any kind of math question. Here's one of the most common math question types that deals with percent change.

The Change-Up, Change-Down

It's a classic trick question to ask what happens if you increase something by a percent and then decrease it by the same percent, as follows:

9. The price of a bicycle that usually sells for $250.00 is marked up 30 percent. If this new price is subsequently discounted by 30 percent, then the final price of the bicycle is

   (A) $200.50
   (B) $216.75
   (C) $227.50
   (D) $250.00
   (E) $265.30

Here's How to Crack It

The easy mistake on this problem type is to assume that the price (after increasing by 30% and then decreasing by 30%) has returned to $250.00, the original amount. Nope! This is the trap answer, and it doesn't actually work out that way, as you'll see if you try it step by step. First, you increase the original price by 30%.

$$\$250.00 + \left(\frac{30}{100} \times \$250.00 \right) =$$

$$\$250.00 + \$75.00 =$$

$$\$325.00$$

Then, discount this price by 30%.

$$\$325.00 - \left(\frac{30}{100} \times \$325.00 \right) =$$

$$\$325.00 - \$97.50 =$$

$$\$227.50$$

The answer is (C). As you can see, the final amount isn't equal to the starting amount. The reason for the difference is that you're increasing the price by 30% of the starting number, and then decreasing by 30% of a *different* number—the new, higher price. The changes will never be of the same *amount*—just the same percent. You end up with a number smaller than your starting number, because the decrease was bigger than the increase. In fact, if you'd done the decrease *first* and then the increase, you would still have gotten the same number, $227.50.

Remember this tip whenever you increase a quantity by a percent and then *decrease* by the same percent. Your final result will always be a bit smaller than your original amount. The same thing is true if you *decrease* a quantity by a percent and then increase by the same percent. You'll get a number a bit lower than your starting number.

REPEATED PERCENT CHANGE

On one common question type, you'll have to work with percent change and exponents together. Occasionally, you'll be required to increase or decrease something by a percent repeatedly. Such questions often deal with growing populations or bank accounts collecting interest. Here's an example:

40. Ruby had $1,250.00 in a bank account at the end of 1990. If Ruby deposits no further money in the account, and the money in the account earns 5 percent interest every year, then to the nearest dollar, how much money will be in the account at the end of 2000 ?

(A) $1,632.00
(B) $1,786.00
(C) $1,875.00
(D) $2,025.00
(E) $2,036.00

Here's How to Crack It

The easy mistake here is to find 5% of the original amount, which in this case would be $62.50. Add $62.50 for each of the ten years from 1990 to 2000 and you've got an increase of $625.00, right? Wrong. That would give you a final total of $1,875.00, but that's the trap answer. Here's the problem—the interest for the first year is $62.50, which is 5% of $1,250. But that means that now there's $1,312.50 in the bank account, so the interest for the second year will be something different. As you can see, this could get messy.

> **Remember to Keep an Eye Out for Traps**
> Notice that $1,875.00 is in the answers. Remember that ETS *loves* to put in numbers that look familiar to you. You'll see partial answers, trap answers, and answers to a question that wasn't even asked. A test question numbered 40 is going to be a difficult one. Always remember to keep an eye out for answers that you can eliminate.

Here's the easy way. The first year's interest can be computed like any ordinary percent change, by adding the percent change to the original amount.

$$\$1,250.00 + (\frac{5}{100} \times \$1,250.00) = \text{total after one year}$$

But there's another way to write that. Just factor out the $1,250.00.

$$\$1,250.00 \times (1 + \frac{5}{100}) = \text{total after one year}$$

$$\$1,250.00 \times (1.05) = \text{total after one year}$$

You can get the total after one year by converting the percent change to a decimal, adding 1, and multiplying the original amount by this number. To get the total after two years, just multiply by that number again.

$$\$1,250.00 \times (1.05) \times (1.05) = \text{total after two years}$$

And so on. So, to figure out how much money Ruby will have after 10 years, all you have to do is multiply her original deposit by 1.05, 10 times. That means multiplying Ruby's original deposit by 1.05 to the 10th power.

$$\$1,250.00 \times (1.05)^{10} = \text{total after 10 years}$$

$$\$1,250.00 \times 1.629 = \text{total after 10 years}$$

$$\$2,036.25 = \text{total after 10 years}$$

So, to the nearest dollar, Ruby will have $2,036.00 after 10 years. The answer is (E).

There's a simple formula you can use to solve repeated percent-increase problems.

> **Final amount** = Original $\times$ (1 + Rate)$^{\text{number of changes}}$

The formula for repeated percent-decrease problems is almost identical. The only difference is that you'll be subtracting the percentage change from 1 rather than adding it.

> **Final amount** = Original $\times$ (1 − Rate)$^{\text{number of changes}}$

Just remember that you've got to convert the rate of change (like an interest rate) from a percentage to a decimal number.

Here's another one. Try it yourself, and then check the explanation below.

43. The weight of a bar of hand soap decreases by 2.5 percent each time it is used. If the bar weighs 100 grams when it is new, what is its weight in grams after 20 uses?

(A) 50.00
(B) 52.52
(C) 57.43
(D) 60.27
(E) 77.85

To Memorize or Not to Memorize?

So, at this point, you're probably starting to get nervous about how many formulas we're giving you and how much you have to memorize. But remember that we're also showing you how to get there. Formulas are designed to save you time. If you ever can't remember a formula, you can still figure out how to do the problem. Notice for repeated percent change, you *can* do it the long way and still get to the right answer accurately. And don't forget your techniques like Ballparking and POE, and there's still more to come!

Here's How to Crack It

You've got all of your starting numbers. The original amount is 100 grams, and the rate of change is 2.5%, or 0.025 (remember to subtract it, because it's a decrease). You'll be going through 20 decreases, so the exponent will be 20. This is how you'd plug these numbers into the formula.

Final amount $= 100 \times (1 - 0.025)^{20}$
$= 100 \times (0.975)^{20}$
$= 100 \times (0.60269)$
Final amount $= 60.27$

The answer is (D). This is an excellent example of a question type that is difficult if you've never seen it before, and easy if you're prepared for it. Memorize the repeated percent-change formulas and practice using them.

DRILL 7: REPEATED PERCENT CHANGE

Try the following practice questions. The answers can be found in Part IV.

35. At a certain bank, savings accounts earn 5 percent interest per year. If a savings account is opened with a $1,000.00 deposit, and no further deposits are made, how much money will the account contain after 12 years?

(A) $ 1,333.33
(B) $ 1,166.67
(C) $ 1,600.00
(D) $ 1,795.86
(E) $12,600.00

43. In 1995, Ebenezer Bosticle created a salt sculpture that weighed 2,000 pounds. If this sculpture loses 4 percent of its mass each year to rain erosion, what is the last year in which the statue will weigh more than 1,000 pounds?

(A) 2008
(B) 2009
(C) 2011
(D) 2012
(E) 2013

AVERAGES

The test uses averages in a variety of question types. Remember, the average is the sum of all the values divided by the number of values you're adding up. Looking at this definition, you can see that every average involves three quantities: the total, the number of things being added, and the average itself.

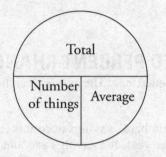

The chart above is called an Average Pie. It's The Princeton Review way of organizing the information found in an average problem. Cover up the "average" section with your thumb. In order to find the average, you divide the total by the "number of things." Now cover up the "number of things" section. You can find it by dividing the total by the average. Finally, you can find the total by multiplying the number of things by the average.

When you run into an average in a SAT Subject Test in Math 1 question, you'll be given two of the three numbers involved. Usually, solving the problem will depend on your supplying the missing number in the Average Pie.

DRILL 8: AVERAGES

Test your understanding of averages with the following questions. The answers can be found in Part IV.

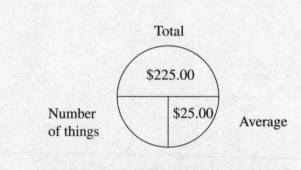

1. People at a dinner paid an average of $25.00 each. The total bill for dinner was $225.00.

   What else do you know? _____

Ways to Remember
Remember that in order to find the average, you divide the total by the number of things. Think of the horizontal line in the Average Pie as one big division bar!

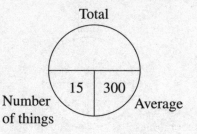

2. The average fruit picker on Wilbury Ranch picked 300 apples on Tuesday. There are 15 fruit pickers at Wilbury Ranch.

   What else do you know? _____

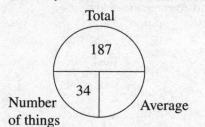

3. If the 34 students in the chess club lie down end to end, they would form a line 187 feet long.

   What else do you know? _____

The Average Pie becomes most useful when you're tackling a multiple-average question—one that requires you to manipulate several averages in order to find an answer. Here's an example:

---

32. Sydney's average score on the first 5 math tests of the year was 82. If she ended the year with a math test average of 88, and a total of 8 math tests were administered that year, what was her average on the last three math tests?

    (A) 99.5
    (B) 98.75
    (C) 98.0
    (D) 96.25
    (E) 94.0

Average Pies and Variables, Never the Twain Shall Meet
There should never be a variable in your Average Pie. You will always be given two of the three numbers you need in your pie. If you can't find two of the three numbers, that means you've missed a step somewhere.

Here's How to Crack It

In this question, there are three separate averages to deal with: Sydney's average on the first five tests, her final average on all 8 tests, and her average for the last three tests. In order to avoid confusion, take these one at a time. Draw the first Average Pie.

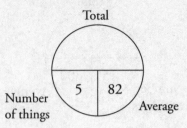

You have the number of things and the average, so you can find the total. You know that Sydney's total for the first test is 410. Fill in that information and draw another pie. For your second pie, the question tells you that Sydney's average on all 8 tests was 88, so you can multiply those numbers to find the total of her 8 scores, or 704. Fill in your second Average Pie below.

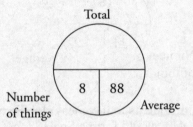

Since you know the total of all 8 tests and the total of the first 5 tests, you can figure out the total of the last three tests:

$$704 - 410 = 294$$

Draw one last pie, using the information that you have:

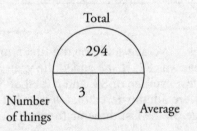

As it turns out, Sydney averaged a 98 on her last three math tests; so the answer is (C).

Multiple-average questions are never terribly difficult. Just draw an Average Pie every time you see the word *average* in the question. Organization is everything on these questions. It's easy to make careless errors if you get your numbers scrambled, so make sure you label the parts of the Average Pie. Notice that you can always add or subtract totals and numbers of things, but you can never add or subtract averages.

DRILL 9: MULTIPLE AVERAGE QUESTIONS

Try these problems. The answers can be found in Part IV.

33. At a charity fund-raiser, the average of the first 19 donations is $485.00. In order for the average of the first 20 donations to be $500.00, what must the amount of the twentieth donation be, in dollars?

(A) $300
(B) $515
(C) $650
(D) $785
(E) $800

35. During the first 20 days of September, the *Tribune* received an average of 4 complaint letters per day. During the last 10 days of September, the *Tribune* received an average of 7 complaint letters per day. What was the *Tribune's* average number of complaint letters per day for the entire month of September?

(A) 5.0
(B) 5.33
(C) 5.67
(D) 6.0
(E) 6.25

36. Over a year, Brendan sold an average of 12 umbrellas per day on rainy days and an average of 3 umbrellas per day on clear days. If the weather was rainy one day in five, and this was not a leap year, what was Brendan's average daily umbrella sales for the year?

(A) 4.8
(B) 5.2
(C) 6.75
(D) 7.3
(E) 9.0

EXPONENTS

An exponent is a simple way of expressing repeated multiplication. You can think of 5^3, for example, as $5 \times 5 \times 5$. In this exponential expression, 5 is referred to as the "base," while 3 is the "exponent." Sometimes a third number is also present, called a "coefficient." In the expression $4b^2$, b is the base, 2 is the exponent, and 4 is the coefficient. Here, b is being squared, but the coefficient, 4, is not affected by the exponent.

For certain questions, you'll need to do some algebraic calculations using exponents. To work with exponents in equations, you just need to remember a few basic rules.

Rules Come from Somewhere

If you ever forget the rules of exponents, remember that you can always expand and cancel. So if you're ever unclear, write it out. Here's a great example:

$$x^2 \cdot x^4 = (x \cdot x)(x \cdot x \cdot x \cdot x)$$

You have six x's. So the answer is x^6.

This also works with dividing:

$$\frac{m^5}{m^3} = \frac{mmmmm}{mmm}$$

Now cancel and you get mm or m^2.

You *never* have to stress about forgetting your rules. They make it easier to get through the problem more quickly, but if you forget, there's always another way. Just remember, when in doubt, expand it out!

Multiplying Exponential Expressions When Bases Are the Same

Exponential terms can be multiplied when their bases are the same. Just leave the bases unchanged and add the exponents.

$$n^3 \times n^5 = n^8 \qquad\qquad 3 \times 3^4 = 3^5$$

Coefficients, if they are present, are multiplied.

$$2b \times 3b^5 = 6b^6 \qquad\qquad \frac{1}{2}c^3 \times 6c^5 = 3c^8$$

Dividing Exponential Expressions When Bases Are the Same

Exponential terms can also be divided when their bases are the same. Once again, the bases remain the same, and the exponents are subtracted.

$$x^8 \div x^6 = x^2 \qquad\qquad 7^5 \div 7 = 7^4$$

Coefficients, if they are present, are divided.

$$6b^5 \div 3b = 2b^4 \qquad\qquad 5a^8 \div 3a^2 = \frac{5}{3}a^6$$

Multiplying and Dividing Exponential Expressions When Exponents Are the Same

There's one special case in which you can multiply and divide terms with different bases—when the exponents are the same. In this case, you can multiply or divide the different bases. Then the bases change and the exponents remain the same.

For multiplication:

$$3^3 \times 5^3 = 15^3 \qquad\qquad x^8 \times y^8 = (xy)^8$$

And for division:

$$33^2 \div 3^2 = 11^2 \qquad\qquad x^{20} \div y^{20} = \left(\frac{x}{y}\right)^{20}$$

If exponential terms have different bases and different exponents, then there's no way to simplify them by adding, subtracting, dividing, or multiplying.

Adding and Subtracting When Bases and Exponential Expressions Are the Same

Terms with exponents can be added or subtracted only when they have the same base and exponent.

$$2a^3 + a^3 = 3a^3 \qquad\qquad 5x^2 - 4x^2 = x^2$$

If they don't have the same base and exponent, exponential terms can never be combined by addition or subtraction.

Raising Powers to Powers

When an exponential term is raised to another power, the exponents are multiplied.

$$(x^2)^8 = x^{16} \qquad\qquad (7^5)^4 = 7^{20}$$

If there is a coefficient included in the term, then the coefficient is also raised to that power.

$$(3c^4)^3 = 27c^{12} \qquad\qquad (5g^3)^2 = 25g^6$$

Using these rules, you should be able to manipulate exponential expressions wherever you find them.

ROOTS

Roots are exponents in reverse. For example, $4 \times 4 = 16$. That means that $4^2 = 16$. It also means that $\sqrt{16} = 4$. Square roots are by far the most common roots on the SAT Subject Test in Math 1. The square root of a number is simply whatever you would square to get that number.

A Horse of a Different Color
Square roots are sometimes called roots of the second power. It's yet another way ETS tries to throw you. It makes a simple concept sound very complicated. But you know better!

You may also encounter other roots: cube roots, fourth roots, fifth roots, and so on. Each of these roots is represented by a radical with a number attached, like $\sqrt[3]{x}$, which means the cube root of x. Roots of higher degrees work just as square roots do. The expression $\sqrt[4]{81}$, for example, equals 3—the number that you'd raise to the 4th power to get 81. Similarly, $\sqrt[5]{32}$ is the number that, raised to the 5th power, equals 32—in this case, 2.

When the number under a radical has a factor whose root is an integer, then the radical can be *simplified*. This means that the root can be pulled out. For example, $\sqrt{48}$ is equal to $\sqrt{16 \times 3}$. Because 16 is a perfect square, its root can be pulled out, leaving the 3 under the radical sign, as $4\sqrt{3}$. That's the simplified version of $\sqrt{48}$.

> ## The Principal Idea
>
> Remember how both 2 and –2 raised to the 4th power equal 16? Well, for the SAT Subject Test in Math 1, a radical refers only to the *principal* root of an expression. When there is only one root, that's the principal root. An example of this is $\sqrt[3]{27}$. The only root of this expression is 3. When you have both a positive *and* a negative root, the positive root is considered to be the principal root and is the only root symbolized by the radical sign. So, even though $2^4 = 16$ and $(-2)^4 = 16$, $\sqrt[4]{16}$ means 2 only, and not –2.

Working with Roots

The rules for manipulating roots when they appear in equations are the same as the rules for manipulating exponents. Roots can be combined by addition and subtraction only when they are roots of the same order (for example, all square roots or all cube roots) and roots of the same number.

$$3\sqrt{5} - \sqrt{5} = 2\sqrt{5} \qquad\qquad 3\sqrt[3]{x} + 2\sqrt[3]{x} = 5\sqrt[3]{x}$$

Roots can be multiplied and divided freely as long as all the roots are of the same order. The resulting product must be kept under the radical.

$$\sqrt{a} \times \sqrt{b} = \sqrt{ab} \qquad\qquad \sqrt[3]{24} \div \sqrt[3]{3} = \sqrt[3]{8} = 2$$

$$\sqrt{18} \times \sqrt{2} = \sqrt{36} = 6 \qquad\qquad \sqrt[4]{5} \div \sqrt[4]{2} = \sqrt[4]{\frac{5}{2}}$$

Be sure to memorize these rules before working with roots.

Roots and Your Calculator

Another important key is the root key. On a scientific calculator it is often the same button as y^x, but you'll have to hit shift first. The symbol is $\sqrt[x]{y}$. So "the 4th root of 81" would be "81 $\sqrt[x]{y}$ 4 = ." Sometimes the calculator will have y^x or $\sqrt[x]{y}$ as x^y or $\sqrt[y]{x}$. They mean the same thing. Just know which number you're supposed to type in first.

The root key in the TI-80 graphing calculator series varies, but the most common symbol is the square root sign, which you can get to by pressing "[SHIFT] x^2." In case you want to find the 3rd, 4th, or other root of a number, there is a button in the [MATH] directory for $\sqrt[3]{}$ or $\sqrt[x]{}$. In the case of the $\sqrt[x]{}$, you have to type in the root you want, then hit [MATH] and $\sqrt[x]{}$, and finally hit your base number. For example, if you wanted to find the 4th root of 81, you'd type "4 [MATH]," then select $\sqrt[x]{}$, then type 81 and press [ENTER]. If you look at it on the screen, it will appear as "4 $\sqrt[x]{}$ 81," which is similar to how you'd write it. You can also use the ^ symbol if you remember that a root is the same as the bottom part of a fractional exponent. We'll go over this in more detail in the fractions section.

Fractional Exponents

A fractional exponent is a way of raising a number to a power and taking a root of the number at the same time. The number on top is the normal exponent. The number on the bottom is the root.

So, in order to raise a number to the $\frac{2}{3}$ power, you would square the number and then take the cube root of your result. You could also take the cube root first and then square the result—it doesn't matter which one you do first, as long as you realize that 2 is the exponent and 3 is the order of the root.

Remember that an exponent of 1 means the number itself, so $x^{\frac{1}{2}}$ is equal to $\sqrt{x}$, the square root of x to the first power. Knowing this will help you handle roots with your calculator. For example, $17^{\frac{1}{3}}$ can be entered into your calculator as $17\verb|^|(1/3)$.

$$27^{\frac{1}{3}} = \sqrt[3]{27} = 3 \qquad\qquad b^{\frac{5}{2}} = \sqrt{b^5}$$

$$8^{\frac{2}{3}} = \sqrt[3]{8^2} = \sqrt[3]{64} = 4 \qquad\qquad x^{\frac{4}{3}} = \sqrt[3]{x^4}$$

SPECIAL EXPONENTS

There are some exponents on the SAT Subject Test in Math 1 that you've got to treat a little differently. Here are some unusual exponents with which you should be familiar.

Zero

Any number (except zero) raised to the power of zero is equal to 1, no matter what you start with. It's a pretty simple rule.

$$5^0 = 1 \qquad\qquad x^0 = 1$$

One

Any number raised to the first power is itself—it doesn't change. In fact, ordinary numbers, written without exponents, are numbers to the first power. You can think of them as having an invisible exponent of 1. That's useful when using the basic exponent rules you've just reviewed. It means that $(x^4 \div x)$ can be written as $(x^4 \div x^1)$, which can prevent confusion when you're subtracting exponents.

$$x = x^1 \qquad\qquad\qquad 4^1 = 4$$

Negative Exponents

Treat a negative exponent exactly like a positive exponent, with one extra step. After you have applied the exponent, flip the number over—that is, you turn the number into its reciprocal.

$$a^{-4} = \frac{1}{a^4} \qquad\qquad\qquad 3^{-2} = \frac{1}{3^2} = \frac{1}{9}$$

$$x^{-1} = \frac{1}{x} \qquad\qquad\qquad \left(\frac{2}{3}\right)^{-1} = \frac{3}{2}$$

The negative sign works the same way on fractional exponents. First, you apply the exponent as you would if it were positive, and then flip it over.

$$x^{-\frac{1}{2}} = \frac{1}{\sqrt{x}} \qquad\qquad\qquad a^{-\frac{3}{2}} = \frac{1}{\sqrt{a^3}}$$

MORE IMPORTANT EXPONENT STUFF

There are a few important things to remember about the effects of exponents on various numbers:

- A positive number raised to any power remains positive. No exponent can make a positive number negative.
- A negative number raised to an odd power remains negative.
- A negative number raised to an even power becomes positive.

In other words, anything raised to an odd power keeps its sign. If a^3 is negative, then a is negative; if a^3 is positive, then a is positive. A term with an odd exponent has only one root. For example, if $a^3 = -27$, there's only one value of a that makes it true: $a = -3$.

On the other hand, anything raised to an even power becomes positive, regardless of its original sign. This means that an equation with an even exponent has two roots. For example, if $b^2 = 25$, then b has two possible values: 5 and –5. It's important to remember that two roots exist for any equation with an even exponent (the only exception is when $b^2 = 0$, in which case b can equal only 0, and b^2 has only one root).

One last thing to remember—since any real number becomes positive when raised to an even exponent, certain equations will have no real roots. For example, the equation $x^2 = -9$ has no real roots. There is no real number which can be squared to produce a negative number. In this equation, x is said to be an imaginary number. The equation is considered to have no real solution. We'll talk about imaginary numbers in Chapter 12.

DRILL 10: EXPONENTS

In the following exercises, find the roots of the exponential expression given. Specify whether each expression has one root, two roots, an infinite number of roots, or no real roots. The answers can be found in Part IV.

1. $b^3 = 27; b =$
2. $x^2 = 121; x =$
3. $n^5 = 32; n =$
4. $c^2 = 10; c =$
5. $x^4 = 81; x =$
6. $x^3 = -8; x =$
7. $d^6 = 729; d =$
8. $n^0 = 1$ (for $n \neq 0$); $n =$

Now try some multiple-choice questions. In the following exercises, expand the exponential expressions. Where the bases are numbers, find the numerical values of the expressions. The answers can be found in Part IV.

9. $4^{\frac{3}{2}} =$

(A) 2.52
(B) 3.64
(C) 8.00
(D) 16.00
(E) 18.67

10. $x^{-\frac{3}{4}} =$

(A) $-\sqrt[5]{x} \cdot x^4$

(B) $-\dfrac{x^3}{x^4}$

(C) $\dfrac{x^4}{x^3}$

(D) $\dfrac{1}{\sqrt[4]{x^3}}$

(E) $-\sqrt[4]{x^3}$

11. $\left(\dfrac{2}{3}\right)^{-2} =$

    (A)   2.25
    (B)   1.67
    (C)   0.44
    (D) −1.50
    (E) −0.44

12. $\left(\dfrac{1}{a}\right)^{-\frac{1}{3}} =$

    (A) $-\dfrac{1}{\sqrt[3]{a}}$

    (B) $\sqrt[-3]{a}$

    (C) $\dfrac{1}{a^3}$

    (D) $-a^3$

    (E) $\sqrt[3]{a}$

13. $5^{\frac{2}{3}} =$

    (A)   2.92
    (B)   5.00
    (C)   6.25
    (D)   8.67
    (E) 11.18

14. $\left(-\dfrac{5}{6}\right)^{0} =$

    (A) −1.2
    (B) −0.8
    (C)   0.0
    (D)   1.0
    (E)   1.2

Comprehensive Arithmetic Drill

The answers can be found in Part IV.

6. If $25x^2 = 16$, then $3(5x)^2 =$

   (A) 9
   (B) 15
   (C) 25
   (D) 48
   (E) 75

9. What is the least common multiple of 180 and 210 ?

   (A)   30
   (B)   360
   (C)   720
   (D) 1,050
   (E) 1,260

11. The price of a television which originally sold for $500 is discounted by 25%. If the new price of the TV is subsequently raised by 25%, what is the final price of the television?

   (A) $375.25
   (B) $450.00
   (C) $468.75
   (D) $500.00
   (E) $575.50

15. In 2010, a minor league baseball team sold an average of 3,215 tickets per game. In 2011, the average tickets sold per game was 2,934. What was the percent decrease in the average number of tickets sold from 2010 to 2011 ?

   (A) 8.7%
   (B) 9.6%
   (C) 12.4%
   (D) 22.9%
   (E) 91.3%

18. If $12^n = 3^5 \cdot 4^5$, what is the value of n ?

   (A) 1
   (B) 5
   (C) 10
   (D) 20
   (E) 25

20. $\dfrac{x^6 y^{-3} z^5}{x^{-2} y^4 z^5} = ?$

   (A) $\dfrac{x^4}{y}$

   (B) $\dfrac{x^4 z}{y}$

   (C) $\dfrac{x^8}{y^7}$

   (D) $\dfrac{x^8 z}{y^7}$

   (E) $\dfrac{x^8}{y}$

21. Steven sold an average (arithmetic mean) of 3 houses per month during the first 5 months of the year. Steven will receive a promotion if he sells 39 houses in 1 year. What must his average sales, in houses per month, be for the remaining 7 months of the year if he is to be promoted?

   (A) 2.1
   (B) 2.8
   (C) 3.1
   (D) 3.4
   (E) 7.2

30. A total of 9 students donated money for a school fundraiser and their average (arithmetic mean) donation was $12. If the average donation for 5 of the students was $16, what was the average donation, for the remaining for students?

   (A) $5
   (B) $6
   (C) $7
   (D) $8
   (E) $9

33. If one-sixth is one-half of three-fourths of a certain number, what is that number?

(A) $\dfrac{3}{16}$

(B) $\dfrac{4}{9}$

(C) $\dfrac{5}{4}$

(D) $\dfrac{3}{2}$

(E) $\dfrac{9}{4}$

41. At the end of 2006, the population of Town *A* was 4,225. If the population increases at a rate of 2.25 percent each year, what will the population of Town *A* be at the end of 2018 ?

(A) 4,538
(B) 4,970
(C) 5,063
(D) 5,518
(E) 6,260

49. A solution is made by mixing acid with water. How many liters of acid should be mixed with 4 liters of water to make a solution that is 24% acid?

(A) 0.26
(B) 0.96
(C) 1.26
(D) 3.45
(E) 5.26

Summary

- Factors are numbers that divide into your original number. Multiples are numbers that your original number divides into.
  - Factors are smaller than or equal to your original number.
  - Multiples are larger than or equal to your original number.

- Make sure that you have a good grasp of PEMDAS and the rules involving even, odd, positive, and negative numbers:
  - even ± even = even
  - even ± odd = odd
  - odd ± odd = even
  - even × even = even
  - even × odd = even
  - odd × odd = odd
  - positive × or ÷ positive = positive
  - negative × or ÷ negative = positive
  - positive × or ÷ negative = negative

- If you have a question that asks for the average, mean, or arithmetic mean, use the Average Pie:

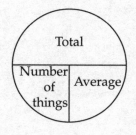

o There are two formulas for percent change:
  • The basic formula for percent change is:

$$\%\,\text{Change} = \frac{\text{Amount Change}}{\text{Original}} \times 100\%$$

  • The formula for repeated percent change is: Final = Original × (1 ± Rate)$^{\#\text{ of changes}}$. If it's a repeated percent increase, you add Rate. If it's a decrease, you subtract Rate.

o Special exponents:
  • Any number, except 0, raised to the 0 power is 1.
  • Raising a number to the first power does not change the number.
  • A negative exponent means take the reciprocal of the number (divide 1 by the number), and then apply the exponent.
  • Fractional exponents are a way of writing exponents and roots together: The top of the fraction is the exponent and the bottom of the fraction is the root.

o For exponents and roots, if you're adding or subtracting, the bases (what's under the root sign) must be the same.

Chapter 6
Algebra

Algebra questions ask you to solve for an unknown amount. In this chapter, we'll show you how ETS uses algebra (and often tries to trick you with it). You'll learn some great techniques to help you avoid ETS traps. We'll also review concepts, such as solving for *x*, inequalities, factoring, simultaneous equations, and quadratic equations.

ALGEBRA ON THE SAT SUBJECT TEST IN MATH 1

Algebra questions will make up about 30 percent of the questions on the SAT Subject Test in Math 1. Many of these questions are best answered by using the simple algebra rules outlined in this chapter. Others can be short-cutted with The Princeton Review techniques, which you'll also find in the following pages.

Definitions

Here are some algebraic terms that may show up on the SAT Subject Test in Math 1. Make sure you're familiar with them. If the meaning of any of these vocabulary words keeps slipping your mind, add those words to your flash cards.

Variable	An unknown quantity in an equation represented by a letter (usually from the end of the alphabet), for example, x, y, or z.
Constant	An unchanging numerical quantity—either a number or a letter that represents a number (usually from the beginning of the alphabet), for example, 5, 7.31, a, b, or k.
Term	An algebraic unit consisting of constants and variables multiplied together, such as $5x$ or $9x^2$.
Coefficient	In a term, the constant before the variable. In ax^2, a is the coefficient. In $7x$, 7 is the coefficient.
Polynomial	An algebraic expression consisting of more than one term joined by addition or subtraction. For example, $x^2 - 3x^2 + 4x - 5$ is a polynomial with four terms.
Binomial	A polynomial with exactly two terms, such as $(x - 5)$.
Quadratic	A quadratic expression is a polynomial with one variable whose largest exponent is a 2, for example, $x^2 - 5x + 6$ or $y = x^2 + 4$.
Root	A root of a polynomial is a value of the variable that makes the polynomial equal to zero. More generally, the roots of an equation are the values that make the equation true. Roots are also known as zeros, solutions, and x-intercepts.

SOLVING EQUATIONS

Many questions on the SAT Subject Test in Math 1 will require you to solve simple algebraic equations. Often these algebraic questions are in the form of word problems. Setting up an equation from the information contained in a word problem is the first step to finding the solution, and it is the step at which many careless mistakes are made. The translation chart on page 78 is very useful for setting up equations from information given in English.

An algebraic equation is an equation that contains at least one unknown—a variable. "Solving" for an unknown means figuring out its value. Generally, the way to solve for an unknown is to isolate the variable—that is, manipulate the equation until the unknown is alone on one side of the equal sign. Whatever's on the other side of the equal sign is the value of the unknown. Take a look at this example.

$$5(3x^3 - 16) - 22 = 18$$

In this equation, x is the unknown. To solve for x, you need to get x alone. You isolate x by undoing everything that's being done to x in the equation. If x is being squared, you need to take a square root; if x is being multiplied by 3, you need to divide by 3; if x is being decreased by 4, you need to add 4, and so on. The trick is to do these things in the right order. Basically, you should follow PEMDAS in reverse. Start by undoing addition and subtraction, then multiplication and division, then exponents and roots, and, last, what's in parentheses.

The other thing to remember is that any time you do something to one side of an equation, you've got to do it to the other side also. Otherwise you'd be changing the equation, and you're trying to rearrange it, not change it. In this example, you'd start by undoing the subtraction.

$$5(3x^3 - 16) - 22 = 18$$
$$+ 22 \quad + 22$$
$$5(3x^3 - 16) = 40$$

Then undo the multiplication by 5, saving what's in the parentheses for last.

$$5\left(3x^3 - 16\right) = 40$$
$$\div 5 \qquad\qquad \div 5$$
$$3x^3 - 16 = 8$$

Once you've gotten down to what's in the parentheses, follow PEMDAS in reverse again—first the subtraction, then the multiplication, and the exponent last.

$$3x^3 - 16 = 8$$
$$+16 \quad +16$$
$$3x^3 = 24$$
$$\div 3 \qquad \div 3$$
$$x^3 = 8$$
$$x = 2$$

At this point, you've solved the equation. You have found that the value of x must be 2. Another way of saying this is that 2 is the root of the equation $5(3x^3 - 16) - 22 = 18$. Equations containing exponents may have more than one root (see page 90, "Exponents," in the previous chapter).

Solving Equations with Absolute Value

The rules for solving equations with absolute value are the same as those we just discussed. The only difference is that, because what's inside the absolute value signs can be positive or negative, you're solving for two different results.

Let's look at an example:

$$20. \quad |x-2| = 17$$

Vocab Review

Remember that a non-negative number can be either a positive number or zero. Since zero is neither positive nor negative, if we said "positive number" that wouldn't include zero.

Now, we know that either $(x - 2)$ is a negative number or a non-negative number. When a number is negative, the absolute value makes it the inverse, or multiplies it by -1 to yield a positive result. If the number is positive, it remains the same after being sent through the absolute value machine. So when we remove the absolute value bars, we're left with two different equations:

$$x - 2 = 17 \qquad \text{or} \qquad x - 2 = -17$$

Now simply solve both equations:

$$
\begin{array}{ccc}
x - 2 = 17 & \text{or} & x - 2 \ = -17 \\
\underline{+ 2 \ + 2} & & \underline{+ 2 \ = + 2} \\
x \quad = 19 & \text{or} & x \quad = -15
\end{array}
$$

And that's all there is to it!

DRILL 1: SOLVING EQUATIONS

Practice solving equations in the following examples. Remember that some equations may have more than one root. The answers can be found in Part IV.

1. If $\dfrac{\left(3x^2 - 7\right)}{17} = 4$, then $x =$

2. If $n^2 = 5n$, then $n =$

3. If $\dfrac{2a - 3}{3} = -\dfrac{1}{2}$, then $a =$

4. If $\dfrac{5s + 3}{3} = 21$, then $s =$

5. If $\dfrac{3(8x - 2) + 5}{5} = 4$, then $x =$

6. If $|2m + 5| = 23$, then $m =$

7. If $\left|\dfrac{r-7}{5}\right| = 4$, then $r =$

FACTORING AND DISTRIBUTING

When manipulating algebraic equations, you'll need to use the tools of factoring and distributing. These are just ways of rearranging equations to make them easier to work with.

Factoring

Factoring simply means finding some factor that is in every term of an expression and "pulling it out." By "pulling it out," we mean dividing each individual term by that factor, and then placing the whole expression in parentheses with that factor on the outside. Here's an example:

$$x^3 - 5x^2 + 6x = 0$$

On the left side of this equation, every term contains at least one x—that is, x is a factor of every term in the expression. That means you can factor out an x:

$$x^3 - 5x^2 + 6x = 0$$
$$x(x^2 - 5x + 6) = 0$$

The new expression has exactly the same value as the old one; it's just written differently, in a way that might make your calculations easier. Numbers as well as variables can be factored out, as seen in the following example.

$$11x^2 + 88x + 176 = 0$$

This equation is, at first glance, a bit of a headache. It'd be nice to get rid of that coefficient in front of the term. In a case like this, check the other terms and see if they share a factor. In fact, in this equation, every term on the left side is a multiple of 11. Because 11 is a factor of each term, you can pull it out:

$$11x^2 + 88x + 176 = 0$$
$$11(x^2 + 8x + 16) = 0$$
$$x^2 + 8x + 16 = 0$$
$$(x + 4)^2 = 0$$
$$x = -4$$

As you can see, factoring can make an equation easier to solve.

Distributing

Distributing is factoring in reverse. When an entire expression in parentheses is being multiplied by some factor, you can "distribute" the factor into each term, and get rid of the parentheses. For example:

$$3x(4 + 2x) = 6x^2 + 36$$

On the left side of this equation the parentheses make it difficult to combine terms and simplify the equation. You can get rid of the parentheses by distributing.

$$3x(4 + 2x) = 6x^2 + 36$$

$$12x + 6x^2 = 6x^2 + 36$$

And suddenly, the equation is much easier to solve.

$$12x + 6x^2 - 6x^2 = 6x^2 - 6x^2 + 36$$

$$12x = 36$$

$$x = 3$$

DRILL 2: FACTORING AND DISTRIBUTING

Practice a little factoring and distributing in the following examples, and keep an eye out for equations that could be simplified by this kind of rearrangement. The answers can be found in Part IV.

3. If $(11x)(50) + (50x)(29) = 4{,}000$, then $x =$

(A) 2,000
(B)   200
(C)   20
(D)   2
(E)   0.2

17. If $ab \neq 0$, $\dfrac{-3b(a+2)+6b}{-ab} =$

(A) −3
(B) −2
(C)   0
(D)   1
(E)   3

36. If $x \neq -1$, $\dfrac{x^5 + x^4 + x^3 + x^2}{x^3 + x^2 + x + 1} =$

    (A) $4x^2$
    (B) x^2
    (C) $4x$
    (D) x
    (E) 4

PLUGGING IN

Plugging In is a technique for short-cutting algebra questions. It works on a certain class of algebra questions in which relationships are defined, but no real numbers are introduced. For example:

19. The use of a neighborhood car wash costs n dollars for a membership and p cents for each wash. If a membership includes a bonus of 4 free washes, which of the following reflects the cost, in dollars, of getting a membership at the car wash and washing a car q times, if q is greater than 4 ?

    (A) $100n + pq - 4p$

    (B) $n + 100pq - 25p$

    (C) $n + pq - \dfrac{p}{25}$

    (D) $n + \dfrac{pq}{100} - \dfrac{p}{25}$

    (E) $n + \dfrac{p}{100} - \dfrac{q}{4}$

To Number or Not to Number?

Let's say you walk into a candy store. The store is selling certain pieces of candy for 5 cents and 10 cents each. You want to get 3 pieces of the 5 cent candy and 6 pieces of the 10 cent candy. You give the cashier a $5 bill. What's your change?

Ok, now let's say you walk into a candy store run by ETS. This store is selling certain pieces of candy for x cents and y cents each. You want to get m pieces of the x cent candy and n pieces of the y cent candy. You give the cashier a $$z$ bill. What's your change?

Which problem would be easier to solve? The one with the numbers! Numbers make everything easier. So why bother with variables when you don't have to?

Here's How to Crack It

In this problem, you see variables in the question and in the answer choices. That's a big clue!

> When you see variables in the answer choices, PLUG IN!

Let's try Plugging In with this problem. We'll start with n, the membership fee.

Plug In an easy number like 3, so that a membership costs $3.00.

Then, Plug In a number for p, the charge per wash. Since this number is in cents, and we'll need to convert it to dollars in the answers, choose a number that can be converted easily to dollars, like 200. Let's make $p = 200$, so a wash costs $2.00.

Last, let's say that q, the number of washes, is 5. That's as easy as it gets. With 4 free washes, you're paying for only 1.

Then, just work out the answer to the question using your numbers. How much does it cost for a membership and 5 washes? Well, that's $3.00 for a membership, 4 washes free, and 1 wash for $2.00. The total is $5.00. That means that if you plug your numbers into the answer choices, the right answer should give you 5. We call that your target number—the number you are looking for in the answer choices. Put a double circle around your target value, so that it stands out from all the other numbers you've written down.

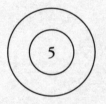

When you plug $n = 3$, $p = 200$, and $q = 5$ into the answer choices, the only answer choice that gives you 5 is (D). That means you've hit your target number, and you're done.

A Big Clue
There will be times when ETS will give you questions that include variables and the phrase "in terms of" (for example, "in terms of x"). This is a big clue that you can Plug In. Cross off the phrase "in terms of x." They're just extra words and you don't need them to solve the problem.

Take a look at one more:

---

20. If $jk \neq 0$, then $\dfrac{jk - \dfrac{j}{k}}{\dfrac{j}{k}} =$

(A) $k^2 - \dfrac{j}{k}$

(B) $j^2 - \dfrac{j^2}{k^2}$

(C) $jk - 1$

(D) $j^2 - 1$

(E) $k^2 - 1$

Here's How to Crack It

When there are variables in the question and the answer choices, Plug In. Re-

member to select numbers that make your math easy. In this case, it's important

to choose numbers that make the fraction $\dfrac{j}{k}$ work out conveniently. Making

$j = 4$ and $k = 2$ turns out well, because it makes $\dfrac{j}{k} = 2$. The expression $\dfrac{jk - \dfrac{j}{k}}{\dfrac{j}{k}}$

then works out to $\dfrac{(4)(2) - 2}{2} = \dfrac{8 - 2}{2} = \dfrac{6}{2} = 3$. To find the correct answer, just go

quickly through the answer choices to find the one that also equals 3 when $j = 4$

and $k = 2$. Only (E) works out equal to 3. Choice (E) is correct.

Hidden Plug-Ins

Let's take a look at the following example:

13. The size of an art collection is tripled, and then 70 percent of the collection is sold. Acquisitions then increase the size of the collection by 10 percent. The size of the art collection is then what percent of its size before these three changes?

    (A) 240%
    (B) 210%
    (C) 111%
    (D) 99%
    (E) 21%

Steps for Plugging In
- Plug In a number for the variable(s)
- Work the steps of the problem and calculate the target value
- Check all five answer choices

Here's How to Crack It

Here's another question in which you aren't given numbers. In this case, you don't know the original size of the art collection. Instead of variables, though, the question and answers contain percents. This is another sign that you can Plug In whatever numbers you like. Because you're working with percentages, 100 is a good number to Plug In—it'll make your math easier.

You start with a collection of 100 items. It's tripled, meaning it increases to 300. Then it's decreased by 70%. That's a decrease of 210, so the collection's size decreases to 90. Then, finally, it increases by 10%. That's an increase of 9, for a final collection size of 99. Since the collection began at 100, it's now at 99% of its original size. The answer is (D). It doesn't matter what number you choose for the original size of the collection—you'll always get the right answer. The trick to choosing numbers is picking ones that make your math easier.

Not Sure When to Plug In? Here Are Some Hints
- The answer choices contain variables, percentages, fractions, or ratios.
- There are unknown quantities or variables in the question.
- The question seems to call for an algebraic equation.
- You see the phrase "in terms of" followed by a variable (for example "in terms of p"). Cross off the phrase "in terms of p," because you don't need it to solve the problem.

The idea behind Plugging In is that if these relationships are true, then it doesn't matter what numbers you put into the question; you'll always arrive at the same answer choice. So the easiest way to get through the question is to Plug In easy numbers, follow them through the question, and see which answer choice they lead you to.

Occasionally, more than one answer choice will produce the correct answer. This often occurs when the question asks for something that "must be true." When that happens, eliminate the answer choices that didn't work out, and Plug In some different kinds of numbers. When Plugging

In more than once, remember ZONEF: zero, one, negatives, extremes, and fractions. You won't have to exhaust this list on any one question, but it will help you remember the kinds of numbers that will help you get to the right answer. The new numbers will produce a new target value. Use this new target value to eliminate the remaining incorrect answer choices. You will rarely have to Plug In more than two sets of numbers.

Plugging In More Than Once
Remember to use ZONEF:

Z - Zero
O - One
N - Negatives
E - Extremes
F - Fractions

When using Plugging In, keep a few simple rules in mind:

- Avoid Plugging In 1 or 0 (unless you have to Plug In more than once), which often makes more than one answer choice produce the same number. For the same reason, avoid Plugging In numbers that appear in the answer choices—they're more likely to cause several answer choices to produce your target value.
- Plug In numbers that make your math easy—2, 3, and 5 are good choices in ordinary algebra. Multiples of 100 are good in percentage questions, and multiples of 60 are good in questions dealing with seconds, minutes, and hours.

Plugging In can be an incredibly useful technique. By Plugging In numbers, you're checking your math as you do the problem. When you use algebra, it takes an extra step to check your work with actual numbers. Also, there are fewer chances to mess up when you Plug In. And you can Plug In when you don't know how to set up an algebraic expression based on a question.

Plugging In is often safer because ETS designs the answer choices so that, if you mess up the algebra, your result will be one of the wrong answers. When your answer matches one of the choices, you think it must be right. Very tempting. Furthermore, all of the answer choices look very similar, algebraically. This is how ETS camouflages correct answers. But when you Plug In, the answers often look very different. Often you'll be able to approximate to eliminate numbers that are obviously too big or too small, without doing a lot of calculation, and that will save you lots of time!

DRILL 3: PLUGGING IN

Try solving the following practice questions by Plugging In. Remember to check all your answer choices, and Plug In a second set of numbers if more than one answer choice produces your target number. The answers can be found in Part IV.

5. The price of an item in a store is p dollars. If the tax on the item is $t\%$, what is the total cost in dollars of n such items, including tax?

(A) npt

(B) $npt + 1$

(C) $\dfrac{np(t+1)}{100}$

(D) $100n(p + pt)$

(E) $\dfrac{np(t+100)}{100}$

8. Vehicle A travels at x miles per hour for x hours. Vehicle B travels a miles per hour faster than Vehicle A, and travels b hours longer than Vehicle A. Vehicle B travels how much farther than Vehicle A, in miles?

(A) $x^2 - ab$

(B) $a^2 + b^2$

(C) $ax + bx + ab$

(D) $x^2 + abx + ab$

(E) $2x^2 + (a + b)x + ab$

17. For any real number n, $|5 - n| - |n - 5| =$

(A) -2

(B) -1

(C) 0

(D) 1

(E) 2

20. If Company A builds a skateboards per week, and Company B builds b skateboards per day, then in m weeks, Company A builds how many more skateboards than Company B ?

(A) $7bm$

(B) $m(a - 7b)$

(C) $7(ma - mb)$

(D) $7m(a - b)$

(E) $\dfrac{m(a - b)}{7}$

23. If $a > 3$ and $b < 3$, then which of the following could be true?

    I. $a - b > 3$

    II. $a + b < 3$

    III. $|a + b| < 3$

(A) I only
(B) III only
(C) I and II only
(D) II and III only
(E) I, II, and III

30. For all real numbers, $x^3 < y^3$. Which of the following must be true?

    I. $x < y$

    II. $x^2 < y^2$

    III. $|x| < |y|$

(A) I only
(B) III only
(C) I and II only
(D) II and III only
(E) I, II, and III

PLUGGING IN THE ANSWERS (PITA)

Plugging In The Answers (PITA) is another approach to solving algebra questions. It uses numbers instead of algebra to find the answer. As you've just seen, Plugging In is useful on questions whose answer choices contain variables, percentages, fractions, or ratios—not actual numbers. PITA, on the other hand, is useful on questions whose answer choices do contain actual numbers.

ETS always organizes answers in numerical order—usually from least to greatest. You can use this to your advantage by combining PITA and POE.

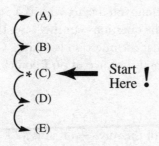

To use PITA on an algebra question, take (C), the middle answer choice, and stick it back into the problem. If it makes all of the statements in the question true, then it's the right answer. If it doesn't, eliminate (C) and try another answer choice. Usually, you'll know from your experience with (C) whether you want to try a smaller or larger answer choice. If (C) is too small, you can eliminate the smaller two choices and try again with the remaining two. Using smart POE can really save you a lot of time. When you find the right answer, you can stop because the answer choices are actual numbers and not variables.

Don't start with (C) if a question asks you for the least or greatest value. Instead, for questions asking about the least value, start with the smallest answer choice. For questions asking about the greatest value, start with the largest answer choice.

Like Plugging In, PITA can open doors for you when you're unsure how to approach a question with algebra. Also, like Plugging In, PITA checks your answers as you pick them, eliminating careless errors. This can be particularly useful at the tough end of the SAT Subject Test in Math 1, as you start getting into hard material. Plugging In and PITA can enable you to solve problems that might otherwise stump you.

Let's take a look at a PITA example.

10. A duck travels from point A to point B. If the duck flies $\frac{3}{4}$ of the way, walks $\frac{1}{9}$ of the way, and swims the remaining 10 kilometers of her trip, what is the total distance in kilometers traveled by the duck?

(A) 36
(B) 45
(C) 56
(D) 72
(E) 108

Here's How to Crack It

To use PITA on this question, you'd start with (C). The answer choices represent the quantity asked for in the question—in this case, the total distance traveled by the duck. Always know what the question is asking. Choice (C), therefore, means that the duck traveled a total distance of 56 kilometers. Follow this information through the problem.

The duck flies $\frac{3}{4}$ of the way. $\frac{3}{4}$ of 56 is 42 kilometers.

The duck walks $\frac{1}{9}$ of the way. $\frac{1}{9}$ of 56 is 6.22 kilometers.

That makes 48.22 kilometers, which leaves 7.78 kilometers in the trip.

BUT the duck swims 10 kilometers!

That means that (C) isn't the right answer. It also tells you that you need a longer trip to fit in all that flying, walking, and swimming; move down to (D), the next largest answer, and try again. At this point, you can also eliminate (A), (B), and (C) because they are too small.

The duck flies $\frac{3}{4}$ of the way. $\frac{3}{4}$ of 72 is 54 kilometers.

The duck walks $\frac{1}{9}$ of the way. $\frac{1}{9}$ of 72 is 8 kilometers.

That makes 62 kilometers, which leaves 10 kilometers in the trip.

And THAT'S exactly how far the duck swims, 10 kilometers. Right answer.

Generally, you'll never have to try more than two answer choices when using PITA thanks to POE—and sometimes, the first answer you try, (C), will be correct. Keep your eyes open for PITA opportunities on the SAT Subject Test in Math 1, particularly when you run into an algebra question that you're not sure how to solve.

> **You Should Try PITA Whenever**
> - there is an unknown or variable in the question, the question asks for an actual value, and the answer choices are all numbers arranged in increasing or decreasing order
> - you have the bizarre urge to translate a word problem into a complicated algebraic equation
> - you find yourself reading a long, convoluted story about some number, and you don't even know what the number is
> - you have no idea how to solve the problem

If, after you Plug In (C), you're not sure which way to go in the answer choices, don't haggle for too long. Just eliminate (C), pick a direction, and go! If you go the wrong way, you'll know pretty quickly, and then you can head the other way.

> **Steps for PITA**
> - Start with (C) and work the steps of the problem.
> - If (C) doesn't work, use POE to decide whether to go higher or lower.
> - When you find the right answer, STOP.

DRILL 4: PLUGGING IN THE ANSWERS (PITA)

Solve the following questions by using PITA. Remember to start with (C), the middle answer choice. The answers can be found in Part IV.

11. Matt has 4 more hats than Aaron and half as many hats as Michael. If the three together have 24 hats, how many hats does Michael have?

   (A) 7
   (B) 9
   (C) 12
   (D) 14
   (E) 18

17. A shipment of 3,200 items is divided into 2 portions so that the difference between the portions is one-half of their average. What is the ratio of the smaller to the larger portion?

   (A) 1:2
   (B) 1:3
   (C) 2:5
   (D) 3:5
   (E) 5:8

27. Three distinct positive integers have a sum of 15 and a product of 45. What is the largest of these integers?

   (A) 1
   (B) 3
   (C) 5
   (D) 9
   (E) 15

Reading Inequality Signs

Here's how you should read the four basic inequality signs:

$a < b$ — a is less than b

$a > b$ — a is greater than b

$a \leq b$ — a is less than or equal to b

$a \geq b$ — a is greater than or equal to b

INEQUALITIES

Inequalities can be treated just like equations. You can add, subtract, multiply, and divide on both sides of the inequality sign. And you still solve by isolating the variable. There is one major difference between solving an equation and solving an inequality.

> Whenever you multiply or divide both sides of an inequality by a negative, flip the inequality sign.

Multiplying across an inequality by a negative flips the signs of all of the terms in the inequality. The inequality sign itself must also flip.

$$-1(4n - 20 > -3n + 15) \qquad\qquad -1(x \geq 5)$$

$$-4n + 20 < 3n - 15 \qquad\qquad -x \leq -5$$

As long as you remember this rule, you can treat inequalities just like equations and use all of your algebra tools to solve them.

DRILL 5: INEQUALITIES

Practice solving inequalities in the following exercises. The answers can be found in Part IV.

1. If $\dfrac{6(5-n)}{4} \leq 3$, then _____

2. If $\dfrac{r+3}{2} < 5$, then _____

3. If $\dfrac{4(1-x)+9}{3} \leq 5$, then _____

4. If $8(3x + 1) + 4 < 15$, then _____

5. If $23 - 4t \geq 11$, then _____

6. If $4n - 25 \leq 19 - 7n$, then _____

7. If $-5(p + 2) < 10p - 13$, then _____

8. If $\dfrac{23s + 7}{10} \geq 2s + 1$, then _____

9. If $-3x - 16 \leq 2x + 19$, then _____

10. If $\dfrac{14s - 11}{9} \geq s - 1$, then _____

WORKING WITH RANGES

Inequalities are also used when discussing the range of possible values a variable could equal. Sometimes you'll see an algebraic phrase in which there are two inequality signs. These are called ranges. Your variable can be any number within a range of numbers, for example, $2 < x < 10$. This means that x can be any number between, but not equal to, 2 and 10. Let's look at this next example:

At a certain amusement park, anyone under 48 inches tall is not permitted to ride the Stupendous Hurlcoaster, because of the amusement park's standard height requirements for roller coasters. Anyone over 84 inches is also prohibited from the ride because he or she may be too tall to fit under the Hurlcoaster's wooden braces. If x is the height of a rider of the Stupendous Hurlcoaster, what is the range of possible values of x ?

The end values of the range are obviously 48 and 84. But are 48 and 84 included in the range themselves, or not? If you read carefully, you'll see that only those under 48 inches or over 84 inches are barred from riding the Hurlcoaster. If you're 48 inches or 84 inches tall, you're perfectly legal. The range of possible values of x is therefore given by $48 \le x \le 84$. Noticing the difference between "greater than" and "greater than or equal to" is crucial to many range questions.

You can add and subtract ranges, as long as their inequality signs point the same way. You can also multiply or divide across a range to produce new information, as long as you obey that basic rule of inequalities—flip the sign if you multiply or divide by a negative number.

DRILL 6: WORKING WITH RANGES

Try the following range questions. The answers can be found in Part IV.

If the range of possible values for x is given by $-5 < x < 8$, find the range of possible values for each of the following:

1. $-x$: _____
2. $4x$: _____
3. $x + 6$: _____
4. $(2 - x)$: _____
5. $\dfrac{x}{2}$: _____

Adding Ranges

Occasionally, a question on the SAT Subject Test in Math 1 will require you to add, subtract, or multiply ranges. Take a look at this example:

> If $3 < a < 10$ and $-6 < b < 3$, what is the range of possible values of $a + b$?

Here, the range of $(a + b)$ will be the sum of the range of a and the range of b. The easy way to do this is to list out the four ways you can combine the endpoints of the two ranges. To do this, take the smallest a and add it to the smallest b. Then, add the smallest a to the biggest b. Then, add the biggest a to the smallest b. Finally, take the biggest a and add it to the biggest b. The biggest and smallest results you get will be the endpoints of the range of $(a + b)$. Watch!

$$3 + -6 = -3$$

$$3 + 3 = 6$$

$$10 + -6 = 4$$

$$10 + 3 = 13$$

The smallest number you found is -3, and the biggest is 13, so the range of possible values looks like the following:

$$-3 < a + b < 13$$

Subtracting Ranges

To subtract one range from another, combine the endpoints just as you did when adding ranges, but in this case, subtract the four combinations of endpoints. Make sure you're subtracting in the order the question asks you to. Let's look at this example.

> If $-4 < a < 5$ and $2 < b < 12$, then what is the range of possible values of $a - b$?

This time, take the smallest a and subtract the smallest b. Then, find the smallest a minus the biggest b, and so on.

$$-4 - 2 = -6$$

$$-4 - 12 = -16$$

$$5 - 2 = 3$$

$$5 - 12 = -7$$

So the range you're looking for is:

$$-16 < a - b < 3$$

Multiplying Ranges

To multiply ranges, follow the same steps, but multiply the endpoints. Let's try one.

> If $-3 < f < 4$ and $-7 < g < 2$, then what is the range of possible values of fg ?

These are the four possible products of the bounds of f and g.

$$(-3)(-7) = 21 \qquad\qquad (-3)(2) = -6$$

$$(4)(-7) = -28 \qquad\qquad (4)(2) = 8$$

The greatest of these values is 21 and the least is -28. So the range of possible values of fg is:

$$-28 < fg < 21$$

And that's all there is to dealing with ranges.

DRILL 7: MORE WORKING WITH RANGES

Absolute Value?
Trouble with absolute value? Pay special attention to the explanations of questions 7 and 8 from this drill.

Try the following range questions. The answers can be found in Part IV.

1. If $-2 \leq a \leq 7$ and $3 \leq b \leq 9$, then what is the range of possible values of $b - a$?

2. If $2 \leq x \leq 11$ and $6 \geq y \geq -4$, then what is the range of possible values of $x + y$?

3. If $-3 \leq n \leq 8$, then what is the range of possible values of n^2 ?

4. If $0 < x < 5$ and $-9 < y < -3$, then what is the range of possible values of $x - y$?

5. If $-3 \leq r \leq 10$ and $-10 \leq s \leq 3$, then what is the range of possible values of $r + s$?

6. If $-6 < c < 0$ and $13 < d < 21$, then what is the range of possible values of cd ?

7. If $|3 - x| \leq 4$, then what is the range of possible values of x ?

8. If $|2a + 7| \geq 13$, then what is the range of possible values of a ?

DIRECT AND INVERSE VARIATION

Direct and inverse variation are specific relationships between quantities. Quantities that vary directly are said to be in *proportion* or *proportional*. Quantities that vary inversely are said to be *inversely proportional*.

Direct Variation

If x and y are in direct variation, that can be said in several ways: x and y are in proportion; x and y change proportionally; or x varies directly with y. All of these descriptions come down to the same thing: if x increases, then y increases. Specifically, they mean that the quantity $\dfrac{x}{y}$ will always have the same numerical value. That's all there is to it. Take a look at a question based on this idea.

> ### A Great Way to Remember
> To remember direct variation, think "direct means divide." So in order to solve, you set up a proportion with a fraction on each side of the equation. Just solve for the one number you don't know. There are two formulas associated with direct variation that may be familiar to you. They are $\dfrac{y_1}{x_1} = \dfrac{y_2}{x_2}$ or $y = kx$, where k is a constant.

---

17. If n and m vary directly, and n is 3 when m is 24, then what is the value of n when m is 11 ?

    (A) 1.375
    (B) 1.775
    (C) 1.95
    (D) 2.0
    (E) 2.125

Here's How to Crack It

To solve the problem, use the definition of direct variation: $\dfrac{n}{m}$ must always have the same numerical value. Set up a proportion.

$$\frac{3}{24} = \frac{n}{11}$$

Solve by cross-multiplying and isolating n.

$$24n = 33$$

$$n = 33 \div 24$$

$$n = 1.375$$

And that's all there is to it. The correct answer is (A). All direct variation questions can be answered this way.

Inverse Variation

If x and y are in inverse variation, this can be said in several ways as well: x and y are in inverse proportion; x and y are inversely proportional; or x varies inversely with y. All of these descriptions come down to the same thing: x increases when y decreases, and decreases when y increases. Specifically, they mean that the quantity xy will always have the same numerical value.

Take a look at this question based on inverse variation:

15. If a varies inversely as b, and $a = 3$ when $b = 5$, then what is the value of a when $b = 7$?

    (A)   2.14
    (B)   2.76
    (C)   3.28
    (D)   4.2
    (E)   11.67

Here's How to Crack It

To answer the question, use the definition of inverse variation. That is, the quantity ab must always have the same value. Therefore, you can set up this simple equation.

$$3 \times 5 = a \times 7$$
$$7a = 15$$
$$a = 15 \div 7$$
$$a = 2.142857$$

So the correct answer is (A). All inverse variation questions on the SAT Subject Test in Math 1 can be handled this way.

DRILL 8: DIRECT AND INVERSE VARIATION

Try these practice exercises using the definitions of direct and inverse variation. The answers can be found in Part IV.

15. If a varies inversely as b, and $a = 3$ when $b = 5$, then what is the value of a when $b = x$?

   (A) $\dfrac{3}{x}$

   (B) $\dfrac{5}{x}$

   (C) $\dfrac{15}{x}$

   (D) $3x$

   (E) $3x^2$

18. If n and m vary directly, and $n = 5$ when $m = 4$, then what is the value of n when $m = 5$?

   (A) 4.0
   (B) 4.75
   (C) 5.5
   (D) 6.25
   (E) 7.75

24. If p varies directly as q, and $p = 3$ when $q = 10$, then what is the value of p when $q = 1$?

   (A) 0.3
   (B) 0.43
   (C) 0.5
   (D) 4.3
   (E) 4.33

26. If y varies directly as x^2, and $y = 24$ when $x = 3.7$, what is the value of y when $x = 8.3$?

   (A) 170.67
   (B) 120.77
   (C) 83.23
   (D) 64.00
   (E) 53.83

WORK AND TRAVEL QUESTIONS

Word problems dealing with work and travel tend to cause a lot of careless mistakes, because the relationships among distance, time, and speed—or among work-rate, work, and time—sometimes confuse test takers. When working with questions about travel, just remember this:

$$distance = rate \times time$$

Look familiar?
If these two formulas seem the same, it's because they are. After all, what is work done if not the distance from the start of work to the end?

When working with questions about work being done, remember this:

$$work\ done = rate\ of\ work \times time$$

DRILL 9: WORK AND TRAVEL QUESTIONS

Answer the following practice questions using these formulas. The answers can be found in Part IV.

11. A factory contains a series of water tanks, all of the same size. If Pump 1 can fill 12 of these tanks in a 12-hour shift, and Pump 2 can fill 11 tanks in the same time, then how many tanks can the two pumps fill, working together, in 1 hour?

    (A) 0.13
    (B) 0.35
    (C) 1.92
    (D) 2.88
    (E) 3.33

12. A projectile travels 227 feet in one second. If there are 5,280 feet in 1 mile, then which of the following best approximates the projectile's speed in miles per hour?

    (A) 155
    (B) 170
    (C) 194
    (D) 252
    (E) 333

18. A train travels from Langston to Hughesville and back in 5.5 hours. If the two towns are 200 miles apart, what is the average speed of the train in miles per hour?

    (A) 36.36
    (B) 72.73
    (C) 109.09
    (D) 110.10
    (E) 120.21

25. Jules can make m muffins in s minutes. Alice can make n muffins in t minutes. Which of the following gives the number of muffins that Jules and Alice can make together in 30 minutes?

    (A) $\dfrac{m+n}{30st}$

    (B) $\dfrac{30(m+n)}{st}$

    (C) $30(mt+ns)$

    (D) $\dfrac{30(mt+ns)}{st}$

    (E) $\dfrac{mt+ns}{30st}$

Average Speed

The "average speed" question is a specialized breed of travel question. Here's what a basic "average speed" question might look like.

15. Roberto travels from his home to the beach, driving at 30 miles per hour. He returns along the same route at 50 miles per hour. If the distance from Roberto's house to the beach is 10 miles, then what is Roberto's average speed for the round-trip in miles per hour?

    (A) 32.5
    (B) 37.5
    (C) 40.0
    (D) 42.5
    (E) 45.0

Won't Get Fooled Again
If an answer choice looks too good to be true, it probably is.

Here's How to Crack It

The easy mistake to make on this question is to simply choose (C), which is the trap answer because it is just the average of the two speeds. Average speed isn't found by averaging speeds, however. Instead, you have to use this formula:

$$\text{average speed} = \frac{\text{total distance}}{\text{total time}}$$

Look Familiar?

This formula may look familiar to you. That's because it's taken from our Average Pie. Another way to work with average speed questions is to use the Average Pie where the total is the total distance and the number of things is the time. So it would look like this:

Total Distance

Average Speed | Total Time

The total distance is easy to figure out—10 miles each way is a total of 20 miles. Total time is a little trickier. For that, you have to use the "distance = rate × time" formula. Here, it's useful to rearrange the equation to read as follows:

$$\text{time} = \frac{\text{distance}}{\text{rate}}$$

On the way to the beach, Roberto traveled 10 miles at 30 mph, which took 0.333 hours, according to the formula. On the way home, he traveled 10 miles at 50 mph, which took 0.2 hours. That makes 20 miles in a total of 0.533 hours. Plug those numbers into the average-speed formula, and you get an average speed of 37.5 mph. The answer is (B).

Here's a general tip for "average speed" questions: On any round-trip in which the traveler moves at one speed heading out and another speed returning, the traveler's average speed will be a little lower than the average of the two speeds. So if you're short on time, you can use this fact to help you with POE.

DRILL 10: AVERAGE SPEED

Try these "average speed" questions. The answers can be found in Part IV.

19. Alexandra jogs from her house to the lake at 12 miles per hour and jogs back by the same route at 9 miles per hour. If the path from her house to the lake is 6 miles long, what is her average speed in miles per hour for the round-trip?

(A) 11.3
(B) 11.0
(C) 10.5
(D) 10.3
(E) 10.1

24. A truck travels 50 miles from Town S to Town T in 50 minutes, and then immediately drives 40 miles from Town T to Town U in 40 minutes. What is the truck's average speed in miles per hour, from Town S to Town U ?

(A)   1
(B) 10
(C) 45
(D) 60
(E) 90

33. Ben travels a certain distance at 25 miles per hour and returns across the same distance at 50 miles per hour. What is his average speed in miles per hour for the round-trip?

(A) 37.5
(B) 33.3
(C) 32.0
(D) 29.5
(E) It cannot be determined from the information given.

SIMULTANEOUS EQUATIONS

It's possible to have a set of equations that can't be solved individually but can be solved in combination. A good example of such a set of equations would be:

$$4x + 2y = 18$$

$$x + y = 5$$

You can't solve either equation by itself. But you can if you put them together. This is called solving simultaneous equations. All you do is stack them and then add or subtract them to find what you're looking for. Often, what you're looking for is another equation. For example, the question that contains the two equations you were given wants to know what the value of $10x + 6y$ is. Do you need to know x or y? No! You just need to know $10x + 6y$. Let's try adding the two equations:

$$
\begin{array}{r}
4x + 2y = 18 \\
+x + y = 5 \\
\hline
5x + 3y = 23
\end{array}
$$

Did adding help? It did! Even though we didn't get what they were asking for, we did get half of what they were asking for. So just multiply the entire equation by 2 and you have your answer: 46.

That Nasty Phrase "In Terms Of"
Remember how we had you cross off the phrase "in terms of" when you plugged in because it doesn't help you at all? Well, solving x "in terms of" y for simultaneous equations doesn't help either. It takes too much time and there is too much room for error to solve in terms of one variable and then put that whole thing into the other equation. And much of the time, that's unnecessary because we don't care what the values of the individual variables are!

Here's another example of a system of simultaneous equations as they might appear on an SAT Subject Test in Math 1 question. Try it.

───────────○───────────

7. If x and y are real numbers such that $3x + 4y = 10$ and $2x - 4y = 5$, then what is the value of x ?

Add It Up
Do you notice how adding brings you close to what the question is asking for?

Here's How to Crack It

$$
\begin{array}{r}
3x + 4y = 10 \\
+ \ \ 2x - 4y = \ 5 \\
\hline
5x \quad\ \ = 15 \\
x \quad\ \ = \ 3
\end{array}
$$

In the question above, instead of solving to find a third equation, you need to find one of the variables. Your job doesn't change: Stack 'em and then add or subtract.

───────────○───────────

This will be the case with every simultaneous equations question. Every once in a while you may want to multiply or divide one equation by a number before you add or subtract.

Try another one. Solve it yourself before checking the explanation.

8. If $12a - 3b = 131$ and $5a - 10b = 61$, then what is the value of $a + b$?

This time adding didn't work, did it? Let's go through and see what subtraction does:

Avoid Subtraction Mistakes
If adding doesn't work and you want to try subtracting, wait! Multiply one of the equations by −1 and add instead. That way you ensure that you don't make any calculation errors along the way.

$$
\begin{array}{r}
12a - \ 3b = 131 \\
-1(5a - 10b) = \ \ 61 \\
\hline
12a - \ 3b \ = 131 \\
-5a + 10b \ = -61 \\
\hline
7a + 7b = 70 \\
a + \ \ b = 10
\end{array}
$$

A little practice will enable you to see quickly whether adding or subtracting will be more helpful. Sometimes it may be necessary to multiply one of the equations by a convenient factor to make terms that will cancel out properly. For example:

6. If $4n - 8m = 6$, and $-5n + 4m = 3$, then $n =$

As before, start by stacking the two equations.

$$4n - 8m = 6$$
$$-5n + 4m = 3$$

Here, it quickly becomes apparent that neither adding nor subtracting will combine these two equations very usefully. However, things look a little brighter when the second equation is multiplied by 2.

$$2(-5n + 4m = 3)$$

$$
\begin{aligned}
4n - 8m &= 6 \\
-10n + 8m &= 6 \\
\hline
-6n &= 12 \\
n &= -2
\end{aligned}
$$

Occasionally, a simultaneous equation can be solved only by *multiplying* all of the pieces together. This will generally be the case only when the equations themselves involve multiplication alone, not the kind of addition and subtraction that the previous equations contained. Take a look at this example:

$$ab = 3 \qquad bc = \frac{5}{9} \qquad ac = 15$$

34. If the above statements are true, what is one possible value of *abc* ?

(A) 5.0
(B) 8.33
(C) 9.28
(D) 18.54
(E) 25.0

# of Equations = # of Variables
We've been talking about two equations each containing two variables. But ETS doesn't stop there. A good rule of thumb is, if the number of equations is equal to the number of variables, you can solve the equations. So count 'em and don't get discouraged! They're always easier than they look!

Here's How to Crack It
This is a tough one. No single one of the three small equations can be solved by itself. In fact, no two of them together can be solved. It takes all three to solve the system, and here's how it's done:

Where's the Trap?
Remember that a number 34 is a difficult question. What do you notice about (E)?

$$ab \times bc \times ac = 3 \times \frac{5}{9} \times 15$$

$$aabbcc = 25$$

$$a^2 b^2 c^2 = 25$$

Once you've multiplied all three equations together, all you have to do is take the square roots of both sides, and you've got a value for *abc*.

$$a^2 b^2 c^2 = 25$$

$$abc = 5, -5$$

And so (A) is the correct answer.

———————————○———————————

DRILL 11: SIMULTANEOUS EQUATIONS

Try answering the following practice questions by solving equations simultaneously. The answers can be found in Part IV.

26. If $a + 3b = 6$, and $4a - 3b = 14$, $a =$

   (A) −4
   (B) 2
   (C) 4
   (D) 10
   (E) 20

31. If $2x - 7y = 12$ and $-8x + 3y = 2$, which of the following is the value of $x - y$?

   (A) 12.0
   (B) 8.0
   (C) 5.5
   (D) 1.0
   (E) 0.8

$$ab = \frac{1}{8}, \; bc = 6, \; ac = 3$$

34. If all of the above statements are true, what is one possible value of *abc* ?

   (A) 3.75
   (B) 2.25
   (C) 2.0
   (D) 1.5
   (E) 0.25

37. If $xyz = 4$ and $y^2 z = 5$, what is the value of $\dfrac{x}{y}$?

   (A) 20.0
   (B) 10.0
   (C) 1.25
   (D) 1.0
   (E) 0.8

FOIL

A binomial is an algebraic expression that has two terms (pieces connected by addition or subtraction). FOIL is how to multiply two binomials together.

The letters of FOIL stand for:

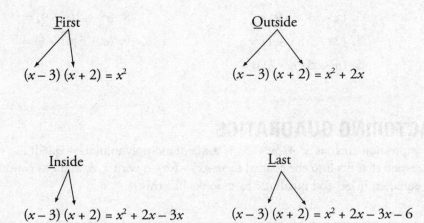

Suppose you wanted to do the following multiplication:

$$(x + 5)(x - 2)$$

You would multiply the two *first* terms together, $(x)(x) = x^2$.
And then the *outside* terms, $(x)(-2) = -2x$.
And then the *inside* terms, $(5)(x) = 5x$.
And finally the two *last* terms, $(5)(-2) = -10$.

String the four products together and simplify them to produce an answer.

$$x^2 - 2x + 5x - 10$$

$$x^2 + 3x - 10$$

And that's the product of $(x + 5)$ and $(x - 2)$.

DRILL 12: FOIL

Practice using FOIL on the following binomial multiplications. The answers can be found in Part IV.

1. $(x - 2)(x + 11) =$
2. $(b + 5)(b + 7) =$
3. $(x - 3)(x - 9) =$
4. $(2x - 5)(x + 1) =$
5. $(n^2 + 5)(n - 3) =$

6. $(3a + 5)(2a - 7) =$
7. $(x - 3)(x - 6) =$
8. $(c - 2)(c + 9) =$
9. $(d + 5)(d - 1) =$

FACTORING QUADRATICS

An expression such as $x^2 + 3x + 10$ is a quadratic polynomial. A quadratic is an expression that fits into the general form $ax^2 + bx + c$, with a, b, and c as constants. An equation in general quadratic form looks like this:

> **General Form of a Quadratic Equation**
>
> $ax^2 + bx + c = 0$

Often, the best way to solve a quadratic equation is to factor it into two binomials—basically FOIL in reverse. Let's take a look at the quadratic you worked with in the previous section, and the binomials that are its factors.

$$x^2 + 3x - 10 = (x + 5)(x - 2)$$

Notice that the coefficient of the quadratic's middle term (3) is the sum of the constants in the binomials (5 and –2), and that the third term of the quadratic (–10) is the product of those constants. That relationship between a quadratic expression and its factors will always be true. To factor a quadratic, look for a pair of constants whose sum equals the coefficient of the middle term, and whose product equals the last term of the quadratic. Suppose you had to solve this equation:

$$x^2 - 6x + 8 = 0$$

Your first step would be to factor the quadratic polynomial. That means looking for a pair of numbers that add up to –6 and multiply to 8. Because their sum is negative but their product is positive, you know that the numbers are both negative. And as always, there's only one pair of numbers that fits the bill—in this case, –2 and –4.

$$x^2 - 6x + 8 = 0$$

$$(x - 2)(x - 4) = 0$$

Since zero multiplied by anything is equal to zero, this equation will be true if $(x - 2) = 0$ or if $(x - 4) = 0$. Therefore,

$$x = \{2, 4\}$$

Two and four are therefore called the zeros of the equation. They are also known as the roots or solutions of the equation.

Once a quadratic is factored, it's easy to solve for x. The product of the binomials can be zero only if one of the binomials is equal to zero—and there are only two values of x that will make one of the binomials equal to zero (2 and 4). The equation is solved.

DRILL 13: FACTORING QUADRATICS

Solve the following equations by factoring the quadratic polynomials. Write down all of the roots of each equation (values of the variable that make the equations true). The answers can be found in Part IV.

1. $a^2 - 3a + 2 = 0$
2. $d^2 + 8d + 7 = 0$
3. $x^2 + 4x - 21 = 0$
4. $3x^2 + 9x - 30 = 0$
5. $2x^2 + 40x + 198 = 0$
6. $p^2 + 10p = 39$
7. $c^2 + 9c + 20 = 0$
8. $s^2 + 4s - 12 = 0$
9. $x^2 - 3x - 4 = 0$
10. $n^4 - 3n^2 - 10 = 0$

Special Quadratic Identities

There are a few quadratic expressions that you should be able to factor at a glance. Because they are useful mathematically, and above all, because ETS likes to put them on the SAT Subject Test in Math 1, you should memorize the following identities:

$$(x + y)^2 = x^2 + 2xy + y^2$$

$$(x - y)^2 = x^2 - 2xy + y^2$$

$$(x + y)(x - y) = x^2 - y^2$$

Here are some examples of these quadratic identities in action.

1. $n^2 + 10n + 25 = (n + 5)(n + 5) = (n + 5)^2$
2. $r^2 - 16 = (r + 4)(r - 4)$
3. $n^2 - 4n + 4 = (n - 2)(n - 2) = (n - 2)^2$

But knowing the quadratic identities will do more for you than just allow you to factor some expressions quickly. ETS writes questions based specifically on these identities. Such questions are easy to solve if you remember these equations and use them, and quite tricky (or even impossible) if you don't. Here's an example.

---

36. If $a + b = 7$, and $a^2 + b^2 = 37$, then what is the value of ab ?

(A)   6
(B)   12
(C)   15
(D)   22
(E)   30

Here's How to Crack It

Algebraically, this is a tough problem to crack. You can't divide $a^2 + b^2$ by $a + b$ and get anything useful. In fact, most of the usual algebraic approaches to questions like these don't work here. Even plugging the answer choices back into the question (PITA) isn't very helpful. What you can do is recognize that the question is giving you all of the pieces you need to build the quadratic identity: $(x + y)^2 = x^2 + 2xy + y^2$. To solve the problem, just rearrange the identity a little and Plug In the values given by the question.

$$(a + b)^2 = a^2 + b^2 + 2ab$$

$$(7)^2 = 37 + 2ab$$

$$49 = 37 + 2ab$$

$$12 = 2ab$$

$$6 = ab$$

And presto, the answer appears. It's not easy to figure out what a or b is specifically—and you don't need to. Just find the value asked for in the question. If you remember the quadratic identities, solving the problem is easy.

DRILL 14: SPECIAL QUADRATIC IDENTITIES

Try solving the following questions using the quadratic identities, and take note of the clues that tell you when the identities will be useful. The answers can be found in Part IV.

17. If $n - m = -3$ and $n^2 - m^2 = 24$, then which of the following is the sum of n and m ?

   (A) −8
   (B) −6
   (C) −4
   (D) 6
   (E) 8

19. If $x + y = 3$ and $x^2 + y^2 = 8$, then $xy =$

   (A) 0.25
   (B) 0.5
   (C) 1.5
   (D) 2.0
   (E) 2.25

24. If the sum of two nonzero integers is 9 and the sum of their squares is 36, then what is the product of the two integers?

   (A)   9.0
   (B) 13.5
   (C) 18.0
   (D) 22.5
   (E) 45.0

Pencil It In
Don't forget to put pencil to paper on these and other algebra questions with lots of steps. Seeing your work will help you better understand the questions and solutions and avoid careless mistakes.

THE QUADRATIC FORMULA

Unfortunately, not all quadratic equations can be factored by the reverse-FOIL method. The reverse-FOIL method is practical only when the roots of the equation are integers. Sometimes, however, the roots of a quadratic equation will be non-integer decimal numbers, and sometimes a quadratic equation will have no real roots at all. Consider the following quadratic equation:

$$x^2 - 7x + 8 = 0$$

There are no integers that add up to −7 and multiply to 8. This quadratic cannot be factored in the usual way. To solve this equation, it's necessary to use the quadratic formula—a formula that produces the root or roots of any equation in the general quadratic form $ax^2 + bx + c = 0$.

$$x = \frac{-b \pm \sqrt{b^2 - 4ac}}{2a}$$

In Case You Were Worried...
On the SAT Subject Test in Math 1, the quadratic formula is necessary only on difficult questions. You may be able to skip over tough quadratic equation questions and avoid having to use the quadratic formula altogether.

The a, b, and c in the formula refer to the coefficients of an expression in the form $ax^2 + bx + c$. For the equation $x^2 - 7x + 8 = 0$, $a = 1$, $b = -7$, and $c = 8$. Plug these values into the quadratic formula and you get the roots of the equation.

$$x = \frac{-(-7) + \sqrt{(-7)^2 - 4(1)(8)}}{2(1)} \qquad x = \frac{-(-7) - \sqrt{(-7)^2 - 4(1)(8)}}{2(1)}$$

$$x = \frac{7 + \sqrt{49 - 32}}{2} \qquad x = \frac{7 - \sqrt{49 - 32}}{2}$$

$$x = \frac{7 + \sqrt{17}}{2} \qquad x = \frac{7 - \sqrt{17}}{2}$$

$$x = 5.56 \qquad\qquad x = 1.44$$

So the equation $x^2 - 7x + 8 = 0$ has two real roots, 5.56 and 1.44.

It's possible to tell quickly, without going all the way through the quadratic formula, how many roots an equation has. The part of the quadratic formula under the radical, $b^2 - 4ac$, is called the *discriminant*. The value of the discriminant gives you the following information about a quadratic equation:

- If $b^2 - 4ac > 0$, then the equation has two distinct real roots.
- If $b^2 - 4ac = 0$, then the equation has one distinct real root and is a perfect square. Actually, it has two identical real roots, which ETS will call a "double root."
- If $b^2 - 4ac < 0$, then the equation has no real roots. Both of its roots are imaginary.

DRILL 15: THE QUADRATIC FORMULA

In the following exercises, use the discriminant to find out how many roots each equation has and whether the roots are real or imaginary. For equations with real roots, find the exact value of those roots using the quadratic formula. The answers can be found in Part IV.

1. $x^2 - 7x + 5 = 0$
2. $3a^2 - 3a + 7 = 0$
3. $s^2 - 6s + 4 = 0$
4. $x^2 - 2 = 0$
5. $n^2 + 5n + 6.25 = 0$

Graphing Calculator to the Rescue

Perhaps the easiest way to find the roots of a hard-to-factor quadratic is to graph it on your calculator and see where the quadratic intersects the x-axis. Your calculator will most likely have several functions that can help you find the answer(s) like "zeros," "intersect," "trace," and/or "table." Consult your calculator's manual and use whatever method you're most comfortable with.

Comprehensive Algebra Drill

The answers can be found in Part IV.

3. If $x + y = 4$ and $x - y = 2$, then $x^2 - y^2 =$

   (A) 4
   (B) 6
   (C) 8
   (D) 12
   (E) 20

9. If $(x + 4)^2 = 63$, then $x =$

   (A) −1.63
   (B) −0.63
   (C) 1.78
   (D) 3.94
   (E) 6.1

15. What are all the values of x for which $|x + 5| < 2$?

   (A) $x > -3$ or $x < -7$
   (B) $x < -7$
   (C) $x > -3$
   (D) $-7 < x < -3$
   (E) $-3 < x < 7$

19. If $a + 3b + 6c = 12$, $-2a + b - c = 5$, and $4a - 2b - 4c = 1$, then $3a + 2b + c =$

   (A) −10
   (B)   0
   (C) 10
   (D) 16
   (E) 18

20. For what value of x is $\dfrac{5x}{4x - 2}$ undefined?

   (A) −1
   (B) $-\dfrac{1}{2}$
   (C) 0
   (D) $\dfrac{1}{2}$
   (E) 1

23. If $x \neq 0$, then $(2^{3x})(8^{2x}) =$

   (A) 2^{5x}
   (B) 2^{6x}
   (C) 2^{9x}
   (D) 8^{5x}
   (E) 16^{5x}

24. A train traveled 500 miles at an average speed of 60 miles per hour. Approximately how much longer would this same 500-mile trip take if the average speed had decreased by 25%?

   (A) $3\dfrac{1}{2}$ hours

   (B) $2\dfrac{7}{8}$ hours

   (C) $2\dfrac{3}{4}$ hours

   (D) $1\dfrac{3}{4}$ hours

   (E) 1 hour

25. If y is directly proportional to x^3 and $y = 1.2$ when $x = 4$, what is the value of y when $x = 12$?

   (A) 0.04
   (B) 22.4
   (C) 32.4
   (D) 37.6
   (E) 40.1

27. If j and k are both odd integers, which of the following must also be an odd integer?

   (A) $(j + k)^5$

   (B) $(j + k)^4$

   (C) $j^5 + k^5 + 1$

   (D) $j^4 + k^4 + 2$

   (E) $\dfrac{j^5 + k^5}{5}$

30. The sum of the two roots of a quadratic equation is 6 and their product is 8. Which of the following could be the equation.

(A) $x^2 - 6x + 8 = 0$
(B) $x^2 + 8x - 6 = 0$
(C) $x^2 - 8x + 6 = 0$
(D) $x^2 + 6x - 8 = 0$
(E) $x^2 - 6x - 8 = 0$

36. The distance, in feet, that an object travels is a function of the time over which it travels. In the equation $d(t) = at + \dfrac{1}{2}bt^2$, $d(t)$ represents the distance, in feet, traveled, t represents the time, in seconds, spent traveling, and a and b are constants. If $a = 10$ m/s and $b = 4$ m/s^2, which of the following is the closest approximation to the time it would take, in seconds, for an object to travel 36 feet?

(A) 0.8
(B) 1.8
(C) 2.4
(D) 4.6
(E) 8.4

Summary

o   Plugging In is a great way to sidestep the landmines that ETS tries to set for you.

o   You can Plug In whenever
  - you see variables, percents, or fractions (without an original amount) in the answers
  - you're tempted to write and then solve an algebraic equation
  - you see the phrase "in terms of" in the question
  - there are unknown quantities or variables in the question

o   Plug In The Answers (PITA) when you have numbers in the answers but don't know where to start or you are still tempted to write an algebraic equation. Don't forget to start with (C), unless the problem asks for the least or greatest value.

o   Inequalities get solved just like equations, but when you multiply or divide by a negative number, flip the inequality sign.

o   When combining ranges, remember to write out all four possibilities.

o   Absolute value questions often have two answers. Write out and solve both equations created by the absolute value.

o   Direct and inverse variation questions ask for the relationships between numbers:
  - Direct: as x goes up, y goes up. Direct means divide. So you'll have an equation with two fractions.
  - Inverse: as x goes up, y goes down. Inverse means multiply. So you'll have an equation with two quantities being multiplied.

o   Work and travel questions often require either the rate equation: distance = rate × time (or work done = rate of work × time), or the Average Pie, which can be used to find average speed.

○ Simultaneous equation questions don't require solving one variable in terms of another. Just stack them and add or subtract to find what you need. Remember that you can multiply or divide before or after you add or subtract to get to what you want.

○ The general form for a quadratic equation is $ax^2 + bx + c = 0$. To find the factors, just reverse FOIL the equation. There are three special quadratics that you should keep an eye out for to save time and brainpower. They are:

- $(x + y)^2 = x^2 + 2xy + y^2$
- $(x - y)^2 = x^2 - 2xy + y^2$
- $(x + y)(x - y) = x^2 - y^2$

○ If you have a quadratic equation that you can't factor, try using the quadratic formula:

$$x = \frac{-b \pm \sqrt{b^2 - 4ac}}{2a}$$

Chapter 7
Plane Geometry

ETS uses the term "plane geometry" to refer to the kind of geometry that is commonly tested on the SAT Subject Test in Math 1—questions about lines and angles, triangles and other polygons, and circles. Simply put, plane geometry is the study of two-dimensional figures in a plane. About 20% of questions on this test concern plane geometry. Don't confuse plane geometry with coordinate geometry, which involves plotting ordered pairs of numbers on a grid, referred to as the "coordinate plane." We'll focus on coordinate geometry in Chapter 9.

DEFINITIONS

Here are some geometry terms that appear on the SAT Subject Test in Math 1. Make sure you're familiar with them. If the meaning of any of these vocabulary words keeps slipping your mind, add that word to your flash cards.

Line	A "line" in plane geometry is perfectly straight and extends infinitely in both directions.
Line Segment	A line segment is a section of a line—still perfectly straight, but having limited length. It has two endpoints.
Ray	A ray has one endpoint and extends infinitely in one direction.
Bisector	Any line that cuts a line segment, angle, or polygon exactly in half. It *bisects* another shape.
Midpoint	The point that divides a line segment into two equal halves.
Equidistant	Having equal distance from two different things.
Plane	A "plane" in plane geometry is a perfectly flat surface that extends infinitely in two dimensions.
Complementary Angles	Angles whose measures add up to 90 degrees.
Supplementary Angles	Angles whose measures add up to 180 degrees; angles that make up a straight line are supplementary.
Parallel Lines	Lines that run in exactly the same direction—they are separated by a constant distance, never growing closer together or farther apart. Parallel lines have the same slope and never intersect.
Perpendicular Lines	Perpendicular lines are at right angles to one another.
Polygon	A flat shape formed by straight line segments, such as a rectangle or triangle.
Regular Polygon	A polygon that has all equal sides and angles. For example, equilateral triangles and squares are regular.
Quadrilateral	A four-sided polygon.
Altitude (height)	A vertical line drawn from the polygon's base to the opposite vertex. Altitudes are always drawn perpendicular to the base.
Area	The amount of space inside a polygon.
Perimeter	The sum of the lengths of a polygon's sides. To prevent confusion with area, think of perimeter as the amount fence it would take to enclose a particular polygon.
Tangent	A tangent line is a line that touches a circle only at one point without crossing it.

Radius	A line segment extending from the center of a circle to a point on that circle. The radius is perpendicular to the tangent line.
Arc	A portion of a circle's edge or circumference.
Chord	A line segment connecting two distinct points on a circle. The diameter forms the largest possible chord of a circle.
Sector	A portion of a circle's area between two radii, like a slice of pie.
Inscribed	A shape that is *inscribed* in another shape is placed inside that shape with the tightest possible fit. For example, a circle inscribed in a square is the largest circle that can be placed inside that square. The two shapes will touch at points, but they'll never overlap.
Circumscribed	A *circumscribed* shape is drawn around another shape with the tightest fit possible. For example, a circle circumscribed around a square is the smallest circle that can be drawn around that square. The two shapes will touch at points, but they'll never overlap.

BASIC RULES OF LINES AND ANGLES

This symbol denotes a 90° angle.

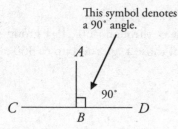

A right angle has a measure of 90°. The angles formed by perpendicular lines are right angles. In the figure above, we see that $AB \perp CD$. The symbol $\perp$ means "perpendicular." Two angles are complementary if they add up to 90°.

Ballparking
In Chapter 2, we discussed Ballparking and how it can help you use POE to eliminate answer choices that are too big or too small. Unless ETS indicates that a figure is NOT drawn to scale, you can assume it is and use Ballparking to eliminate impossible lengths, angles, and areas (such as shaded regions). If a figure is not drawn to scale, you should redraw it according to any information ETS gives you. If, on the other hand, no figure is given at all, you'll want to make sure to draw one yourself so you can solve the problem more easily. Try to draw your figure to scale as closely as possible—you may be able to ballpark and eliminate answer choices that are the wrong size.

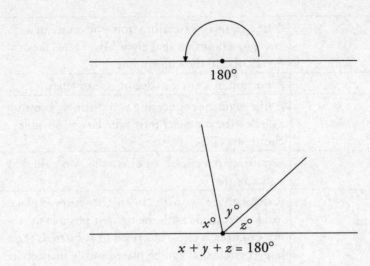

$x + y + z = 180°$

An angle opened up into a straight line (called a "straight angle") has a measure of 180°. If a number of angles makes up a straight line, then the measures of those angles add up to 180 and are said to be supplementary.

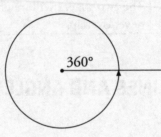

Any line rotated through a full circle moves through 360°. If a group of angles makes up a full circle, then the measures of those angles add up to 360°.

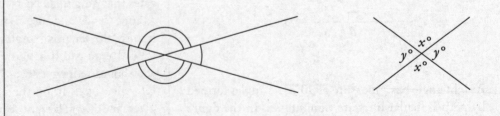

As you can see in the previous diagram, when two lines cross, opposite angles are equal (these are called "vertical angles"). Adjacent angles form straight lines and, therefore, add up to 180°.

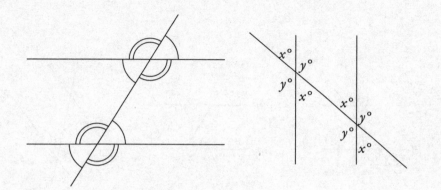

Transected parallel lines: When two parallel lines are crossed by a third line, that third line transects the parallel lines. You probably learned a whole mess of rules with confusing names for this sort of situation. However, all those rules boil down to three ideas:

1. All big angles are equal.
2. All small angles are equal.
3. Any big angle plus any small angle equals 180⁰.

When parallel lines are crossed by a third line, two kinds of angles are formed—little angles and big angles. All of the little angles are congruent or equal, all of the big angles are congruent, and any little angle plus any big angle equals 180°.

ETS will sometimes use the parallel symbol as well. For example, $AC \parallel DE$ means that AC is parallel to DE. Think of the two l's in *parallel* to help you remember this.

Likewise, the symbol for perpendicular is ⊥, as in $GH \perp JK$. It's easy to remember this symbol because it looks like perpendicular lines: two lines meeting to form right angles.

> ## What's with All the Symbols?
> In geometry questions, ETS sometimes will write out the geometric phrase "line segment AB." Sometimes, however, the test writers will use only geometric symbols or write these kinds of things in "code form." So line segment AB would be $\overline{AB}$. This is just one more way ETS tries to confuse you or throw you off your game.

DRILL 1: BASIC RULES OF LINES AND ANGLES

In the following exercises, find each measure. The answers can be found in Part IV.

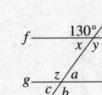

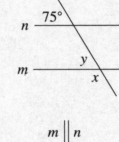

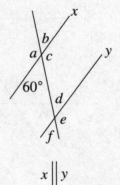

$$f \parallel g \qquad\qquad m \parallel n \qquad\qquad x \parallel y$$

1. x _____   a _____   2. x _____   3. a _____   d _____
   y _____   b _____   y _____   b _____   e _____
   z _____   c _____   c _____   f _____

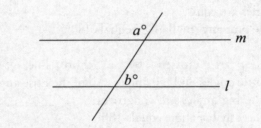

8. If line *l* and line *m* are parallel, then *a* + *b* =

   (A) 90°
   (B) 180°
   (C) 270°
   (D) 360°
   (E) It cannot be determined from the information given.

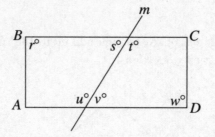

13. If line *m* intersects rectangle *ABCD* as shown, then which of the following is equal to *t* ?

(A) *v*
(B) *w*
(C) *r* + *s*
(D) *w* − *v*
(E) *r* + *w* − *s*

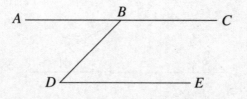

16. If $AC \parallel DE$, then which of the following is the difference between the degree measures of ∠*DBC* and ∠*BDE* ?

(A)   0°
(B)   45°
(C)   90°
(D) 180°
(E) It cannot be determined from the information given.

TRIANGLES

Triangles appear in the majority of plane geometry questions on the SAT Subject Test in Math 1. What's more, triangle techniques are useful in solving questions that don't obviously relate to triangles, such as coordinate geometry and solid geometry questions. The following rules are some of the most important in plane geometry.

The Rule of 180°

For starters, the three angles of any triangle add up to 180°. This rule helps to solve a great many plane geometry questions.

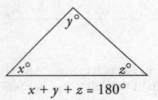

$$x + y + z = 180°$$

The Proportionality of Triangles

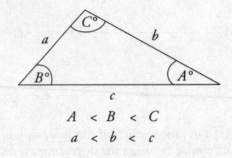

$$A < B < C$$
$$a < b < c$$

Opposite Side? Huh?
If you have trouble figuring out which side is opposite a certain angle in a triangle, remember this simple rule: The opposite side is the side that doesn't touch the angle you're talking about.

In a triangle, the smallest angle is always opposite the shortest side; the middle angle is opposite the middle side; and the largest angle is opposite the longest side. If a triangle has sides of equal length, then the opposite angles will have equal measures.

The Third Side Rule

The *Third Side Rule:* The length of any side of a triangle must be between the sum and the difference of the lengths of the other two sides.

Beware!
The Third Side Rule is commonly used to create tricky triangle questions.

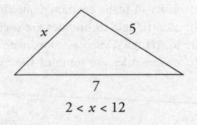

$$2 < x < 12$$

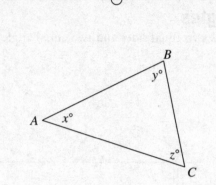

Note: Figure not drawn to scale

33. In the figure above, if $\overline{AC} = 11$, $\overline{BC} = 6$, and $x > z$, then which one of the following could be the length of $\overline{AB}$?

(A) 4
(B) 5
(C) 5.5
(D) 6
(E) 8.5

Here's How to Crack It

Start by labeling the diagram with what you know:

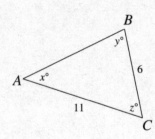

The relationship of side lengths within a triangle is the same as the relationship of the opposite angles. Therefore, if $x > z$, then $\overline{BC} > \overline{AB}$. $\overline{AB}$ must therefore be less than 6; eliminate (D) and (E).

Next, use the Third Side Rule. $\overline{AB}$ must be greater than the difference of $\overline{AC}$ and $\overline{BC}$, but less than the sum. $11 - 6 = 5$, and $11 + 6 = 17$, so $5 < \overline{AB} < 17$. Eliminate (A) and (B) and choose (C).

Isosceles Triangles

An isosceles triangle has two equal sides and two equal angles.

Isosceles and the Third Side

Watch out for questions that employ the Third Side Rule in isosceles triangles.

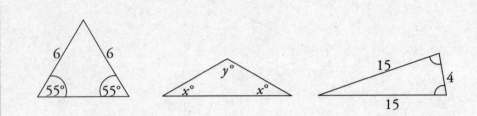

Equilateral Triangles

An equilateral triangle has three equal sides and three equal angles. Each angle has a measure of 60°.

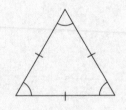

DRILL 2: THIRD SIDE RULES

The answers can be found in Part IV.

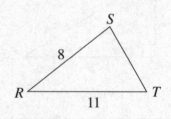

12. Which of the following expresses the possible values of *p*, if *p* is the perimeter of *RST* ?

    (A) $3 < p < 19$
    (B) $3 < p < 22$
    (C) $19 < p < 22$
    (D) $19 < p < 38$
    (E) $22 < p < 38$

17. An isosceles triangle has sides of lengths 5, 11, and *x*. How many possible values of *x* exist?

    (A) One
    (B) Two
    (C) Three
    (D) Four
    (E) More than four

18. The distance between points *A* and *D* is 6, and the distance between *D* and *F* is 4. Which of the following is NOT a possible value for the distance between *F* and *A* ?

    (A) 3
    (B) 4
    (C) 7
    (D) 9
    (E) 11

Right Triangles

Right triangles are, not surprisingly, triangles that contain right angles. The sides of right triangles are referred to by special names. The sides that form the right angle are called the legs of the triangle and the longest side, opposite the right angle, is called the hypotenuse. There are many techniques and rules for right triangles that won't work on just any triangle. The most important of these rules is the relationship between sides described by the Pythagorean Theorem.

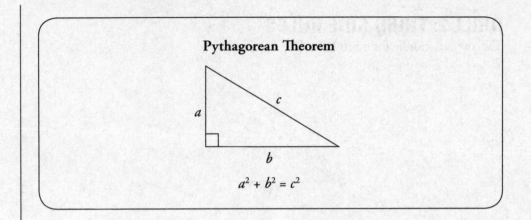

Pythagorean Theorem

$$a^2 + b^2 = c^2$$

Keep in mind when you use the Pythagorean Theorem that the c always represents the hypotenuse.

DRILL 3: THE PYTHAGOREAN THEOREM

In the following triangles, use the Pythagorean Theorem to fill in the missing sides of the triangles shown. The answers can be found in Part IV.

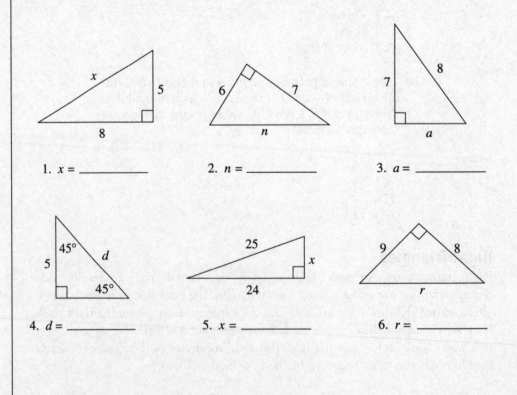

1. $x = $ _____

2. $n = $ _____

3. $a = $ _____

4. $d = $ _____

5. $x = $ _____

6. $r = $ _____

Area of Triangles

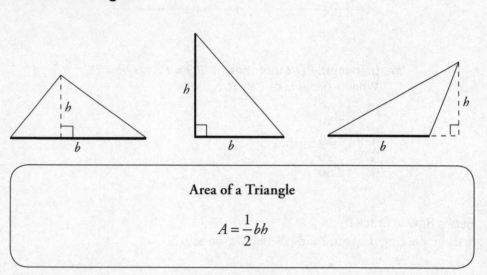

Area of a Triangle

$$A = \frac{1}{2}bh$$

Notice that the height, or altitude, of a triangle can be inside the triangle, outside the triangle, or formed by a side of the triangle. In each case, the height is always perpendicular to the base. The height of a triangle must sometimes be computed with the Pythagorean Theorem.

Area of an Equilateral Triangle

The height of an equilateral triangle can be found by dividing it into two 30°-60°-90° triangles, but you can save yourself the time and trouble if you memorize the following formula:

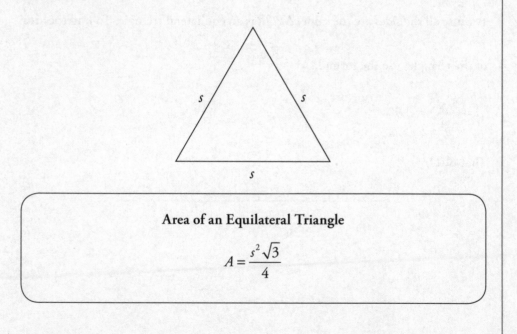

Area of an Equilateral Triangle

$$A = \frac{s^2\sqrt{3}}{4}$$

Here's an example of an equilateral triangle question.

─────────────── ○ ───────────────

24. In triangle PQR (not shown), $\overline{PQ} = \overline{PR} = \overline{QR} = 3$.
What is the area of $\triangle PQR$?

(A) 15.59
(B) 7.79
(C) 4.50
(D) 3.90
(E) 2.60

Here's How to Crack It

Start by drawing the figure and labeling the sides:

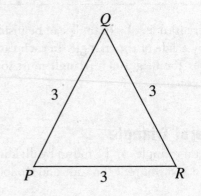

Because all the sides are the same, $\triangle PQR$ is an equilateral triangle. To find the area

of the triangle, use the formula $A = \dfrac{s^2 \sqrt{3}}{4}$:

$$A = \frac{3^2 \sqrt{3}}{4} = 3.90$$

That is (D).

─────────────── ○ ───────────────

DRILL 4: AREAS OF TRIANGLES

Try the following practice questions about the areas of triangles. The answers can be found in Part IV.

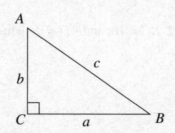

9. If the area of $\triangle ABC$ is equal to $3b$, then $a =$

   (A) $\dfrac{3}{4}$

   (B) $\dfrac{3}{2}$

   (C) 3

   (D) 4

   (E) 6

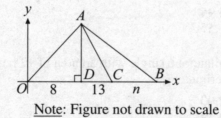

Note: Figure not drawn to scale

15. If $\triangle OAD$ and $\triangle ABC$ are of equal area, then $n =$

   (A) 8
   (B) 16
   (C) 18
   (D) 21
   (E) 24

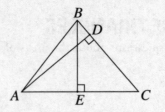

37. If $AC = 12$, $BC = 10$, and $AD = 9$, then $BE =$

(A) 7.0
(B) 7.5
(C) 8.0
(D) 8.5
(E) 9.0

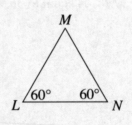

38. If $\triangle LMN$ has a perimeter of 24, then what is the area of $\triangle LMN$?

(A) 13.86
(B) 20.78
(C) 27.71
(D) 36.95
(E) 41.57

44. An equilateral triangle with an area of 12 has what perimeter?

(A) 12.00
(B) 13.39
(C) 15.59
(D) 15.79
(E) 18.66

SPECIAL RIGHT TRIANGLES

There are a few right triangles with special characteristics that ETS loves to test over and over again. The test writers may get creative and try to hide these triangles, but if you know to look out for them, you'll work these questions more efficiently and score more!

Pythagorean Triplets

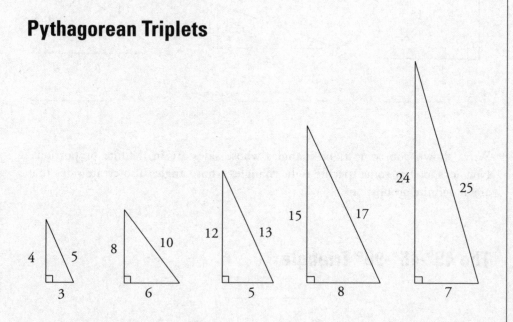

There are only a few right triangles whose sides all have integer lengths. These special triangles are called "Pythagorean triplets." What is important is that ETS puts these triangles on the test a lot. Memorize them and keep an eye out for them.

If a right triangle has two sides that fit the proportions of a Pythagorean triplet, then you can automatically fill in the third side. The multiples of these basic proportions will also be Pythagorean triplets. For example, a right triangle with legs 30 and 40 will have a hypotenuse of 50, because it's simply a 3:4:5 triangle with all the sides multiplied by 10.

Triplet Families
Can you figure out the original triplet that a 25-60-65 sided triangle and a 30-40-50 sided triangle came from? The first is a multiple of a 5-12-13 right triangle, and the second is a multiple of a 3-4-5 right triangle. This means that a 5-12-13 triangle is similar to a 25-60-65 triangle. The same is true of a 3-4-5 and a 30-40-50.

DRILL 5: PYTHAGOREAN TRIPLETS

Use the proportions of the Pythagorean triplets to complete the triangles below. The answers can be found in Part IV.

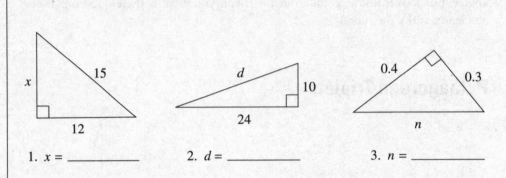

1. $x =$ _____   2. $d =$ _____   3. $n =$ _____

We've shown you some right triangles whose sides are in definite proportions. Now let's look at some specific right triangles whose angles also create sides that are in definite proportions.

The 45°-45°-90° Triangle

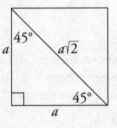

If you cut a square along its diagonal, you end up with two 45°-45°-90° triangles. Notice that this is an isosceles right triangle. The relation of the sides to the hypotenuse will always be the same.

The ratio of the sides of a 45°-45°-90° will always be $a : a : a\sqrt{2}$, where a is the length of one leg. The legs will be equal and the hypotenuse will always be equal to the length of a leg times $\sqrt{2}$. You can use this ratio for questions that ask for the length of either the leg or the hypotenuse. If the question gives you the length of the hypotenuse, just divide by $\sqrt{2}$ to find the length of each leg.

Remember that you can use the Pythagorean Theorem on most right triangle problems. However, if you recognize that a triangle is a 45°-45°-90°, this is a great shortcut to use to find the lengths.

Questions asking about the diagonal of a square are really 45°-45°-90° triangle questions in disguise. If you cut a square by its diagonal, you get two 45°-45°-90° triangles. Let's see how this is tested.

———————————◯———————————

34. If the diagonal of square *FGHJ* is equal to 8, then what is the area of square *FGHJ* ?

    (A) 80
    (B) 72
    (C) 64
    (D) 40
    (E) 32

Here's How to Crack It

As with all plane geometry questions in which you aren't given a figure, the first step is to draw one. Your figure should look something like this:

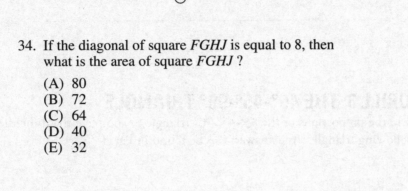

Since you know that questions that ask about the diagonals of square are really asking about 45°-45°-90° triangles, you can use the special right triangle to find the side of the square. If the diagonal of the square is 8, and the diagonal equals $s\sqrt{2}$, then each side is equal to $\dfrac{8}{\sqrt{2}}$. Plug $\dfrac{8}{\sqrt{2}}$ into the formula for the area of the square and solve.

$$A = s^2$$

$$A = \left(\dfrac{8}{\sqrt{2}}\right)^2$$

$$A = \dfrac{64}{2}$$

$$A = 32$$

Choice (E) is the correct answer. Notice that (C) is the value you'd get if you assumed that each side of the square was equal to 8. This is a common mistake that test-takers make. Remember to use the 45°-45°-90° on all questions involving the diagonal of a square.

DRILL 6: THE 45°-45°-90° TRIANGLE

Use the proportions of the 45°-45°-90° triangle to complete the dimensions of the following triangles. The answers can be found in Part IV.

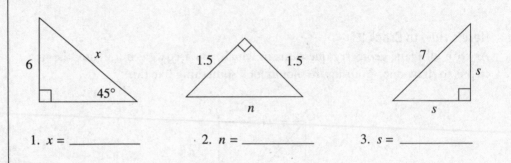

1. $x = $ _____

2. $n = $ _____

3. $s = $ _____

The 30°-60°-90° Triangle

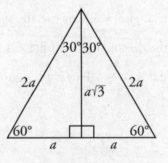

As with 45°-45°-90° triangles, all right triangles with angles of 30°, 60°, and 90° have sides in a definite proportion. In a 30°-60°-90° triangle, the hypotenuse is twice as long as the shorter leg. The length of the longer leg is equal to the length of the shorter leg times $\sqrt{3}$. So the ratio of the sides is $a : a\sqrt{3} : 2a$, where a is the length of the shorter leg of the triangle. If you are given the length of the longer leg, what can you do? That's right, just divide the leg and the hypotenuse by $\sqrt{3}$.

DRILL 7: THE 30°-60°-90° TRIANGLE

Use the proportions of the 30°-60°-90° triangles to complete the dimensions of the following triangles. The answers can be found in Part IV.

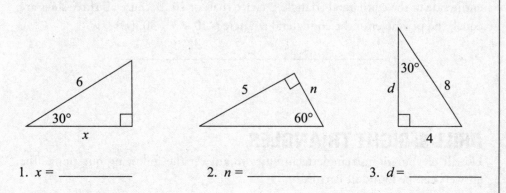

1. $x =$ _____

2. $n =$ _____

3. $d =$ _____

Questions about equilateral triangles often require you to find the height of the triangle. When you draw the altitude (height) of an equilateral triangle, you create two 30°-60°-90° triangles. As with questions about the diagonal of a square, questions about the height or area of an equilateral triangle will be much easier if you know the proportions of 30°-60°-90° triangles. Here's an example.

———————○———————

34. An equilateral triangle has a height of $5\sqrt{3}$. What is the perimeter of the triangle?

(A) 10
(B) 15
(C) $15\sqrt{3}$
(D) 30
(E) $25\sqrt{3}$

Here's How to Crack It
First, draw and label the question:

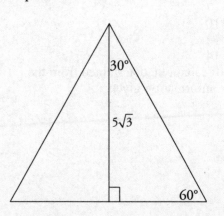

When you draw in the altitude of an equilateral triangle, you create two 30°-60°-90° triangles. The altitude is opposite the 60° angle, so in the 30°-60°-90° triangle, it's the side equal to $a\sqrt{3}$. Therefore, in this case, $a = 5$. But be careful! The side of the 30°-60°-90° triangle opposite the 30° angle is equal to 5, which means the entire side of the equilateral triangle is twice that, or 10. Because all three sides are equal, the perimeter of the equilateral triangle is $10 \times 3 = 30$, (D).

DRILL 8: RIGHT TRIANGLES

Use all of your right-triangle techniques to answer the following questions. The answers can be found in Part IV.

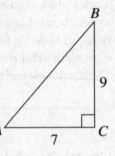

7. The perimeter of triangle *ABC* has how many possible values?

(A) One
(B) Two
(C) Three
(D) Four
(E) Infinitely many

13. A right triangle with a side of length 6 and a side of length 8 also has a side of length *x*. What is *x* ?

(A) 7
(B) 10
(C) 12
(D) 14
(E) It cannot be determined from the information given.

16. A straight 32-foot ladder is leaned against a vertical wall so that it forms a 30° angle with the wall.
To what height in feet does the ladder reach?

(A) 9.24
(B) 16.00
(C) 27.71
(D) 43.71
(E) 54.43

19. An isosceles right triangle has a perimeter of
23.9. What is the area of this triangle?

(A) 16.9
(B) 24.5
(C) 25.0
(D) 33.8
(E) 49.0

Similar Triangles

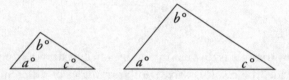

Triangles are said to be "similar" when they have the same angle measures. Basically, similar triangles have exactly the same shape, although they may be different
sizes. Their sides, therefore, are in the same proportion.

> Corresponding sides and heights of similar triangles are proportional.

For example, two 30°-60°-90° triangles of different sizes would be similar. If the
short side of one triangle were twice as long as the short side of the other, then you
could expect all of the larger triangle's dimensions to be twice the smaller triangle's dimensions. Similar triangles don't have to be right triangles, however. Sides
of triangles will be related proportionally whenever they have identical angle
measures.

Proportionality
Here's a quick reminder:
Not only are all
30°-60°-90° triangles
similar to each other,
but so are all
45°-45°-90° triangles. Also,
the Pythagorean triplets
that we mentioned are
similar to their multiples.

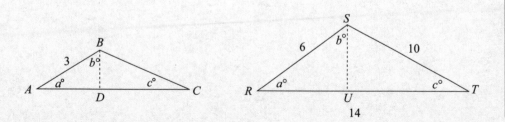

In the figure on the previous page, both triangles have angles measuring *a*, *b*, and *c*. Because they have the same angles, you know they're similar triangles. Side *RS* of the large triangle and side *AB* of the smaller triangle are corresponding sides; each is the short side of its triangle. You can use the lengths of those two sides to figure out the proportion between the triangles. The length of *AB* is 3 and the length of *RS* is 6. So, *RS* is twice as long as *AB*. You can expect every side of *RST* to be twice as long as the corresponding side of *ABC*. That makes *BC* = 5 and *AC* = 7. Also, the height of triangle *RST* will be twice as long as the height of triangle *ABC*.

More Similarity

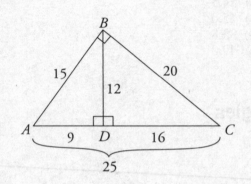

Whenever a right triangle is divided in two by a height drawn from the right angle to the opposite side, the result is three similar triangles of different sizes. The sides of the three triangles will be proportional. Let's separate the triangles so you can see them more clearly.

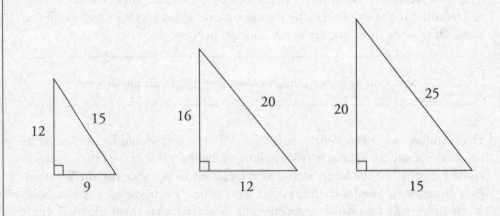

Let's look at one.

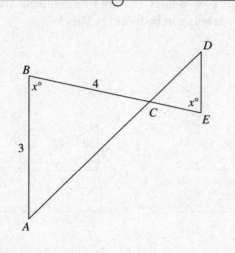

37. In the figure above, $\overline{AB} = 3$ and $\overline{BC} = 4$. What is

the value of $\dfrac{DE}{CE}$?

(A) $\dfrac{3}{4}$

(B) $\dfrac{3}{5}$

(C) $\dfrac{4}{3}$

(D) $\dfrac{5}{4}$

(E) $\dfrac{5}{3}$

Here's How to Crack It

The two triangles both have an angle that is $x°$. They also have equal angles at

point C. Therefore, the remaining angle must also be equal, so the two triangles are

similar. To find the ratio $\dfrac{DE}{CE}$, you can find the ratio of the corresponding sides of

triangle ABC. $\overline{DE}$ is opposite the angle at point C, so its corresponding side is $\overline{AB}$.

$\overline{CE}$ is opposite the unlabeled angle at point D, so it's corresponding side is opposite

the unlabeled angle A, which is $\overline{BC}$. Therefore, $\dfrac{DE}{CE} = \dfrac{AB}{BC} = \dfrac{3}{4}$, which is (A).

DRILL 9: SIMILAR TRIANGLES

Use the proportionality of similar triangles to complete the dimensions of the triangles below. The answers can be found in Part IV.

1.

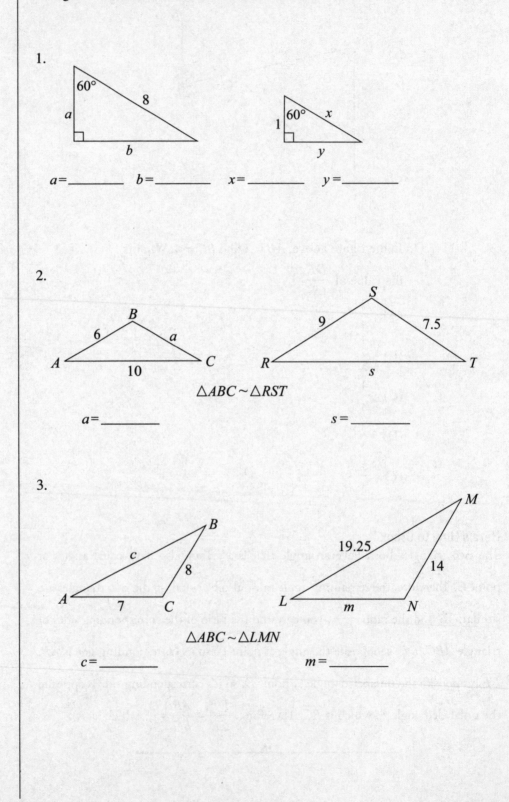

a = _____ b = _____   x = _____   y = _____

2.

$\triangle ABC \sim \triangle RST$

a = _____   s = _____

3.

$\triangle ABC \sim \triangle LMN$

c = _____   m = _____

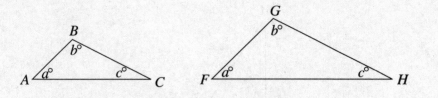

37. *FG* is twice as long as *AB*. If the area of triangle *FGH* is 0.5, what is the area of triangle *ABC* ?

(A) 0.13
(B) 0.25
(C) 0.50
(D) 1.00
(E) 2.00

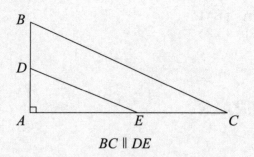

BC ∥ *DE*

40. If the length of *DB* is half of the length of *AD* and *BC* ∥ *DE*, then the area of triangle *ADE* is what fraction of the area of triangle *ABC* ?

(A) $\dfrac{5}{9}$

(B) $\dfrac{1}{2}$

(C) $\dfrac{4}{9}$

(D) $\dfrac{1}{4}$

(E) $\dfrac{1}{9}$

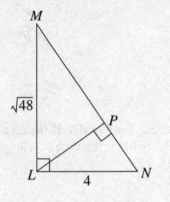

New Rule?
Can you figure out a rule about the relationship between the areas of similar triangles? The areas and perimeters are proportional in the same way that the sides are proportional.

45. What is the area of $\triangle LPN$?

(A) 3.46
(B) 6.93
(C) 8.00
(D) 11.31
(E) 13.86

QUADRILATERALS

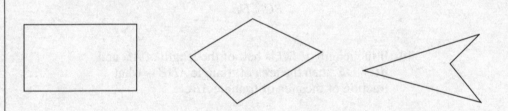

A quadrilateral is any shape formed by four intersecting lines in a plane. The internal angle measures of a quadrilateral always add up to 360°.

Parallelograms

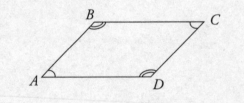
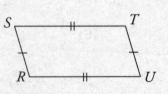

A parallelogram is a quadrilateral whose opposite sides are parallel. Rectangles are parallelograms, but a parallelogram does not need to have right angles. Parallelograms have the following characteristics:

- Opposite angles in a parallelogram are equal.
- Adjacent angles in a parallelogram are supplementary; they add up to 180°.
- Opposite sides in a parallelogram are of equal length.
- The diagonals of a parallelogram bisect each other.

The area of a parallelogram is given by this formula:

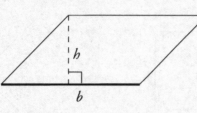

Area of a Parallelogram

$$A = bh$$

Rectangles

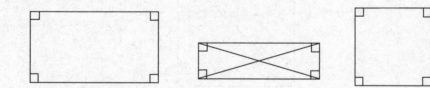

A rectangle is just a parallelogram with four right angles. Rectangles have all the properties of parallelograms. In addition,

- each of the four interior angles measures 90°.
- the diagonals of a rectangle are of equal length.

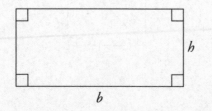

Connect the Dots

Notice that the area of a parallelogram is twice the area of a triangle. So you can always figure out one formula if you forget the other!

Height? There's No Height!

If you're having trouble finding the height in a parallelogram involving area, you can often use Pythagorean Theorem or one of the special right triangles.

Since all rectangles are parallelograms, the area of a rectangle is given by the same formula as that of a parallelogram.

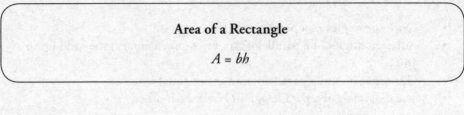

Area of a Rectangle

$A = bh$

Squares

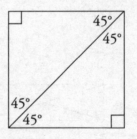

A square is a rectangle with four sides of equal length. (If you are asked to draw a rectangle, drawing a square is a legitimate response.)

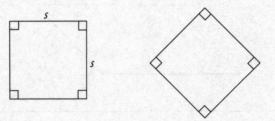

A diagonal in a square divides the square into two 45°-45°-90° triangles. The area of a square is given by either one of these formulas:

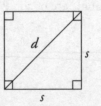

What's with All This Memorization?!

Notice that the area of a square, s^2, is just the base times the height, which is the formula for area of a parallelogram and area of a rectangle. Because the base and height of a square are the same, we give you a shortcut formula, but it's really no different from the others. So, no need to memorize it. You can always figure it out!

The second, less-known formula for the area of a square can be used to shortcut questions that would otherwise take many more steps and require you to use a 45°-45°-90° triangle.

Trapezoids

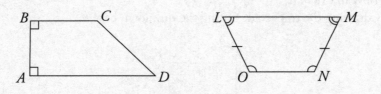

A trapezoid is a quadrilateral whose top and bottom are parallel but differ in length.

The area of a trapezoid is given by the following formula:

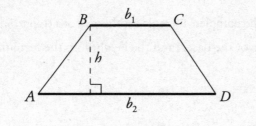

Let's look at a trapezoid question.

---

24. Trapezoid *WXYZ* (not shown) has an area of 30, a height of 5, and one base with length 3. What is the length of the other base?

    (A)   3
    (B)   6
    (C)   9
    (D)   10
    (E)   12

Here's How to Crack It

Start by drawing the trapezoid, calling the unknown base b_2:

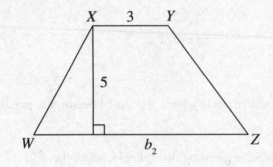

Next, write down the complete formula for the area of a trapezoid: $A = \left(\dfrac{b_1 + b_2}{2}\right)h$.

Fill in the area, one of the bases, and the height into the formula:

$$30 = \left(\dfrac{3 + b_2}{2}\right)5$$

Solve the equation for b_2. Begin by dividing both sides by 5:

$$\dfrac{30}{5} = \dfrac{\left(\dfrac{3 + b_2}{2}\right)5}{5}$$

$$6 = \dfrac{3 + b_2}{2}$$

Multiply both sides by 2:

$$6(2) = \frac{3 + b_2}{2}(2)$$

$$12 = 3 + b_2$$

Finally, subtract 3 from both sides:

$$12 - 3 = 3 + b_2 - 3$$

$$9 = b_2$$

That matches (C).

———————————————◯———————————————

DRILL 10: QUADRILATERALS

Try the following practice questions using quadrilateral formulas. The answers can be found in Part IV.

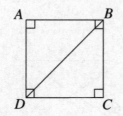

22. If $AB = BC$ and $DB = 5$, then the area of $ABCD =$

    (A) 12.50
    (B) 14.43
    (C) 17.68
    (D) 35.36
    (E) 43.30

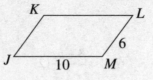

34. If the measure of ∠KJM is 60°, what is the area of parallelogram JKLM ?

   (A) 18.34
   (B) 25.98
   (C) 34.64
   (D) 51.96
   (E) 60.00

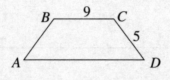

40. The bases of trapezoid ABCD differ in length by 6, and the perimeter of the trapezoid is 34. What is the area of ABCD ?

   (A) 45.0
   (B) 48.0
   (C) 54.0
   (D) 60.0
   (E) 62.5

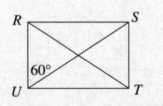

45. If the area of rectangle RSTU is 62.35, then RT + SU =

   (A) 18.8
   (B) 24.0
   (C) 32.0
   (D) 36.0
   (E) 40.8

OTHER POLYGONS

The SAT Subject Test in Math 1 may occasionally require you to deal with polygons other than triangles and quadrilaterals. Here are the names of the other polygons you're likely to see:

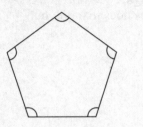

pentagon: a five-sided polygon

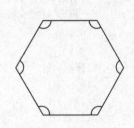

hexagon: a six-sided polygon

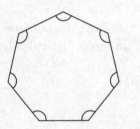

heptagon: a seven-sided polygon

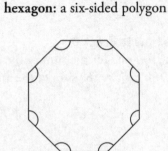

octagon: an eight-sided polygon

All of the polygons pictured above are *regular* polygons. That means that their sides and angles are all of the same size.

You know that the internal angles of a triangle add up to 180° and that the internal angles of a quadrilateral add up to 360°. But what about the angles of a hexagon or an octagon? You can compute the sum of a polygon's internal angles using this formula:

Sum of the Angles of an *n*-sided Polygon

Sum of Angles = $(n - 2) \times 180°$

Using this formula, you can figure out that the angles of a hexagon (a 6-sided figure) would have a sum of (4×180) degrees. That's 720°. If you know that the figure is a regular hexagon, then you can even figure out the measure of each angle: $720° \div 6 = 120°$.

Here's an example.

_____◯_____

13. If the sum of the interior angles of a polygon is 1,800°, then how many sides does that polygon have?

(A) 5
(B) 6
(C) 10
(D) 12
(E) 18

Here's How to Crack It

Use the formula for the sum of the angles of an n-sided polygon: Sum of Angles = $(n - 2)180°$. Make the sum of the angles 1,800° and solve algebraically:

$$1,800° = (n - 2)180°$$

$$\frac{1,800°}{180°} = \frac{(n - 2)180°}{180°}$$

$$10 = n - 2$$

$$12 = n$$

That is (D).

_____◯_____

Just Make Triangles!

This formula may seem random and now you're stressing about all the memorizing you're going to have to do. But in reality, you don't have to know the formula. Now you're saying "What?! If we don't have to know it, why are we memorizing it?!" There are almost always ways around knowing formulas. It's great if you can memorize this, but if you can't, then count the triangles! Start at one vertex of the polygon you're looking at and create triangles by drawing a line from that same vertex to every other vertex in the figure, like this:

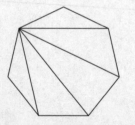

Now just count the triangles. For our picture, there are 5 triangles. You already know that there are 180° in a triangle. So there must be 5 × 180°, or 900°, in the polygon. Notice that 5 is 7 − 2 and 180 is just the number of degrees in a triangle. Funny, you just created the formula for the sum of the angles in a polygon!

Here's how it might be tested.

19. A nonagon is a polygon with nine sides. What is the average measure, in degrees, of the interior angles of a nonagon?

(A) 120°
(B) 140°
(C) 160°
(D) 1,260°
(E) 1,440°

Here's How to Crack It
Start by drawing a 9-sided figure:

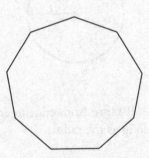

Next, start drawing some triangles! It's easiest to draw all the triangles sharing one vertex of the nonagon:

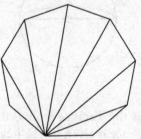

There are 7 triangles, and each triangle has interior angles which add up to 180°. Therefore, a nonagon has interior angles which add up to 180° × 7 = 1,260°. The question wants to know what the average degree measure of the interior angles of a nonagon is, so you need to divide by the number of angles, 9: 1,260° ÷ 9 = 140°, which is (B).

CIRCLES

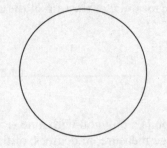

A circle is defined as the set of all the points located at a certain distance from a given center point. A point that is said to be on a circle is a point on the edge of the circle, not contained within the circle.

The *radius* is the distance from the center to the edge of the circle.

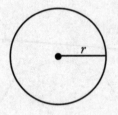

The *diameter* of a circle is the distance from edge to edge through the circle's center. The diameter is twice as long as the radius.

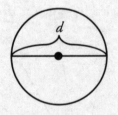

The *circumference* of a circle is the distance around the circle—essentially, the circle's perimeter. The circumference is given by the following formula:

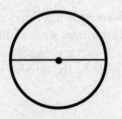

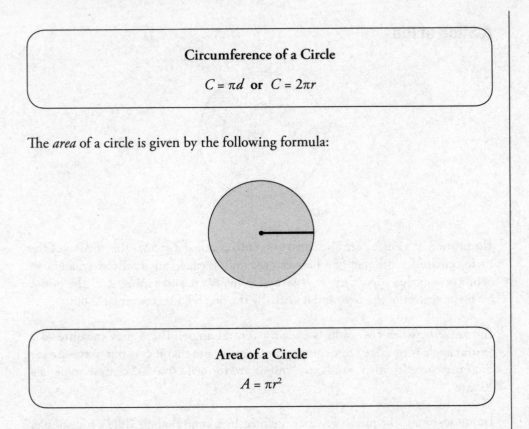

> **Circumference of a Circle**
>
> $C = \pi d$ **or** $C = 2\pi r$

The *area* of a circle is given by the following formula:

> **Area of a Circle**
>
> $A = \pi r^2$

DRILL 11: CIRCLES

Use formulas to complete the dimensions of the following circles. The answers can be found in Part IV.

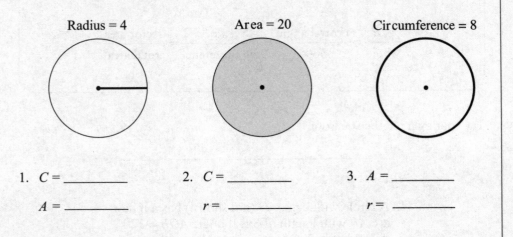

Radius = 4 Area = 20 Circumference = 8

1. $C =$ _____   2. $C =$ _____   3. $A =$ _____

    $A =$ _____ $r =$ _____ $r =$ _____

A Slice of Pie

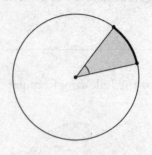

The portion of a circle's area between two radii is called a sector. The portion of the circle's circumference that falls between the radii is called an arc. Between any two points on a circle's edge, there are two arcs, a major arc and a minor arc. The minor arc is the shorter of the two, and it's usually the one ETS is concerned about.

The angle between two radii is called a central angle. The degree measure of a central angle is equal to the degree measure of the arc that it cuts out of the circle's circumference. In other words, the minor arc formed by a 40° central angle is a 40° arc.

To put it simply, the piece of a circle defined by a central angle (like a slice of pie) takes the same fraction of everything. A 60° central angle, for instance, takes one-sixth of the circle's 360°; the arc that is formed will be one-sixth of the circumference; the sector that is formed will be one-sixth of the circle's area. In other words:

$$\frac{\text{part}}{\text{whole}} = \frac{\text{central angle}}{360°} = \frac{\text{arc}}{\text{circumference}} = \frac{\text{sector area}}{\text{total area}}$$

Try your own pie-slice question.

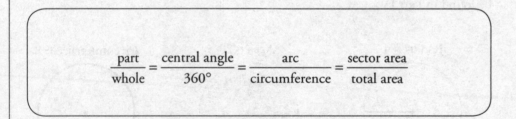

34. A circle with center O (not shown) has a minor arc AB with length of 3π. If angle $AOB = 120°$, then what is the area of circle O ?

   (A) 4.5π
   (B) 6.75π
   (C) 9π
   (D) 20.25π
   (E) 81π

Here's How to Crack It

Start by drawing the circle, arc, and central angle:

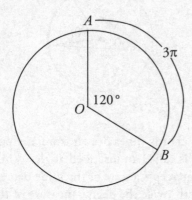

Use the proportion $\dfrac{\text{central angle}}{360°} = \dfrac{\text{arc}}{\text{circumference}}$ to find the circumference:

$$\frac{120°}{360°} = \frac{3\pi}{\text{circumference}}$$

Cross-multiply then divide to solve for circumference:

$$120(\text{circumference}) = 360(3\pi)$$

$$\text{circumference} = 9\pi$$

To find the area, you need the radius. The formula for circumference using radius is $2\pi r$, so make this equal to the circumference and solve for r:

$$2\pi r = 9\pi$$

$$r = 4.5$$

Finally, use the area formula, πr^2, to solve for the area:

$$\pi(4.5)^2 = 20.25\pi$$

That matches (D).

Inscribed Angles

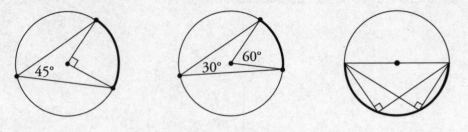

An angle formed by two chords (lines drawn from any point on the circle to any other point on the circle) is called an inscribed angle. While a central angle with a certain degree measure intercepts an arc of the same degree measure, an inscribed angle intercepts an arc with twice the degree measure of the angle. For example, a 30° central angle intercepts a 30° arc, while a 30° inscribed angle intercepts a 60° arc.

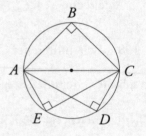

Any time you draw two lines, one from each endpoint of the diameter, to the same point on the semicircle, the lines will meet at a right angle. In other words, any angle inscribed in a semicircle is a right angle.

Here's an example.

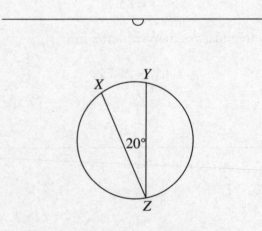

36. The radius of the circle shown above is 18. What is the length of minor arc *XY* ?

(A) 2π
(B) 4π
(C) 8π
(D) 18π
(E) 36π

Here's How to Crack It

To find the arc, you will need to know the central angle. Draw in the center (call it *O*) and the central angle and label the radii as 18:

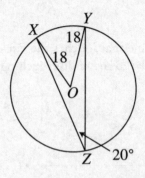

Angle *XOY* is the central angle inside the inscribed angle *XZY*. Therefore, angle *XOY* is twice angle *XZY*, or 2(20°) = 40°. If the radius is 18, you can use 2π*r* to find the circumference: 2π(18) = 36π. At this point, you can use Ballparking to eliminate (D) and (E), since the arc is only a small portion of the total circumference.

Now that you know the central angle and the circumference, you can use

$$\frac{\text{central angle}}{360°} = \frac{\text{arc}}{\text{circumference}}$$ to solve for arc:

$$\frac{40°}{360°} = \frac{\text{arc}}{36π}$$

$$36π(40°) = \text{arc}(360°)$$

$$\frac{36π(40°)}{360°} = \text{arc}$$

$$\text{arc} = 4π$$

That is equal to (B).

Tangent Lines

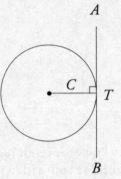

A *tangent line* to a circle is a line that touches the circle at only one point. A tangent line is always perpendicular to the radius touching the same point.

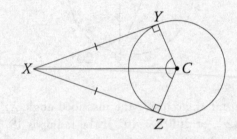

From any point outside a circle, there are two separate tangent lines to that circle. The distances to the two points of tangency are equal, and the radii to the points of tangency make equal angles with the line connecting the external point to the circle's center.

Take a look at a question about tangency.

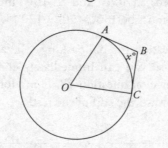

48. In the figure above, $\overline{AB}$ and $\overline{BC}$ are tangent to the circle with center O at points A and C, respectively. If the area of the sector AOC is 6π and the diameter of the circle is 12, then what is the value of x ?

(A) 30
(B) 60
(C) 90
(D) 120
(E) 150

Here's How to Crack It

Start by labeling the given information into the diagram. Remember that lines tangent to the circle create right angles with the radius at the point of intersection. Also, if the diameter is 12, then $\overline{OA}$ and $\overline{OC}$ are both 6:

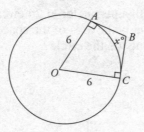

$OABC$ is a quadrilateral, so its interior angles add up to 360°. Because $\angle OAB$ and $\angle OCB$ are both right angles, the other two angles, $\angle AOC$ and $\angle ABC$, must add up to 180°.

You know that the area of sector AOC is 6π. If the radius of the circle is 6, then the area is $\pi(6)^2$, or 36π. Using the proportion $\dfrac{\text{central angle}}{360°} = \dfrac{\text{sector area}}{\text{total area}}$, you can solve for the central angle AOC:

$$\frac{\angle AOC}{360°} = \frac{6\pi}{36\pi}$$

$$\angle AOC \, (36\pi) = 360° \, (6\pi)$$

$$\angle AOC = \frac{360° \, (6\pi)}{36\pi} = 60°$$

As we previously discussed, $\angle AOC$ and $\angle ABC$ must add up to 180°. If $\angle AOC = 60°$, then $\angle ABC$ must be $180° - 60° = 120°$, which is (D).

This question is a great question for Ballparking. The angle marked $x°$ is clearly greater than a right angle, so you can immediately eliminate (A), (B), and (C). This gives you a 50/50 chance on question 48. Don't forget to ballpark on geometry questions, especially toward the end of the test!

Overlapping Figures

ETS likes to combine different shapes in a single problem. You've already seen this idea in the case of 45°-45°-90° triangles and squares and 30°-60°-90° triangles and equilateral triangles. There are a few key points about questions involving multiple figures:

- Figure out how the shapes are related. Typically, there will be some line (or feature like a diameter or diagonal) that both shapes share.
- Look to solve a couple of easier problems and then add or subtract values rather than solve for goofy shapes directly.

Let's look at an example:

---

22. A square with a perimeter of 24 circumscribes a circle. What is the area of the space inside the square but outside the circle?

   (A) 4.27
   (B) 5.15
   (C) 7.73
   (D) 17.15
   (E) 20.55

Here's How to Crack It

Start by drawing the figure. Because all the sides of the square are the same, if the perimeter of the square is 24, then the sides of the square are $24 \div 4 = 6$:

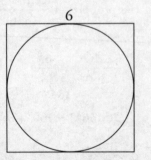

To find the area inside the square but outside the circle, instead of solving for the wedge shapes in the corner directly, take the area of the square and subtract the area of the circle. If the side of the square is 6, then the area of the square is 6^2, or 36. To find the area of the circle, you need the radius. Draw a radius on your diagram:

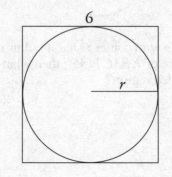

The radius is half of the diameter, and the diameter of the circle is equal to the side of the square. Therefore, the radius of the circle is 3. The area of the circle is $\pi(3)^2$, or 9π. To find the area of the space between the circle and the square, subtract: $36 - 9\pi = 7.73$, which is (C).

DRILL 12: MORE CIRCLES

Try the following practice questions using the rules and techniques for circles. The answers can be found in Part IV.

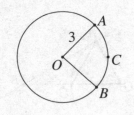

Note: Figure not drawn to scale

12. In the circle with center O, if the length of minor arc ACB is 4.71, which of the following best approximates the measure of $\angle AOB$?

    (A) 60.0°
    (B) 72.0°
    (C) 86.4°
    (D) 90.0°
    (E) 98.6°

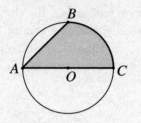

29. If the circle with center O has a radius of 5 and the measure of $\angle BAC$ is 45°, then what is the area of the shaded region?

(A) 32.13
(B) 31.52
(C) 26.70
(D) 25.41
(E) 24.26

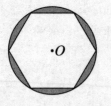

31. A regular hexagon is inscribed in the circle with center O. If the circle has a radius of 4, what is the area of the shaded region?

(A) 8.3
(B) 8.7
(C) 9.0
(D) 9.4
(E) 10.2

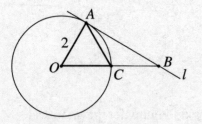

43. Line l is tangent to the circle with center O at A, and $OA = AC$. What is the length of AB ?

(A) 1.73
(B) 2.83
(C) 3.46
(D) 4.74
(E) 5.20

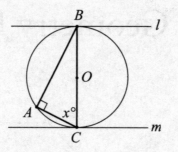

Note: Figure not drawn to scale.

45. The right angle *CAB* is inscribed in the circle
with center *O* and diameter *BC*. Lines *l* and *m*
are tangent to the circle at *B* and *C,* respectively.
Which of the following must be true?

   I. *AB < BC*

  II. *x* = 60

  III. *l* and *m* meet when extended to the
right.

(A) I only
(B) III only
(C) I and II only
(D) II and III only
(E) I, II, and III

Comprehensive Plane Geometry Drill

The answers can be found in Part IV.

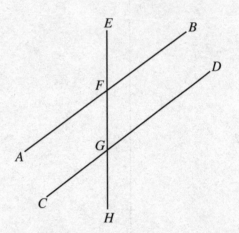

Note: Figure not drawn to scale.

3. In the figure above, if ∠EFB and ∠CGF are supplementary, then which of the following must be true?

(A) $\overline{AB} \parallel \overline{CD}$
(B) $\overline{AB} \perp \overline{CD}$
(C) $\angle EFB + \angle CGF = 90°$
(D) $\overline{AB} \parallel \overline{EF}$
(E) $\overline{EH} \perp \overline{AB}$

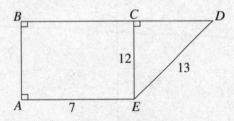

Note: Figure not drawn to scale

5. What is the perimeter of quadrilateral *ABDE* shown above?

(A) 32
(B) 39
(C) 44
(D) 56
(E) 114

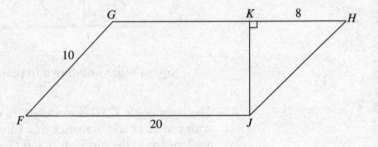

9. If *FG* = 10, *FJ* = 20, and *KH* = 8, then what is the area of parallelogram *FGHJ* above?

(A) 120
(B) 140
(C) 160
(D) 180
(E) 200

11. Triangle *ABC* (not shown) is isosceles, and *AB* = 7. Which of the following could be the perimeter of triangle *ABC* ?

  I. 14
  II. 18
  III. 28

(A) I only
(B) II only
(C) I and II only
(D) II and III only
(E) I, II, and III

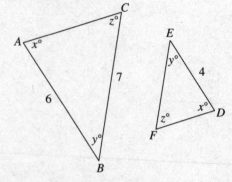

15. In the figure above, what is the length of $\overline{EF}$?

(A) 2.67
(B) 4
(C) 4.5
(D) 4.67
(E) 5

24. A printmaker wants to triple the area of a square print. If the current print has an area of 50 cm², then what will be the side length of the new, larger print?

(A) 4.08 cm
(B) 7.07 cm
(C) 10.00 cm
(D) 12.25 cm
(E) 21.21 cm

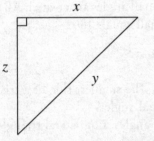

Note: Figure not drawn to scale.

32. Given the triangle shown above, which of the following must be true?

(A) $\left(\dfrac{x+y}{2}\right)\sqrt{2} = z$

(B) $x^2 + y^2 = z^2$

(C) $y = x\sqrt{2}$

(D) $x = z$

(E) $\sqrt{y^2 - z^2} = x$

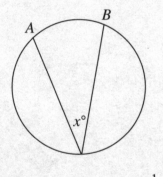

36. In the circle above, minor arc AB is $\dfrac{1}{5}$ the length of the circumference. What is the value of x ?

(A) 30
(B) 36
(C) 60
(D) 72
(E) 144

45. A circle with center O (not shown) has a perimeter of 12π. $\overline{WX}$ is a diameter of circle O, and $\overline{YZ}$ is a chord on the circle parallel to $\overline{WX}$ and with a length of 6. What is the area of sector WOY ?

(A) 6.28
(B) 12.57
(C) 15.59
(D) 18.85
(E) 31.18

48. The diagonal of square $ABCD$ (not shown) is 1.76 m longer than side AB. What is the area of square $ABCD$?

(A) 4.24 m²
(B) 6 m²
(C) 18 m²
(D) 25.46 m²
(E) 36 m²

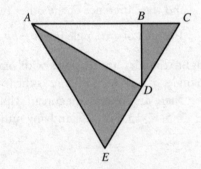

50. In the figure above, triangle ACE is an equilateral triangle with area 15.59, D is the midpoint of $\overline{CE}$, and $\overline{BD} \perp \overline{AC}$. What is the area of the shaded region?

(A) 5.85
(B) 7.79
(C) 9.74
(D) 10.13
(E) 10.53

Summary

o   Some rules about lines and angles:
  - A 90° angle is formed by two lines perpendicular to each other.
  - There are 180° in a line.
  - When two straight lines intersect, the angles created opposite each other are equal. The adjacent angles (two angles beside each other along the same straight line) have a sum of 180°.

o   When parallel lines are transected by a third line, big angles and small angles are created. All the big angles are equal, all the small angles are equal, and a big plus a small equals 180°.

o   Triangles form the largest set of plane geometry questions on the test.
  - The sum of the angles in a triangle is 180°.
  - The longest side of a triangle is across from the largest angle. The smallest side of a triangle is across from the smallest angle. Equal sides are across from equal angles.
  - Isosceles triangles have at least two equal sides and two equal angles. Equilateral triangles have three equal sides and three equal angles.
  - The Third Side Rule states that the length of any side of a triangle must be between the sum and the difference of the other two sides.
  - The area of a triangle is $A = \dfrac{1}{2}bh$. The height must be perpendicular to the base.

o   Right triangles are triangles with one 90° angle. The Pythagorean Theorem states that, in a right triangle, $a^2 + b^2 = c^2$, where c is the hypotenuse of the triangle and a and b are the two legs.
  - There are some Pythagorean triplets that are helpful to have in your back pocket. They are 3-4-5, 5-12-13, 7-24-25, and any multiples of these as well.

- Special right triangles are helpful in simplifying the math. They often provide an easier route to the correct solution than using the Pythagorean Theorem, so look closely for opportunities to use them. The following is a list of special right triangles:
  - The sides of a 45°-45°-90° triangle have a very specific ratio: $x : x : x\sqrt{2}$, where x is the length of each leg.
  - The sides of a 30°-60°-90° triangle have a very specific ratio: $x : x\sqrt{3} : 2x$, where x is the length of the shorter leg.

- Similar triangles have the same angle measures. The corresponding sides and heights of similar triangles are proportional.

- Quadrilaterals are four-sided figures. The sum of the angles in a quadrilateral is 360°.
  - Parallelograms have two sets of equal, parallel lines. The area of a parallelogram is $A = bh$, where the base is perpendicular to the height.
  - Rectangles are parallelograms with four right angles.
  - Squares are rectangles with four equal sides.
  - Trapezoids are four-sided figures whose top and bottom are parallel but different in length. The area of a trapezoid is $A = \left(\dfrac{b_1 + b_2}{2}\right)h$, where b_1 is one base and b_2 is the other.

- The sum of the angles of an n-sided polygon is $(n - 2) \times 180°$.

- Here are some things to remember about a circle:
  - A circle contains a total of 360°.
  - The radius is the distance from the center of the circle to any point on the circle.
  - The diameter is a straight line drawn from one point on a circle through the center to another. Its length is twice the radius.
  - The circumference of the circle is the distance around the circle. You can think of it as the perimeter of the circle. Its formula is $C = \pi d$. You may also know it as $C = 2\pi r$.
  - The formula for area of a circle is $A = \pi r^2$.

- A sector is a slice of pie of the circle. The part of the circumference that the sector contains is called an arc and is in the same proportion to the circumference as the angle of the sector is to 360°.
- A central angle is an angle whose vertex is the center of the circle. An inscribed angle has its vertex on the circle and its two endpoints on the circle. Its angle is half of what the central angle is to those same two endpoints.
- Any angle inscribed in a semicircle is a right angle.
- A line tangent to the circle touches the circle in only one place and is always perpendicular to the radius drawn to the point of tangency.

o When dealing with overlapping figures, look for where the shapes share a line or dimension. Also, look to solve for simple shapes and add or subtract the results when asked to solve for strange shapes or areas.

Chapter 8
Solid Geometry

Questions about solid geometry frequently test plane geometry techniques. They're difficult mostly because the added third dimension makes them harder to visualize. You're likely to run into three or four solid geometry questions on the SAT Subject Test in Math 1, however, so it's important to practice. If you're not the artistic type and have trouble drawing cubes, cylinders, and so on, it's worthwhile to practice sketching the shapes in the following pages. The ability to make your own drawing is often helpful.

On Solid Geometry, the same basic approach applies:

1) Draw a figure (if none is provided).
2) Label all information on the figure.
3) Write down complete formulas

As you will see, the basic approach works just as well on Solid Geometry as it does in Plane Geometry!

PRISMS

Prisms are three-dimensional figures that have two parallel bases that are polygons. Cubes and rectangular solids are examples of prisms that ETS often asks about. In general, the volume of a prism is given by the following formula:

Volume of a Prism

$$V = Bh$$

In this formula, B represents the area of either base of the prism (the top or the bottom), and h represents the height of the prism (perpendicular to the base). The formulas for the volume of a rectangular solid, a cube, and a cylinder all come from this basic formula.

RECTANGULAR SOLIDS

A rectangular solid is simply a box; it is also sometimes called a rectangular prism. It has three distinct dimensions: *length*, *width*, and *height*. The volume of a rectangular solid (the amount of space it contains) is given by this formula:

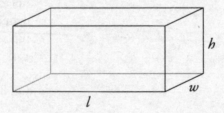

Volume of a Rectangular Solid

$$V = lwh$$

The surface area (*SA*) of a rectangular solid is the sum of the areas of all of its faces. A rectangular solid's surface area is given by the following formula.

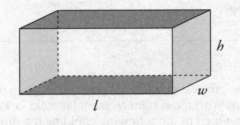

The volume and surface area of a solid make up the most basic information you can have about that solid (volume is tested more often than surface area). You may also be asked about *lengths* within a rectangular solid—edges and diagonals. The dimensions of the solid give the lengths of its edges, and the diagonal of any *face* of a rectangular solid can be found using the Pythagorean Theorem. There's one more length you may be asked about—the long diagonal (or space diagonal) that passes from corner to corner through the center of the box. The length of the long diagonal is given by this formula:

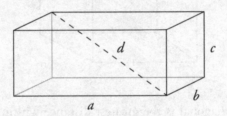

This is the Pythagorean Theorem with a third dimension added, and it works just the same way. This formula will work in any rectangular box. The long diagonal is the longest straight line that can be drawn inside any rectangular solid.

Let's look at a question.

---

30. If the greatest possible distance between two points within a certain rectangular solid is 12, then which of the following could be the dimensions of this solid?

    (A) $3 \times 3 \times 9$
    (B) $3 \times 6 \times 7$
    (C) $3 \times 8 \times 12$
    (D) $4 \times 7 \times 9$
    (E) $4 \times 8 \times 8$

Here's How to Crack It

As with all geometry questions, the first step is to draw your own figure if one isn't provided. Your figure should look something like this:

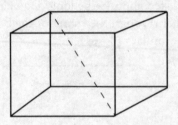

Notice that the long diagonal is the greatest distance within a rectangular solid. The length of the long diagonal can be found using the Super Pythagorean Theorem, $a^2 + b^2 + c^2 = d^2$, where a, b, and c are the dimensions of the solid and d is the length of the diagonal.

Plug In the Answers to find the possible dimensions of the rectangular solid. Start with (C) and plug the given dimensions into the Super Pythagorean Theorem: $3^2 + 8^2 + 12^2 = d^2$, so $d = \sqrt{217}$, which is 14.73. According to the problem, d should equal 12, so eliminate (C).

It may be difficult to tell which answer choice you should try next, so just pick a direction. Choice (D) gives you $4^2 + 7^2 + 9^2 = d^2$. Therefore, $d = \sqrt{146} = 12.08$. You're getting closer, so try (E) next. Choice (E) gives you $4^2 + 8^2 + 8^2 = d^2$. $d = \sqrt{144} = 12$, so (E) is the correct answer. Remember that when using PITA, you can stop when you find the right answer, so there's no need to test out (A) and (B).

CUBES

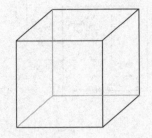

A cube is a rectangular solid that has the same length in all three dimensions. All six of its faces are squares. This simplifies the formulas for volume, surface area, and the long diagonal.

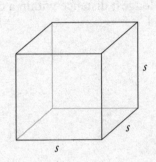

Volume of a Cube

$$V = s^3$$

Surface Area of a Cube

$$SA = 6s^2$$

Face Diagonal of a Cube

$$f = s\sqrt{2}$$

Long Diagonal of a Cube

$$d = s\sqrt{3}$$

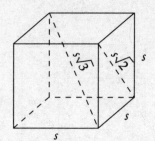

Let's try an example.

---

24. What is the longest distance within a cube with a volume of 64 ?

(A) 5.66
(B) 6.93
(C) 11.31
(D) 13.86
(E) 22.63

Here's How to Crack It

Start by drawing a cube. The longest distance within a cube will be a long diagonal:

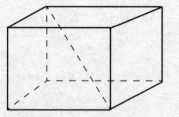

Use the formula for volume to find the side length: $V = s^3$, so $64 = s^3$, $s = \sqrt[3]{64} = 4$.

To find the long diagonal, use the formula $d = s\sqrt{3} : d = 4\sqrt{3} = 6.93$, which is (B).

Triangles in Rectangular Solids

Many questions about rectangular solids are actually testing triangle rules. Such questions generally ask for the lengths of the diagonals of a box's faces, the long diagonal of a box, or other lengths. These questions are usually solved using the Pythagorean Theorem or the Super Pythagorean Theorem.

Let's look at an example.

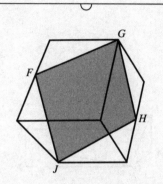

32. In the figure above, the edge of the cube is equal to 5. If G and J are vertices of the cube, and F and H are midpoints of their respective edges, then what is the perimeter of the shaded region?

    (A) 11.18
    (B) 22.36
    (C) 31.25
    (D) 62.5
    (E) 125

Here's How to Crack It

The first step is to label the figure with the information provided in the problem. If the edge of the cube is equal to 5, then the distance from the vertex to the midpoint is 2.5. Once you label the figure, you'll realize that you can use the Pythagorean Theorem to solve for the side of the square.

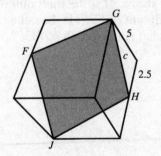

$5^2 + 2.5^2 = 31.25$, so $c = s\sqrt{31.25} = \sqrt{5.59}$. Therefore, the perimeter of the shaded region is 5.59 × 4 = 22.36. Choice (B) is the correct answer. Notice that (C) is a partial answer.

DRILL 1: TRIANGLES IN RECTANGULAR SOLIDS

Here are some practice questions using triangle rules in rectangular solids. The answers can be found in Part IV.

32. What is the length of the longest line that can be drawn in a cube of volume 27 ?

    (A) 3.0
    (B) 4.2
    (C) 4.9
    (D) 5.2
    (E) 9.0

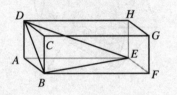

36. In the rectangular solid shown above, if $AB = 4$, $BC = 3$, and $BF = 12$, what is the perimeter of triangle EDB ?

    (A) 27.33
    (B) 28.40
    (C) 29.20
    (D) 29.50
    (E) 30.37

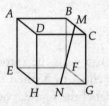

39. In the cube above, M is the midpoint of BC, and N is the midpoint of GH. If the cube has a volume of 1, what is the length of MN ?

    (A) 1.23
    (B) 1.36
    (C) 1.41
    (D) 1.73
    (E) 1.89

CYLINDERS

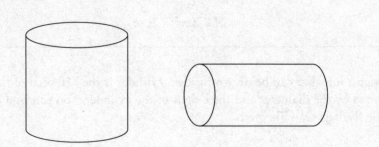

A cylinder is like a prism but with a circular base. It has two important dimensions—radius and height. Remember that volume is the area of the base times the height. In this case, the base is a circle. The area of a circle is πr^2. So the volume of a cylinder is $\pi r^2 h$.

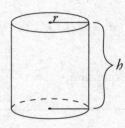

Volume of a Cylinder

$$V = \pi r^2 h$$

The surface area of a cylinder is found by adding the areas of the two circular bases to the area of the rectangle you'd get if you unrolled the side of the cylinder. That boils down to the following formula:

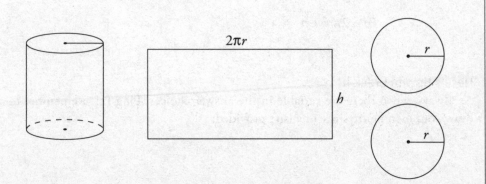

Surface Area of a Cylinder

$$SA = 2\pi r^2 + 2\pi r h$$

The longest line that can be drawn inside a cylinder is the diagonal of the rectangle formed by the diameter and the height of the cylinder. You can find its length with the Pythagorean Theorem.

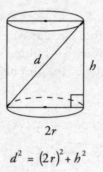

$$d^2 = (2r)^2 + h^2$$

Here is an example of a cylinder question.

49. The height of a cylinder is equal to one-half of n, where n is equal to one-half of the cylinder's diameter. What is the surface area of this cylinder in terms of n ?

(A) $\dfrac{3\pi n^2}{2}$

(B) $2\pi n^2$

(C) $3\pi n^2$

(D) $2\pi n^2 + \dfrac{\pi n}{2}$

(E) $2\pi n^2 + n$

Here's How to Crack It

As always, when there are variable in the answer choices, Plug In! Remember to draw your own figure since one isn't provided:

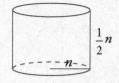

Let's make the diameter equal to 8. Therefore, $n = 4$ and the height is equal to 2. Notice that n is equal to the radius of the cylinder. Plug these values into the surface area formula: $SA = 2\pi r^2 + 2\pi rh$, so $SA = 2\pi(4)^2 + 2\pi(4)(2)$. The surface area equals 48π. Now plug $n = 4$ into each answer choice to see which one equals 48π.

Choice (C) equals 48π, so it is the correct answer. Remember, when Plugging In, you must check all five answer choices.

CONES

If you take a cylinder and shrink one of its circular bases down to a point, then you have a cone. A cone has three significant dimensions which form a right triangle—its radius, its height, and its *slant height,* which is the straight-line distance from the tip of the cone to a point on the edge of its base. The formulas for the volume and surface area of a cone are given in the information box at the beginning of the SAT Subject Test in Math 1. The formula for the volume of a cone is pretty straightforward:

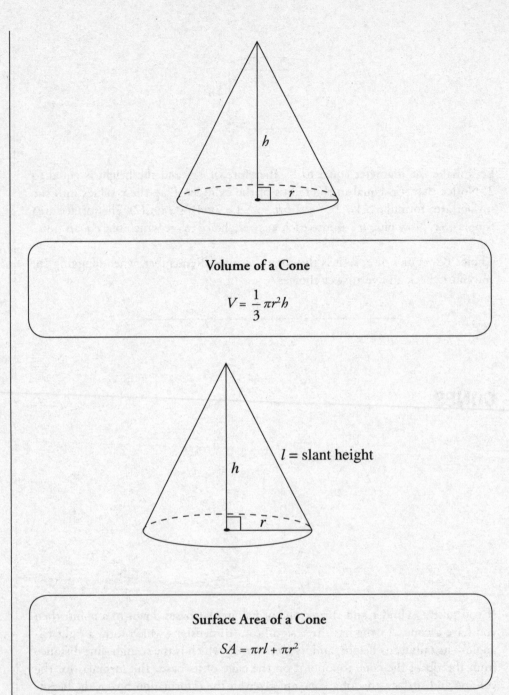

Volume of a Cone

$$V = \frac{1}{3}\pi r^2 h$$

Connect the Dots

Notice that the volume of a cone is just one-third of the volume of a circular cylinder. Make memorizing easy!

Surface Area of a Cone

$$SA = \pi r l + \pi r^2$$

The lateral area of a cone is just the area of the sloping sides. It's not the complete surface area because it doesn't include the area of the circular base. If you want to calculate only the lateral area, just use the first half of the formula above.

Let's look at an example problem.

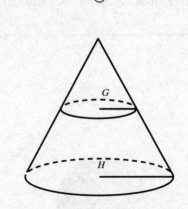

42. In the figure above, points *G* and *H* are the centers of the bases of the cones. If the ratio of the radius of the smaller cone to the larger cone is 1 to 3, what is the ratio of the volume of the smaller cone to the volume of the larger cone?

(A) $\dfrac{1}{27}$

(B) $\dfrac{1}{9}$

(C) $\dfrac{1}{3}$

(D) $\dfrac{1}{2}$

(E) It cannot be determined from the information given.

Here's How to Crack It
Remember when the answer choices contain fractions or ratios, you can Plug In. Plug In 1 for the radius of the small cone and 3 for the radius of the large cone (Plugging In the given ratio makes the math easy). Since the smaller cone is contained within the larger cone, the cones are similar and the ratio of the heights is also 1 to 3. Plug In 1 and 3 for the heights of the smaller and larger cone, respectively.

For the smaller cone, $V = \dfrac{1}{3}\pi r^2 h = \dfrac{1}{3}\pi(1)^2\,(1) = \dfrac{1}{3}\pi.$

For the larger cone, $V = \dfrac{1}{3}\pi r^2 h = \dfrac{1}{3}\pi(3)^2\,(3) = 9\pi.$

Therefore, the relationship of the volume of the smaller cone to the larger cone is $\dfrac{\dfrac{1}{3}}{9} = \dfrac{1}{27}$, so (A) is the correct answer. Choices (C) and (E) are trap answers.

SPHERES

A sphere is simply a hollow ball. It can be defined as all of the points in space at a fixed distance from a central point. The one important measure in a sphere is its radius. The formulas for the volume and surface area of a sphere are given to you at the very beginning of the SAT Subject Test in Math 1. That means that you don't need to have them memorized, but here they are anyway:

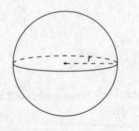

Volume of a Sphere

$$V = \frac{4}{3}\pi r^3$$

Surface Area of a Sphere

$$SA = 4\pi r^2$$

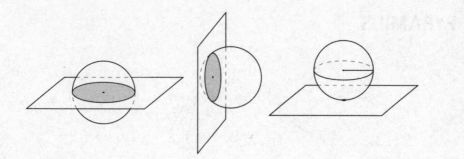

The intersection of a plane and a sphere always forms a circle unless the plane is *tangent* to the sphere, in which case the plane and sphere touch at only one point.

Take a look at this example.

37. The volume of a sphere is equal to 972π cubic centimeters. What is the surface area of the sphere in cubic centimeters?

(A) 108π
(B) 162π
(C) 324π
(D) 486π
(E) 729π

Here's How to Crack It

The first step is to calculate the radius of the sphere from the given volume.

$$V = \frac{4}{3}\pi r^3 = 972\pi$$

$$\frac{4}{3}r^3 = 972$$

$$r^3 = 729$$

$$r = 9$$

Now, plug the radius into the surface area formula.

$$SA = 4\pi r^2$$

$$SA = 324\pi$$

Choice (C) is the correct answer.

PYRAMIDS

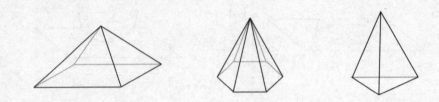

A pyramid is a little like a cone, except that its base is a polygon instead of a circle. Pyramids don't show up very often on the SAT Subject Test in Math 1. When you do run into a pyramid, it will almost always have a rectangular base. Pyramids can be pretty complicated solids, but for the purposes of this test, a pyramid has just two important measures—the area of its base and its height. The height of a pyramid is the length of a line drawn straight down from the pyramid's tip to its base. The height is perpendicular to the base. The volume of a pyramid is given by this formula.

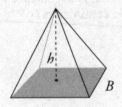

Connect the Dots
Notice that the volume of a pyramid is just one-third of the volume of a prism. This makes memorizing easy!

Volume of a Pyramid

$$V = \frac{1}{3} Bh$$

(B = area of base)

It's not really possible to give a general formula for the surface area of a pyramid because there are so many different kinds. At any rate, the information is not generally tested on the SAT Subject Test in Math 1. If you should be called upon to figure out the surface area of a pyramid, just figure out the area of each face using polygon rules and add them up.

Here's an example of a pyramid question.

---

48. The side of a square base of a pyramid has a length of 10 and a parallel cross section has sides of length 5. If the distance from the cross section to the tip of the pyramid is 7, what is the altitude of the pyramid?

    (A) 7
    (B) 14
    (C) 20
    (D) 21
    (E) 25

Here's How to Crack It

First, draw your own figure. Yours should look something like this:

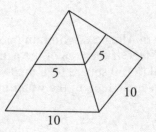

Next, set up a proportion. The ratio of the sides of the cross section and the base is $\frac{5}{10}$, or $\frac{1}{2}$. If the height of the pyramid is x, then the distance to the cross section from the tip of the pyramid is $x - 7$. Therefore, $\frac{1}{2} = \frac{x-7}{x}$. You can either use PITA to solve or cross-multiply to solve for x. If you cross-multiply, you get $x = 2x - 14$. Therefore, $x = 14$, which is (B).

TRICKS OF THE TRADE

Here are some of the most common solid geometry question types you're likely to encounter on the SAT Subject Test in Math 1.

Volume Questions

Many solid geometry questions test your understanding of the relationship between a solid's volume and its other dimensions—sometimes including the solid's surface area. To solve these questions, just plug the numbers you're given into the solid's volume formula.

DRILL 2: VOLUME

Try the following practice questions. The answers can be found in Part IV.

17. The volume and surface area of a cube are equal. What is the length of an edge of this cube?

    (A) 1
    (B) 2
    (C) 4
    (D) 6
    (E) 9

24. A rectangular solid has a volume of 30, and its edges have integer lengths. What is the greatest possible surface area of this solid?

    (A) 62
    (B) 82
    (C) 86
    (D) 94
    (E) 122

28. The water in Allegra's swimming pool has a depth of 7 feet. If the area of the pentagonal base of the pool is 150 square feet, then what is the volume, in cubic feet, of the water in her pool?

    (A) 57
    (B) 50
    (C) 1,050
    (D) 5,250
    (E) It cannot be determined from the information given.

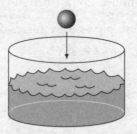

43. A sphere of radius 1 is totally submerged in a cylindrical tank of radius 4, as shown. The water level in the tank rises a distance of h. What is the value of h ?

    (A) 0.072
    (B) 0.083
    (C) 0.096
    (D) 0.108
    (E) 0.123

18. A cube has a surface area of 6x. What is the volume of the cube?

(A) $x^{\frac{2}{3}}$

(B) $x^{\frac{3}{2}}$

(C) $6x^2$

(D) $36x^2$

(E) x^3

36. A sphere has a radius of r. If this radius is increased by b, then the surface area of the sphere is increased by what amount?

(A) b^2
(B) $4\pi b^2$
(C) $8\pi rb + 4\pi b^2$
(D) $8\pi rb + 2rb + b^2$
(E) $4\pi r^2 b^2$

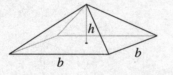

40. If the pyramid shown has a square base with edges of length b, and $b = 2h$, then which of the following is the volume of the pyramid?

(A) $\dfrac{h^3}{3}$

(B) $\dfrac{4h^3}{3}$

(C) $4h^3$

(D) $8h^2 - h$

(E) $\dfrac{8h^3 - 4h}{3}$

Inscribed Solids

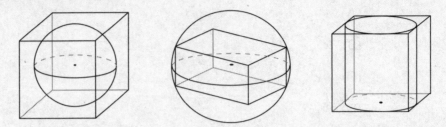

Some questions on the SAT Subject Test in Math 1 will be based on spheres inscribed in cubes or cubes inscribed in spheres (these are the most popular inscribed shapes). Occasionally, you may also see figures such as a rectangular solid inscribed in a sphere or a cylinder inscribed in a rectangular box. These questions will give you information about one of the shapes and ask you to solve for a value related to the other shape. The trick to these questions is always figuring out how to get from the dimensions of one of the solids to the dimensions of the other.

The following are a few basic tips that can speed up your work on inscribed solids questions.

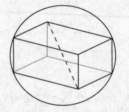

- When a cube or rectangular solid is inscribed in a sphere, the long diagonal of that solid is equal to the diameter of the sphere.

- When a cylinder is inscribed in a sphere, the sphere's diameter is equal to the diagonal of the rectangle formed by the cylinder's heights and diameter.

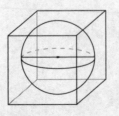

- When a sphere is inscribed in a cube, the diameter of the sphere is equal to the length of the cube's edge.

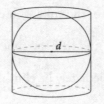

- If a sphere is inscribed in a cylinder, both solids have the same diameter.

Most inscribed solids questions fall into one of the preceding categories. If you run into a situation not covered by these tips, just look for the way to get from the dimensions of the inner shape to those of the external shape, or vice versa.

Here's an example.

---

46. A cube is inscribed in a sphere of radius 6. What is the volume of the cube?

(A) $36\sqrt{3}$

(B) 36π

(C) 216

(D) $192\sqrt{3}$

(E) $216\sqrt{3}$

Here's How to Crack It
Start by drawing the figure. The situation described will look something like this:

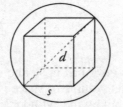

When a cube is inscribed in a sphere, the long diagonal of the cube is equal to the

diameter of the sphere. Since the sphere has a radius of 6 and a diameter of 12,

you know that the cube has a long diagonal of 12. The long diagonal of a cube is

related to the side of a cube using the formula $d = s\sqrt{3}$. You can use that formula to find the length of a side: $s = \dfrac{d}{\sqrt{3}}$. In this case, $s = \dfrac{12}{\sqrt{3}} = \dfrac{12}{1.732} = 6.93$. Once you know the length of one side of the cube, you can easily find the cube's volume using the formula $V = s^3$. You'll find that the cube has a volume of 332.55. At this point, (A), (B), and (C) can immediately be eliminated by Ballparking, as they are much smaller than this. To choose between (D) and (E), just calculate the decimal value of one of them. Since $192\sqrt{3} = 332.55$, (D) is the correct answer.

DRILL 3: INSCRIBED SOLIDS

Here are some practice inscribed solids questions. The answers can be found in Part IV.

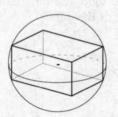

32. A rectangular solid is inscribed in a sphere as shown. If the dimensions of the solid are 3, 4, and 6, then what is the radius of the sphere?

    (A) 2.49
    (B) 3.91
    (C) 4.16
    (D) 5.62
    (E) 7.81

35. A cylinder is inscribed in a cube with an edge of length 2. What volume of space is enclosed by the cube but not by the cylinder?

    (A) 1.41
    (B) 1.56
    (C) 1.72
    (D) 3.81
    (E) 4.86

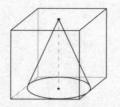

38. A cone is inscribed in a cube of volume 1 in such a way that its base is inscribed in one face of the cube. What is the volume of the cone?

(A) 0.21
(B) 0.26
(C) 0.33
(D) 0.42
(E) 0.67

Solids Produced by Rotation

Three types of solids can be produced by the rotation of simple two-dimensional shapes—spheres, cylinders, and cones. Questions about solids produced by rotation are generally fairly straightforward; they usually test your ability to visualize the solid generated by the rotation of a flat shape. Sometimes, rotated solids questions begin with a shape in the coordinate plane—that is, rotated around one of the axes or some other line. Practice will help you figure out the dimensions of the solid from the dimensions of the original flat shape.

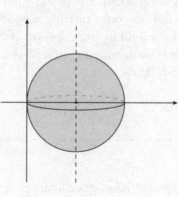

A sphere is produced when a circle is rotated around its diameter. This is an easy situation to work with, as the sphere and the original circle will have the same radius. Find the radius of the circle, and you can solve for the volume or the surface area of the sphere.

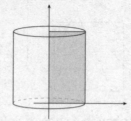

A cylinder is formed by the rotation of a rectangle around a central line *or* one edge.

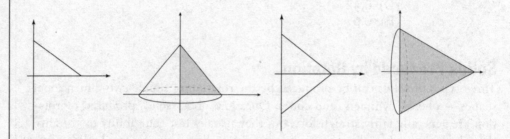

A cone is formed by rotating a right triangle around one of its legs (think of it as spinning the triangle) or by rotating an isosceles triangle around its axis of symmetry. Another way of thinking about it is if you spun the triangle in the first figure above around the *y*-axis (so you're rotating around the leg that's sitting on the *y*-axis) you would get the second figure. Likewise, if you spun the third figure above around the *x*-axis (so you're rotating around the axis of symmetry), you would end up with the fourth figure.

Let's look at a sample question.

50. Circle *O* lies on the *xy*-coordinate plan with its center at the origin. Point (−4, 3) lies on circle *O*. If circle *O* were to be rotated about its center in three dimensions, what would be the volume of the resulting figure?

(A)   78.54
(B)   268.08
(C)   314.16
(D)   339.29
(E)   523.60

Here's How to Crack It
Start by drawing a coordinate plane with a circle at the origin and point (−4, 3) on the circle:

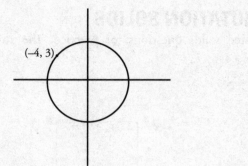

If the circle is rotated around its center in three dimensions, the resulting shape would be a sphere. To find the volume of a sphere, you need its radius, which in this case will be the same as the radius of the circle. To find the radius of the circle, find the distance from the origin to the point (–4, 3). You could use the Pythagorean Theorem, or you could notice that you can make a 3:4:5 right triangle between the origin and that point (see the next chapter for more on distance in coordinate geometry):

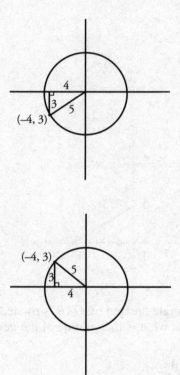

The radius of the circle (and therefore the radius of the sphere) is 5. The volume of the sphere is given by the equation $V = \frac{4}{3}\pi r^3$, so make $r = 5$ and solve: $V = \frac{4}{3}\pi 5^3$, which is (E).

DRILL 4: ROTATION SOLIDS

Try these rotated solids questions for practice. The answers can be found in Part IV.

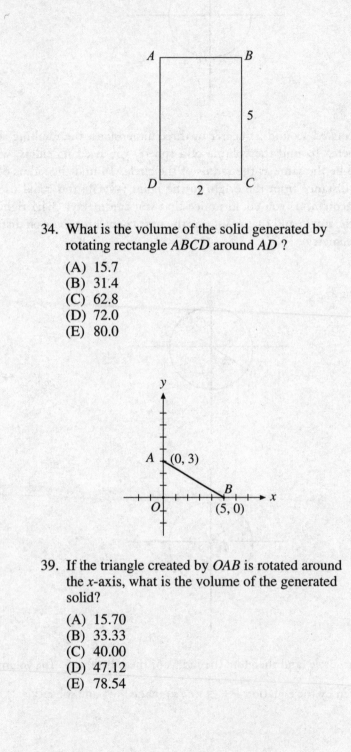

34. What is the volume of the solid generated by rotating rectangle *ABCD* around *AD* ?

    (A) 15.7
    (B) 31.4
    (C) 62.8
    (D) 72.0
    (E) 80.0

39. If the triangle created by *OAB* is rotated around the *x*-axis, what is the volume of the generated solid?

    (A) 15.70
    (B) 33.33
    (C) 40.00
    (D) 47.12
    (E) 78.54

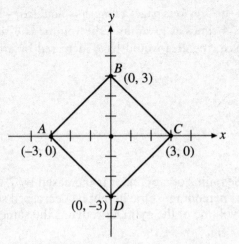

46. What is the volume generated by rotating square
ABCD around the *y*-axis?

(A) 24.84
(B) 28.27
(C) 42.66
(D) 56.55
(E) 84.82

Changing Dimensions

Some solid geometry questions will ask you to figure out what happens to the volume of a solid if all of its lengths are increased by a certain factor or if its area doubles, and so on. To answer questions of this type, just remember a basic rule.

> When the lengths of a solid are increased by a certain factor, the surface area of the solid increases by the square of that factor, and the volume increases by the cube of that factor. This rule is true only when the solid's shape doesn't change—its length must increase in *every* dimension, not just one. For that reason, cubes and spheres are most often used for this type of question because their shapes are constant.

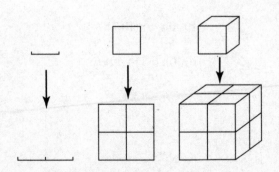

In the illustration on the previous page, a length is doubled, which means that the corresponding area is 4 times as great, and the volume is 8 times as great. If the length had been tripled, the area would have increased by a factor of 9, and the volume by a factor of 27.

Let's try one.

---

50. If the radius of a cylinder is increased by 7%, by what percent must the height be decreased so that the volume of the cylinder remains the same?

(A) 7%
(B) 8.7%
(C) 12.7%
(D) 26%
(E) 30%

Here's How to Crack It

Plug In! Since you aren't given the values for the height or radius of the cylinder and you are given percentages in the answer choices, you can plug in your own numbers. The number 10 makes the math a lot easier when working with percentages, so plug in $r = 10$ and $h = 10$.

Solve for the volume of the cylinder:

$$V = \pi r^2 h$$

$$V = \pi(10)^2(10)$$

$$V = 1000\pi$$

Now, calculate the radius of the new cylinder. If the radius increases by 7%, the new radius is equal to 10.7. Since we are looking for the new height required to keep the volume the same, set the volume equal to 1000π and solve for h:

$$V = 1000\pi = \pi r^2 h$$

$$1000\pi = \pi(10.7)^2 h$$

$$1000\pi = 114.49\pi h$$

$$h = 8.73$$

Notice that (B) is 8.7% but that's the value of the new height not the percent change, so (B) is a partial answer. You need to use the percent change formula to calculate the percent decrease of the height:

$$\text{Percent Change} = \frac{\text{amount change}}{\text{original}} \times 100\%$$

$$\text{Percent Change} = \frac{10 - 8.73}{10} \times 100\%$$

$$\text{Percent Change} = 12.7\%$$

Choice (C) is the correct answer. Notice that (A) is a trap answer.

This problem required you to use the percent change formula in conjunction with the formula for the volume of a cylinder. ETS makes questions more difficult by requiring knowledge of multiple concepts. So remember, percent change isn't just for arithmetic questions. Geometry questions can also test your knowledge of percent change.

DRILL 5: CHANGING DIMENSIONS

Try these practice questions. The answers can be found in Part IV.

13. If the radius of sphere A is one-third as long as the radius of sphere B, then the volume of sphere A is what fraction of the volume of sphere B?

(A) $\dfrac{1}{3}$

(B) $\dfrac{1}{4}$

(C) $\dfrac{1}{9}$

(D) $\dfrac{1}{12}$

(E) $\dfrac{1}{27}$

18. A rectangular solid with length l, width w, and height h has a volume of 24. What is the volume of a rectangular solid with length $\dfrac{l}{2}$, width $\dfrac{w}{2}$, and height $\dfrac{h}{2}$?

    (A) 18
    (B) 12
    (C) 6
    (D) 3
    (E) 2

21. If the surface area of a cube is increased by a factor of 2.25, then its volume is increased by what factor?

    (A) 1.72
    (B) 3.38
    (C) 4.50
    (D) 5.06
    (E) 5.64

Comprehensive Solid Geometry Drill

The answers can be found in Part IV.

24. If the volume of a cube is 100, how long is the diagonal of the cube?

    (A) 4.64
    (B) 6.56
    (C) 8.04
    (D) 10.42
    (E) 13.76

29. A rectangular solid has a length of 6, a width of 3, and a height of 4. If each dimension is decreased by 20%, what is the volume of the resulting solid?

    (A) 36.86
    (B) 46.08
    (C) 57.60
    (D) 72.00
    (E) 124.42

30. In a certain cube, the ratio of surface area (in square units) to the volume (in cubic units) is 3 to 1. What is the length of the side of the cube (in units)?

    (A) 1
    (B) 2
    (C) 3
    (D) 4
    (E) 5

34. A sphere and a cube have equal volumes. If the diameter of the sphere is 8, what is the surface area of the cube?

    (A) 6.5
    (B) 41.6
    (C) 210.6
    (D) 249.5
    (E) 268.1

38. A pyramid has a square base with an area of 16 and a height of 6. If the height were to increase by 50% and the volume of the pyramid was to remain constant, what would be the value of the side of the base?

    (A) 1.64
    (B) 3.27
    (C) 3.56
    (D) 5.65
    (E) 10.67

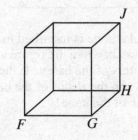

39. In the figure above, the cube has edge of length 4. What is the distance from vertex F to the midpoint of edge HJ ?

    (A) 2
    (B) $\sqrt{20}$
    (C) $4\sqrt{2}$
    (D) 6
    (E) $\sqrt{30}$

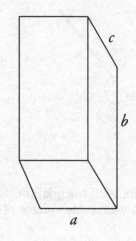

40. In the figure above, if $a = \frac{1}{2}b$ and $b = 5c$, what is the volume of the rectangular solid in terms of a ?

    (A) $\frac{3}{4}a^3$

    (B) $\frac{3}{5}a^3$

    (C) $\frac{4}{5}a^3$

    (D) a^3

    (E) $\frac{5}{4}a^3$

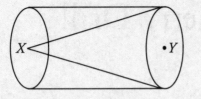

42. A right circular cone is inscribed in a right circular cylinder as shown in the figure above. *X* and *Y* are the centers of the bases. If the height of the cylinder is 4 and the radius of the base is 5, what is the volume of the cone?

(A) 51.33
(B) 83.77
(C) 104.72
(D) 251.33
(E) 314.16

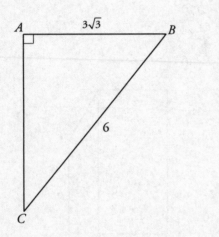

43. In the figure above, if triangle *ABC* is rotated about side *AB*, what is the volume of the cone that is generated?

(A) 12.5π
(B) $9\pi\sqrt{3}$
(C) 18π
(D) 20π
(E) $18\pi\sqrt{3}$

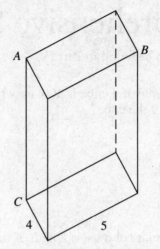

47. In the figure above, if two sides of a rectangular solid have lengths 4 and 5 as shown, and $BC = 15$, what is the length of *AC* ?

(A) 6.4
(B) 13.6
(C) 14.2
(D) 16.0
(E) 21.4

50. A sphere has a volume of 8,000 cubic units. If a right cylinder with a diameter equal to its height is inscribed inside the sphere, then what is the volume of the cylinder?

(A) 530
(B) 3,818
(C) 4,243
(D) 13,328
(E) 35,682

Summary

o   Solid geometry questions are often plane geometry questions in disguise.

o   For the purposes of the SAT Subject Test in Math 1, prisms are 3-dimensional figures with two parallel, identical bases. The bases can be any shape from plane geometry.

o   The general formula for the volume of a prism is the area of the base, which is often referred to as B, times the height, h.

o   Rectangular Prisms:
  • The formula for the volume of a rectangular prism is $V = lwh$.
  • The formula for the surface area of a rectangular prism is $SA = 2lw + 2wh + 2lh$. You're really just finding the area of each side and adding them together.
  • The Super Pythagorean Theorem, which is helpful is solving questions about the long diagonal of a rectangular prism, is $a^2 + b^2 + c^2 = d^2$.

o   Cubes:
  • Remember that a cube is just a rectangular prism whose length, width, and height are equal. If you forget one of the cube formulas, just use the rectangular prism formula.
  • The volume of a cube is $V = s^3$.
  • The surface area of a cube is $SA = 6s^2$.
  • The long diagonal of a cube is $d = s\sqrt{3}$.

o   Cylinders:
  • A cylinder is a prism whose bases are circles.
  • The volume of a cylinder is $V = \pi r^2 h$.
  • The surface area of a cylinder is $SA = 2\pi r^2 + 2\pi rh$. If you forget this formula, remember that you'll need the area of the two circles and the area of the other piece, which rolled out (like a roll of paper towels), is a rectangle whose sides are the circumference of the circle and the height.

- Cones
  - A cone is similar to a cylinder except that one of its bases is merely a point.
  - The formula for the volume of a cone is $V = \frac{1}{3}\pi r^2 h$, where the height must be perpendicular to the base.
  - The formula for the surface area of a cone is $SA = \pi r l + \pi r^2$, where l is the slant height.

- Spheres
  - A sphere is a hollow ball.
  - The formula for the volume of a sphere is $V = \frac{4}{3}\pi r^3$.
  - The formula for the surface area of a sphere is $SA = 4\pi r^2$.

- Pyramids
  - Pyramids are like cones, but the base is a polygon.
  - The formula for the volume of a pyramid is $V = \frac{1}{3}Bh$.

- Inscribed figures always have a line or curve that connects the inner figure to the outer figure.

- Questions about solids produced by rotation usually test your ability to visualize the solid created by the rotation of a flat shape.

- When the lengths of a solid are increased by factor, the surface area of the solid increases by the square of that factor and the volume increases by the cube of that factor.

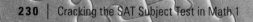

Chapter 9
Coordinate
Geometry

About 12 percent of the questions on the SAT Subject Test in Math 1 will concern graphs on the coordinate plane. Most of these questions are about lines, slopes, and distances. Simple circles and parabolas can appear on the test as well. The techniques in this chapter will prepare you for all major coordinate geometry question types.

DEFINITIONS

Here are some coordinate geometry terms that appear on the SAT Subject Test in Math 1. Make sure you're familiar with them. If the meaning of any of these vocabulary words keeps slipping your mind, add that word to your flash cards.

Coordinate Plane	A system of two perpendicular axes used to describe the position of a point using a pair of coordinates—also called the *rectangular coordinate system*, or the *Cartesian plane.*
Slope	For a straight line, the ratio of vertical change to horizontal change. Also known as "rise over run."
x-axis	The horizontal axis of the coordinate plane.
y-axis	The vertical axis of the coordinate plane.
Origin	The intersection of the x- and y-axes, with coordinates $(0, 0)$.
x-intercept	The x-coordinate of the point at which a line or other function intersects the x-axis. These values are also known as *zeros, roots,* or *solutions.* At the x-intercept, $y = 0$.
y-intercept	The y-coordinate of the point at which a line or other function intersects the y-axis. At the y-intercept, $x = 0$.

THE COORDINATE PLANE

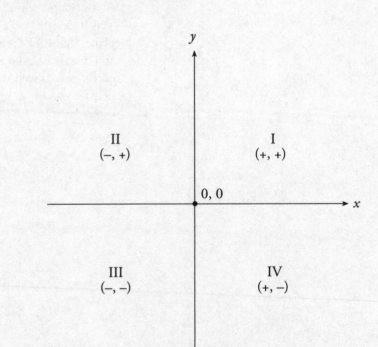

The plane is divided into four regions by two perpendicular axes called the *x*- and *y*-axes. These axes are like rulers that measure horizontal distances (the *x*-axis) and vertical distances (the *y*-axis). Okay, now follow along with the picture. Each axis has a positive direction and a negative direction; up and right are positive, down and left are negative. The four regions created by the axes are known as *quadrants*. The quadrants are numbered from I to IV, starting on the upper right and moving counterclockwise.

The location of every point on the coordinate plane can be expressed by a pair of *coordinates* that show the point's position with relation to the axes. The *x*-coordinate is always given first, followed by the *y*-coordinate: (2, 3), for example. This is called a coordinate pair—it is read as "two *right*, three *up*." These coordinates reflect the distance on each axis from the *origin*, or intersection of the axes.

The Coordinate Plane
The coordinate plane is a perfectly flat surface that extends an infinite distance in two dimensions. Oh, and it doesn't exist. It's just an abstract idea, a way of seeing mathematical relationships visually.

DRILL 1: THE COORDINATE PLANE

On the coordinate plane below, match each coordinate pair to the corresponding point on the graph and identify the quadrant in which the point is located. The answers can be found in Part IV.

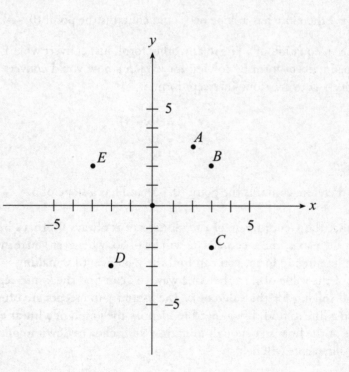

1. (–3, 2)   Point _____, Quadrant _____
2. (2, 3)   Point _____, Quadrant _____
3. (3, –2)   Point _____, Quadrant _____
4. (–2, –3) Point _____, Quadrant _____
5. (3, 2)   Point _____, Quadrant _____

THE EQUATION OF A LINE

Most of the coordinate geometry questions on the SAT Subject Test in Math 1 will deal with the equations and graphs of lines. The equation of a line can show up on the test in many forms. The more common form is called the slope-intercept formula, and it is shown here:

> **Slope-Intercept Form of the Equation of a Line**
>
> $$y = mx + b$$

You may have seen this before. In this form, m and b are constants; m is the slope and b is the y-intercept. An equation in this form might look like: $y = \frac{2}{3}x - 4$. So $m = \frac{2}{3}$ and $b = -4$.

Let's talk a little about the y-intercept. This is the y-coordinate of the point at which the line intersects the y-axis. So, the slope-intercept formula of a line gives you the slope of the line and a specific point on the line, the y-intercept. The line $y = \frac{2}{3}x - 4$ therefore has a slope of $\frac{2}{3}$ and contains the point $(0, -4)$.

If you see an equation of a line in any other form, just convert what ETS gives you into slope-intercept form by solving for y. Here's how you'd convert the equation $y + 2 = 3(x - 1)$ to the slope-intercept form.

$$y + 2 = 3(x - 1)$$
$$y + 2 = 3x - 3$$
$$y = 3x - 5$$

The line therefore contains the point $(0, -5)$ and has a slope of 3.

Notice that the x-coordinate of the y-intercept is always 0. That's because at any point on the y-axis, the x-coordinate will be 0. So, whenever you're given the equation of a line in any form, you can find the y-intercept by making $x = 0$ and then solving for the value of y. In the same way, you can find the x-intercept by making $y = 0$ and solving for the value of x. The x- and y-intercepts are often the easiest points on a line to find. If you need to identify the graph of a linear equation, and the slope of the line isn't enough to narrow your choices down to one, finding the x- and y-intercepts will help.

To graph a line, simply plug a couple of x-values into the equation of the line and plot the coordinates that result. The y-intercept is generally the easiest point to plot. Often, the y-intercept and the slope are enough to graph a line accurately enough or to identify the graph of a line.

Let's look at an example.

---

5. Which of the following could be the equation of the line with an x-intercept of -3 and a y-intercept of 5 ?

(A) $y = \dfrac{5}{3}x - 3$

(B) $y = 3x + 5$

(C) $y = \dfrac{3}{5}x - 3$

(D) $y = \dfrac{5}{3}x + 5$

(E) $y = \dfrac{3}{5}x + 5$

Here's How to Crack It

All of the answers are in $y = mx + b$ format. If the line has a y-intercept of 5, you know that the b variable must equal 5; eliminate (A) and (C). To determine the answer, you could find the slope using the two given points (more on that in the next section), or you could Plug In the points given. If the x-intercept is -3, that means that $x = -3$ when $y = 0$. Or, in other words, point $(-3, 0)$ is on the line. Make $x = -3$ in each of the remaining answer choices and eliminate each answer which does not make $y = 0$. The only answer in which $y = 0$ when $x = -3$ is (D).

DRILL 2: EQUATION OF A LINE

Try the following practice questions. The answers can be found in Part IV.

7. If a line with a slope of 0.6 contains the point $(3, 1)$, then it must also contain which of the following points?

(A) $(-2, -2)$
(B) $(-1, -4)$
(C) $(0, 0)$
(D) $(2, -1)$
(E) $(3, 4)$

10. The line $y - 1 = 5(x - 1)$ contains the point $(0, n)$. What is the value of n ?

(A) 0
(B) –1
(C) –2
(D) –3
(E) –4

11. What is the slope of the line whose equation is $2y - 13 = -6x - 5$?

(A) –5
(B) –3
(C) –2
(D) 0
(E) 3

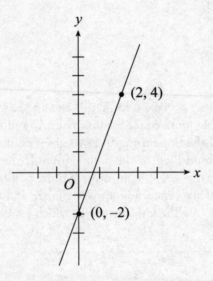

19. If the line $y = mx + b$ is graphed above, then which of the following statements is true?

(A) $m < b$

(B) $m = b$

(C) $2m = 3b$

(D) $2m + 3b = 0$

(E) $m = \dfrac{2b}{3}$

Let's Talk About Slope

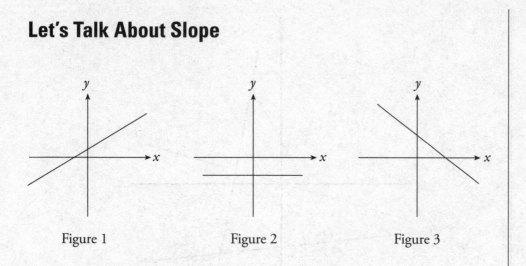

Figure 1   Figure 2   Figure 3

Often, slope is all you need to match the equation of a line to its graph. To begin with, it's easy to distinguish positive slopes from negative slopes. A line with a positive slope is shown in Figure 1 above; it goes uphill from left to right. A line with zero slope is shown in Figure 2; it's horizontal, and neither rises nor falls. A line with a negative slope is shown in Figure 3; it goes downhill from left to right.

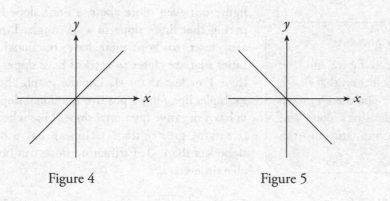

Figure 4   Figure 5

A line with a slope of 1 rises at a 45° angle, as shown in Figure 4. A line with a slope of −1 falls at a 45° angle, as shown in Figure 5.

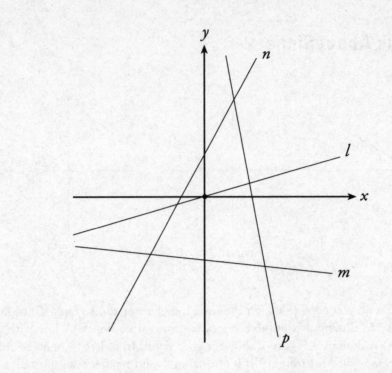

Because a line with a slope of 1 or –1 forms a 45° angle with either axis, you can figure out even more about a line's slope by comparing that line's slope to a 45° angle. Lines that are closer to horizontal have fractional slopes. Lines that are closer to vertical have slopes greater than 1 or less than –1. On the graph above, for example, line *l* has a positive fractional slope. Line *m* has a negative fractional slope. Line *n* has a positive slope greater than 1. Line *p* has a negative slope less than –1. Estimating slope can be a valuable time-saver.

You Have Two Points, You Have It All!
Using the slope formula, you can figure out the slope of any line given only two points on that line—which means that you can figure out the complete equation of the line. Just find the line's slope and plug the slope and one point's coordinates into the point-slope equation of a line.

Remember that the equation of a line gives you the slope without requiring calculation. But what if you're only given the coordinates of a couple of points on a line? Since the slope of a line is rise (change in *y*) over run (change in *x*), the coordinates of two points on a line provide you with enough information to figure out a line's slope. All you need is the following formula:

Slope Formula

$$m = \frac{y_2 - y_1}{x_2 - x_1}$$

Slopes can also help you determine the relationship between lines in a coordinate plane.

- The slopes of parallel lines are identical.
- The slopes of perpendicular lines are opposite reciprocals.

That means that if line l has a slope of 2, then any line parallel to l will also have a slope of 2. Any line perpendicular to l will have a slope of $-\dfrac{1}{2}$.

Let's look at an example.

Flip It!
Opposite reciprocal means flip the number over and reverse the sign.

8. Line l passes through the points (3, −0.5) and (−2, 4). If line m is parallel to line l, then which of the following could be the equation of line m ?

(A) $y = 0.9x - 3$
(B) $y = -0.9x + 5$
(C) $y = 1.1x - 7.5$
(D) $y = -1.1x - 11.1$
(E) $y = 4.5x + 8.4$

Here's How to Crack It
Parallel lines have the same slope. To find the slope of line l, use the slope formula:
$m = \dfrac{y_2 - y_1}{x_2 - x_1}$:

$$m = \frac{4 - (-0.5)}{-2 - 3} = \frac{4.5}{-5} = -0.9$$

Because all of your answers are in $y = mx + b$ form, you only need to look at the x coefficient to find the line with the same slope. The choice that matches is (B).

DRILL 3: SLOPE

The answers can be found in Part IV.

4. What is the slope of the line that passes through the origin and the point $(-3, 2)$?

   (A) -1.50
   (B) -0.75
   (C) -0.67
   (D) 1.00
   (E) 1.50

17. Lines l and m are perpendicular lines that intersect at the origin. If line l passes through the point $(2, -1)$, then line m must pass through which of the following points?

   (A) $(0, 2)$
   (B) $(1, 3)$
   (C) $(2, 1)$
   (D) $(3, 6)$
   (E) $(4, 0)$

23. Which of the following could be the graph of
    $2(y + 1) = -6(x - 2)$?

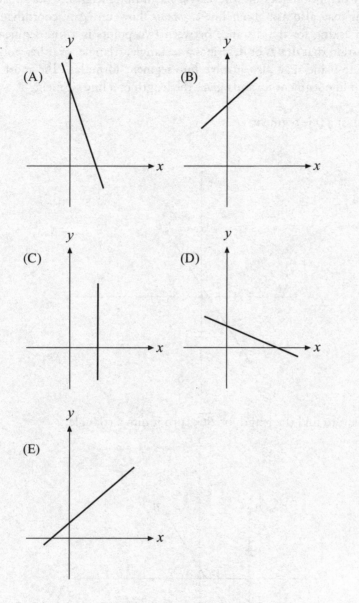

(A)

(B)

(C)

(D)

(E)

47. Line f and line g are perpendicular lines with
    slopes of x and y, respectively. If $xy \neq 0$, which of
    the following are possible values of $x - y$?

    I.   0.8
    II. 2.0
    III. 5.2

    (A) I only
    (B) I and II only
    (C) I and III only
    (D) II and III only
    (E) I, II, and III

Line Segments

A line by definition goes on forever—it has infinite length. Coordinate geometry questions may also ask about line *segments,* however. Any coordinate geometry question asking for the distance between two points is a line segment question. Any question that draws or describes a rectangle, triangle, or other polygon in the coordinate plane may also involve line segment formulas. The most commonly requested line segment formula gives the length of a line segment.

Let's look at a line segment:

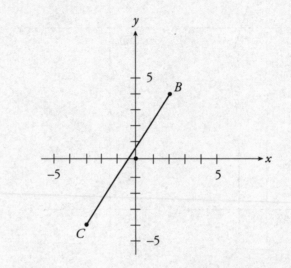

If you want to find the length of $\overline{BC}$, turn it into a triangle:

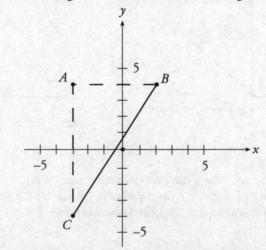

We've added in point A to illustrate the point. You know how to find the hypotenuse of a triangle, right? Pythagorean Theorem! It's easy to find the distance from A to B, just count across. The distance is 5. The distance between A and C is 8. Using the Pythagorean Theorem, we can fill in $5^2 + 8^2 = 89$. So the length of $\overline{BC}$ is $\sqrt{89}$. If you ever forget the distance formula, remember that all you have to do is make a triangle. After all, that's how the distance formula was created in the first place!

The Distance Formula

For the two points (x_1, y_1) and (x_2, y_2),

$$d = \sqrt{(x_2 - x_1)^2 + (y_2 - y_1)^2}$$

Now let's take a look at the same triangle we were working with and use the distance formula.

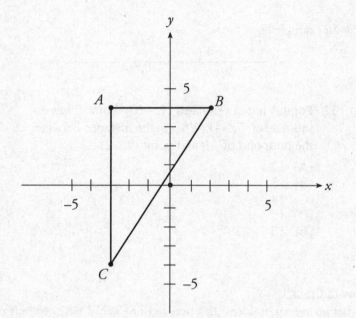

How Did We Get There?
Look carefully at the distance formula. Notice anything familiar? If you square both sides, it's just the Pythagorean Theorem!

The coordinates of B are (2, 4). The coordinates of C are (–3, –4). If you plug these coordinates into the distance formula, you get

$$d = \sqrt{(2 - (-3))^2 + (4 - (-4))^2}$$
$$d = \sqrt{(5)^2 + (8)^2}$$
$$d = \sqrt{25 + 64}$$
$$d = \sqrt{89}$$
$$d = 9.434$$

Notice that you would get the same answer by counting the vertical distance between B and C (8) and the horizontal distance between B and C (5), and using the Pythagorean Theorem to find the diagonal distance.

The other important line segment formula is used to find the coordinates of the middle point of a line segment with endpoints (x_1, y_1) and (x_2, y_2).

Coordinate Geometry | **243**

The midpoint formula
finds the average of
the x-coordinates and
the average of the
y-coordinates.

Coordinates of the Midpoint of a Line Segment

For the two points (x_1, y_1) and (x_2, y_2),

$$M = \left(\frac{x_1 + x_2}{2}, \frac{y_1 + y_2}{2} \right)$$

The midpoint and distance formulas used together can answer any line segment question.

Let's look at an example.

---

32. Point A has coordinates $(1, -10)$. Point B has co-ordinates $(-7, -4)$. What is the distance between the midpoint of $\overline{AB}$ and point $(9, -2)$?

   (A) 12
   (B) 13
   (C) 14
   (D) 15
   (E) 16

Here's How to Crack It

As with other geometry problems, it's best to draw coordinate geometry problems if no figure is given:

To find the midpoint of $\overline{AB}$, take the averages of the x-coordinates to find x, and the averages of the y-coordinates to find y:

Midpoint of $\overline{AB}$ = $\left(\dfrac{-7+1}{2}, \dfrac{-4+(-10)}{2} \right) = (-3, -7)$

Plot that point and connect it to (9, –2):

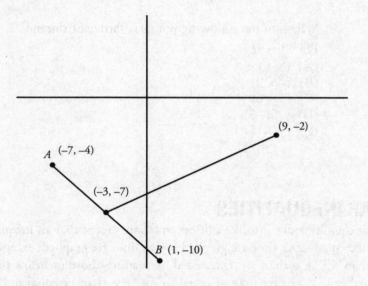

To find this distance, you can either use the distance formula $\left(d = \sqrt{(x_2 - x_1)^2 + (y_2 - y_1)^2} \right)$ or draw a triangle. The triangle has an x distance of 12 and a y distance of 5; it's a 5:12:13 Pythagorean triplet, so the distance between (–3, –7) and (9, –2) is 13, which is (B).

DRILL 4: LINE SEGMENTS
The answers can be found in Part IV,

12. What is the distance between the origin and the point (–5, 9) ?

    (A)   5.9
    (B)   6.7
    (C)   8.1
    (D) 10.3
    (E) 11.4

19. Point A has coordinates $(-4, 3)$, and the midpoint of AB is the point $(1, -1)$. What are the coordinates of B?

(A) $(-3, 4)$
(B) $(-4, 5)$
(C) $(4, -5)$
(D) $(5, -4)$
(E) $(6, -5)$

27. Which of the following points is farthest from the point $(2, 2)$?

(A) $(8, 8)$
(B) $(-6, 2)$
(C) $(4, -6)$
(D) $(-5, -3)$
(E) $(9, 4)$

LINEAR INEQUALITIES

A linear inequality looks just like a linear equation, except that an inequality sign replaces the equal sign. They are graphed just as lines are graphed, except that the "greater than" or "less than" is represented by shading above or below the line. If the inequality is a "greater than or equal to" or "less than or equal to," then the line itself is included and is drawn as a solid line. If the inequality is a "greater than" or "less than," then the line itself is not included; the line is drawn as a dotted line, and only the shaded region is included in the inequality. Take a look at some examples.

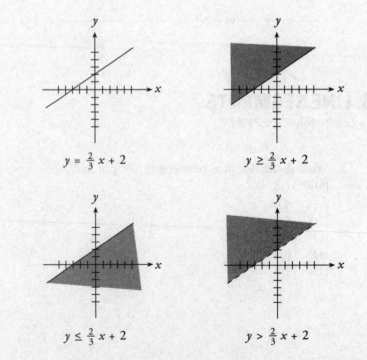

$y = \frac{2}{3}x + 2$

$y \geq \frac{2}{3}x + 2$

$y \leq \frac{2}{3}x + 2$

$y > \frac{2}{3}x + 2$

Let's see how linear inequalities might be tested in a question.

○

34. Which of the following is the graph of the inequality $y < -2x + 5$?

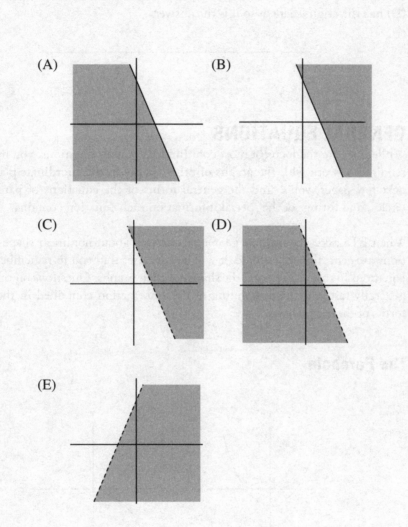

(A)

(B)

(C)

(D)

(E)

Here's How to Crack It

The inequality needs to have a negative slope; (E) shows a line with a positive slope, so eliminate (E). The inequality is less than, not less than or equal to, so the line should be dotted; eliminate (A) and (B).

To choose between (C) and (D), you need to know what side of the line should be shaded. The best way to approach this situation is to Plug In a point. Choose one that is shaded on one graph but not on the other. Plug the coordinates into the inequality and see if the point is true or false in the inequality. The origin is probably the easiest point to choose, as it is clearly not shaded in (C) and shaded in (D). So, take the inequality and make $x = 0$ and $y = 0$:

$$0 < -2(0) + 5$$

$$0 < 5$$

This is true, which means that $(0, 0)$ must be included in the inequality. Choice (D) has the origin shaded, so it is the answer.

GENERAL EQUATIONS

While lines are the focus of most coordinate geometry questions, you may also be required to work with the graphs of other shapes in the coordinate plane. In the next few pages, you'll find the general forms of the equations of parabolas and circles, and listings of the special information each equation contains.

When ETS asks a coordinate geometry question about nonlinear shapes, the questions are generally very simple. It will be very useful to you to remember the basic equations in this chapter and the shapes of their graphs. Questions on this material generally test your understanding of the information contained in the standard forms of these equations.

The Parabola

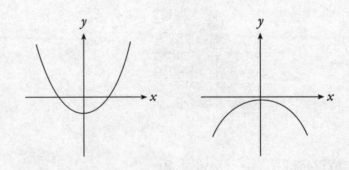

A parabola takes the form of a single curve opening either upward or downward, becoming increasingly steep as you move away from the center of the curve. Parabolas are the graphs of *quadratic* functions, which were discussed in Chapter 6. The equation of a parabola can come in two forms. Here is the one that will make you happiest on the test.

> ## Standard Form of the Equation of a Parabola
>
> $$y = a(x - h)^2 + k$$

In this formula, a, h, and k are constants. The following information can be gotten from the equation of a parabola in standard form:

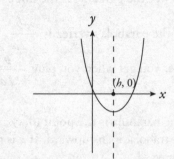

The axis of symmetry of the parabola is the line $x = h$.

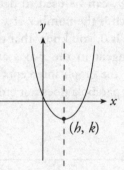

The vertex of the parabola is the point (h, k).

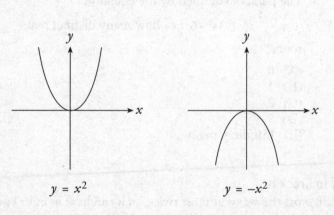

If a is positive, the parabola opens upward. If a is negative, the parabola opens downward.

> **General Form of the Equation of a Parabola**
>
> $$y = ax^2 + bx + c$$

In this formula, a, b, and c are constants. The following information can be gotten from the equation of a parabola in general form:

- The axis of symmetry of the parabola is the line $x = -\dfrac{b}{2a}$.

- The x-coordinate of the parabola's vertex is $-\dfrac{b}{2a}$. The y-coordinate of the vertex is whatever you get when you plug $-\dfrac{b}{2a}$ into the equation as x.

- The y-intercept of the parabola is the point $(0, c)$.

- If a is positive, the parabola opens upward. If a is negative, the parabola opens downward.

Since a parabola is simply the graph of a quadratic equation, the quadratic formula can be used to find the roots (x-intercepts or zeros), if any, of the parabola. The discriminant, or $b^2 - 4ac$, can be used to determine how many distinct real roots the quadratic has, which is the number of x-intercepts the parabola has. For example, if the discriminant is 0, you know that the parabola has one root, which means that the graph is tangent to the x-axis at the vertex of the parabola. If the discriminant is positive, the graph intercepts the x-axis at two points. If the discriminant is negative, the parabola does not cross the x-axis.

Let's try an example.

---

43. The parabola defined by the equation $y = -\dfrac{3}{8}x^2 + 3x - 6$ has how many distinct real roots?

(A) 0
(B) 1
(C) 2
(D) 3
(E) Infinitely many

Here's How to Crack It

A parabola can cross the x-axis at most twice, so it can have at most two real roots; eliminate (D) and (E). To find the number of real roots, determine the discriminant: $b^2 - 4ac$. If the discriminant is less than 0, there are no real roots, if it is equal to 0, there is one root, and if it is greater than 0, there are two roots. The equation is already in the general form of a parabola, so $a = -\dfrac{3}{8}$, $b = 3$, and $c = -6$:

$$3^2 - 4\left(-\dfrac{3}{8}\right)(-6) = 0$$

Because the discriminant is equal to 0, there is exactly one distinct real root; the answer is (B).

———————————○———————————

DRILL 5: PARABOLA EQUATIONS
The answers can be found in Part IV.

34. What is the minimum value of $f(x)$ if
    $f(x) = x^2 - 6x + 8$?
    (A) -3
    (B) -2
    (C) -1
    (D) 0
    (E) 2

37. What are the coordinates of the vertex of the

    parabola defined by the equation $y = \dfrac{1}{2}x^2 + x + \dfrac{5}{2}$?
    (A) $(-2, 4)$
    (B) $(-1, 2)$
    (C) $(1, 2)$
    (D) $(2, 4)$
    (E) $(2, -4)$

38. At which of the following x-values does the
    parabola defined by $y = (x - 3)^2 - 4$ cross the
    x-axis?
    (A) -3
    (B) 3
    (C) 4
    (D) 5
    (E) 9

The Circle

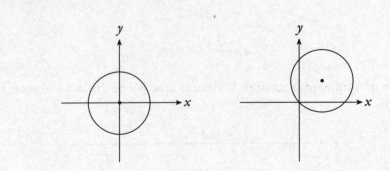

The circle is that round shape you know and love. Below is the formula for a circle.

Standard Form of the Equation of a Circle

$$(x - h)^2 + (y - k)^2 = r^2$$

In this formula, *h, k,* and *r* are constants. The following information can be learned from the equation of a circle in standard form:

- The center of the circle is the point (h, k).
- The length of the circle's radius is r.

And that's all there is to know about a circle. Once you know its radius and the position of its center, you can sketch the circle yourself or identify its graph easily. It's also a simple matter to estimate the radius and center coordinates of a circle whose graph is given, and make a good guess at the equation of that circle. One last note: If the circle's center is the origin, then $(h, k) = (0, 0)$. This greatly simplifies the equation of the circle.

Equation of a Circle with Center at Origin

$$x^2 + y^2 = r^2$$

Let's check out an example.

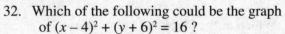

32. Which of the following could be the graph
of $(x - 4)^2 + (y + 6)^2 = 16$?

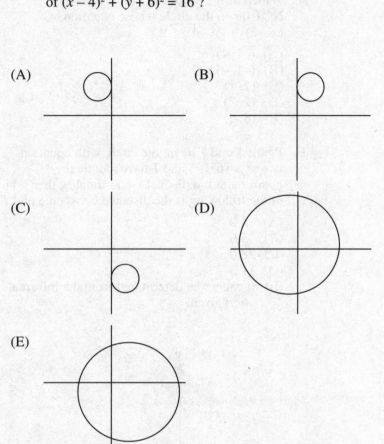

(A)

(B)

(C)

(D)

(E)

Here's How to Crack It

The equation given is the general equation of a circle: $(x - h)^2 + (y - k)^2 = r^2$, where the center of the circle is at (h, k) and the radius is r. In this case, the center of the circle is at $(4, -6)$ (watch those negative signs in the general equation!), so you can eliminate (A), (B), and (D), because the centers of those circles are the wrong quadrant. If $r^2 = 16$, then the radius of the circle is 4. Because the x coordinate of the center of the circle is 4, the circle should be tangent to the y-axis. That leaves you with (C).

DRILL 6: CIRCLE EQUATIONS

The answers can be found in Part IV.

30. Which of the following points does NOT lie on the circle whose equation is $(x - 2)^2 + (y - 4)^2 = 9$?

    (A) $(-1, 4)$
    (B) $(-1, -1)$
    (C) $(2, 1)$
    (D) $(2, 7)$
    (E) $(5, 4)$

34. Points S and T lie on the circle with equation $x^2 + y^2 = 16$. If S and T have identical y-coordinates but distinct x-coordinates, then which of the following is the distance between S and T ?

    (A) 4.0
    (B) 5.6
    (C) 8.0
    (D) 11.3
    (E) It cannot be determined from the information given.

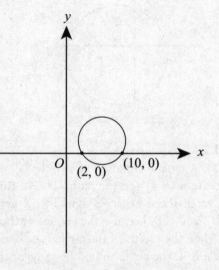

50. Which of the following equations could represent the circle shown in the figure above?

    (A) $x^2 + y^2 - 14x - 8y + 40 = 0$
    (B) $x^2 + y^2 - 14x + 8y + 40 = 0$
    (C) $x^2 + y^2 - 12x - 6y + 20 = 0$
    (D) $x^2 + y^2 - 10x + 8y + 16 = 0$
    (E) $x^2 + y^2 + 4x - 6y - 12 = 0$

TRIAXIAL COORDINATES: THINKING IN 3-D

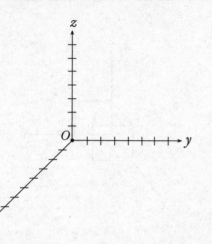

On the difficult final third of the SAT Subject Test in Math 1, you may run into a twist on the coordinate plane—a coordinate *space*. A third dimension can be added to the coordinate plane by introducing a third axis (often referred to as the *z*-axis) that passes through the origin at right angles to both the *x*-axis and the *y*-axis. While the *x*- and *y*-axes define the location of a point in a plane, the *x*-, *y*-, and *z*-axes define the location of a point in a three-dimensional space.

Such a system of three axes is called a *three-dimensional coordinate system,* a *triaxial coordinate system,* or a *coordinate space.* Sometimes it's not called anything at all; ETS will simply show you a diagram of a three-dimensional graph, or a set of triple coordinates, and expect you to understand what you're seeing. The coordinates of a point in three dimensions are given in this form: (*x, y, z*). The point (3, 4, 5) is located 3 units along the *x*-axis, 4 units along the *y*-axis, and 5 units along the *z*-axis. Always check the labels on the axes if you're given a diagram, because there's no firm convention about which axis is pictured in which position.

If you are given two points in 3-D, (x_1, y_1, z_1) and (x_2, y_2, z_2), then the distance, d, between them is given by the following formula:

Distance in a Three-Dimensional Space

$$d = \sqrt{(x_2 - x_1)^2 + (y_2 - y_1)^2 + (z_2 - z_1)^2}$$

Most of these three-dimensional coordinate questions require you to calculate a distance between two points in a 3-D coordinate system. Just use the formula.

Connect the Dots
This formula is equivalent to the Super Pythagorean Theorem: $a^2 + b^2 + c^2 = d^2$.

Let's look at an example.

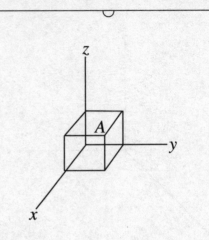

40. In the triaxial coordinate system shown above, a cube with volume 125 has one vertex at the origin, one edge on the x-axis, one edge on the y-axis, and one edge on the z-axis. What is the distance from the origin to point A ?

(A) 5.00
(B) 7.07
(C) 8.66
(D) 10.00
(E) 11.18

Here's How to Crack It

The formula for volume of a cube is $V = s^3$, so if the volume is 125, then the side must be $\sqrt[3]{125}$, which is 5. Point A is at the vertex opposite the origin, so you can use the Super Pythagorean Theorem to find the distance: $a^2 + b^2 + c^2 = d^2$:

$$5^5 + 5^5 + 5^5 = d^2$$

$$75 = d^2$$

$$8.66 = d$$

That is (C).

DRILL 7: TRIAXIAL COORDINATES

Try the following practice questions. The answers can be found in Part IV.

29. What is the distance between the origin and the point (5, 6, 7) ?

    (A)   4.24
    (B)   7.25
    (C) 10.49
    (D) 14.49
    (E) 18.00

34. Sphere O has a radius of 6, and its center is at the origin. Which of the following points is NOT inside the sphere?

    (A) (–3, 5, 1)
    (B) (–4, –4, 3)
    (C) (5, –2, 2)
    (D) (4, 1, –4)
    (E) (2, –4, –3)

Comprehensive Coordinate Geometry Drill

The answers can be found in Part IV.

7. Which of the following graphs is a linear function that has a positive x-intercept and a negative slope?

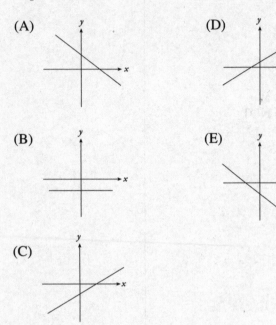

(A)

(B)

(C)

(D)

(E)

8. A line contains the points (4, 13) and (–4, 7). What is the slope of the line?

(A) 0.51
(B) 0.75
(C) 0.81
(D) 1.22
(E) 1.33

17. What is the equation of a line with an x-intercept of 2 and a y-intercept of 8 ?

(A) $y = 4x - 8$
(B) $y = 0.25x + 2$
(C) $y = -4x + 2$
(D) $y = 4x + 2$
(E) $y = 0.25x - 8$

18. What is the y-intercept of the linear equation $3y - 5x - 8 = 0$?

(A) $\dfrac{3}{8}$

(B) $\dfrac{5}{8}$

(C) $\dfrac{8}{5}$

(D) $\dfrac{8}{3}$

(E) 8

25. If $f(x) = 2x^2 - 3x + 5$, for what value of x will $f(x)$ have its minimum value?

(A) $-\dfrac{3}{2}$

(B) $-\dfrac{3}{4}$

(C) $-\dfrac{3}{5}$

(D) $\dfrac{3}{4}$

(E) $\dfrac{3}{8}$

29. On the xyz-coordinate plane, what is the distance between (–3, 8, 2) and (7, –4, 3) ?

(A) 5.75
(B) 7.55
(C) 9.95
(D) 15.65
(E) 16.62

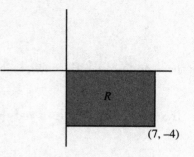

(7, –4)

30. In the figure above, rectangle R contains all points (x, y). What is the area of a rectangle that contains all points (x + 2, 3y) ?

(A) 28
(B) 36
(C) 84
(D) 90
(E) 108

31. In the coordinate plane, points A (3, 7), B (5, –4), C (0, 0), and D (–3, –2) can be connected to form line segments. Which of the following line segments has the greatest length?

(A) $\overline{AB}$
(B) $\overline{AC}$
(C) $\overline{BC}$
(D) $\overline{BD}$
(E) $\overline{CD}$

35. In the coordinate plane, the midpoint of the line segment formed by points (12, y) and (x, 7) is (5, 8). What is the distance between the endpoints?

(A) 7.07
(B) 8.00
(C) 14.14
(D) 16.00
(E) 20.25

44. If the graph of $y = 3x^2 + bx + 12$ is tangent to the x-axis, then which of the following could be the value of b ?

(A) –12
(B) –9
(C) –4
(D) 0
(E) 4

47. Circle A is centered at (5, –2) and has a radius of 3. Circle B is centered at (–1, 1) and has a radius of r. If circle A and circle B are externally tangent, then what is the value of r ?

(A) 2.00
(B) 3.71
(C) 4.12
(D) 6.71
(E) 9.71

Summary

○ The coordinate plane is created by the perpendicular intersection of the x- and y-axes. This intersection creates four quadrants.

○ The slope-intercept form of the equation of a line is $y = mx + b$. The slope of the line is m and the y-intercept is b.

○ To find the slope of a line, take two points on the line and put them into the formula: $m = \dfrac{y_2 - y_1}{x_2 - x_1}$.

○ The distance formula comes from the Pythagorean Theorem. It is $d = \sqrt{(x_2 - x_1)^2 + (y_2 - y_1)^2}$.

○ To find the coordinates of the midpoint of a line, take the average of the endpoints. The formula is

$$M = \left(\dfrac{x_1 + x_2}{2}, \dfrac{y_1 + y_2}{2} \right).$$

○ The standard form of the equation of a parabola is $y = a(x - h)^2 + k$, where (h, k) is the vertex of the parabola. The general form of a parabola is a quadratic equation: $y = ax^2 + bx + c$. Use the general form to find the axis of symmetry, the vertex, and whether the parabola opens up or down.

○ The standard form of the equation of a circle is $(x - h)^2 + (y - k)^2 = r^2$, where (h, k) is the center of the circle.

○ The 3-D coordinate plane has 3 axes: x, y, and z. The formula for the distance of a line in three-dimensional space comes from the Super Pythagorean Theorem. It is $d = \sqrt{(x_2 - x_1)^2 + (y_2 - y_1)^2 + (z_2 - z_1)^2}$.

Chapter 10
Trigonometry

There will be about 4 questions on the SAT Subject Test in Math 1 on trigonometry. Most trigonometry questions you will see will test your understanding of the definitions of sine, cosine, and tangent and how the functions apply to right triangles. You may also see algebra problems using trigonometric functions which test your knowledge of trigonometric identities. You do NOT need to know how to apply trigonometry to non-right triangles or graph these functions, so don't worry about that!

DEFINITIONS

Here are some trigonometric terms that appear on the SAT Subject Test in Math 1. Make sure you're familiar with them. If the meaning of any of these vocabulary words keeps slipping your mind, add that word to your flash cards.

Acute Angle	An angle whose measure in degrees is between 0 and 90, exclusive.
Obtuse Angle	An angle whose measure in degrees is between 90 and 180, exclusive.
Theta	The symbol θ (pronounced thay-tuh) is a variable, just like x and y, used to represent the measure of an angle in trigonometry.
arc–	Prefix added to trigonometric functions, meaning *inverse*. Also indicated by the use of an exponent to the power of -1 (such as "$\sin^{-1}$"). The inverse of a trigonometric function takes the ratio of the corresponding sides and gives you the angle.

THE BASIC FUNCTIONS

The basis of trigonometry is the relationship between the parts of a right triangle. When you know the measure of one of the acute angles in a right triangle, you know all the angles in that triangle. For example, if you know that a right triangle contains a 20° angle, then you know all three angles—the right triangle must have a 90° angle, and because there are 180° in a triangle, the third angle must measure 70°. You don't know the lengths in the triangle, but you know its shape and its proportions.

A right triangle that contains a 20° angle can have only one shape, though it can be any size. The same is true for a right triangle containing any other acute angle. That's the fundamental idea of trigonometry. Once you know the measure of an acute angle in a right triangle, you know that triangle's proportions.

Similar Right Triangles
Remember that similar triangles have the same angles. So, any right triangle that contains a 20° angle will be similar to all other right triangles with a 20° angle.

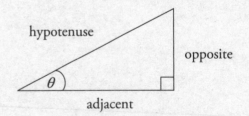

The three basic functions in trigonometry—the sine, cosine, and tangent—are ways of expressing proportions in a right triangle (that's the ratio of one side to another). They may sound familiar to you. Or maybe you've heard of a little phrase called SOHCAHTOA?

Let's break it down.

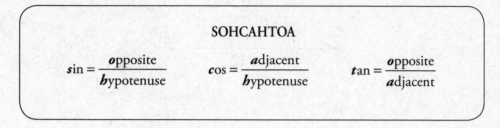

$$\textbf{SOHCAHTOA}$$

$$\textit{s}in = \frac{\textit{o}\text{pposite}}{\textit{h}\text{ypotenuse}} \qquad \textit{c}os = \frac{\textit{a}\text{djacent}}{\textit{h}\text{ypotenuse}} \qquad \textit{t}an = \frac{\textit{o}\text{pposite}}{\textit{a}\text{djacent}}$$

Sine

The sine of an angle is the ratio of the opposite side to the hypotenuse. The sine function of an angle θ is abbreviated sin θ. The value of sine must be between -1 and 1, inclusive.

Cosine

The cosine of an angle is the ratio of the adjacent side to the hypotenuse. The cosine function of an angle θ is abbreviated cos θ. As with sine, the value of cosine must be between -1 and 1, inclusive.

Tangent

The tangent of an angle is the ratio of the opposite side to the adjacent side. The tangent function of an angle θ is abbreviated tan θ. Unlike sine and cosine, tangent may be any value, positive or negative.

These three functions form the basis of everything else in trigonometry. All of the more complicated functions and rules in trigonometry can be derived from the information contained in SOHCAHTOA.

Let's look at a question using SOHCAHTOA.

It's All About Proportions
A trigonometric function of any angle comes from the proportions of a right triangle containing that angle. For any given angle, there is only one possible set of proportions.

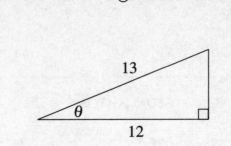

4. In the triangle above, what is the value of sin θ ?

(A) $\dfrac{5}{13}$

(B) $\dfrac{5}{12}$

(C) $\dfrac{12}{13}$

(D) $\dfrac{13}{12}$

(E) $\dfrac{13}{5}$

Here's How to Crack It

SOHCAHTOA tells you that $\sin = \dfrac{\text{opposite}}{\text{hypotenuse}}$. The length of the hypotenuse is given, so you need to determine the length of the opposite side. You could use the Pythagorean Theorem, but notice you have 2 sides of a 5:12:13 right triangle. Therefore, the side opposite θ must be 5 units long. Therefore, $\sin θ = \dfrac{5}{13}$, (A).

(Note: if you remember that the value of sine must be between −1 and 1, inclusive, then you can eliminate (D) and (E) right off the bat. If you're short on time, you can sometimes POE trigonometry questions asking about sine or cosine, but NOT tangent!)

What Your Calculator Can Do for You

Tables of sine, cosine, and tangent values are programmed into your calculator—that's what the "sin," "cos," and "tan" keys do.

- If you press one of the three trigonometric function keys and then enter an angle measure, your calculator will give you the function (sine, cosine, or tangent) of that angle. Just make sure that your calculator is in degree mode. This operation is written:

  $\sin 30° = 0.5$ $\qquad$ $\cos 30° = 0.866$ $\qquad$ $\tan 30° = 0.577$

- Your calculator can also take a trig function value and tell you what angle would produce that value. Press the "2nd" key, then press "sin," "cos," or "tan," then enter the decimal or fraction you're given, and your calculator will give you the measure of that angle. This is called taking an inverse function, and it's written:

  $\sin^{-1} (0.5) = 30°$ $\qquad$ $\cos^{-1} (0.866) = 30°$ $\qquad$ $\tan^{-1} (0.577) = 30°$
  OR
  $\arcsin (0.5) = 30°$ $\qquad$ $\arccos (0.866) = 30°$ $\qquad$ $\arctan (0.577) = 30°$

The expressions "$\sin^{-1} (0.5)$" and "$\arcsin (0.5)$" have the same meaning. Both mean "the angle whose sine is 0.5." While ordinary trig functions take angle measures and output ratios, inverse trig functions take ratios and produce the corresponding angle measures; they work in reverse.

Finding Trig Functions in Right Triangles

On the SAT Subject Test in Math 1, the three basic trigonometric functions always occur in right triangles—particularly the Pythagorean triplets from Chapter 7.

DRILL 1: TRIG FUNCTIONS IN RIGHT TRIANGLES

Use the definitions of the sine, cosine, and tangent to fill in the requested quantities in the following triangles. The answers can be found in Part IV.

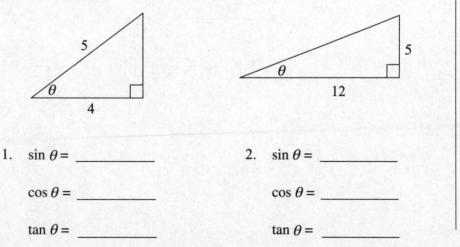

1. $\sin \theta =$ _____

   $\cos \theta =$ _____

   $\tan \theta =$ _____

2. $\sin \theta =$ _____

   $\cos \theta =$ _____

   $\tan \theta =$ _____

Check Your Calculator
For some scientific calculators, you need to enter things in reverse order. To find sin 30°, for example, you would type "30" first and then hit "sin." To find $\sin^{-1}(0.5)$, you would type "0.5" first and then hit "2nd" and "sin."

Special Right Triangles
Be on the lookout for special right triangles on trigonometry questions!

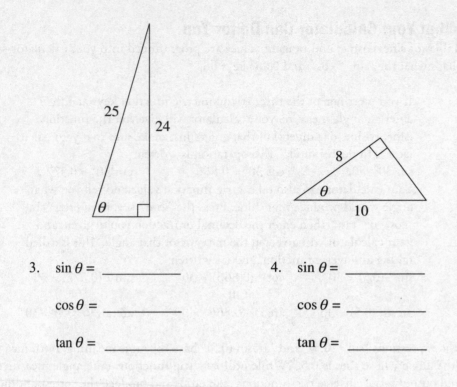

3. $\sin \theta = \underline{\hspace{2cm}}$

    $\cos \theta = \underline{\hspace{2cm}}$

    $\tan \theta = \underline{\hspace{2cm}}$

4. $\sin \theta = \underline{\hspace{2cm}}$

    $\cos \theta = \underline{\hspace{2cm}}$

    $\tan \theta = \underline{\hspace{2cm}}$

Completing Triangles

The preceding examples have all involved figuring out the values of trigonometric functions from lengths in a right triangle. Slightly more difficult trigonometry questions may require you to go the other way and figure out lengths or measures of angles using trigonometry. For example:

Check Your Mode
On this test, your calculator should always be in degree mode.

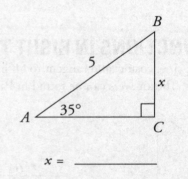

$x = \underline{\hspace{2cm}}$

Because we're dealing with the hypotenuse and the side that is opposite the angle, the best definition to use is sine.

$$\sin = \frac{opposite}{hypotenuse}$$

$$\sin 35° = \frac{x}{5}$$

$$5(\sin 35°) = x$$

$$5(0.5736) = x$$

$$2.8679 = x$$

$\overline{BC}$ of $\triangle ABC$ therefore has a length of 2.8679.

The Unknown
In triangle ABC, you know only two quantities—the length of AB and the measure of $\angle A$. This question, unlike previous examples, doesn't give you enough information to use the Pythagorean Theorem. What you need is an equation that relates the information you have (AB and $\angle A$) to the information you don't have (x). Use the SOHCAHTOA definitions to set up an equation. Solve that equation, and you find the value of the unknown.

You can use a similar technique to find the measure of an unknown angle in a right triangle. For example:

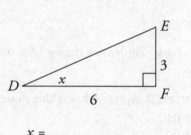

$$x = \underline{\hspace{4cm}}$$

In triangle DEF, you know $\overline{EF}$ and $\overline{DF}$. $\overline{EF}$ is the side that is opposite the angle we're looking for, and $\overline{DF}$ is the side that is adjacent to that same angle. So the best definition to use is tangent.

$$\tan = \frac{opposite}{adjacent}$$

$$\tan x = \frac{EF}{FD}$$

$$\tan x = \frac{3}{6}$$

$$\tan x = 0.5$$

To solve for x, take the *inverse tangent* of both sides of the equation. On the left side, that just gives you x. The result is the angle whose tangent is 0.5.

$$\tan^{-1}(\tan x) = \tan^{-1}(0.5)$$

$$x = 26.57°$$

The measure of $\angle D$ is therefore 26.57°.

Let's look at a couple of problems which show how these concepts may be tested.

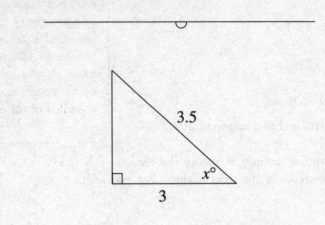

Note: Figure not drawn to scale

18. In the triangle above, what is the value of x ?

 (A) 18.02
 (B) 31.00
 (C) 40.60
 (D) 49.40
 (E) 59.00

Here's How to Crack It
You are given the hypotenuse and the leg adjacent to the angle with degree measure x, so you want to use cosine. First, set up the problem using SOHCAHTOA:

$$\cos x° = \frac{3}{3.5}$$

Next, take the $\cos^{-1}$ of each side. Remember that $\cos^{-1}(\cos x°) = x$:

$$\cos^{-1}(\cos x°) = \cos^{-1}\left(\frac{3}{3.5}\right)$$

Use the 2nd function of cos on your calculator to find $\cos^{-1}\dfrac{3}{3.5}$:

$$x = \cos^{-1}\left(\frac{3}{3.5}\right) = 31.00$$

The answer is (B).

⊖

Let's look at another problem.

⊖

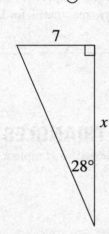

27. In the triangle above, what is the value of x ?

    (A)   3.29
    (B)   3.72
    (C)   6.18
    (D) 13.17
    (E) 14.91

Here's How to Crack It
You are given the sides opposite from and adjacent to the known angle, so you want to use tangent. Set up the problem using SOHCAHTOA:

$$\tan 28° = \frac{7}{x}$$

Use algebra to isolate x by multiplying both sides by x then dividing both sides by tan 28°:

$$x \tan 28° = 7$$

$$x = \frac{7}{\tan 28°}$$

Use your calculator to solve for x. The answer is 13.17, (D).

Another approach to this question would be to Ballpark. The known angle is 28°, so the other "unknown" angle must be bigger (in fact, 62°). x is opposite a larger angle than the side with measure 7, so x must be greater than 7. You can eliminate (A), (B), and (C). Choices (D) and (E) are pretty close to each other, but a 50/50 shot on a question you didn't do any "real math" for is pretty good!

DRILL 2: COMPLETING TRIANGLES

Use the techniques you've just reviewed to complete the following triangles. The answers can be found in Part IV.

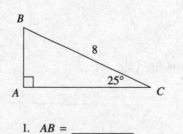
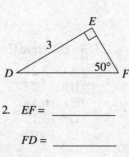

1. $AB =$ _____

   $CA =$ _____

   $\angle B =$ _____

2. $EF =$ _____

   $FD =$ _____

   $\angle D =$ _____

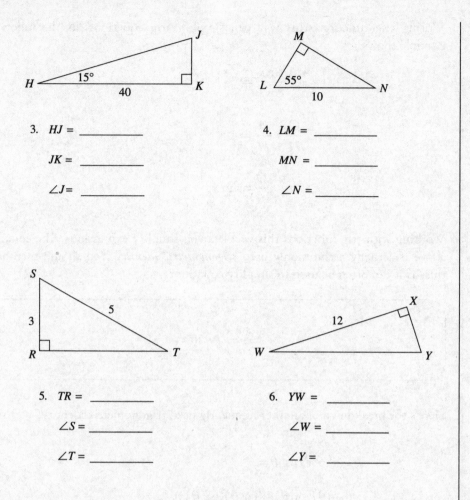

3. HJ = _____

    JK = _____

    ∠J = _____

4. LM = _____

    MN = _____

    ∠N = _____

5. TR = _____

    ∠S = _____

    ∠T = _____

6. YW = _____

    ∠W = _____

    ∠Y = _____

TRIGONOMETRIC IDENTITIES

Some SAT Subject Test in Math 1 questions will ask you to do algebra with trigonometric functions. These questions usually involve using the SOHCAHTOA definitions of sine, cosine, and tangent. Often, the way to simplify equations that are mostly made up of trigonometric functions is to express the functions as follows:

$$\sin = \frac{O}{H} \qquad \cos = \frac{A}{H} \qquad \tan = \frac{O}{A}$$

Writing trig functions this way can simplify trig equations, as the following example shows:

$$\frac{\sin x}{\cos x} =$$

$$\frac{O}{H} \div \frac{A}{H} =$$

$$\frac{O}{A} = \tan x$$

Working with trig functions this way lets you simplify expressions. The equation above is actually a commonly used *trigonometric identity*. You should memorize this, as it can often be used to simplify equations.

$$\frac{\sin x}{\cos x} = \tan x$$

Here's the breakdown of another frequently used trigonometric identity:

$$\sin^2 \theta + \cos^2 \theta =$$

$$(\sin\theta)(\sin\theta) + (\cos\theta)(\cos\theta) =$$

$$\left(\frac{O}{H}\right)\left(\frac{O}{H}\right) + \left(\frac{A}{H}\right)\left(\frac{A}{H}\right) =$$

$$\frac{O^2}{H^2} + \frac{A^2}{H^2} =$$

$$\frac{O^2 + A^2}{H^2} = 1$$

That last step may seem a little baffling, but it's really simple. This equation is based on a right triangle, in which O and A are legs of the triangle, and H is the hypotenuse. Consequently, you know that $O^2 + A^2 = H^2$. That's just the Pythagorean Theorem. That's what lets you do the last step, in which $\frac{O^2 + A^2}{H^2} = 1$. This completes the second commonly used identity that you should memorize.

$$\sin^2 \theta + \cos^2 \theta = 1$$

In addition to memorizing these two identities, you should practice working algebraically with trig functions in general. Some questions may require you to use the SOHCAHTOA definitions of the trig functions; others may require you to use the two identities you've just reviewed. Take a look at these examples:

---

35. If $\sin x = 0.707$, then what is the value of $(\sin x) \cdot (\cos x) \cdot (\tan x)$?

    (A) 1.0
    (B) 0.707
    (C) 0.5
    (D) 0.4
    (E) 0.207

Here's How to Crack It

This is a tricky question. To solve it, simplify that complicated trigonometric expression. Writing in the SOHCAHTOA definitions works just fine, but in this case it's even faster to use one of those identities.

$$(\sin x) \cdot (\cos x) \cdot (\tan x) =$$
$$(\sin x) \cdot (\cos x) \cdot \left(\frac{\sin x}{\cos x} \right) =$$
$$(\sin x) \cdot (\sin x) =$$
$$\sin^2 x =$$

Now it's a simpler matter to answer the question. If $\sin x = 0.707$, then $\sin^2 x = 0.5$. The answer is (C).

Take a look at this one:

---

36. If $\sin a = 0.4$, and $1 - \cos^2 a = x$, then what is the value of x ?

    (A) 0.8
    (B) 0.6
    (C) 0.44
    (D) 0.24
    (E) 0.16

Here's How to Crack It

Here again, the trick to the question is simplifying the complicated trig expression. Since $\sin^2 \theta + \cos^2 \theta = 1$, you can rearrange any of those terms to rephrase it. Using the second trig identity, you can quickly take these steps:

$$1 - \cos^2 a = x$$
$$\sin^2 a = x$$
$$(0.4)^2 = x$$
$$x = 0.16$$

And that's the answer. Choice (E) is correct.

Using the SOHCAHTOA definitions and the two trigonometric identities reviewed in this section, simplify trigonometric expressions to answer the following sample questions.

Plugging In on Trigonometry

As we discussed before, Plugging In is a great technique to attack questions involving algebraic expressions. Because many Trigonometry questions are really just algebra questions, you can Plug In on these questions as well.

When you Plug In on these questions, choose a value for your variable (remember that θ is just a fancy way of expressing a variable). As with Plugging In on other algebra questions, you want to avoid values for your variable which would result in multiple answers which work. In Trigonometry, avoid choosing values which are multiples of 45 (because $\sin 45° = \cos 45°$ and $\tan 45° = 1$).

Finally, there is one last trick to be aware of when Plugging In for trigonometry. When you want to find the value of an expression such as $\sin^2 20°$, first find the value of $\sin 20°$ and then square the result:

$$\sin^2 20° = (\sin 20°)^2 = 0.342^2 = 0.117$$

Let's see how Plugging In works in a problem.

---

40. $\dfrac{\tan \theta - \sin \theta \cos \theta}{\tan \theta} =$

(A) 1
(B) $\sin \theta$
(C) $\tan \theta$
(D) $\sin^2 \theta$
(E) $\cos^2 \theta$

Here's How to Crack It

Plug In for θ. Make $\theta = 20°$ and use your calculator to find the value of the expression:

$$\frac{\tan 20° - \sin 20° \cos 20°}{\tan 20°} = \frac{0.364 - (0.342)(0.940)}{0.364} = 0.117$$

This is your target; circle it! Next, check each answer choice by plugging in 20° for θ. The only answer which matches is (D).

———————————————◯———————————————

Use SOHCAHTOA, the two trigonometric identities, or Plugging In to answer the following questions.

DRILL 3: TRIGONOMETRIC IDENTITIES

Try the following practice questions. The answers can be found in Part IV.

25. $(1 - \sin x)(1 + \sin x) =$
    (A) $\cos x$
    (B) $\sin x$
    (C) $\tan x$
    (D) $\cos^2 x$
    (E) $\sin^2 x$

31. $\dfrac{\tan x \cos x}{\sin x} =$
    (A) $\dfrac{1}{\tan x}$

    (B) $\dfrac{1}{\cos x}$

    (C) 1

    (D) $\cos^2 x$

    (E) $\tan x$

39. $\dfrac{1}{\cos x} - (\sin x)(\tan x) =$
    (A) $\cos x$
    (B) $\sin x$
    (C) $\tan x$
    (D) $\cos^2 x$
    (E) $\sin^2 x$

42. $\dfrac{\tan x - \sin x \cos x}{\tan x} =$

(A) $1 - \cos x$
(B) $1 - \sin x$
(C) $\tan x + 1$
(D) $\cos^2 x$
(E) $\sin^2 x$

50. $\dfrac{\sin\theta\tan\theta - \sin^2\theta\,\cos\theta}{\sin^2\theta\,\cos\theta} =$

(A) $\sin\theta\cos\theta$
(B) $\sin\theta - \cos\theta$
(C) $\sin^2\theta$
(D) $\cos^2\theta$
(E) $\tan^2\theta$

DEGREES AND RADIANS

ETS will rarely ask about radians on the SAT Subject Test in Math 1. Radians are an alternative to using degrees to measure angles. One degree is defined as $\dfrac{1}{360}$ of a full circle. One radian, on the other hand, is the measure of an angle that intercepts an arc exactly as long as the circle's radius. Since the circumference of a circle is 2π times the radius, the circumference is about 6.28 times as long as the radius, and there are about 6.28 radians in a full circle.

Because a number like 6.28 isn't easy to work with, angle measurements in radians are usually given in multiples or fractions of π. For example, there are exactly 2π radians in a full circle. There are π radians in a semicircle. There are $\dfrac{\pi}{2}$ radians in a right angle. Because 2π radians and 360° both describe a full circle, you can relate degrees and radians with the following proportion:

$$\frac{\text{degrees}}{360} = \frac{\text{radians}}{2\pi}$$

To convert degrees to radians, just plug the number of degrees into the proportion and solve for radians. The same technique works in reverse for converting radians to degrees. The figures on the next page show what the unit circle looks like in radians, compared to the unit circle in degrees.

Radians

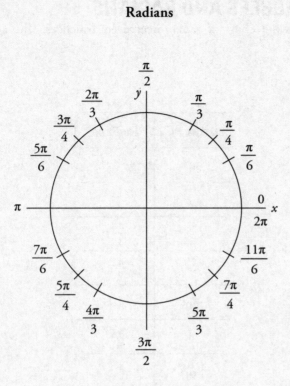

Degrees

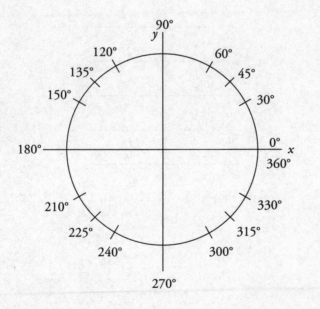

DRILL 4: DEGREES AND RADIANS

Fill in the following chart of radian-degree equivalences. The answers can be found in Part IV.

Degrees	Radians
30°	
45°	
	$\frac{\pi}{3}$
	$\frac{\pi}{2}$
120°	
	$\frac{3\pi}{4}$
150°	
	π
	$\frac{5\pi}{4}$
240°	
	$\frac{3\pi}{2}$
300°	
315°	
330°	$\frac{11\pi}{6}$
	2π

Comprehensive Trigonometry Drill

The answers can be found in Part IV.

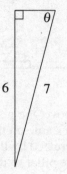

14. In the figure above, what is the value of cos θ ?

(A) $\dfrac{\sqrt{13}}{7}$

(B) $\dfrac{\sqrt{13}}{6}$

(C) $\dfrac{6}{7}$

(D) $\dfrac{7}{6}$

(E) $\dfrac{7\sqrt{13}}{13}$

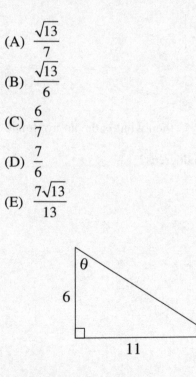

19. In the figure above, what is the value of θ in degrees?

(A) 28.61
(B) 33.06
(C) 49.09
(D) 56.94
(E) 61.39

23. If $\tan^2 \theta = 4.60$, then $\cos\dfrac{\theta}{5} =$

(A) 0.225
(B) 0.268
(C) 0.423
(D) 0.963
(E) 0.974

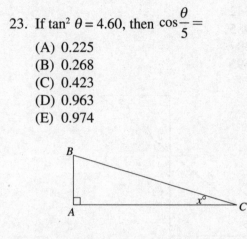

24. In the figure above, if x = 19 and AC = 10, then AB =

(A) 1.63
(B) 3.26
(C) 3.44
(D) 9.46
(E) 29.04

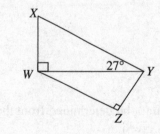

29. In the figure above, if XY ∥ WZ and WY = 8, then YZ =

(A) 3.63
(B) 4.08
(C) 7.13
(D) 8.98
(E) 17.62

38. If $0 < \theta < \dfrac{\pi}{2}$ and $\cos \theta = 0.173$, then $\sin\dfrac{\theta}{4} =$

(A) −0.641
(B) 0.342
(C) 0.985
(D) 1.397
(E) 5.693

42. In the figure above, the pillar on the left is 25 feet tall, the dragon statue on the right is 250 feet tall, and the angle created by the line from the center of the top of the pillar to the center of the top of the dragon statue is 50°. What is the approximate distance, in feet, from the middle of the pillar to the middle of the statue?

(A) 145
(B) 188
(C) 210
(D) 268
(E) 298

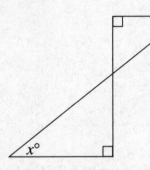

40. In the figure above, $\sin x° = \dfrac{3}{5}$. Which of the following is equal to $\cos y°$?

(A) $\dfrac{3}{5}$

(B) $\dfrac{3}{4}$

(C) $\dfrac{4}{5}$

(D) $\dfrac{5}{4}$

(E) It cannot be determined from the information given.

46. If $\dfrac{4\cos^2 \theta}{3} = 1$, then what is the approximate value of θ in degrees?

(A) 30
(B) 37
(C) 41
(D) 60
(E) 90

47. Where defined, $\dfrac{\sin^2 x - \cos^2 x}{\sin^4 x - \cos^4 x} =$

(A) 0

(B) 1

(C) $\sin^2 x$

(D) $\cos^2 x$

(E) $\tan^2 x$

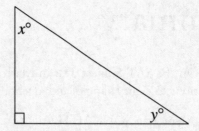

Note: Figure not drawn to scale

50. Given the triangle above, which of the following must be true?

    I. $\sin x° = \cos y°$

    II. $\tan x° > \tan y°$

    III. $\sin^2 x + \sin^2 y = 1$

(A) I only

(B) II only

(C) I and III only

(D) II and III only

(E) I, II, and III

Summary

o   On the SAT Subject Test in Math 1, you only need to know how to apply the trigonometric functions to right triangles and algebraic expressions. Be sure your calculator is in degree mode!

o   Memorize SOHCAHTOA!

- $\sin = \dfrac{\text{opposite}}{\text{hypotenuse}}$
- $\cos = \dfrac{\text{adjacent}}{\text{hypotenuse}}$
- $\tan = \dfrac{\text{opposite}}{\text{adjacent}}$

o   Whenever you have a right triangle question involving trigonometry, figure out which trig function you need, set up the problem (on the page with your pencil!) and solve from there.

o   Inverse trigonometric functions can be indicated by either the prefix *arc-* or by the exponent –1. These are used to determine the angle when you know two sides of the triangle.

o   There are two trigonometric identities that are useful on the SAT Subject Test in Math 1.

- $\tan = \dfrac{\sin}{\cos}$
- $\sin^2 x + \cos^2 x = 1$

o   On algebra questions using trigonometric functions, you can either use your algebra skills (keeping in mind the above identities) or Plug In for the angle (remember that θ is just a fancy variable). If you Plug In, avoid multiples of 45°.

o   Very rarely will you see a trigonometry question using radians. Radians are an alternative way to express the size of an angle. You can convert radians to degrees by using the proportion

$$\frac{\text{degrees}}{360} = \frac{\text{radians}}{2\pi}.$$

Chapter 11
Functions

ETS will test you on two types of functions. The first type of function is in $f(x)$ or mathematical notation, such as the following:

$$f(x) = (x + 3)^2 - x^2 \qquad f(a) = |7a - 12|$$

These functions require you to know some rules about the properties of functions and their graphs. This chapter will take you through what you need to know. The second type of function is what ETS calls "algebraic functions," but we call these problems "weird functions" because they use a strange symbol to represent a series of algebraic operations. Here are a couple of examples:

$$¥x = (x + 3)^2 - x^2 \qquad \left\|\overline{\overline{a}}\right\| = |7a - 12|$$

"Weird functions" are generally testing your basic math skills, including math vocabulary and PEMDAS. We'll cover them because they do show up on the SAT Subject Test in Math 1, but you're more likely to encounter functions in mathematical notation.

DEFINITIONS

Here are some terms concerning algebraic functions that appear on the SAT Subject Test in Math 1. Make sure you're familiar with them. If the meaning of any of these vocabulary words keeps slipping your mind, add that word to your flash cards.

Domain	The set of values that may be put into a function.
Range	The set of values that can be produced by a function.
Even Function	A function for which $f(x) = f(-x)$—even functions are symmetrical across the y-axis.
Odd Function	A function for which $-f(x) = f(-x)$—odd functions have origin symmetry, which means that they are the same when reflected across the origin.
Root	Values in a function's domain at which the function equals zero—a root is also called a *zero, solution,* or *x-intercept* of a function.
Asymptote	A line that the graph of a function approaches but never reaches.
Nonnegative	The values of a function that are greater than or equal to zero.

FUNCTIONS IN MATHEMATICAL NOTATION

On many questions, ETS will give you functions with letters like f and g, which look like the ones you've probably studied in school. A function is a type of relationship between two sets of numbers called the domain and range of the function. Specifically, a function is a relation in which every element in the domain corresponds to only one element in the range; for every x in the function, there is only one possible $f(x)$ (or y, on a graph).

The most basic function questions test only your understanding of functions and the algebra required to work with them. Here are some examples of basic functions.

$$f(x) = |x^2 - 16| \qquad\qquad g(x) = \frac{1}{4}(x - 2)^3$$

$$t(a) = a(a - 6) + 8 \qquad\qquad p(q) = \frac{3 - q}{q}$$

The best way to think of a function is that it's like a machine. It spits out a different result depending on what you put into it. As long as you follow the directions of the machine, it will spit out the right response for you. The test may bring up a couple of phrases: independent variable and dependent variable. The *independent variable* is what you put into the machine. You could put anything in; it doesn't rely on anything, so it's *independent*. The *dependent variable* is what your machine spits out. What it is depends on what's put into the machine. That's why it's the *dependent variable*. On a graph, the independent variable is on the *x*-axis and the dependent variable is on the *y*-axis.

When questions ask you to work with functions in mathematical notation, you'll be required to do one of two things: plug numbers into a function and get a numerical answer, or plug variables into a function and get an algebraic answer. For example, given the function $g(x) = (x + 2)^2$, you could run into two types of questions:

3. If $g(x) = (x + 2)^2$, what is the value of $g(4)$?

    (A) 8
    (B) 12
    (C) 16
    (D) 36
    (E) 64

Here's How to Crack It

Answering this question is a simple matter of Plugging In. Plug 4 into the given function for *x* to get $(4 + 2)^2$ and then simplify to get 36. Choice (D) is the correct answer.

Here, on the other hand, is an algebraic version of the same question:

13. If $g(x) = (x + 2)^2$, what is the value of $g(x + 2)$?

    (A) $x^2 + 4$
    (B) $x^2 + 6$
    (C) $x^2 + 4x + 4$
    (D) $x^2 + 4x + 6$
    (E) $x^2 + 8x + 16$

$f(x) = y$
Sometimes it helps to think of $f(x)$ as being equal to *y*. Both are the result you get when you put a number into the equation.

Here's How to Crack It

To solve this problem, just Plug In a number for x. Let's pick $x = 3$, and plug that in to $g(x + 2)$. You need to find $g(3 + 2) = g(5)$, which is $(5 + 2)^2 = 49$, your target value. Now, plug $x = 3$ into the answer choices to see which equals 49. Choice (E) is the correct answer. Remember to check all five answer choices when Plugging In.

You may also have to work with a *split function*—sometimes called a *piecewise function*. A split function is one that has different definitions, depending on some condition that is part of the function. Here are a couple of examples of split functions:

$$y(x) = \begin{cases} x^2, & x > 0 \\ 1, & x = 0 \\ -x^2, & x < 0 \end{cases} \qquad f(x) = \begin{cases} 5x, & \text{if } x \text{ is odd} \\ 4x, & \text{if } x \text{ is even} \end{cases}$$

Functions of this type are fairly straightforward. It's just necessary to check the conditions of the function before plugging values in to make sure you're using the right definition.

ETS may also give you the value of $f(x)$ and ask you to find the value of x that gives that particular value. Here's an example:

---

11. If $f(x) = x^4 + 3$, for what value of x is $f(x) = 10$?

   (A) 0.53
   (B) 0.84
   (C) 1.29
   (D) 1.63
   (E) 7.00

Here's How to Crack It

Plug In the Answers! Start with (C) and plug in 1.29 for x to see if $f(1.29) = 10$. $f(1.29) = 1.29^4 + 3 = 2.77 + 3 = 5.77$. Eliminate (C), and also eliminate (A) and (B) because these answers are even smaller. Next, try (D): $f(1.63) = 1.63^4 + 3 = 7.06 + 3 = 10.06$. This is close to 10 with rounding, so (D) is correct. Remember, when you PITA, you can stop when you find the answer that works, so there's no reason to test out (E).

DRILL 1: GENERAL FUNCTIONS

Practice working with functions in the following questions. The answers can be found in Part IV.

14. If $f(x) = x^2 - x^3$, then $f(-1) =$

(A) -2
(B) -1
(C) 0
(D) 1
(E) 2

17. If $f(z) = \sqrt{z^2 + 8z}$, then how much does $f(z)$ increase as z goes from 7 to 8 ?

(A) 0.64
(B) 1.07
(C) 2.96
(D) 3.84
(E) 5.75

26. If $g(t) = t^3 + t^2 - 9t - 9$, then $g(3) =$

(A) -9
(B) 0
(C) 9
(D) 27
(E) 81

29. If $f(x, y) = \dfrac{xy}{x + y}$, which of the following is equal to $f(3, -6)$?

(A) -48
(B) -6
(C) 3
(D) 6
(E) 18

30. If $h(x) = x^2 + x - 2$, and $h(n) = 10$, then n could be which of the following?

(A) -4
(B) -3
(C) -1
(D) 1
(E) 2

33. The function f is given by $f(x) = x \cdot [x]$, where $[x]$ is defined to be the greatest factor of x that does not equal x. What is $f(75)$?

    (A)   25
    (B)   225
    (C)   625
    (D) 1,125
    (E) 1,875

$$g(x) = \begin{cases} 2|x| & \text{if } x \leq 0 \\ -|x| & \text{if } x > 0 \end{cases}$$

34. What is the value of $g(-y)$ if $y = 3$?

    (A) −6.0
    (B) −3.0
    (C) −1.5
    (D) 1.5
    (E) 6.0

Weird Functions

These are what ETS calls "algebraic functions" but really they're just functions that contain strange symbols rather than the standard mathematical notation. ETS will try to frighten you with weird characters, but as long as you can follow the directions and Plug In, you'll have little trouble with these questions.

Here's an example.

―――――○―――――

13. If $\lozenge a \lozenge = a^2 - 5a + 4$, then $\lozenge 6 \lozenge =$

    (A) 6
    (B) 8
    (C) 10
    (D) 12
    (E) 14

Here's How to Crack It
Answer this question by plugging 6 into the definition of the function anytime you see a.

$$(6)^2 - 5(6) + 4 =$$
$$36 - 30 + 4 =$$
$$10$$

The answer is (C).

―――――○―――――

Don't be confused if a question requires you to plug something strange into a function. Just follow the instructions, and the answer will become clear as you work the problem.

Try the following question.

———————————————○———————————————

17. If $\&y = y^2 - 6$, then which of the following equals $\&(y + 6)$?

(A) y^2
(B) $y^2 - 36$
(C) $2y - 36$
(D) $y^2 + 12y + 30$
(E) $y^2 + 12y + 42$

Here's How To Crack It

To find the answer, just Plug In a number. Let's pick $y = 2$. That means that we want to find the value of $\&(2 + 6)$ which is $\&8$. Plugging 8 into the definition gives you:

$$(8)^2 - 6 = 58$$

Now just Plug In 2 for y in the answer choices to see which one becomes 58, which is your target value. Choice (D) is the correct answer. Remember to check all five answer choices when Plugging In.

———————————————○———————————————

DRILL 2: WEIRD FUNCTIONS

Practice your techniques on the following function questions. The answers can be found in Part IV.

34. If $[x] = -\left|x^3\right|$, then $[4] - [3] =$
(A) −91
(B) −37
(C)   1
(D)   37
(E)   91

35. If ¥c is defined as $5(c - 2)^2$, then ¥5 + ¥6 =

 (A) ¥7
 (B) ¥8
 (C) ¥9
 (D) ¥10
 (E) ¥11

$$\S a = \begin{cases} a \text{ if } a \text{ is even} \\ -a \text{ if } a \text{ is odd} \end{cases}$$

36. §1 + §2 + §3 . . . §100 + §101 =

 (A) −151
 (B) −51
 (C)   0
 (D) 50
 (E) 51

Compound Functions

A compound function is a combination of two or more functions, in sequence. It's essentially a function of a function—you take the output of the first function and put it into the second function. For example:

$$f(x) = x^2 + 10x - 3 \qquad\qquad g(x) = \frac{1}{\sqrt{x + 22}}$$

$$g(f(x)) = \frac{1}{\sqrt{x^2 + 10 + 19}}$$

The expressions $g(f(x))$ is a compound function made up of the functions $f(x)$ and $g(x)$. As with any algebraic expression with parentheses, you start with the inner-most part. To find $g(f(x))$ for any x, calculate the value of $f(x)$, and plug that value into $g(x)$. The result is $g(f(x))$. Like questions based on simple algebraic functions, compound-function questions come in two flavors—questions that require you to plug numbers into compound functions and do the arithmetic, and questions that require you to plug terms with variables into compound functions and find an algebraic answer. For example:

Remember the Machines?
Earlier, we called functions machines that take one value and produce another value. You can think of compound functions as a series of machines. The first machine (the inside function) performs its operations on the input, and then the output of this machine is used as the input for the second machine (the outside function).

$$f(x) = x^2 + 10x + 3$$

$$g(x) = \frac{1}{\sqrt{x+22}}$$

34. What is the value of $g(f(-4))$?

    (A) 0.15
    (B) 1.00
    (C) 2.75
    (D) 3.00
    (E) 6.56

Here's How to Crack It

To find the value of $g(f(-4))$, just plug -4 into $f(x)$; you should find that $f(-4) = -21$. Then, plug -21 into $g(x)$. You should find that $g(-21) = 1$. The correct answer is (B).

The more complicated type of compound-function question asks you to find the algebraic expression of a compound function. Essentially, that means you'll be combining the definitions of two functions. Try the following example:

$$f(x) = x^2 + 10x + 3$$

$$g(x) = \frac{1}{\sqrt{x+22}}$$

34. Which of the following is $g(f(x))$?

    (A) $\dfrac{1}{x-5}$

    (B) $\dfrac{1}{x+5}$

    (C) $\dfrac{1}{\sqrt{x^2+10x+3}}$

    (D) $\dfrac{1}{x^2+10x+3}$

    (E) $\dfrac{1}{\left(x+5\right)^2}$

Here's How to Crack It

Instead of doing a lot of complicated algebra, just pick an easy number to Plug In for x. Remember, when you have variables in your answer choices, you can Plug In. Let's try $x = 3$. So we're looking for $g(f(3))$. Work from the inside out.

$f(3) = 3^2 + 10(3) + 3 = 42$ so $g(f(3)) = g(42)$.

$g(42) = \dfrac{1}{\sqrt{42 + 22}} = \dfrac{1}{\sqrt{64}} = \dfrac{1}{8}$, the target value. Plugging In $x = 3$ into the answer choices, you find that (B) hits that target.

DRILL 3: COMPOUND FUNCTIONS

Practice working with compound functions in the following questions. The answers can be found in Part IV.

17. If $f(x) = 3x$ and $g(x) = x + 4$, what is the difference between $f(g(x))$ and $g(f(x))$?

    (A) 0
    (B) 2
    (C) 4
    (D) 8
    (E) 12

24. If $f(x) = |x| - 5$ and $g(x) = x^3 - 5$, what is $f(g(-2))$?

    (A) −18
    (B) −5
    (C) 0
    (D) 3
    (E) 8

25. If $f(x) = 5 + 3x$ and $f(g(x)) = 17$, then $g(x) =$

    (A) 3
    (B) 4
    (C) 56
    (D) $3 + 5x$
    (E) $5 + 3x$

$$f(x) = x^2 + 10x + 25$$

$$g(x) = \sqrt{x} + 4$$

32. Which of the following is $g(f(x))$?

(A) $x - 1$
(B) $x + 1$
(C) $x + 7$
(D) $x + 9$
(E) $x^2 - 2x - 1$

$$f(x) = \sqrt{x}$$

$$g(x) = x^3 - 2$$

36. What is the positive difference between $f(g(3))$ and $g(f(3))$?

(A) 0.7
(B) 0.9
(C) 1.8
(D) 3.4
(E) 6.8

Inverse Functions

Inverse functions are just opposites; they are functions that undo each other. Here's a simple example.

$$f(x) = 5x \qquad\qquad f^{-1}(x) = \frac{x}{5}$$

Here, the function $f(x)$ multiplies x by 5. Its inverse, symbolized by $f^{-1}(x)$, divides x by 5. Any number put through one of these functions and then the other would come back to where it started. Here's a slightly more complex pair of inverse functions:

$$f(x) = 5x + 2 \qquad\qquad f^{-1}(x) = \frac{x - 2}{5}$$

Here, the function $f(x)$ multiplies x by 5 and then adds 2. The inverse function $f^{-1}(x)$ does the opposite steps in reverse order, subtracting 2 and then dividing by 5. Let's add one more step:

$$f(x) = \frac{5x + 2}{4} \qquad\qquad f^{-1}(x) = \frac{4x - 2}{5}$$

Now, the function $f(x)$ multiplies x by 5, adds 2, and then divides by 4. The inverse function $f^{-1}(x)$ once again does the reverse; it multiplies by 4, subtracts 2, and then divides by 5. An inverse function always does the opposite of each operation in the original function, in reverse order.

More Machines

Once again, we have two machines. This time, you take your starting number and put it through the first machine. When you take the result of the first machine and put it into the second machine, something magical happens: you end up with your starting number! This is what is meant by inverse functions: the functions "undo" each other, returning you to your starting value.

$f(g(x)) = x$

Compound functions and inverse functions are often used together in questions on the SAT Subject Test in Math 1. It's the defining characteristic of inverse functions that they have opposite effects— they undo each other. For that reason, whenever you see the statement $f(g(x)) = x$, you know that the functions $f(x)$ and $g(x)$ are inverse functions. When a value of x is put through one function and then the other, it returns to its original value. That means that whatever changes $f(x)$ makes are undone by $g(x)$. The statement $f(g(x)) = x$ means that $g(x) = f^{-1}(x)$.

The typical inverse-function question gives you the definition of a function and asks you to identify the function's inverse. Let's look at an example.

---

40. If $f(x) = \dfrac{x}{4} + 3$ and $f(g(x)) = x$, which of the following is $g(x)$?

    (A) $x - \dfrac{3}{4}$

    (B) $x - 12$

    (C) $4x - 3$

    (D) $4x - 12$

    (E) $4(x + 12)$

Here's How to Crack It

In this question, the statement $f(g(x)) = x$ tells you that $f(x)$ and $g(x)$ are inverse functions. Finding $g(x)$, then, amounts to finding the inverse of $f(x)$. You could do this by picking out the function that does the opposite of the operations in $f(x)$, in reverse order; but there's an easier way. By definition, inverse functions undo each other. In practice, this means that if you plug an easy number into $f(x)$ and get a result, the inverse function will be the function that turns that result back into your original number.

For example, given the function $f(x)$, you might decide to Plug In 8, which is a number that makes the math easy:

$$f(x) = \frac{x}{4} + 3$$

$$f(8) = \frac{8}{4} + 3$$

$$f(8) = 2 + 3$$

$$f(8) = 5$$

You find that $f(x)$ turns 8 into 5. The inverse function $g(x)$ will be the one that does the reverse—that is, turns 5 into 8. To find $g(x)$, plug 5 into each of the answer choices. The answer choice that gives you 8 will be the correct answer. In this case, the correct answer is (D).

Invert *x* and *y*

If it doesn't look like Plugging In will help you, another great way to find the inverse of a function is to switch *x* and *y*, or *f*(*x*). So if the original function is $f(x) = 3x - 4$, move it all around. First, replace $f(x)$ with *y* so you can see it all more easily. Now you have $y = 3x - 4$. Switch *x* and *y*: $x = 3y - 4$. Now solve for *y*: $x + 4 = 3y$; and $\dfrac{x+4}{3} = y$. As a final touch, replace *y* with $f^{-1}(x)$: $f^{-1}(x) = \dfrac{x+4}{3}$. Now you have the inverse of $f(x) = 3x - 4$.

DRILL 4: INVERSE FUNCTIONS

Practice your inverse-function techniques on these questions. The answers can be found in Part IV.

22. If $f(x) = \dfrac{4x-5}{2}$ and $f(g(x)) = x$, then $g(x) =$

(A) $2x + \dfrac{5}{4}$

(B) $\dfrac{2x+5}{4}$

(C) $x + \dfrac{5}{2}$

(D) $\dfrac{x}{4} + \dfrac{2}{5}$

(E) $\dfrac{5x+2}{4}$

33. If $f(x) = 4x^2 - 12x + 9$ for $x \geq 0$, what is $f^{-1}(9)$?

(A) 1
(B) 3
(C) 5
(D) 12
(E) 16

35. If $f(3) = 9$, then $f^{-1}(4) =$

(A) –2
(B) 0
(C) 2
(D) 16
(E) It cannot be determined from the information given.

DOMAIN AND RANGE

Some function questions will ask you to make statements about the domain and range of functions. With a few simple rules, it's easy to figure out what limits there are on the domain or range of a function.

Domain
An easy way to think about it is that the domain is all the possible values of *x*.

Domain

The domain of a function is the set of values that may be put into a function without violating any laws of math. When you're dealing with a function in the $f(x)$ form, the domain includes all of the allowable values of *x*. Sometimes a function question will limit the function's domain in some way, like the following:

For all integers n, $f(n) = (n-2)\pi$. What is the value of $f(7)$?

In this function, the independent variable n is limited; n can only be an integer. The domains of most functions, however, are not obviously limited. Generally, you can put whatever number you want into a function; the domain of many functions is all real numbers. Only certain functions have domains that are mathematically limited. To figure out the limits of a function's domain, you need to use a few basic rules. Here are the laws that can limit a function's domain.

Mathematical Impossibilities for Domain
- **A fraction having a denominator of zero:** Any values that would make the bottom of a fraction equal to zero must be excluded from the domain of that function.
- **The square root of a negative number:** Any values that would make a number under a square root sign negative must be excluded from the domain of that function.
- **Any even-numbered root of a negative number:** This refers to $\sqrt[4]{}$, $\sqrt[6]{}$, etc. No value in the domain can make the function include an even-numbered root of a negative number.

Whenever a function contains a fraction, a square root, or another even-numbered root, it's possible that the function will have a limited domain. Look for any values that would make denominators zero, or even-numbered roots negative. Those values must be eliminated from the domain. Take a look at these examples.

$$f(x) = \frac{x+5}{x}$$

In this function, there is a variable in the denominator of a fraction. This denominator must not equal zero, so the domain of the function of $f(x)$ is $\{x \neq 0\}$.

$$g(x) = \frac{x}{x+5}$$

Once again, this function has a variable in the denominator of a fraction. In this case, the value of x that would make the denominator equal to zero is -5. Therefore, the domain of $g(x)$ is $\{x \neq -5\}$.

$$t(a) = 4\sqrt{a}$$

This function has a variable under a square root sign. The quantity under a square root sign must not be negative, so the domain of $t(a)$ is $\{a \geq 0\}$.

$$s(a) = 3\sqrt{10 - a}$$

Here again, you have a function with a variable under a square root. This time, the values that would make the expression negative are values great than 10; all of these values must be eliminated from the function's domain. The domain of $s(a)$ is therefore $\{a \leq 10\}$.

A function can involve both fractions and square roots. Always pay careful attention to any part of a function that could place some limitation on the function's domain. It's also possible to run into a function where it's not easy to see what values violate the denominator rule or the square root rule. Generally, factoring is the easiest way to make these relationships clearer. For example:

$$f(x) = \frac{1}{x^3 + 2x^2 - 8x}$$

Here, you've got variables in the denominator. You know this is something to watch out for, but it's not obvious what values might make the denominator equal zero. To make it clearer, factor the denominator.

$$f(x) = \frac{1}{x(x^2 + 2x - 8)}$$

$$f(x) = \frac{1}{x(x + 4)(x - 2)}$$

Now, things are much clearer. Whenever quantities are being multiplied, the entire product will equal zero if any one piece equals zero. Any value that makes the denominator equal zero must be eliminated from the function's domain. In this case, the values 0, −4, and 2 all make the denominator zero. The domain of $f(x)$ is $\{x \neq -4, 0, 2\}$. Take a look at one more example.

$$g(x) = \sqrt{x^2 + 4x - 5}$$

Once again, you've got an obvious warning sign—variables under a radical. Any values of x that make the expression under the radical sign negative must be eliminated from the domain. To make it clear which values to exclude from the domain, factor the expression.

$$g(x) = \sqrt{(x + 5)(x - 1)}$$

The product of two expression can be negative only when one of the expressions is negative and the other positive. If both expressions are positive, their product is positive. If both expressions are negative, their product is still positive. So the domain of $g(x)$ must contain only values that make $(x + 5)$ and $(x - 1)$ both negative or both nonnegative. The left binomial will always be greater, so if $(x + 5)$ is negative, then $(x - 1)$ will also be negative. $(x - 5)$ is negative when $x < -5$, so both expressions are negative when $x < -5$. Similarly, because $(x - 1)$ will be nonnegative when $x \geq 1$, both expressions are nonnegative when $x \geq 1$. The domain of $g(x)$ is therefore $\{x \leq -5\}$ or $\{x \geq 1\}$.

Domain Notation

The domain of a function is generally described using the variable x. A function $f(x)$ whose domain includes only values greater than 0 and less than 24 could be described in the following ways:

- The domain of $f(x)$ is $\{0 < x < 24\}$.
- The domain of f is the set $\{x: 0 < x < 24\}$.

A function in the form $f(x)$ can be referred to either as $f(x)$ or simply as f.

Range

The range of a function is the set of possible values that can be produced by the function. When you're dealing with a function in the $f(x)$ form, the range consists of all the allowable values of $f(x)$. The range of a function, like the domain, is limited by a few laws of mathematics. Here are the major rules that limit a function's range.

> Mathematical Impossibilities for Range
> - **An even exponent produces only nonnegative numbers:** Any term raised to an even exponent must be positive or zero.
> - **The square root of a quantity represents only the positive root:** Like even powers, a square root can't be negative. The same is true for other even-numbered roots ($\sqrt[4]{}$, $\sqrt[6]{}$, etc.).
> - **Absolute values produce only nonnegative values.**

Range
An easy way to think about it is that the range is all possible values of y. In the case of functions, the range is all the possible values of $f(x)$.

These three operations—even exponents, even roots, and absolute values—can produce only nonnegative values. Consider these three functions.

$$f(x) = x^4 \qquad\qquad f(x) = \sqrt{x} \qquad\qquad f(x) = |x|$$

These functions all have the same range, $\{f(x) \geq 0\}$. These are the three major mathematical operations that often limit the ranges of functions. They can operate in unusual ways. The fact that a term in a function must be nonnegative can affect the entire function in different ways. Take a look at the following examples.

$$f(x) = -x^4 \qquad\qquad f(x) = -\sqrt{x} \qquad\qquad f(x) = -|x|$$

Each of these functions once again contains a nonnegative operation, but in each case the sign is now flipped by a negative sign. The range of each function is now $\{f(x) \leq 0\}$. In addition to being flipped by negative signs, ranges can also be slid upward or downward by addition and subtractions. Take a look at these examples.

$$f(x) = x^4 - 5 \qquad f(x) = \sqrt{x} - 5 \qquad f(x) = |x| - 5$$

Each of these functions contains a nonnegative operation that is then decreased by 5. The range of each function is consequently also decreased by 5, becoming $\{f(x) \geq -5\}$. Notice the pattern: A nonnegative operation is flipped, the sign of the range also flips. When a quantity added to the operation, the same quantity is added to the range. These changes can also be made in combination.

$$g(x) = \frac{-x^2 + 6}{2}$$

In this function, the sign of the nonnegative operation is flipped, 6 is added, and the whole thing is divided by 2. As a result, the range of $g(x)$ is $\{g(x) \leq 3\}$. The range of x^2, which is $\{y : y \geq 0\}$, has its sign flipped, is increased by 6, and is then divided by 2.

Range Notation

Ranges can be represent in several ways. If the function $f(x)$ can produce values between -10 and 10, then a description of its range could look like any of the following:

- The range of $f(x)$ is given by $\{f : -10 < f(x) < 10\}$.
- The range of $f(x)$ is $\{-10 < f(x) < 10\}$.
- The range of $f(x)$ is the set $\{y : -10 < y < 10\}$.

Solving a Range Question

Now that you've learned about ranges, let's try out a question. Take a look at the following example.

Why Do I See *y*?
Because a function's range is represented on the *y*-axis when the function is graphed, the range is sometimes described using the variable *y*, even when *y* doesn't appear in the function.

25. If $f(x) = |-x^2 - 8|$ for all real numbers x, then which of the following sets is the range of f?

(A) $\{y: y \geq -8\}$
(B) $\{y: y > 0\}$
(C) $\{y: y \geq 0\}$
(D) $\{y: y \leq 8\}$
(E) $\{y: y \geq 8\}$

Here's How to Crack It

Start out with what you know about the equation. Since the result of absolute value is a nonnegative number, you can eliminate (A) right away. There is no maximum value, so you can eliminate (D) because it states the range must be less than or equal to 8. Now look at x^2. We know that there's no maximum that x^2 can be, but there is a minimum. The smallest x^2 can be is 0. If $x^2 = 0$, then the result inside the absolute value sign would be -8. This means that when $x = 0$, $f(x) = 8$. So the answer is (E). Now you may be thinking, what about the negative sign? Well, a negative minus a negative makes a number more negative and it's in absolute value so it would get more positive. The smallest number that this machine can produce is 8.

Plugging In on Range Questions

Because all questions on the SAT Subject Test in Math 1 are multiple choice, you can always Plug In and use POE on range questions. It may take a little longer, but it gives you a chance to score another point. So, if you're confused by the process of finding the range, or not sure what steps to take on a particular range question, Plug In.

Let's take another look at question 25 on this page. If you Plugged In $x = 3$, you would find that $f(3) = 17$. From that information you could eliminate (D). If you Plugged In 0, you'd see that $f(0) = 8$. If you Plugged In numbers less than 0, you'd see that $f(x)$ never gets smaller than 8. The answer is (E). You still get the right answer!

FUNCTIONS WITHIN INTERVALS: DOMAIN MEETS RANGE

A question that introduces a function will sometimes ask about that function only within a certain interval. This interval is a set of values for the variable in the x position.

Remember?
Don't forget that x represents the independent variable!

For example:

- If $f(x) = 4x - 5$ for $[0, 10]$, then which of the following sets represent the range of f?
- If $f(x) = 4x - 5$ for $0 \leq x \leq 10$, what is the range of f?

These two questions present the same information and ask the same question. The second version simply uses a different notation to describe the interval, or domain, in which $f(x)$ is being looked at.

The examples given in bullet points also demonstrates the most common form of a function-interval question, in which you're given a domain for the function and asked for the range. Whenever the function has no exponents, finding the range is easy. Just plug the upper and lower extremes of the domain into the function. The results will be the upper and lower bounds of the range. In the example given in bullet points, the function's range is the set {y: $-5 \leq y \leq 35$}.

The interval that you are given means that, for that particular question, you have a different set of values for the function's domain.

Be Careful!
You have to be alert when domains or ranges are given in this notation, because it's easy to mistake intervals in this form for coordinate pairs.

DRILL 5: DOMAINS AND RANGES

Practice your domain and range techniques on the following questions. The answers can be found in Part IV.

24. If $f(x) = \dfrac{1}{x^3 - x^2 - 6x}$, then which of the following sets is the domain of f?

   (A) {x: $x \neq -2, 0, 3$}
   (B) {x: $x \neq 0$}
   (C) {x: $x > -2$}
   (D) {x: $x > 0$}
   (E) {x: $x > 3$}

27. If $g(x) = \sqrt{x^2 - 4x - 12}$, then the domain of g is given by which of the following?

   (A) {x: $x \geq -2$}
   (B) {x: $x \neq 3, 4$}
   (C) {x: $-2 \leq x \leq 6$}
   (D) {x: $-2 < x < 6$}
   (E) {x: $x \leq -2$ or $x \geq 6$}

30. If $t(a) = \dfrac{a^2 + 5}{3}$, then which of the following sets is the range of t?

   (A) {y: $y \neq 0$}
   (B) {y: $y \geq 0$}
   (C) {y: $y \geq 0.60$}
   (D) {y: $y \geq 1.67$}
   (E) {y: $y \geq 2.24$}

34. If $f(x) = 4x + 3$ for $-1 \leq x \leq 4$, then which of the following gives the range of f?

   (A) {y: $-4 \leq y \leq 7$}
   (B) {y: $-4 \leq y \leq 19$}
   (C) {y: $-1 \leq y \leq 7$}
   (D) {y: $-1 \leq y \leq 19$}
   (E) {y: $1 \leq y \leq 19$}

GRAPHING FUNCTIONS

All of the function techniques covered in this chapter so far have dealt with the algebra involved in doing functions. Most of the function questions on the SAT Subject Test in Math 1 will be algebra questions like the ones you've seen so far. However, you might also encounter questions that ask about the graph of a particular function.

Graphical function questions require you to relate an algebraic function to the graph of that function in some way. Here are some of the tasks you might be required to do on one of these questions.

- Match a function's graph with the function's domain or range.
- Match the graph of a function with the function's algebraic definition.
- Decide whether statements about a function are true or false, based on its graph.

None of these tasks is very difficult, as long as you're prepared for them. The next few pages will tell you everything you need to know.

Looking at a Graph

When a function $f(x)$ is graphed, the x-axis represents the values of x. The y-axis represents the values of $f(x)$. When you look at the coordinates (x, y) of any point on the function's graph, x represents a value in the function's domain (the input of the function), and y represents the function of that value (the output of the function).

Identifying Graphs of Functions

The most useful tool for identifying the graph of a function is the *vertical-line test*. Remember that a function is a relation of a domain and a range, in which each value in the domain matches up with only one value in the range. Simply put, there's only one $f(x)$, or y, for each x. Graphically, that means that any vertical line drawn through the x-axis can intersect a function only once. If you can intersect a graph more than once with a vertical line, it isn't a function. Here's the vertical-line test in action.

This is a function, because no vertical line can intersect it more than once. All straight lines are functions, with only one exception. A vertical line is not a function, because another vertical line would intersect it at an infinite number of points.

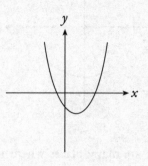

This is also a function. Any parabola that opens up or down is a function.

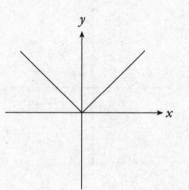

This is the graph of $y = |x|$, and it's a function as well.

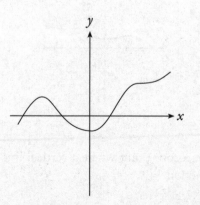

This complicated curve also passes the vertical-line test for functions.

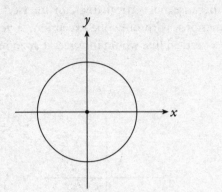

This is not a function; there are many places where a vertical line can intersect a circle twice.

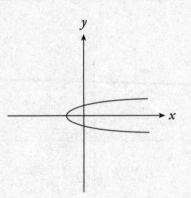

This isn't a function either. Although this graph is parabolic in shape, it fails the vertical-line test.

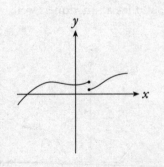

Nope. It's close, but there's one point where a vertical line can intersect this graph twice—it can't be a function.

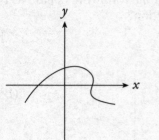

This curve is also not a function. It's possible to cross this curve more than once with one vertical line.

DRILL 6: GRAPHS OF FUNCTIONS

Use the vertical-line test to distinguish functions from nonfunctions in the following practice questions. The answers can be found in Part IV.

9. Which of the following could NOT be the graph of a function?

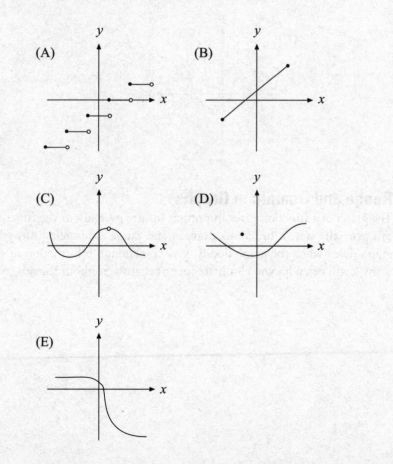

15. Which of the following could NOT be the graph of a function?

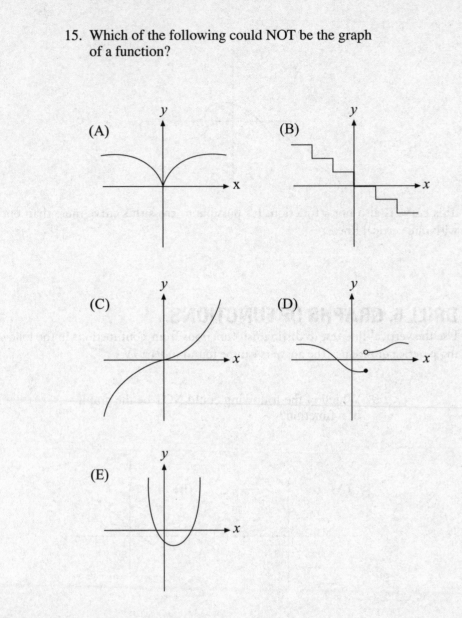

(A)

(B)

(C)

(D)

(E)

Range and Domain in Graphs

The graph of a function gives important information about the function itself. You can generally state a function's domain and range accurately just by looking at its graph. Even when the graph doesn't give you enough information to state them exactly, it will often let you eliminate incorrect answers about the range and domain.

Take a look at the following graphs of functions and the information they provide:

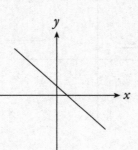

If you followed this line to the left, it would continue to rise forever. Likewise, if you followed it to the right, it would continue to fall. The range of this line (the set of y-values it occupies) goes on forever; the range is said to be "all real numbers." Because the line also continues to the left and right forever, there are no x-values that the line does not pass through. The domain of this function, like its range, is the set of all real numbers.

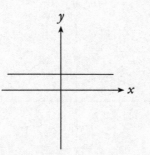

The same thing is true of all linear functions (whose graphs are straight lines); their ranges and domains include all real numbers. There's only one exception. A horizontal line extends forever to the left and right (through all x-values) but has only one y-value. Its domain is therefore all real numbers, while its range contains only one value.

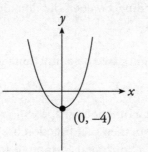

(0, –4)

The domain of this function is the set of all real numbers, because parabolas continue widening forever. Its range, however, is limited. The parabola extends upward forever, but it never descends lower along the y-axis than $y = -4$. The range of this function is therefore $\{y: y \geq -4\}$. Graphs of functions containing asymptotes don't show up on the SAT Subject Test in Math 1 all that often, but it's a good idea to understand how asymptotes affect the domain and range of a function.

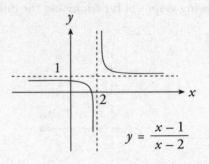

$$y = \frac{x-1}{x-2}$$

This function has two asymptotes. Asymptotes are lines that the function approaches but never reaches. They mark values in the domain or range at which the function does not exist or is undefined. The asymptotes on this graph mean that it's impossible for x to equal 2, and it's impossible for y to equal 1. The domain of $f(x)$ is therefore $\{x: x \neq 2\}$, and the range is $\{y: y \neq 1\}$.

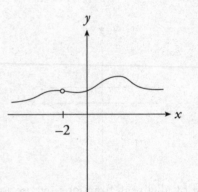

The hole in this function's graph means that there's an x-value missing at that point. The domain of any function whose graph sports a little hole like this one must exclude the corresponding x-value. The domain of this function, for example, would simply be $\{x: x \neq -2\}$.

To estimate range and domain based on a function's graph, just use common sense and remember these rules:

- If something about a function's shape will prevent it from continuing forever up and down, then that function has a limited range.
- If the function has a horizontal asymptote at a certain y-value, then that value is excluded from the function's range.
- If anything about a function's shape will prevent it from continuing forever to the left and right, then that function has a limited domain.

- If a function has a vertical asymptote or hole at a certain *x*-value, then that value is excluded from the function's domain.
- If you are asked to identify an asymptote, Plug In very large positive and negative numbers for *x* or *y* and see what values the other variable approaches. Try 1, 1,000, −1, −1,000, etc.
- Sometimes you can Plug In the Answers (PITA) and see which values of *x* or *y* don't make sense in the equation.
- Graphing the function on your calculator may be the easiest approach.

DRILL 7: RANGE AND DOMAIN IN GRAPHS

Test your understanding of range and domain with the following practice questions. The answers can be found in Part IV.

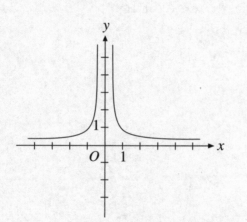

17. If the graph of $y = f(x)$ is shown above, which of the following could be the domain of f?

(A) $\{x : x \neq 0\}$
(B) $\{x : x > 0\}$
(C) $\{x : x \geq 0\}$
(D) $\{x : x > 1\}$
(E) $\{x : x \geq 1\}$

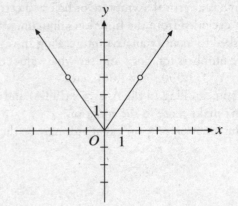

24. Which of the following could be the domain of the function graphed above?

   (A) $\{x : x \neq 2\}$

   (B) $\{x : -2 < x < 2\}$

   (C) $\{x : x < -2 \text{ or } x > 2\}$

   (D) $\{x : |x| \neq 2\}$

   (E) $\{x : |x| > 2\}$

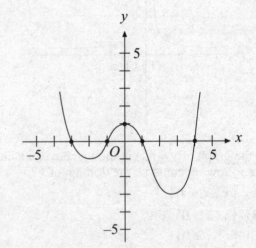

28. If $y = g(x)$ is graphed above, which of the following sets could be the range of $g(x)$?

   (A) $\{y : y \leq -1\}$

   (B) $\{y : y \geq -1\}$

   (C) $\{y : y \geq -3\}$

   (D) $\{y : -3 \leq y \leq -1\}$

   (E) $\{y : y \leq -3 \text{ or } y \geq -1\}$

37. Which of the following lines is an asymptote of the graph of $y = 3e^{-2x} + 5$?

(A) $x = 0$
(B) $x = -2$
(C) $y = 5$
(D) $y = 0$
(E) $y = -6$

48. Which of the following lines is an asymptote of the graph of $y = \dfrac{1-x}{x-2}$?

   I. $x = 2$

  II. $y = -\dfrac{1}{2}$

  III. $y = -1$

(A) I only
(B) II only
(C) III only
(D) I and II only
(E) I and III only

Roots of Functions in Graphs

The roots of a function are the values that make the function equal to zero. Hence, the roots are also called zeros or solutions of the function. To find the roots of a function $f(x)$ algebraically, you simply set $f(x)$ equal to zero and solve for x. The values of x that make $f(x) = 0$ are the roots of the function.

Graphically, the roots of a function are the values of x at which the graph crosses the x-axis, that is, the x-intercepts. That makes them easy to spot on a graph. If you are asked to match a function to its graph, it's often helpful to find the roots of the function using algebra; then it's a simple matter to compare the function's roots to the x-intercepts on the graph. Take a look at this function:

$$f(x) = x^3 + 3x^2 - 4x$$

If you factor it to find its roots, you get:

$$f(x) = x(x + 4)(x - 1)$$

The roots of $f(x)$ are therefore $x = -4$, 0, and 1. You can expect the graph of $y = f(x)$ to cross the x-axis at those three x-values. If you are having trouble factoring the function, you can always graph it on your calculator to find the roots or Plug In the Answers to see which ones make $f(x) = 0$.

DRILL 8: ROOTS OF FUNCTIONS

Try the following practice questions by working with the roots of functions. The answers can be found in Part IV.

16. Which of the following is a zero of
    $f(x) = 2x^2 - 7x + 5$?

    (A) 1.09
    (B) 1.33
    (C) 1.75
    (D) 2.50
    (E) 2.75

19. The function $g(x) = x^3 + x^2 - 6x$ has how many distinct roots?

    (A) 1
    (B) 2
    (C) 3
    (D) 4
    (E) It cannot be determined from the information given.

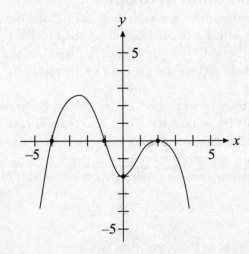

25. If the graph of $y = f(x)$ is shown above, which of the following sets represents all the roots of $f(x)$?

    (A) $\{x = -2, 0, 2\}$
    (B) $\{x = -4, -1, 0\}$
    (C) $\{x = -1, 2\}$
    (D) $\{x = -4, -1, 2\}$
    (E) $\{x = -4, -1\}$

SYMMETRY IN FUNCTIONS

Symmetry Across the *y*-axis (Even Functions)

When a function contains exponents and fractions *and* you're given an interval, you'll have to take the question in two steps. First, Plug In the upper and lower limits of the domain of the function. Then, use the range techniques from the previous section to see whether there are other limits on the function's range. If the paper were folded along the *y*-axis, the left and right halves of the graph would meet perfectly. Functions with symmetry across the *y*-axis are sometimes called even functions. This is because functions with only even exponents have this kind of symmetry, even though they are not the only even functions.

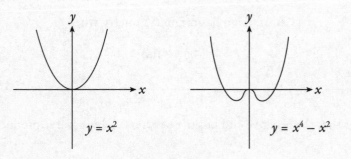

Even Functions

This is the algebraic definition of symmetry across the *y*-axis:

A function is symmetrical across the *y*-axis when

$$f(-x) = f(x)$$

This means that the negative and positive versions of any *x*-value produce the same *y*-value.

Origin Symmetry (Odd Functions)

A function has origin symmetry when one half of the graph is identical to the other half and reflected across the point (0, 0). Functions with origin symmetry are sometimes called odd functions, because functions with only odd exponents (as well as some other functions) have this kind of symmetry.

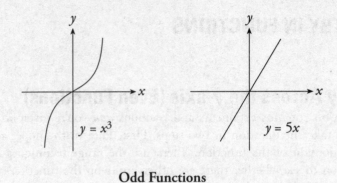

$y = x^3$

$y = 5x$

Odd Functions

This is the algebraic definition of origin symmetry:

> A function has origin symmetry when
>
> $$f(-x) = -f(x)$$

This means that the negative and positive versions of any x-value produce opposite y-values.

Symmetry Across the *x*-axis

Some equations will produce graphs that are symmetrical across the x-axis. These equations can't be functions, however, because each x-value would then have to have two corresponding y-values. A graph that is symmetrical across the x-axis automatically fails the vertical-line test.

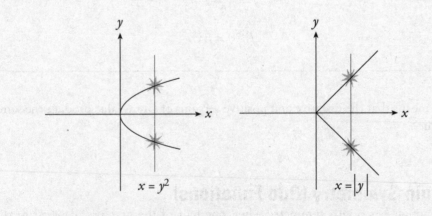

$x = y^2$

$x = |y|$

Questions asking about symmetry generally test basic comprehension of these definitions. It's also important to understand the connection between these algebraic definitions and the appearance of graphs with different kinds of symmetry.

DRILL 9: SYMMETRY IN FUNCTIONS

Try these practice questions. The answers can be found in Part IV.

6. Which of the following graphs is symmetrical with respect to the *x*-axis?

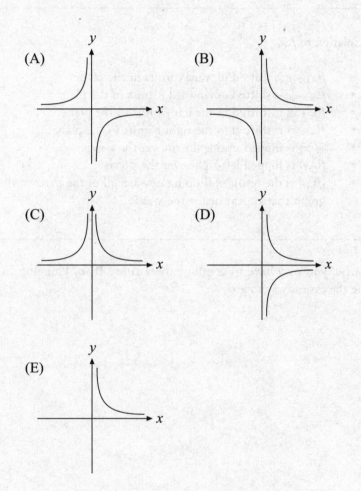

(A)

(B)

(C)

(D)

(E)

17. If an even function is one for which *f*(*x*) and *f*(–*x*) are equal, then which of the following is an even function?

   (A) $g(x) = 5x + 2$

   (B) $g(x) = x$

   (C) $g(x) = \dfrac{x}{2}$

   (D) $g(x) = x^3$

   (E) $g(x) = -|x|$

Movement of a Function

When giving you a function question, ETS may decide to fool around with the variable. Sometimes you'll be asked how this affects the graph of the function. For example, ETS may show you $f(x)$ and ask you about the graph of $|f(x)|$. You can either Plug In points or know the following rules.

In relation to $f(x)$:

- $f(x) + c$ is shifted upward c units in the plane
- $f(x) - c$ is shifted downward c units in the plane
- $f(x + c)$ is shifted to the left c units in the plane
- $f(x - c)$ is shifted to the right c units in the plane
- $-f(x)$ is flipped upside down over the x-axis
- $f(-x)$ is flipped left-right over the y-axis
- $|f(x)|$ is the result of flipping upward all of the parts of the graph that appear below the x-axis

Of course, you may have to combine these rules. If so, Plugging In some points may be the easiest way to go.

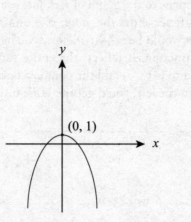

(0, 1)

45. The graph of $y = f(x)$ is shown above. Which of the following is the graph of $y = -f(x + 1)$?

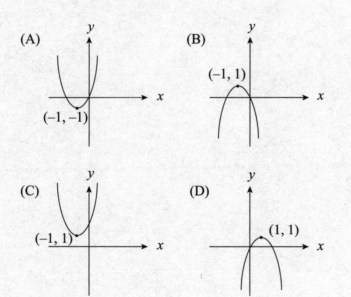

(A)

(–1, –1)

(B)

(–1, 1)

(C)

(–1, 1)

(D)

(1, 1)

(E)

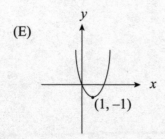

(1, –1)

Mirror, Mirror on the Axis
A function that seems to have a mirror image reflected in the y-axis is symmetrical across the y-axis.

Here's How to Crack It

To figure out what happens to the graph of $f(x)$, just use the rules on page 316. The $x + 1$ inside the parentheses shifts the graph one unit to the left. If this were the final answer, the vertex would be at $(-1, 1)$. Now you have to take care of the negative sign outside the function. It reflects the entire function across the x-axis, so the vertex gets reflected to $(-1, -1)$ and the parabola opens upward. If you reflected first and then shifted to the left, you'd get the same result. The answer is (A).

Comprehensive Functions Drill

The answers can be found in Part IV.

1. If $f(x) = -x^2 - 3x + 5$, then $f(-4) =$

   (A) −23
   (B) −4
   (C) 1
   (D) 9
   (E) 33

8. If $h(x) = x^2 - 3$, then $h(x + 2) =$

   (A) $x - 1$
   (B) $x^2 + 1$
   (C) $x^2 + 4$
   (D) $x^2 + 4x + 1$
   (E) $x^2 + 4x + 4$

10. If $f(x) = \dfrac{x^2 - 2x}{3}$ and $f(a) = 5$, then which of the following could be the value of a ?

    (A) −5
    (B) −3
    (C) 0
    (D) 3
    (E) 8

12. If $\square x$ is the greatest integer less than or equal to x, then what is the value of $\square(\square(\square 0.5)))$?

    (A) −2
    (B) −1
    (C) 0
    (D) 0.5
    (E) 1

15. If $f(x) = 0.7x - 2.5$ for $[-8, 3]$, then which of the following sets represents the range of f?

    (A) $\{y: -8.1 \le y \le -4.6\}$
    (B) $\{y: -8.1 \le y \le -0.4\}$
    (C) $\{y: -5.6 \le y \le -4.6\}$
    (D) $\{y: -5.6 \le y \le 3.1\}$
    (E) $\{y: -5.6 \le y \le 4.6\}$

$$f(x) = \frac{x^2 + 3}{2}$$

$$g(x) = 5x - 4$$

16. What is the value of $g(f(3))$?

    (A) 6
    (B) 11
    (C) 26
    (D) 62
    (E) 116

22. If $f(x) = \dfrac{(x - 3)^3}{5}$ and $f(g(x)) = x$, then $g(x) =$

    (A) $5\sqrt[3]{x} - 3$
    (B) $5\sqrt[3]{x} + 3$
    (C) $\sqrt[3]{5x}$
    (D) $\sqrt[3]{5x} - 3$
    (E) $\sqrt[3]{5x} + 3$

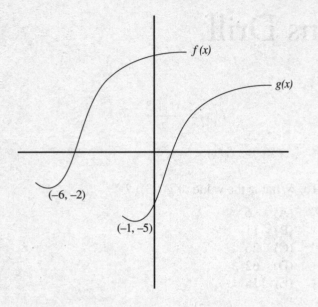

f(x)

g(x)

(−6, −2)

(−1, −5)

36. The graphs of $f(x)$ and $g(x)$ are shown above. Which of the following gives the equation of $g(x)$ in terms of $f(x)$?

(A) $g(x) = f(x - 5) - 3$
(B) $g(x) = f(x + 5) - 3$
(C) $g(x) = f(x - 3) + 5$
(D) $g(x) = f(x) - 8$
(E) $g(x) = f(x - 5) + 3$

40. If $f(x) = 2x^2 + x$ and $g(x) = 3x - 1$, then what is $f(g(x))$?

(A) $6x^2 + 3x - 1$
(B) $6x^2 + 3x$
(C) $9x^2 - 6x - 1$
(D) $18x^2 - 9x - 1$
(E) $18x^2 - 9x + 1$

42. If $f(x) = \ln x$, then which of the following is the domain of $f(x)$?

(A) $\{x : x \neq 0\}$
(B) $\{x : x \leq 0\}$
(C) $\{x : x \geq 0\}$
(D) $\{x : x > -2.5\}$
(E) $\{x : x > 0\}$

48. If $f(x) = x^4 + 6x^3 - x^2 - 30x$, then which of the following is NOT a root of $f(x)$?

(A) −5
(B) −3
(C) 0
(D) 2
(E) 3

Summary

o Mathematical functions relate two sets of numbers: the domain and the range. Think of it like a machine. You put in one number (from the domain) and the function spits out another number (in the range).

o Functions with weird symbols are what ETS calls algebraic functions. Follow the directions of the function.

o A compound function is a combination of two or more functions. It's like having two machines. You put your number in one machine, and you take the result from that and put it into the second machine.

o Inverse functions are opposites. Here are a couple of specifics:
  - An example of what inverse functions do is the following: If you put 5 into your first machine and get 12, then you put 12 into the inverse of that machine, you'll get 5.
  - Inverse functions will be symbolized either by $f^{-1}(x)$, or $f(g(x)) = x$.
  - Inverse function questions can be solved, either by Plugging In or by replacing $f(x)$ with y, switching x and y in the equation and solving.

o Domain is all the possible values of x in a given function. These are the numbers you put into the function. They are independent.

o Range is all the possible values of y (or $f(x)$) in a given function. These are the numbers you get out of the function. They are dependent.

o In order to figure out if a graph is a function, use the vertical-line test. The line will touch only one point on the graph if the graph is a function.

o When answering domain and range questions with graphs, take a look to see what values x can't be and what values y can't be.

o The roots of a function will make the function equal to 0 when you substitute them for the independent variable. Graphically, a function crosses the x-axis at its root values.

○ There are a few types of symmetry discussed in this chapter. An easy way to think about symmetry is this: If you physically folded your paper along the line of symmetry and all the points on both sides touched, the graph would be symmetrical along that line.

- A function is symmetrical across the y-axis when $f(-x) = f(x)$. This is called an even function.
- A function has origin symmetry when $f(-x) = -f(x)$. This is called an odd function.
- A graph that is symmetrical across the x-axis isn't a function, because it fails the vertical-line test.

○ You may see questions that ask about the movement of a function. If the number is outside the parentheses of the function, the graph shifts along the y-axis. If it is inside the parentheses, the graph shifts along the x-axis.

Chapter 12
Miscellaneous

You will see 2 or 3 questions about Statistics on the SAT Subject Test in Math 1. Statistics questions cover a range of topics about manipulating groups of numbers. Mean, median, and mode, permutations and combinations, and probability may show up. Data may be presented in various charts and graphs. Most of the questions are straightforward once you've learned the content, but because these questions are rare, focus on this chapter only after you've mastered the preceding material.

The most difficult portion of the SAT Subject Test in Math 1 may contain questions about seemingly random topics. These questions deal with content often covered in a Precalculus course. As with Statistics, the questions are often fairly direct once you understand the concepts, but because these questions are quite rare, only focus on this material once the rest of the book is mastered.

STATISTICS DEFINITIONS

Here are some terms dealing with sets and statistics that appear on the SAT Subject Test in Math 1. Make sure you're familiar with them. If the meaning of any of these vocabulary words keeps slipping your mind, add that word to your flash cards.

Mean	An average—also called an arithmetic mean.
Median	The middle value in a list of numbers when the numbers are arranged in order. When there is an even number of values in the list, the median is the average of the two middle values.
Mode	The value that occurs most often in a list.
Range	The result when you subtract the smallest value from the largest value in a list.
Standard Deviation	A measure of the variation of the values in a list.
Combination	A grouping of distinct objects in which order is not important.
Permutation	An arrangement of distinct objects in a definite order.

WORKING WITH STATISTICS

The science of statistics is all about working with large groups of numbers and trying to see patterns and trends in those numbers. To look at those numbers in different ways, statisticians use a variety of mathematical tools. And, just to keep you guessing, ETS tests your knowledge of several of these tools. The three most commonly tested statistical measures are the mean, the median, and the mode.

Mean

The mean (or "arithmetic mean") of a set is simply its average value—the sum of all its elements divided by the number of elements. To calculate averages, use the Average Pie we discussed in Chapter 5.

Median

The median is the middle value of a set. To find a set median, you must first put all of its elements in order. If the set has an odd number of elements, then there will be one value in the exact middle, which is the median value. If the set has an even number of elements, then there will be two middle values; the median value is the average of these two middle values.

Mode

The mode of a set is simply the value that occurs most often in that list.

Many statistics questions require you to work with all three of these measures. The calculations involved are usually not very difficult. However, the real challenge of these questions is simply understanding these terms and knowing how to use them. Similarly, there are two more statistical terms that you may be required to know for certain questions—range and standard deviation.

Range

A less commonly tested, but still important, statistical measure is range. The range of a set is the positive difference between the set's highest and lowest values. You can also think of range as the distance on the number line between these two values. Remember that distance is always positive.

Many statistics questions require you to work with all of these concepts. The calculations involved are usually not very difficult. However, the real challenge of working these problems is simply understanding these terms and knowing how to use them.

Let's look at a question testing these concepts.

19. In a set of seven numbers, the mean is 7, the median is 7, and the only mode is 7. Which of the following must be true about this set?

   I. There are fewer 5's than 7's in the set.

   II. The sum of the set is less than 50.

   III. The range of the set is greater than 7.

   (A) I only
   (B) II only
   (C) I and II only
   (D) I and III only
   (E) I, II, and III

Here's How to Crack It

Take the statements one at a time and see if you know it's true from the provided information. For Statement I, if 7 is the only mode, that means there cannot be any other number which occurs more often than 7. Therefore, there must be fewer 5s than 7s in the set. Statement I must be true; eliminate (B).

For the second statement, if the set has 7 numbers and a mean of 7, you can use the Average Pie to find the sum of the set:

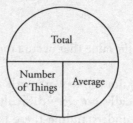

So, filling in what you know (the number of things and the average) lets you multiply and find the total:

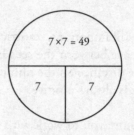

49 is less than 50, so Statement II must be true; eliminate (A) and (D).

For Statement 3, if the median is 7, you know if you line up the 7 numbers in order, 7 would be in the middle:

$$\underline{\quad} \quad \underline{\quad} \quad \underline{\quad} \quad \overset{7}{\underline{\quad}} \quad \underline{\quad} \quad \underline{\quad} \quad \underline{\quad}$$

You also know from the fact that the mean is 7 that all seven must add up to 49 and that there must be at least one more 7 for the mode to be 7. What you don't know, however, is what any of the other numbers MUST be. For example, all seven of the numbers could be 7:

$$\overset{7}{\underline{\quad}} \quad \overset{7}{\underline{\quad}} \quad \overset{7}{\underline{\quad}} \quad \overset{7}{\underline{\quad}} \quad \overset{7}{\underline{\quad}} \quad \overset{7}{\underline{\quad}} \quad \overset{7}{\underline{\quad}}$$

This would give a range of zero. Conversely, you could have a set with extremely small and large values:

$$\overset{-500}{\underline{\quad}} \quad \overset{0}{\underline{\quad}} \quad \overset{7}{\underline{\quad}} \quad \overset{7}{\underline{\quad}} \quad \overset{7}{\underline{\quad}} \quad \overset{28}{\underline{\quad}} \quad \overset{500}{\underline{\quad}}$$

This set has a mean (the numbers add up to 49), median, and mode of 7, yet the range is now 500 − (−500) = 1000. As you can see, for range, you need to know the first and last numbers, but as shown above the first and last numbers of this set can be anything, so long as the other conditions are met. The range may or may not be greater than 7; Statement III is not necessarily true. Eliminate (E) and choose (C).

DRILL 1: STATISTICS

Try the following practice question on statistical definitions. The answers can be found in Part IV.

25. List M contains ten elements whose sum is zero. Which of the following statements must be true?

   I. The mean of the elements in M is zero.
   II. The median of the elements in M is zero.
   III. The mode of the elements in M is zero.

(A) None
(B) I only
(C) I and II only
(D) II and III only
(E) I, II, and III

38. The mean and median of the annual salaries of the seven employees at Ricojack Technologies is $42,000. If an eighth employee is hired at an annual salary of $38,000, and no employee leaves Ricojack Technologies, then which of the following must be true about the annual salaries of the eight employees of Ricojack Technologies?

(A) The mean and the median of the annual salaries of the eight employees are less than $42,000.
(B) The mean of the annual salaries of the eight employees is less than $42,000, and the median of the annual salaries of the eight employees is $42,000.
(C) The mean of the annual salaries of the eight employees is less than $42,000, but the median of the annual salaries cannot be determined from the provided information.
(D) The mean of the annual salaries of the eight employees cannot be determined from the provided information, and the median of the annual salaries of the eight employees is less than $42,000.
(E) Neither the mean nor the median of the annual salaries of the eight employees can be determined from the provided information.

PLOTS, CHARTS, AND GRAPHS

On the SAT Subject Test in Math 1, ETS may present data in a number of different ways. Once you understand the basics of how to read these different types of plots, charts, and graphs, these questions are typically not too complicated.

Stem-and-Leaf Plots

ETS may ask you about a stem-and-leaf plot once in a while. The good news is that the questions are usually pretty simple if you understand the basic concepts.

Suppose that a class earned these quiz scores: 65, 70, 70, 78, 80, 81, 84, 86, 89, 89, 93, 93, 93, 98, 100.

A stem-and-leaf plot would show the data like this:

```
 6 | 5
 7 | 0  0  8
 8 | 0  1  4  6  9  9
 9 | 3  3  3  8
10 | 0
```

The tens digits are listed vertically, and then each ones digit is listed horizontally. For example, the row that reads "7| 0 0 8" means "70, 70, 78". This forms a sort of bar graph, but we have actual numbers instead of bars.

Let's look at how ETS might use a stem-and-leaf plot in a question.

```
 5 | 5  6
 6 | 2  3  6
 7 |
 8 | 0  0  2  9
 9 | 5  7
10 | 0
```

7. The stem-and-leaf plot above shows the final exam scores of the students in a Chemistry class. What was the approximate average (arithmetic mean) final score of the class?

    (A) 76
    (B) 77
    (C) 78
    (D) 79
    (E) 80

Here's How to Crack It

To find the average, you need to find the sum of the scores and divide by the number of scores. In a stem-and-leaf plot, each number on the right gives you one score. So, the first line, "5 | 5 6," tells you that you have scores 55 and 56 as part of your set. The line "7 | " tells you that there were no scores in the range of 70–79, inclusive. Your set would therefore be:

$$55, 56, 62, 63, 66, 80, 80, 82, 89, 95, 97, 100$$

You add them up and find that the sum is 925. There are 12 scores, so you divide: $925 \div 12 = 77.08$, which is closest to (B).

Boxplots

Unlike a stem-and-leaf plot, a boxplot does not show you all scores. Instead, a boxplot breaks the scores into what are known as quartiles.

The fifteen test scores 65, 70, 70, 78, 80, 81, 84, 86, 89, 89, 93, 93, 93, 98, 100 would be represented in a boxplot as follows:

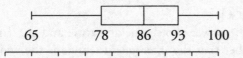

Each part of the boxplot represents 25% of the data. Here, 78 is the *first quartile*, or Q_1, 86 is the median (sometimes called the *second quartile*, or Q_2), and 93 is the *third quartile*, or Q_3. The only other thing you need to know is that the *interquartile range* is the range of the middle 50%: $Q_3 - Q_1$, or the width of the box. In this example, that's $93 - 78 = 15$.

Let's see an example of how ETS might test your understanding of boxplots.

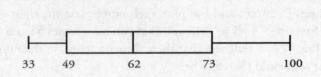

33   49   62   73   100

23. A hamburger stand recorded the number of hamburgers sold each day over a 200-day time period. The results are shown in the boxplot above. Which of the following CANNOT be inferred from the information provided?

(A) The interquartile range of daily hamburgers sold is 24.
(B) For 50 days, the hamburger stand sold between 33 and 49 hamburgers daily, inclusive.
(C) The median number of daily hamburgers sold was 62.
(D) The range of daily hamburgers sold was 67.
(E) The mean number of daily hamburgers sold was 62.

Here's How to Crack It

Work through each answer choice one at a time and see if the boxplot supports it. For (A), remember that the interquartile range is the width of the box. So to determine the interquartile range, just subtract the two numbers at each end of the box: 73 – 49 = 24. This matches (A), but you're looking for what is not supported, so eliminate (A).

Next, for (B) you need to remember that the data represents 200 days. Therefore, each quartile will represent 200 ÷ 4 = 50 days. 33 is the least number of hamburgers sold, and 49 is the first quartile. Therefore, this range represents one quarter of the elements, or 50 days. Choice (B) is true, so eliminate it.

For (C), you just need to look at the bar in the middle of the box, because that bar represents the median. The median is in fact 62, so eliminate (C).

For (D), you need to calculate the range. As you saw earlier, the range is the difference between the greatest and least values. You can determine these values by taking the extremes of the boxplot and subtracting: 100 – 33 = 67. This supports (D), so eliminate (D) and choose (E).

Choice (E) is not supported by the data because you do not know the actual values and therefore cannot determine the total. Because you are unable to determine the total, you cannot find the mean, so this answer cannot be inferred from the boxplot.

Charts

Sometimes ETS will present information in chart form. Be careful when reading charts and ALWAYS read the titles on each column!

Number of runs per innings per player
2015 Parc Jarry Open

Runs per innings	Number of players
5	11
6	25
7	17
8	25
9	11
10	25
11	11
12	8
13	11

22. What is the product of the modes of the number of runs per innings at the 2015 Parc Jarry Open?

(A)   11
(B)   48
(C)   80
(D)   480
(E) 6,435

Here's How to Crack It

You need to first figure out the modes of the number of runs per innings. Note that there are multiple modes here; that means there are multiple numbers of runs per innings with the most occurrences. To find this information, look at the titles of the columns. The second column is titled "Number of players," so the rows with the highest number of players will have the most occurrences. Working down this column, you find that 6, 8, and 10 each have 25 players with those numbers of runs per innings, so the modes of the set of data are 6, 8, and 10. Finally, the problem wants the product of the modes, so you multiply: 6 × 8 × 10 = 480, (D).

Graphs

You may also see statistical information in graphical form. As with charts, be sure to check out the labels. In particular, it is important to read the axes, as they'll let you know how to interpret what you're seeing.

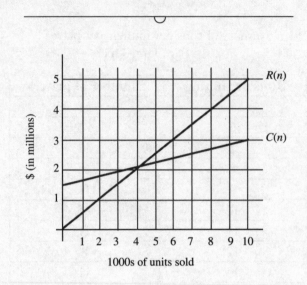

24. In the graph shown above, $R(n)$ represents revenue per n units sold, and $C(n)$ represents cost per n units sold. If $P(n)$ (not shown) represents profit, and $P(n) = R(n) - C(n)$, then what is the approximate value, in dollars, of $P(2,000)$?

   (A)   −800,000
   (B)   −800
   (C)   800,000
   (D)   4,000,000
   (E) 850,000,000

Here's How to Crack It

If $P(n) = R(n) - C(n)$, then $P(2,000) = R(2,000) - C(2,000)$. So you'll need to find $R(2,000)$ and $C(2,000)$ on the graph. It may seem like you're going to have to derive equations for $R(n)$ and $C(n)$ to find their values at $n = 2,000$. Before doing so, however, look at the axes. Note that the vertical (y-) axis is in millions of dollars and the horizontal (x-) axis is in 1000s of units sold. So rather than having to find equations of $R(n)$ and $C(n)$, you can just look at where the 2 is on the x-axis, because that's where 2,000 units were sold. Therefore, $R(2,000) = \$1,000,000$ and $C(2,000) = \$1,800,000$ or so (remember the y-axis is in millions of dollars). So $P(2,000) = \$1,000,000 - \$1,800,000 = -\$800,000$, which is (A).

Other Charts and Graphs

ETS may sometimes be creative when presenting information and do something other than what you've just read about. In these circumstances, be sure to read ALL the labels provided (including any "key" or "legend" that the information may have) and pay attention to what the question is asking you to do.

PROBABILITY

Probability is a mathematical expression of the likelihood of an event. The basis of probability is simple. The likelihood of any event is discussed in terms of all of the possible outcomes. To express the probability of a given event, x, you would count the number of possible outcomes, count the number of outcomes that give you what you want, and arrange them in a fraction, like this:

$$\text{Probability of } x = \frac{\text{number of outcomes that are } x}{\text{total number of possible outcomes}}$$

Every probability is a fraction. The largest a probability can be is 1. A probability of 1 indicates total certainty. The smallest a probability can be is 0, meaning that it's something that cannot happen. Most probabilities you'll be asked to find on the test are fractions between 0 and 1. Figuring out the probability of any single event is usually simple. When you flip a coin, there are only two possible outcomes, heads and tails. The probability of getting heads is therefore 1 out of 2, or $\frac{1}{2}$. When you roll a die, there are six possible outcomes, 1 through 6; the odds of getting a 6 is therefore $\frac{1}{6}$. The odds of getting an even result when rolling a die are $\frac{1}{2}$ since there are three even results in six possible outcomes. Here's a typical example of a simple probability question.

Not!
You can find the probability that something WILL NOT happen by subtracting the probability that it WILL happen from 1. For example, if the weatherperson tells you that there is a 0.3 probability of rain today, then there must be a 0.7 probability that it won't rain, because $1 - 0.3 = 0.7$.

11. A bag contains 7 blue marbles and 14 marbles that are not blue. If one marble is drawn at random from the bag, what is the probability that the marble is blue?

(A) $\dfrac{1}{7}$

(B) $\dfrac{1}{3}$

(C) $\dfrac{1}{2}$

(D) $\dfrac{2}{3}$

(E) $\dfrac{3}{7}$

Here's How to Crack It

Here, there are 21 marbles in the bag, 7 of which are blue. The probability that a marble chosen at random would be blue is therefore $\dfrac{7}{21}$, or $\dfrac{1}{3}$. The correct answer is (B).

Probability of Multiple Events

Some advanced probability questions require you to calculate the probability of more than one event. Here's a typical example:

23. If a fair coin is flipped three times, what is the probability that the result will be tails exactly twice?

(A) $\dfrac{1}{8}$

(B) $\dfrac{1}{5}$

(C) $\dfrac{3}{8}$

(D) $\dfrac{5}{8}$

(E) $\dfrac{2}{3}$

Here's How to Crack It

When the number of possibilities involved is small enough, the easiest and safest way to do a probability question like this is to write out all of the possibilities and count the ones that give you what you want. Here are all the possible outcomes of flipping a coin three times.

heads, heads, heads	tails, tails, tails
heads, heads, tails	tails, tails, heads
heads, tails, heads	tails, heads, tails
heads, tails, tails	tails, heads, heads

As you can see by counting, only three of the eight possible outcomes produce tails exactly twice. The chance of getting exactly two tails is therefore $\frac{3}{8}$. The correct answer is (C).

———————◯———————

Sometimes, however, you'll be asked to calculate probabilities for multiple events when there are too many outcomes to write out easily. Consider, for example, this variation on an earlier question.

———————◯———————

41. A bag contains 7 blue marbles and 14 marbles that are not blue. What is the probability that the first three marbles drawn at random from this bag will be blue?

(A) $\frac{1}{3}$

(B) $\frac{1}{9}$

(C) $\frac{1}{21}$

(D) $\frac{1}{38}$

(E) $\frac{1}{46}$

Here's How to Crack It

Three random drawings from a bag of 21 objects produce a huge number of possible outcomes. It's not practical to write them all out. To calculate the likelihood of three events combined, you need to take advantage of a basic rule of probability.

The probability of multiple events occurring together is the product of the probabilities of the events occurring individually.

In order to calculate the probability of a series of events, calculate the odds of each event happening separately and multiply them together. This is especially important in processes like drawings, because each event affects the odds of following events. This is how you'd calculate the probability of those three marble drawings.

The first drawing is just like the simple question you did earlier; there are 7 blue marbles out of 21 total—a probability of $\frac{1}{3}$.

For the second drawing, the numbers are different. There are now 6 blue marbles out of a total of 20, making the probability of drawing another blue marble $\frac{6}{20}$, or $\frac{3}{10}$.

For the third drawing, there are now 5 blue marbles remaining out of a total of 19. The odds of getting a blue marble this time are $\frac{5}{19}$.

To calculate the odds of getting blue marbles on the first three random drawings, just multiply these numbers together.

$$\frac{1}{3} \times \frac{3}{10} \times \frac{5}{19} = \frac{1}{38}$$

The odds of getting three blue marbles is therefore $\frac{1}{38}$, and the answer is (D). This can also be expressed as a decimal, as 0.026. ETS often asks for answers in decimal form on the test, just to make sure you haven't forgotten how to push the little buttons on your calculator. Just bear with them.

DRILL 2: PROBABILITY

Try the following practice questions about probability. The answers can be found in Part IV.

13. If the probability that it will rain is $\frac{5}{12}$, then what is the probability that it will NOT rain?

   (A) $\frac{7}{12}$

   (B) $\frac{5}{7}$

   (C) $\frac{12}{7}$

   (D) $\frac{12}{5}$

   (E) It cannot be determined from the information given.

16. In an experiment, it is found that the probability that a released bee will land on a painted target is $\frac{2}{5}$. It is also found that when a bee lands on the target, the probability that the bee will attempt to sting the target is $\frac{1}{3}$. In this experiment, what is the probability that a released bee will land on the target and attempt to sting it?

   (A) $\frac{2}{15}$

   (B) $\frac{1}{5}$

   (C) $\frac{2}{5}$

   (D) $\frac{1}{3}$

   (E) $\frac{6}{5}$

Day	Daily Cookie Production	Number Burned
Monday	256	34
Tuesday	232	39
Wednesday	253	41

20. The chart above shows the cookie production at MunchCo for three days. What is the probability that a cookie made on one of these three days will be burned?

(A) $\dfrac{1}{26}$

(B) $\dfrac{2}{13}$

(C) $\dfrac{1}{7}$

(D) $\dfrac{3}{13}$

(E) It cannot be determined from the information given.

24. If two six-sided dice are rolled, each having faces numbered 1 to 6, what is the probability that the product of the two numbers rolled will be odd?

(A) $\dfrac{1}{6}$

(B) $\dfrac{1}{4}$

(C) $\dfrac{1}{3}$

(D) $\dfrac{1}{2}$

(E) $\dfrac{7}{12}$

44. In a basketball-shooting contest, if the probability that Heather will make a basket on any given attempt is $\frac{4}{5}$, then what is the probability that she will make at least one basket in three attempts?

(A) $\dfrac{12}{125}$

(B) $\dfrac{64}{125}$

(C) $\dfrac{124}{125}$

(D) 1

(E) $\dfrac{12}{5}$

PERMUTATIONS, COMBINATIONS, AND FACTORIALS

Questions about permutations and combinations are rare on the SAT Subject Test in Math 1. As is the case with many of the odds and ends of precalculus, questions about permutations and combinations are rarely mathematically difficult; they just test your understanding of the concepts and ability to work with them. Both permutations and combinations are simply ways of counting groups of numbers.

Simple Permutations

A permutation is an arrangement of objects of a definite order. The simplest sort of permutation question might ask you how many different arrangements are possible for 6 different chairs in a row, or how many different 4-letter arrangements of the letters in the word FUEL are possible. Both of these simple questions can be answered with the same technique.

Just draw a row of boxes corresponding to the positions you have to fill. In the case of the chairs, there are six positions, one for each chair. You would make a sketch like the following:

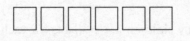

Then, in each box, write the number of objects available to put into that box. Keep in mind that objects put into previous boxes are no longer available. For the chair-arranging example, there would be 6 chairs available for the first box; only 5 left for the second box; 4 for the third, and so on, until only one chair remained to be put into the last position. Finally, just multiply the numbers in the boxes together, and the product will be the number of possible arrangements, or permutations.

There are 720 possible permutations of a group of 6 chairs. This number can also be written as "6!"—that's not a display of enthusiasm—the exclamation point means *factorial*. The number is read "six factorial," and it means $6 \cdot 5 \cdot 4 \cdot 3 \cdot 2 \cdot 1$, which equals 720. A factorial is simply the product of a series of integers counting down to 1 from the specified number. For example, the number 70! means $70 \cdot 69 \cdot 68 \ldots 3 \cdot 2 \cdot 1$.

The number of possible arrangements of any group with n members is simply $n!$. In this way, the number of possible arrangements of the letters in FUEL is 4!, because there are 4 letters in the group. That means $4 \cdot 3 \cdot 2 \cdot 1$ arrangements, or 24. If you sketched 4 boxes for the 4 letter positions and filled in the appropriate numbers, that's exactly what you'd get.

Let's look at an example problem.

---

3. 10 children are standing in a line. In how many ways could the 10 children be arranged in line?

(A) 55
(B) 100
(C) 1024
(D) 3,628,800
(E) 10,000,000,000

Here's How to Crack It
First, sketch out ten boxes in a row for the ten students:

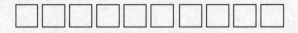

Next, write in how many children are available for each spot in line. Remember that each time you "place" a child the number of children available decreases by 1:

Finally, multiply the numbers together: $10 \cdot 9 \cdot 8 \cdot 7 \cdot 6 \cdot 5 \cdot 4 \cdot 3 \cdot 2 \cdot 1 = 3,628,800$, which is (D).

Advanced Permutations

Permutations get a little trickier when you work with smaller arrangements. For example, what if you were asked how many 2-letter arrangements could be made from the letters in FUEL? It's just a modification of the original counting procedure. Sketch 2 boxes for the 2 positions. Then fill in the number of letters available for each position. As before, there are 4 letters available for the first space, and 3 for the second. The only difference is that you're done after two spaces.

$$\boxed{4}\ \boxed{3} = 12$$

As you did before, multiply the numbers in the boxes together to get the total number of arrangements. You should find that there are 12 possible 2-letter arrangements from the letters in FUEL.

Let's look at another problem.

---

23. There are seven competitors in the final round of a biathlon competition. First place will receive a gold medal, second place will receive a silver medal, and third place will receive a bronze medal. How many different arrangements of medal winners are possible?

(A)   35
(B)   210
(C)   840
(D) 5,040
(E) 30,240

Here's How to Crack It
You only need to figure out the arrangements of the medal winners, so you need three boxes:

$$\boxed{}\ \boxed{}\ \boxed{}$$

Input the number of options for each space and multiply:

$$7 \quad 6 \quad 5 = 210$$

The answer is (B).

That's all there is to permutations. The box-counting procedure is the safest way to approach them. Just sketch the number of positions available, and fill in the number of objects available for each position, from first to last—then multiply those numbers together.

Combinations

Combinations differ from permutations in just one way. In combinations, order doesn't matter. A permutation question might ask you to form different numbers from a set of digits. Order would certainly matter in that case, because 135 is very different from 513. Similarly, a question about seating arrangements would be a permutation question, because the word "arrangements" tells you that order is important. So questions that ask about "schedules" or "orderings" require you to calculate the number of *permutations*.

Which One to Use?
Combination and permutation questions can be very similar in appearance. Always ask yourself carefully whether sequence is important in a certain question before you proceed.

Combination questions, on the other hand, deal with groupings in which order isn't important. Combination questions often deal with the selection of committees. Josh, Lisa, Andy isn't any different from Andy, Lisa, Josh, as far as committees go. In the same way, a question about the number of different 3-topping pizzas you could make from a 10-topping list would be a combination question, because the order in which the toppings are put on is irrelevant. Questions that refer to "teams" or "pairs" are therefore asking about the number of possible *combinations*.

Calculating Combinations

Calculating combinations are surprisingly straight-forward. All you have to do is throw out duplicate answers that count as separate permutations, but not as separate combinations. For example, let's make a full-fledged combination question out of that pizza example.

pepperoni	sausage
meatballs	anchovies
green peppers	onion
mushrooms	garlic
tomato	broccoli

36. If a pizza must have 3 toppings chosen from the list above, and no topping may be used more than once on a given pizza, how many different kinds of pizza can be made?

(A) 720
(B) 360
(C) 120
(D) 90
(E) 30

Here's How to Crack It

To calculate the number of possible combinations, start by figuring out the number of possible *permutations*.

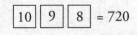 $\boxed{10}\ \boxed{9}\ \boxed{8} = 720$

That tells you that there are 720 possible 3-topping permutations that can be made from a list of 10 toppings. You're not done yet, though. Because this is a list of permutations, it contains many arrangements that duplicate the same group of elements in different orders. For example, those 720 permutations would include these:

pepperoni, mushrooms, onion	mushrooms, onion, pepperoni
pepperoni, onion, mushrooms	onion, pepperoni, mushrooms
mushrooms, pepperoni, onion	onion, mushrooms, pepperoni

All six of these listings are different permutations of the same group. In fact, for every 3-topping combination, there will be 6 different permutations. You've got to divide 720 by 6 to get the true number of combinations, which is 120. The correct answer is (C).

So, how do you know what number to divide permutations by to get combinations? It's simple. For the 3-position question above, we divided by 6, which is 3!. That's all there is to it. To calculate a number of possible combinations, calculate the possible permutations first, and divide that number by the number of positions, factorial. Take a look at one more:

29. How many different 4-person teams can be made from a roster of 9 players?

(A) 3,024
(B) 1,512
(C) 378
(D) 254
(E) 126

Here's How to Crack It

This is definitely a combination question. Start by sketching 4 boxes for the 4 team positions.

☐☐☐☐

Then fill in the number of possible contestants for each position, and multiply them together. This gives you the number of possible *permutations*.

 9 | 8 | 7 | 6 | = 3,024

Finally, divide this number by 4! for the 4 positions you're working with. This gets rid of different permutations of identical groups. You divide 3,024 by 24 and get the number of possible combinations, 126. The correct answer is (E).

DRILL 3: PERMUTATIONS, COMBINATIONS, AND FACTORIALS

Try the following practice questions about permutations, combinations, and factorials. The answers can be found in Part IV.

27. How many different 4-student committees can be chosen from a panel of 12 students?

(A)   236
(B)   495
(C) 1,980
(D) 11,880
(E) 20,736

32. In how many different orders may 6 books be placed on a shelf?

(A)   36
(B)   216
(C)   480
(D)   720
(E) 46,656

45. How many 7-person committees consisting of 4 females and 3 males may be assembled from a pool of 17 females and 12 males?

(A)   523,600
(B) 1,560,780
(C) 1.26×10^7
(D) 7.54×10^7
(E) 7.87×10^9

GROUP QUESTIONS

Group questions are a very specific type of counting problem. They don't show up very frequently on the SAT Subject Test in Math 1, but when they do, they are straightforward problems if you're prepared for them. Otherwise, they can be a bit confusing.

Here's a sample group question.

---

34. At Bedlam Music School, 64 students are enrolled in the gospel choir, and 37 students are enrolled in the handbell choir. Fifteen students are enrolled in neither group. If there are 100 students at Bedlam, how many students are enrolled in both the gospel choir and the handbell choir?

(A) 12
(B) 16
(C) 18
(D) 21
(E) 27

Here's How to Crack It

As you can see, part of the difficulty of such problems lies in reading them—they're confusing. The other trick lies in the actual counting. If there are students in both the gospel choir and the handbell choir, then when you count the members of both groups, you're counting some kids twice—the kids who are in both groups. To find out how many students are in both groups, just use the group problem formula.

For question 34, this formula gives you $100 = 64 + 37 + 15 - \text{Both}$. Solve this, and you get Both = 16. The correct answer is (B).

The group problem formula will work for any group question with two groups. Just Plug In the information you know, and solve for the piece that's missing.

DRILL 4: GROUP QUESTIONS

Use the group formula on the following practice questions. The answers can be found in Part IV.

25. At Buford Prep School, 253 students are enrolled in French, and 112 students are enrolled in Latin. 23 students are enrolled in both Latin and French. If there are 530 students at Buford Prep School, how many students are enrolled in neither French nor Latin?

    (A) 188
    (B) 342
    (C) 388
    (D) 484
    (E) 507

28. On the Leapwell gymnastics team, 14 gymnasts compete on the balance beam, 12 compete on the uneven bars, and 9 compete on both the balance beam and the uneven bars. If 37 gymnasts compete on neither the balance beam nor the uneven bars, how many gymnasts are on the Leapwell team?

    (A) 45
    (B) 51
    (C) 54
    (D) 63
    (E) 72

42. In a European tour group, $\frac{1}{3}$ of the tourists speak Spanish, $\frac{2}{5}$ of the tourists speak French, and $\frac{1}{2}$ of the tourists speak neither language. What fraction of the tourists in the tour group speak both Spanish and French?

(A) $\frac{2}{15}$

(B) $\frac{7}{30}$

(C) $\frac{1}{3}$

(D) $\frac{1}{2}$

(E) $\frac{14}{15}$

MISCELLANEOUS TOPICS

The remainder of this chapter covers topics that may appear on the SAT Subject Test in Math 1. When these topics do appear, they tend to be in the last third of the test. If you feel as if you've mastered the rest of this book, these topics are the final frontier to achieving an amazing score. If you're still struggling with some of the previous material, you will be better served by going back and reviewing those chapters.

LOGARITHMS

Exponents can also be written in the form of logarithms. For example, $\log_2 8$ represents the exponent that turns 2 into 8. In this case, the "base" of the logarithm is 2. It's easy to make a logarithmic expression look like a normal exponential expression. Here you can say $\log_2 8 = x$, where x is the unknown exponent that turns 2 into 8. Then you can rewrite the equation as $2^x = 8$. Notice that, in this equation, 2 is the base of the exponent, just as it was the base of the logarithm. Logarithms can be rearranged into exponential form using the following definition:

Definition of a Logarithm

$$\log_b n = x \Leftrightarrow b^x = n$$

Let's look at an example.

---

27. If $\log_3 x = 9$, then $x =$

    (A)   2
    (B)   3
    (C)   27
    (D)   729
    (E) 19,683

Here's How to Crack It

Rewrite the problem in exponent notation using the information above:

$$\log_3 x = 9 \Leftrightarrow 3^9 = x$$

To solve for x, simply use your calculator to find 3^9, which is 19,683, (E).

A logarithm that has no written base is assumed to be a base-10 logarithm. Base-10 logarithms are called "common logarithms," and are so frequently used that the base is often left off. Therefore, the expression "log 1,000" means $\log_{10} 1{,}000$. Most calculations involving logarithms are done in base-10 logs. When you punch a number into your calculator and hit the "log" button, the calculator assumes you're using a base-10 log. There will be times when you're dealing with other bases. A nifty formula allows you to use your calculator to evaluate logs with other bases.

> **Change of Base Formula**
>
> $$\log_B A = \frac{\log A}{\log B}$$

For example, $\log_7 54$ can be entered into your calculator as $\log(54)/\log(7)$, which gives you 2.0499.

Let's look at an example.

39. $\log_\pi 7.9 =$

    (A) 0.400
    (B) 0.497
    (C) 0.898
    (D) 1.395
    (E) 1.806

Here's How to Crack It

Use the Change of Base formula: $\log_\pi 7.9 = \dfrac{\log 7.9}{\log \pi}$. Then use your trusty calculator: $\dfrac{\log 7.9}{\log \pi} = \dfrac{0.898}{0.497} = 1.807$, which is closest to (E).

For the SAT Subject Test in Math 1, that's all you need to know about logarithms! So long as you can convert problems from log into exponents and use the Change of Base formula, you will be able to crack these questions when they appear on the test.

DRILL 5: LOGARITHMS

Test your understanding of the definition of a logarithm with the following exercises. The answers can be found in Part IV.

1. $\log_2 32 =$ _____
2. $\log_3 x = 4: x =$ _____
3. $\log 1000 =$ _____
4. $\log_b 64 = 3: b =$ _____
5. $x^{\log_x y} =$ _____
6. $\log_7 1 =$ _____
7. $\log_x x =$ _____
8. $\log_x x^{12} =$ _____
9. $\log 37 =$ _____
10. $\log 5 =$ _____

Natural Logarithms

On the SAT Subject Test in Math 1, you may run into a special kind of logarithm called a natural logarithm. Natural logarithms are logs with a base of e, a constant that is approximately equal to 2.718.

A Nifty Trick!
So you know how any number to the first power is that same number? For example, $4^1 = 4$. Well, that means that $\log_4 4 = 1$. Any log that has the same base as number is going to equal 1. So any time you see that, no work is necessary. Pretty cool, huh?

The constant e is a little like π. It's a decimal number that goes on forever without repeating itself, and, like π, it's a basic feature of the universe. Just as π is the ratio of a circle's circumference to its diameter, no matter what, e is a basic feature of growth and decay in economics, physics, and even in biology.

The role of e in the mathematics of growth and decay is a little complicated. Don't worry about that, because you don't need to know very much about e for the SAT Subject Test in Math 1. Just memorize a few rules and you're ready to go.

Natural logarithms are so useful in math and science that there's a special notation for expressing them. The expression ln x (which is read as "ell-enn x") means the log of x to the base e, or $\log_e x$. That means that there are three different ways to express a natural logarithm.

> ## Definitions of a Natural Logarithm
>
> $$\ln n = x \iff \log_e n = x \iff e^x = n$$

You can use the definitions of a natural logarithm to solve equations that contain an e^x term. Since e equals 2.718281828..., there's no easy way to raise it to a specific power. By rearranging the equation into a natural logarithm in "ln x" form, you can make your calculator do the hard work for you. Here's a simple example:

---

19. If $e^x = 6$, then $x =$

    (A) 0.45
    (B) 0.56
    (C) 1.18
    (D) 1.79
    (E) 2.56

Calculator Tip

On some scientific calculators, you'll punch in 6 first, and then hit the "ln x" key

Here's How to Crack It

The equation in the question, $e^x = 6$, can be converted directly into a logarithmic equation using the definition of a logarithm. It would then be written as $\log_e 6 = x$, or ln $6 = x$. To find the value of x, just hit the "LN" key on your calculator and punch in 6. You'll find that $x = 1.791759$. The correct answer is (D).

VISUAL PERCEPTION

Some questions on the SAT Subject Test in Math 1 ironically do not appear to test mathematical skills in any conventional sense of the phrase. One type of non-mathematical question on the test is the visual perception question, which asks you to visualize (that is, draw) a picture of a situation described in two or three dimensions.

The only technique for such questions is to draw your best representation of the situation described and use that as a guide in eliminating answers. You don't have to be a great artist, but a simple diagram will go a long way.

24. Which of the following equations describes the set of points equidistant from the lines described by the equations $y = 2x + 7$ and $y = 2x + 1$?

   (A) $y = 4x + 8$
   (B) $y = 4x + 6$
   (C) $y = 2x + 8$
   (D) $y = 2x + 6$
   (E) $y = 2x + 4$

This is asked in words because if there were a picture, it would be too easy. So make it easier by drawing a picture.

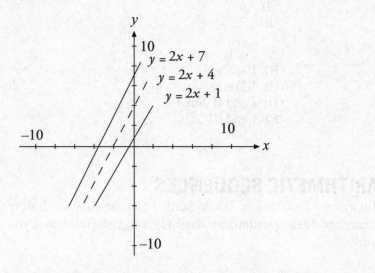

If you draw points halfway between the two lines, you get another line. It's parallel to the other two, slope its slope is 2; eliminate (A) and (B). Also, it's halfway between the two, so its y-intercept is halfway between 7 and 1. That's a y-intercept of 4, so (E) is the answer.

DRILL 6: VISUAL PERCEPTION

Try the following practice questions about visual perception. The answers can be found in Part IV.

27. Lines l, m, n, and o are all distinct lines which lie in the same plane. If line l is perpendicular to line m, line m is parallel to line o, and line o is perpendicular to line n, which of the following must be true?

    I.   Line l is parallel to line n.
    II. Line n is perpendicular to line l.
    III. Line n is parallel to line m.

(A) I only
(B) II only
(C) III only
(D) I and III only
(E) I, II, and III

42. Which of the following could be the number of circles created by the intersection of a sphere and a cube?

    I.   5
    II. 6
    III. 7

(A) I only
(B) II only
(C) III only
(D) I and II only
(E) I and III only

ARITHMETIC SEQUENCES

The average SAT Subject Test in Math 1 has one question dealing with arithmetic sequences. These questions are relatively straightforward once you know how they work.

The people at ETS define an arithmetic sequence as "one in which the difference between successive terms is constant." Real human beings just say that an arithmetic sequence is what you get when you pick a starting value and add the same number again and again.

Here are some sample arithmetic sequences.

$$\{a_n\} = 1, 7, 13, 19, 25, 31, \ldots$$
$$\{b_n\} = 3, 13, 23, 33, 43, 53, \ldots$$
$$\{c_n\} = 12, 7, 2, -3, -8, -13, \ldots$$

It's not hard to figure out what difference separates any two terms in a sequence. To continue a sequence, you would just continue adding that difference. The larger letter in each case is the name of the sequence (these are sequences a, b, and c). The subscript, n, represents the number of the term in the sequence. The expression a_4, for example, represents the fourth term in the a sequence, which is 19. The expression b_7 means the seventh term in the b sequence, which would be 63.

The typical arithmetic sequence question asks you to figure out the difference between any two successive terms in the sequence, and then calculate the value of a term much farther along. There's just one trick to that—to calculate the value of a_{26}, for example, start by figuring out the difference between any two consecutive terms. You'll find that the terms in the a sequence increase at intervals of 6. Now here's the trick: To get to the 26th term in the sequence, you'll start with a_1, which is 1, and increase it by 6 twenty-five times. The term $a_{26} = 1 + (25 \times 6)$, or 151. It's like climbing stairs in a building; to get to the fifth floor, you climb 4 flights. To get to the 12th floor, you climb 11 flights, and so on. In the same way, it takes 11 steps to get to the 12th term in a sequence from the first term. To get to the nth term in a sequence, take $(n - 1)$ steps from the first term.

Here's another example—to figure out the value of c_{17}, start with 12 and add –5 sixteen times. The value of $c_{17} = 12 + (16 \times -5)$, or –68. That's all there is to calculating values in arithmetic sequences.

Here's the algebraic definition of the nth term of an arithmetic sequence, if the starting value is a_1 and the difference between any two successive terms is d.

The nth Term of an Arithmetic Sequence

$$a_n = a_1 + (n - 1)d$$

Let's look at a problem.

---

14. If the first term of an arithmetic sequence is 3 and the third term is 10, then what is the 30th term of the sequence?

(A) 73
(B) 101.5
(C) 104.5
(D) 108
(E) 213.5

Here's How to Crack It

First, you need to determine the difference between terms. You are given the first and third terms of the sequence, so you have a couple of options. You could use the nth term of an arithmetic sequence formula and solve for d. Or, you could realize that the second term must be halfway between the first and third terms, so you can find the second term by taking the average of the first and third terms:

$$\frac{3+10}{2} = 6.5$$

If 6.5 is the second term, then the difference between terms is $6.5 - 3 = 3.5$. Now, to find the 30th term, the best approach is to use the formula $a_n = a_1 + (n-1)d$. $a_1 = 3$, $n = 30$, and $d = 3.5$:

$$a_{30} = 3 + (30-1)3.5 = 104.5$$

This is (C).

Finding the Sum of an Arithmetic Sequence

You might be asked to figure out the sum of the first 37 terms of an arithmetic sequence, or the first 48 terms, and so on. To figure out the sum of a chunk of an arithmetic sequence, take the average of the first and last terms in that chunk, and multiply by the number of terms you're adding up. For example,

$$\{a_n\} = 5, 11, 17, 23, 29, 35,\ldots$$

What is the sum of the first 40 terms of a_n?

The first term of a_n is 5. The fortieth term is 239. The sum of these terms will be the average of these two terms, 122, multiplied by the number of terms, 40. The product of 122 and 40 is 4,880. That's the sum of the first 40 terms of the sequence. Here's the algebraic definition of the sum of the first n terms of an arithmetic sequence, where the difference between any two successive terms is d.

Sum of the First n Terms of an Arithmetic Sequence

$$\text{sum} = n\left(\frac{a_1 + a_n}{2}\right)$$

Let's look at an example.

---○---

48. An arithmetic sequence has an initial value of 2
and a constant difference of 3. What is the sum of
the first 45 terms of this sequence?

(A) 2,970
(B) 3,060
(C) 3,197
(D) 5,940
(E) 6,120

Here's How to Crack It

First, you need to determine what the 45th term in the sequence is. Use the formula $a_n = a_1 + (n - 1)d$, where $a_1 = 2$, $n = 45$, and $d = 3$:

$$a_{45} = 2 + (45 - 1)3 = 134$$

Next, use the formula for the sum of an arithmetic sequence: $\text{sum} = n\left(\dfrac{a_1 + a_n}{2}\right)$:

$$\text{sum} = 45\left(\dfrac{2 + 134}{2}\right) = 3,060$$

This matches (B).

---○---

DRILL 7: ARITHMETIC AND GEOMETRIC SEQUENCES

Try the following practice questions about arithmetic and geometric sequences. The answers can be found in Part IV.

14. In an arithmetic sequence, the second term is 4
and the sixth term is 32. What is the fifth term in
the sequence?

(A)   8
(B) 15
(C) 16
(D) 24
(E) 25

19. In the arithmetic sequence a_n, $a_1 = 2$ and $a_7 = 16$. What is the value of a_{33}?

(A) 72.00
(B) 74.33
(C) 74.67
(D) 75.14
(E) 76.67

LOGIC

Every now and then, you will come upon a question asked in simple English that seems to have nothing at all to do with math. This is a logic question. Here's a typical example.

---

24. If every precious stone is harder than glass, which of the following statements must also be true?

(A) Glass can be a precious stone.
(B) Every stone harder than glass is a precious stone.
(C) No stone is exactly as hard as glass.
(D) Some stones softer than glass are precious stones.
(E) Every stone softer than glass is not a precious stone.

Here's How to Crack It

This is madness. There's no math here at all. However, there is a rule here for you to work with. The rule states that given one statement, there's only one other statement that is logically necessary, the contrapositive. This is what the contrapositive states:

> **The Contrapositive**
>
> Given the statement $A \rightarrow B$, you also know $\sim B \rightarrow \sim A$.

In English, that means that the statement "If A, then B" also tells you that "If not B, then not A." To find the contrapositive of any statement, switch the order of the first and second parts of the original statement, and negate their meaning. But you can't be sure of anything else. For example, "If not A" doesn't necessarily mean "then not B." And "if B" doesn't necessarily mean "then A." This is how you'd find the contrapositive of the statement, "Every precious stone is harder than glass." Start by making sure that you clearly see what the two parts of the original statement are.

$$\text{stone is precious} \rightarrow \text{stone harder than glass}$$

Then switch the order of the statement's parts, and negate their meanings:

$$\text{stone not harder than glass} \rightarrow \text{stone is not precious}$$

This is the contrapositive. Once you've found it, just check the answer choices for a statement with an equivalent meaning. In this case, (E) is equivalent to the contrapositive. Trap answers will typically say things like "Every stone that is harder than glass is precious" or "Every stone that is not precious is softer than glass."

———————————◯———————————

Almost all logic questions test your understanding of the contrapositive. There are just a couple of other points that might come up in logic questions.

- If you see the statement "Some *A* are *B*," then you also know that "Some *B* are *A*." For example, "Some teachers are pretty cool people" also means that "Some pretty cool people are teachers."
- To disprove the claim, "*X* might be true," or "*X* is possible," you must show that *X* is never, ever true, in any case, anywhere.
- To disprove the claim, "*X* is true," you only need to show that there's one exception, somewhere, sometime.

In other words, a statement that something *may* be true is very hard to disprove; you've got to demonstrate conclusively that there's no way it could be true. On the other hand, a statement that something is *definitely* true is easy to disprove; all you have to do is find one exception. If you remember the three bullet points above and the contrapositive, you'll be prepared for any logic question on the SAT Subject Test in Math 1.

DRILL 8: LOGIC

Exercise your powers of logic on these practice questions. The answers can be found in Part IV.

28. At Legion High School in a certain year, no sophomore received failing grades. Which of the following statements must be true?

    (A) There were failures in classes other than the sophomore class.
    (B) Sophomores had better study skills than other students that year.
    (C) No student at Legion High School received failing grades that year.
    (D) Any student who received failing grades was not a sophomore.
    (E) There were more passing grades in the sophomore class than in other classes.

33. "If one commits arson, a building burns." Which of the following is a contradiction to this statement?

    (A) Many people would refuse to commit arson.
    (B) A building did not burn, and yet arson was committed.
    (C) Some buildings are more difficult to burn than others.
    (D) A building burned, although no arson was committed.
    (E) Arson is a serious crime.

35. In a necklace of diamonds and rubies, some stones are not genuine. If every stone that is not genuine is a ruby, which of the following statements must be true?

    (A) There are more diamonds than rubies in the necklace.
    (B) The necklace contains no genuine rubies.
    (C) No diamonds in the necklace are not genuine.
    (D) Diamonds are of greater value than rubies.
    (E) The necklace contains no genuine diamonds.

IMAGINARY NUMBERS

Almost all math on the SAT Subject Test in Math 1 is confined to real numbers. Only a few questions deal with the square roots of negative numbers—imaginary numbers. For the sake of simplicity, imaginary numbers are expressed in terms of i. The quantity i is equal to the square root of -1. It's used to simplify the square roots of negative numbers. ETS will remind you of this in the question by saying "If $i = \sqrt{-1}$" or "If $i^2 = 1$." For example, here's how i can be used to simplify square roots of negative numbers.

$$\sqrt{-25} = \sqrt{25}\sqrt{-1} = 5\sqrt{-1} = 5i$$
$$\sqrt{-48} = \sqrt{48}\sqrt{-1} = \sqrt{16}\sqrt{3}\sqrt{-1} = 4i\sqrt{3}$$
$$\sqrt{-7} = \sqrt{7}\sqrt{-1} = i\sqrt{7}$$

Computing Powers of i

You may run into a question that asks you to find the value of i^{34}, or something equally outrageous. This may seem difficult or impossible at first, but, as usual, there's a trick to it. The powers of i repeat in a cycle of 4 values, over and over.

$$i^1 = i \qquad i^5 = i$$
$$i^2 = -1 \qquad i^6 = -1$$
$$i^3 = -i \qquad i^7 = -i$$
$$i^4 = 1 \qquad i^8 = 1$$

And so on. These are the only four values that can be produced by raising i to an integer power. To find the value of i^{34}, either write out the cycle of four values up to the 34th power, which would take less than a minute, or, more simply, divide 34 by 4. You find that 34 contains eight cycles of 4, with a remainder of 2. The eight cycles of 4 just bring you back to where you started. It's the remainder that's important. The remainder of 2 means that the value of i^{34} is equal to the value of i^2, or -1. In order to raise i to any power, just divide the exponent by 4 and use the remainder as your exponent.

Let's look at a problem.

27. If $i = \sqrt{-1}$, then $i^{85} =$

    (A) -1
    (B) 0
    (C) 1
    (D) i
    (E) $-i$

Here's How to Crack It

First, i to any power must equal i, $-i$, 1, or -1, so eliminate (B). Next, you need to find the remainder when the exponent is divided by 4. Break out your long division skills:

$$
\begin{array}{r}
21\,r1 \\
4\overline{)85} \\
\underline{8} \\
5 \\
\underline{4} \\
1
\end{array}
$$

If there is a remainder of 1, then $i^{85} = i^1 = i$, which is (D).

Doing Algebra with i

Algebra that includes complex numbers is no different from ordinary algebra. You just need to remember that i raised to an exponent changes in value, which can have some odd effects in algebra.

Here's an example.

$$
\begin{aligned}
(x - 3i)(2x + 6i) &= \\
2x^2 - 6ix + 6ix + 18i^2 &= \\
2x^2 - 18i^2 &= \\
2x^2 - 18(-1) &= \\
2x^2 + 18
\end{aligned}
$$

As with most algebra problems on this test, you can Plug In for the variables (remember that i is not a variable) and solve the problem that way. If you do so, you may have to simplify i at the end of working the problem by using the method in the section Computing Powers of i.

Some calculators can help you on these questions if you're Plugging In. On the TI-84, press MODE and go to the 7th row. The second option in that row, $a + bi$, lets your calculator deal with imaginary numbers. Pressing 2ND->"." lets you input i into your calculator, and the calculator will simplify the powers of i for you.

Let's try a problem.

———————————◯———————————

41. $\dfrac{(7+4i)(7-4i)}{(2i+1)(2i-1)} =$

   (A) -65
   (B) -13
   (C) $14 + 4i$
   (D) $-14 - 4i$
   (E) 13

Here's How to Crack It

Begin by using the FOIL method in the numerator and denominator of the fraction. (Note that you may notice that both the numerator and denominator are the common quadratic $(a + b)(a - b) = a^2 - b^2$, which can speed things up):

$$\frac{(7+4i)(7-4i)}{(2i+1)(2i-1)} = \frac{49 - 28i + 28i - 16i^2}{4i^2 - 2i + 2i - 1} = \frac{49 - 16i^2}{4i^2 - 1}$$

$i^2 = -1$, so you can substitute -1 for i^2 wherever it appears and solve:

$$\frac{49 - 16(-1)}{4(-1) - 1} = \frac{49 + 16}{-4 - 1} = \frac{65}{-5} = -13$$

This result matches (B).

———————————◯———————————

DRILL 9: IMAGINARY NUMBERS

Test your understanding of imaginary numbers with the following practice questions. The answers can be found in Part IV.

25. If $i^2 = -1$, then what is the value of i^{51} ?

   (A) 0
   (B) -1
   (C) $-i$
   (D) i
   (E) 1

36. If $i^2 = -1$, then which of the following expressions is NOT equal to zero?

(A) $i^0 - i^{12}$
(B) $i + i^3$
(C) $i^4 + i^{10}$
(D) $i^{11} - i^9$
(E) $i^8 - i^{12}$

40. $\dfrac{(2 + 4i)(2 - 4i)}{5} =$

(A) 2.2
(B) 4.0
(C) 4.6
(D) 5.0
(E) 8.4

MATRICES

Matrices are a way of presenting information. Matrix questions are rare on the SAT Subject Test in Math 1, but there are a couple of different things which ETS may ask you to do.

Matrix Multiplication

The simplest sort of multiplication you may be asked to do with a matrix is to multiply a matrix by a single term. In these cases, the product is a matrix the same size as the original matrix, and each position is multiplied by the single term.

For example:

$$3 \begin{bmatrix} 2 & 1 \\ 4 & 2 \\ 0 & 5 \end{bmatrix} = \begin{bmatrix} 3 \times 2 & 3 \times 1 \\ 3 \times 4 & 3 \times 2 \\ 3 \times 0 & 3 \times 5 \end{bmatrix} = \begin{bmatrix} 6 & 3 \\ 12 & 6 \\ 0 & 15 \end{bmatrix}$$

The more complicated type of matrix multiplication involves multiplying two matrices together. Unlike other types of multiplication in math, order matters when you multiply matrices; i.e., matrix A × matrix B won't typically equal matrix B × matrix A. You can only multiply matrices when the first matrix has the same number of columns as the second matrix has rows. The product matrix will have the same number of rows as the first matrix and the same number of columns as the second matrix.

To illustrate:

$$\begin{bmatrix} - & - \\ - & - \\ - & - \end{bmatrix} \times \begin{bmatrix} - & - & - \\ - & - & - \end{bmatrix} = \begin{bmatrix} - & - & - \\ - & - & - \\ - & - & - \end{bmatrix}, \text{ but } \begin{bmatrix} - & - & - \\ - & - & - \end{bmatrix} \times \begin{bmatrix} - & - \\ - & - \\ - & - \end{bmatrix} = \begin{bmatrix} - & - \\ - & - \end{bmatrix}$$

Now, to determine what goes into the product matrix, you will need to follow some rules. The first row, first column position of the product matrix is the *dot product* of the first row of the first matrix and the first column of the second matrix. The dot product is the sum of the products of the row and column matched by position:

$$\begin{bmatrix} a & b & c \\ - & - & - \end{bmatrix} \times \begin{bmatrix} u & - \\ w & - \\ y & - \end{bmatrix} = \begin{bmatrix} (au + bw + cy) & - \\ - & - \end{bmatrix}$$

In other words, the first element in the row of the first matrix is multiplied by the first element in the column of the second matrix, the second element by the second, and the third by the third. Then you add them up, and that goes into the first row, first column of the product matrix.

The easy way to remember where each dot product ends up in your product matrix is that the **first row, first column** of your product is the **first row** of the first matrix multiplied by the **first column** of your second matrix. The **first row, second column** of the product will be the **first row** of the first times the **second column** of the second, and so on:

$$\begin{bmatrix} a & b & c \\ d & e & f \end{bmatrix} \times \begin{bmatrix} u & v \\ w & x \\ y & z \end{bmatrix} = \begin{bmatrix} (au + bw + cy) & (av + bx + cz) \\ (du + ew + fy) & (dv + ex + fz) \end{bmatrix}$$

Let's see how this works out in a real question.

$$50. \begin{bmatrix} 2 & -1 \\ 0 & x \end{bmatrix} \begin{bmatrix} 3 & y & 0 \\ x & 2 & -2 \end{bmatrix} =$$

(A) $\begin{bmatrix} 6-x & 2y-2 & 2 \\ x^2 & 2x & -2x \end{bmatrix}$

(B) $\begin{bmatrix} 6-x & x^2 \\ 2y-2 & 2x \\ 2 & -2x \end{bmatrix}$

(C) $\begin{bmatrix} x^2 & 2x & -2x \\ 6-x & 2y-2 & 2 \end{bmatrix}$

(D) $\begin{bmatrix} 6-x & 2y-2 & 2 \\ x^2 & 2x & -2x \\ 3x & 2y & 0 \end{bmatrix}$

(E) $\begin{bmatrix} 6 & -y \\ 0 & -2x \end{bmatrix}$

Here's How to Crack It

There's a lot going on in this problem, so using Process of Elimination will be the key to working this problem efficiently. First, the product matrix must have the same number of rows as the first matrix. The first matrix has two rows; eliminate (B) and (D). The product matrix must have the same number of columns as the second matrix. The second matrix has three columns; eliminate (E).

The last two choices are the right size. Note, however, that the first row, first column of (A) and (C) are different, so you only need to figure out that first position to finish the problem. The first row, first column will be the dot product of the first row of the first matrix times the first column of the second matrix: (2 • 3) + (–1 • x) = 6 – x. Choice (A) has 6 – x in the first row, first column, so it's your answer.

You could also Plug In for x and y on this problem and use your calculator. Look at the next section to learn how to multiply matrices the easy way!

Matrices and Your Calculator

Many calculators can do operations on matrices. The first step for any matrix question will be to input the matrices in your calculator. On the TI-84, press 2ND-> x^{-1} to access the MATRIX menu. The first submenu is titled NAMES; however, you need to start under the EDIT submenu.

The EDIT submenu looks identical to the NAMES submenu, but here you can, well, edit the matrices. To edit a matrix, first input the size of the matrix (rows by columns). Press ENTER after you finish inputting the size of the matrix. Use ENTER to move on to the next position after inputting the value. Use the QUIT function to leave this menu after you are finished.

To multiply matrices, simply enter both matrices in the EDIT submenu, select the first matrix under NAMES, use the normal multiplication key, select the second matrix, and press ENTER. Your calculator will do all the hard work of determining dot products for you.

DRILL 10: MATRICES

Try this sample problem. The answers can be found in Part IV.

30. If matrix X has dimension 3×2, matrix Y has dimension 2×5, and $XY = Z$, then matrix Z must have dimension

    (A) 2×2
    (B) 2×5
    (C) 3×2
    (D) 3×5
    (E) 6×10

Comprehensive Miscellaneous Drill

The answers can be found in Part IV.

2	0 0 0 1 2
3	1 2
4	
5	2 3 9
6	1 8
7	2 9

6. What is the median of the set of data shown in the stem-and-leaf plot above?

(A) 20
(B) 32
(C) 42
(D) 44
(E) 52

"If you complete the marathon in under 5 hours, then you must have prepared adequately for the marathon."

15. If the statement above is true, then which of the following MUST be true?

(A) If you did not prepare adequately for the marathon, then you will not complete the marathon in under 5 hours.
(B) If you do not complete the marathon in under 5 hours, then you did not prepare adequately for the marathon.
(C) If you prepare adequately for the marathon, then you will complete the marathon in under 5 hours.
(D) Proper preparation and planning prevents poor marathon performance.
(E) If you fail to complete the marathon, then it is proven that you did not prepare at all for the marathon.

18. If $\log_x 256 = 8$, then $x =$

(A) 2
(B) 10
(C) 16
(D) 32
(E) 64

Questions 25 and 26 refer to the table below.

Weekly Salaries of Employees of Jazzstar, Inc.

■ Weekly Salaries of Employees of Jazzstar, Inc.

25. Approximately what percent of employees at Jazzstar Inc. have a weekly salary of more than $800 ?

(A) 23%
(B) 35%
(C) 40%
(D) 45%
(E) 60%

26. What is the median weekly salary at Jazzstar Inc.?

(A) $650
(B) $700
(C) $750
(D) $800
(E) $850

34. A standard piece of A4 paper is a rectangle with dimensions 210 by 297 mm. Sandra makes an open-topped box by cutting four squares, each with side length 10 mm, from each of the four corners of the piece of paper and folding up the sides. What is the volume of the resulting open-topped box?

(A) 52,630 mm^3
(B) 62,370 mm^3
(C) 526,300 mm^3
(D) 574,000 mm^3
(E) 623,700 mm^3

35. Nathalie's collection of nail polish consists of 4 bottles of blue nail polish, 7 bottles of green nail polish, 5 bottles of mauve nail polish, and 10 bottles of red nail polish. If Nathalie were to select 2 bottles of nail polish, one at a time and without replacement, at random from her collection, what is the probability that she selects a bottle of mauve nail polish followed by a bottle of blue nail polish?

(A) $\dfrac{5}{169}$

(B) $\dfrac{2}{65}$

(C) $\dfrac{4}{25}$

(D) $\dfrac{5}{26}$

(E) $\dfrac{9}{26}$

38. If the fourth term of an arithmetic sequence is 22, and the sixth term of the same sequence is 32, then what is the sum of the seventh through seventy-seventh terms of the sequence, inclusive?

(A) 37
(B) 387
(C) 14,840
(D) 14,555
(E) 15,052

42. A high school class of 55 students goes to the Magical SAT Wonderland amusement park. All 55 students ride the Sine Wave Spectacular, the Matrix Mixer, or both. If 37 students ride the Sine Wave Spectacular and 23 students ride both the Sine Wave Spectacular and the Matrix Mixer, then how many students ride the Matrix Mixer but NOT the Sine Wave Spectacular?

(A) 14
(B) 18
(C) 32
(D) 41
(E) 64

47. Karl is deciding how to staff his factory for a project. The project will require 3 machinists and 4 laborers. If Karl has 7 machinists and 6 laborers available to work on the project, then how many possible groups of machinists and laborers are available for the project?

(A) 40
(B) 504
(C) 525
(D) 570
(E) 75,600

50. If $\begin{bmatrix} x & y \\ 0 & z \end{bmatrix} \times \begin{bmatrix} 1 & 0 \\ 1 & 0 \end{bmatrix} = \begin{bmatrix} 0 & 0 \\ 0 & 0 \end{bmatrix}$, then which of the following MUST be true?

(A) $x = 0$
(B) $y = 0$
(C) $x = y$
(D) $x = -y$
(E) $xyz \neq 0$

Summary

o Statistics is about working with large groups of numbers and looking for patterns and trends in those numbers.
  - The mean is the average value of a set.
  - The median is the middle value of a set when the values of the set are in chronological order.
  - The mode is the value that occurs the most in a set.

o Range is the positive difference between the least and greatest values in a set. You can think of range as the distance between the least and greatest values on the number line.

o Probability is the number of ways to get what you want divided by the total number of possible outcomes.

o The probability of multiple events occurring can be calculated either by writing them all out or by multiplying the individual probabilities together.

o Permutations and combinations are somewhat rare on the SAT Subject Test in Math 1, but the concepts are fairly straightforward
  - A permutation is the number of ways you can arrange objects in a definitive order. Make spaces for each object you're arranging, fill in the number of options for each space, then multiply.
  - A combination is the number of ways you can group the objects. Order doesn't matter. Start by finding the permutation as stated above, then divide by the factorial of the number of spaces.

o Group questions require one formula: Total = Group 1 + Group 2 + Neither − Both.

o A logarithm is just another way to express exponents. Go from logarithms to exponents by using $\log_b n = x \Leftrightarrow b^x = n$.

o Visual Perception problems are about reading carefully, drawing what ETS is telling you, and using Ballparking and POE.

o   There are a few things you need to know for arithmetic sequences:
    •   An arithmetic sequences is created by adding a number to the previous term in the sequence.
    •   The nth term of an arithmetic sequence can be found using the formula $a_n = a_1 + (n - 1)d$, where d is the constant difference between terms.
    •   The sum of the first n terms of a sequence can be found with the formula $n\left(\dfrac{a_1 + a_n}{2}\right)$.

o   The main thing you need to know for logic questions is the contrapositive. If the initial statement is "If A then B," then the contrapositive is "If not B then not A." The contrapositive is *always* true if the initial statement is true.

o   The definition of i is $\sqrt{-1}$. There are two ways ETS may test imaginary numbers:
    •   The powers of i follow a repeating pattern: $i^1 = i$, $i^2 = -1$, $i^3 = -i$, and $i^4 = 1$. To find the value of i to an exponent greater than 4, divide the exponent by 4 and use the remainder as the exponent for i.
    •   You may need to multiply complex numbers or algebraic expressions with i. Remember to FOIL and simplify i in the last step, or Plug In if necessary and use your calculator.

o   Matrix problems are rare on this test. There are a couple of things to keep in mind. If you're intent on tackling these problems, learn the rules for matrix multiplication or learn how to make your calculator do the work for you!

Part IV
Drills: Answers
and Explanations

CHAPTER 5: ARITHMETIC DRILL EXPLANATIONS

Drill 1: Prime Factors, p. 71

1. $64 = 2 \times 2 \times 2 \times 2 \times 2 \times 2$

2. $70 = 2 \times 5 \times 7$

3. $18 = 2 \times 3 \times 3$

4. $98 = 2 \times 7 \times 7$

5. $68 = 2 \times 2 \times 17$

6. $51 = 3 \times 17$

Drill 2: Factors, p. 72

3. **B** 21 can also be written as 3×7, and 18 as $2 \times 3 \times 3$. The smallest number that contains both is $2 \times 3 \times 3 \times 7$, or 126.

7. **E** 53 is a prime number; its largest prime factor is 53. None of the other answers contains so large a prime factor. Choice (A) is (2)(5)(17), so its greatest prime factor is 17. Choice (B) is (3)(3)(13), so its greatest prime factor is 13. Choice (C) is (2)(2)(2)(11), so its greatest prime factor is 11. Choice (D) is (2)(31), so its greatest prime factor is 31.

9. **C** The smallest integer divisible by 10 and 32 is 160, and the smallest integer divisible by 6 and 20 is 60. The difference between them is 100. Remember to factor each time, as shown in question 3.

Drill 3: Positive and Negative Numbers, p. 74

15. **A** Start with I. You know from the rules that an odd number times an odd number is an odd number. So I has to be true. Use POE to eliminate (B). Now let's skip down to III for a moment. You know from I that odd times odd equals odd. You also know that odd plus odd is even. And an even times an even is even. So III will be an even number. Since III isn't true, eliminate (D) and (E). Look at II. Remember that the question asks which of the following *must* be an odd *integer*. Since an odd integer divided by an odd integer isn't always an integer, you can eliminate (C). If you ever forget a rule, you can always try a couple of numbers.

18. **D** The statement $cd < 0$ means that one of the numbers is positive and one negative; that's the only way to get a negative product. Try your own numbers to eliminate answer choices. If you try $c = 1$ and $d = -3$, only (A) and (D) are true. Switch them and try $c = -3$ and $d = 1$, and only (D) remains true.

20.   **C**   Use your rules. Choice (A) would be an even times an odd, which is even. Choice (B) would be an odd times an even (even result), plus an even, squared, which would remain even. Choice (C) would be even minus one, which results in an odd number. Choice (D) would be an odd plus an even, which is odd, and (E) would be an odd divided by an even, which may not be an integer. So you're down to (C) and (D). Since y is negative, it is possible that (D) would yield a negative number. The answer must be (C). Again, you can always try out sample numbers to prove the rules.

Drill 4: PEMDAS and Your Calculator, p. 76

1.   5

2.   35

3.   12

4.   35

5.   0

Drill 5: Word Problems and Translation, p. 79

1. $6.5 = \dfrac{x}{100} \cdot 260 \, ; \, x = 2.5$

2. $20 = \dfrac{n}{100} \cdot 180 \, ; \, n = 11$

3. $\dfrac{30}{100} \cdot \dfrac{40}{100} \cdot 25 = x \, ; \, x = 3$

4. $x = \sqrt{\dfrac{1}{3} \cdot 48} \, ; \, x = 4$

5. $\sqrt{y} = \dfrac{1}{8} \cdot y \, ; \, y = \dfrac{1}{64} y^2 \, ; \dfrac{1}{y} = \dfrac{1}{64} \, ; y = 64$

Drill 6: Percent Change, p. 80

2.   **B**   You already know that the difference is going to be 25. Set up your formula: $\dfrac{25}{150} \cdot 100 = 16.67$. Thus, adding 25 gallons to 150 gallons is a 16.67% increase.

5.   **B**   The decrease from 5 to 4 is a 20% decrease, and the increase from 4 to 5 is a 25% increase. The difference is 5%.

12.   **C**   Using the formula $12 = (150 \div x)100$, you get $x = 1,250$, so 1,250 must have been the original amount. $1,250 + 150 = 1,400$. Be careful to read "after the deposit" in the question.

Drill 7: Repeated Percent Change, p. 85

35.   **D**   Using the formula, you get $1,000(1.05^{12}) = 1,795.856$.

43.   **C**   This question is a little trickier. For each annual decrease of 4%, you must multiply by 0.96. The easiest way to solve the question is to start with 2,000 and keep multiplying until the result is less than 1,000—just count the number of decreases it takes. The seventeenth annual decrease makes it less than 1,000, so the sixteenth is the last one that is not less than 1,000—and 1995 + 16 = 2011. You can also use logs (see Chapter 12).

Drill 8: Averages, p. 86

1.   There were 9 people at dinner.

2.   All told, 4,500 apples were picked.

3.   The average height of a chess club member is 5.5 feet.

Drill 9: Multiple Average Questions, p. 89

33.   **D**   Nineteen donations averaging $485 total $9,215. Twenty donations averaging $500 total $10,000. The difference is $785.

35.   **A**   The *Tribune* received 80 letters in the first 20 days and 70 for the last 10 days. That's a total of 150 in 30 days, or $150 \div 30 = 5$ letters per day on average.

36.   **A**   One day in five out of a year is 73 days. At 12 a day, that's 876 umbrellas sold on rainy days. The rest of the year (292 days) is clear. At 3 umbrellas a day, that's another 876 umbrellas. A total of 1,752 umbrellas in 365 days makes a daily average of 4.8 umbrellas.

Drill 10: Exponents, p. 95

1. $b = 3$ (1 root)

2. $x = 11, -11$ (2 roots)

3. $n = 2$ (1 root)

4. $c = \sqrt{10}, -\sqrt{10}$ (2 roots)

5. $x = 3, -3$ (2 roots)

6. $x = -2$ (1 root)

7. $d = 3, -3$ (2 roots)

8. n = any real number; everything to the 0 power is 1.

9. **C** Remember that the top is the exponent and the bottom is the root. So in your calculator, put in 4^(3/2). This is the same as cubing 4 and then taking the square root of your result (or taking the square root of 4 and then cubing that result). Any way you slice it, the answer is 8.

10. **D** Remember your rules. A negative exponent means flip it. And a fractional exponent means the top is the exponent and the bottom is the root. You may have ended up with $\dfrac{1}{\left(\sqrt[4]{x}\right)^3}$, which isn't wrong. It just happens to not be in the answers. The only correct answer is $\dfrac{1}{\left(\sqrt[4]{x^3}\right)}$.

11. **A** Flip and square it: $\left(\dfrac{3}{2}\right)^2 = 2.25$. Don't forget your parentheses in your calculator.

12. **E** Flip and take the third root.

13. **A** In your calculator it goes, either as is (with parentheses) or if you need to take more steps, just remember that the numerator is the exponent and the denominator is the root. Or notice that $\sqrt[3]{25}$ must be less than $\sqrt{25}$ and use POE.

14. **D** What's anything raised to the zero power? That's right, 1.

Comprehensive Arithmetic Drill, p. 97

6. **D** First, simplify the expression $3(5x)^2$ to be $3(25x^2)$. From this, the value of 16 can be plugged in for the term $25x^2$—as given by the first equation—to get $3(16)$, or 48. Thus, (D) is the correct answer. If your first instinct was to solve for x in the first equation, that is also possible. Divide both sides of the first equation by 25 to get $x^2 = \dfrac{16}{25}$. Then, take the square root to of both sides to get $x = 0.8$. Plug $x = 0.8$ into the second equation to solve the expression.

$$3(5 \times 0.8)^2 = 48$$

9. **E** "Multiples" are a given number that is multiplied by other positive integers, so the least common multiple of 180 and 210 would be bigger than 180. Eliminate (A), which is a factor or divisor of both given numbers. The easiest way to approach the question from here is to Plug In the Answers. Check each one to see if it is divisible by both 180 and 210. Only (E) is, so it is the correct answer. You could also list multiples of both numbers until you found a common multiple, which would be time consuming.

11. **C** The original price of the television is discounted by 25%, which is $125, so the new price is $375. The new price of the television is raised by 25% of $375, which is $93.75, so the final price of the television is $468.75.

15. **A** Use the percent change formula to calculate the percent decrease in tickets from 2010 to 2011.

Percent Change $= \dfrac{difference}{original} \times 100\%$. The difference from 2010 to 2011 was 281 tickets per game, so Percent Change $= \dfrac{281}{3,215} \times 100\%$. Therefore, the percent decrease from 2010 to 2011 is 8.7%.

18. **B** $3^5 \cdot 4^5$ can be simplified to $(3 \cdot 4)^5$, which is 12^5, so $n = 5$.

20. **C** Remember the rules of exponents (MADSPM) when dealing with negative exponents. For this question, because there are exponents in both the numerator and denominator, you must subtract the exponents since you are dividing the bases. Therefore, for the exponent for x, you get $6 - (-2) = 8$. Eliminate (A) and (B). For the exponent for y, $-3 - 4 = -7$, which is equivalent to y^7 in the denominator. Eliminate (D). Finally, for the exponent for z, $5 - 5 = 0$, and any term that has an exponent of zero is always equal to 1. Therefore, eliminate (D), and the correct answer is (C).

21. **D** Use the Average Pie to determine the number of houses Steven sold in 5 months. If Steven sold an average of 3 houses per month, then he sold 15 total houses in the first 5 months. If Steven needs to sell 39 houses total, he must sell 24 houses over the next 7 months to get his promotion. Use another Average Pie to calculate the average number of houses Steven must sell per month for the remainder of the year to earn his promotion. 24 houses ÷ 7 months = 3.4 houses per month.

30. **C** Use the Average Pie to calculate the total money donated by the 9 students: 9 × $12 = $108. Then, use another Average Pie to calculate the total amount donated by the 5 students: 5 × $16 = $80. Subtract $80 from $108 dollars to calculate the total amount donated by the remaining 4 students, which is $28. Now, use another Average Pie to calculate the average donation for the 4 remaining students: $28 ÷ 4 = $7.

33. **B** Translate the English phrase to the math equivalents to get $\dfrac{1}{6} = \dfrac{1}{2} \cdot \dfrac{3}{4}x$. Simplify the right side of the equation.

$$\dfrac{1}{6} = \dfrac{3}{8}x$$

Multiply both sides of the equation by $\dfrac{8}{3}$.

$$\dfrac{8}{18} = x$$

Reduce the fraction to get $x = \dfrac{4}{9}$.

41. **D** Use the repeated percent-increase formula to solve for the total population after 12 years. Final Amount = Original × (1 + Rate)$^{number\ of\ changes}$. Final Amount = $4,225 \times (1 + 0.0225)^{12}$. Therefore, the population is 5,518 at the end of 2018.

49.   C   If the solution must be 24% acid, then it will contain 76% water. Since the volume of water equals 4 liters, calculate the total volume of the solution using the expression $\frac{76}{100} \cdot x = 4$. Solve the equation to get $x = 5.26$. 5.26 liters is the total volume, so subtract the volume of water (4 liters) to get 1.26 liters of acid.

CHAPTER 6: ALGEBRA DRILL EXPLANATIONS

Drill 1: Solving Equations, p. 104

1. $x = \{5, -5\}$

If you're having trouble, think of peeling away the layers of the left side until you get to just x. So you're going to multiply by 17, then add 7, then divide by 3, then take the square root of both sides. Remember that when you take the square root of both sides, you'll end up with two answers: positive and negative.

2. $n = \{0, 5\}$

This is tricky. You most likely found that the answer is 5. Remember that you can divide both sides by n only if n isn't 0. So you also have to consider that n could be 0. In this case, it can.

3. $a = 0.75$

Peel away those layers.

4. $s = 12$

Keep peeling.

5. $x = 0.875$

Make sure you didn't cancel the 5's. You can cancel only when numbers are being multiplied or divided, not added or subtracted. Did you get $\frac{7}{8}$? Same thing!

6. $m = 9$ or $m = -14$

Because the left side of the equation is inside absolute value signs, you know it can be either positive or negative. So set up two equations! In the first equation, set $2m + 5$ equal to 23. In the second equation, set $2m + 5$ equal to -23. Then solve each equation for m. These are your two possible values for m.

7. $r = 27$ or $r = -13$

Set this problem up just like question 6. The value inside the absolute value signs can be either positive or negative, so write an equation for each scenario. Solve each equation to come up with the two possible values for r.

Drill 2: Factoring and Distributing, p. 106

3.   **D**   This equation can be rearranged to look like: $50x(11 + 29) = 4,000$. This is done simply by factoring out 50 and x. Once you've done that, you can add 11 and 29 to produce $50x(40) = 2,000x = 4,000$. Therefore, $x = 2$.

17.   **E**   Here, distributing makes your math easier. Distributing $-3b$ into the expression $(a + 2)$ on top of the fraction gives you $\dfrac{-3ab - 6b + 6b}{-ab}$, which simplifies to $\dfrac{-3ab}{-ab}$, which equals 3.

36.   **B**   The trap in this question is to try to cancel similar terms on the top and bottom—but that's not possible, because these terms are being added together, and you can cancel only in multiplication. Instead, factor out x^2 on top of the fraction. That gives you $\dfrac{x^2 \left(x^3 + x^2 + x + 1 \right)}{x^3 + x^2 + x + 1}$. The whole mess in parentheses cancels out (now that it's being multiplied), and the answer is x^2.

Drill 3: Plugging In, p. 112

5.   **E**   Plug in $p = 20$, $t = 10$, and $n = 3$. That's 3 items for $20.00 each with 10% tax. Each item would then cost $22.00, and three would cost $66.00. Only (E) equals $66.00.

8.   **C**   Plug in $x = 5$, $a = 2$, and $b = 3$. That means Vehicle A travels at 5 mph for 5 hours, or 25 miles. Vehicle B travels at 7 mph for 8 hours, or 56 miles. That's a difference of 31 miles. Only (C) equals 31.

17.   **C**   Plug in $n = 3$, then $5 - 3 = 2$ and $3 - 5 = -2$. These numbers have the same absolute value, so the difference between them is zero.

20.   **B**   Plug in $a = 10$, $b = 1$, and $m = 4$. That means that Company A builds 10 skateboards a week and 40 skateboards in 4 weeks. Company B builds 7 skateboards in a week (1 per day), or 28 in 4 weeks. That's a difference of 12 between the two companies. Only (B) equals 12 when you plug in $a = 10$, $b = 1$, and $m = 4$.

23. **E** Plug in $a = 4$ and $b = 2$. Okay, all three fail. Try some different-sized numbers like $a = 10$ and $b = 2$. Now I works; eliminate (B) and (D). Try to make $a + b$ small; plug in $a = 4$ and $b = -4$. Now II and III work; eliminate (A) and (C).

30. **A** Plug in $x = 2$ and $y = 3$. Oh well—they all work! Try $x = -3$ and $y = -2$. Now II fails; eliminate (C), (D), and (E). III also fails; eliminate (B).

Drill 4: Plugging In The Answers (PITA), p. 116

11. **D** The answer choices represent Michael's hats. Start with (C): If Michael has 12 hats, then Matt has 6 hats and Aaron has 2. That adds up to 20, not 24—you need more hats, so move on to the next bigger answer, (D). Michael now has 14 hats, meaning Matt has 7 and Aaron has 3. That adds up to 24, so you're done.

17. **D** There's a little shortcut you can take if you remember the Average Pie. Since the total is 3,200 and you have two parts, you know that the average will be 1,600. This means that the difference will be 800. Work through the answer choices, starting with (C). A ratio of 2:5 has 7 parts. Divide 3,200 by 7. Each part would be 457.14—it doesn't work out with whole numbers, so it can't be right. Then move on to (D); a ratio of 3:5 has 8 parts, each of which would be 400. That means the shipment is divided into shares of 1,200 and 2,000. Their difference is 800, and their average is 1,600, which is what you're looking for!

27. **D** Start with (C); if the largest of the three integers is 5, then the total of the other two integers would have to be $15 - 5$, or 10. No two numbers less than 5 have a sum of 10, so eliminate (A), (B), and (C). If you plug in (D), 9 is the largest number. For the product of all three integers to be 45, the product of the other two integers must be 5. So these two integers can only be 5 and 1. Now find the sum of all three numbers: $9 + 5 + 1 = 15$, so (D) is the correct answer.

Drill 5: Inequalities, p. 117

1. $n \geq 3$

2. $r < 7$

3. $x \geq -\dfrac{1}{2}$

4. $x < \dfrac{1}{8}$

5. $t \leq 3$

6. $n \leq 4$

7. $p > \dfrac{1}{5}$

8. $s \geq 1$

9. $x \geq -7$

10. $s \geq \dfrac{2}{5}$

Drill 6: Working with Ranges, p. 118

1. $-8 < -x < 5$

2. $-20 < 4x < 32$

3. $1 < (x + 6) < 14$

4. $7 > (2 - x) > -6$

5. $-2.5 < \dfrac{x}{2} < 4$

Drill 7: More Working with Ranges, p. 120

1. $-4 \leq b - a \leq 11$

2. $-2 \leq x + y \leq 17$

3. $0 \leq n^2 \leq 64$

4. $3 < x - y < 14$

5. $-13 \leq r + s \leq 13$

6. $-126 < cd < 0$

7. $-1 \leq x \leq 7$ Because the absolute value is less than 4, whatever's inside the absolute value must be between −4 and 4. Therefore, $-4 \leq 3 - x \leq 4$. Start solving this by subtracting 3 from all three sides: $-7 \leq -x \leq 1$. Then divide through by −1 (remember to flip the direction of the inequality signs because you're dividing by a negative number): $7 \geq x \geq -1$.

8. $a \leq -10$ or $a \geq 3$ Because the absolute value is greater than 13, the stuff inside the absolute value must be either less than −13 or greater than 13. Therefore, you have two inequalities: $2a + 7 \leq -13$ or $2a + 7 \geq 13$. Solve each inequality separately.

Drill 8: Direct and Inverse Variation, p. 123

15. **C** There are variables in the answers, so Plug In! Quantities in inverse variation always have the same product. That means that $ab = 3 \cdot 5$, or 15, always. Plug in a number for x, such as 10. Now set up your proportion: $3 \cdot 5 = a \cdot 10$. So $10a = 15$, and $a = 2.5$. Plug $x = 10$ into the answers and find the answer choice that gives you 2.5. Only (C) does.

18. **D** Remember your formulas. Direct means divide. Quantities in direct variation always have the same proportion. In this case, that means that $\dfrac{n}{m} = \dfrac{5}{4}$. When $m = 5$, solve the equation $\dfrac{5}{4} = \dfrac{n}{5}$. Multiply both sides by 5 and you'll find that $n = 6.25$.

24. **A** Direct variation means the proportion is constant, so that $\dfrac{p}{q} = \dfrac{3}{10}$. To find the value of p when $q = 1$, solve the equation $\dfrac{3}{10} = \dfrac{p}{1}$; p must be 0.3.

26. **B** Remember that direct means divide. Set up your proportion: $\dfrac{24}{3.7^2} = \dfrac{y}{8.3^2}$. If you simplify this, you get 120.77, which is (B). Be careful. If you answered (E), you forgot that the direct variation was between y and x^2, not y and x.

Drill 9: Work and Travel Questions, p. 124

11. **C** The important thing to remember here is that when two things or people work together, their work rates are added up. Pump 1 can fill 12 tanks in 12 hours, and Pump 2 can fill 11 tanks in 12 hours. That means that together, they could fill 23 tanks in 12 hours. To find the work they would do in 1 hour, just divide 23 by 12. You get 1.91666....

12. **A** To translate feet per second to miles per hour, take it one step at a time. First, find the feet per hour by multiplying 227 feet per second by the number of seconds in an hour (3,600). You find that the projectile travels at a speed of 817,200 feet per hour. Then divide by 5,280 to find out how many miles that is. You get 154.772.

18. **B** The train travels a total of 400 miles (round-trip) in 5.5 hours. Now that you know distance and time, plug them into the formula and solve to find the rate: $400 = r \times 5.5$, so $r = 72.73$.

25. **D** Plug In! Say Jules can make 3 muffins in 5 minutes ($m = 3$, $s = 5$). Say Alice can make 4 muffins in 6 minutes ($n = 4$, $t = 6$). That means that Jules can make 18 muffins in 30 minutes, and Alice can make 20 muffins in 30 minutes. Together, they make 38 muffins in 30 minutes. That's your target number. Take the numbers you plugged in to the answers and find the one that gives you 38. Choice (D) does the trick.

Drill 10: Average Speed, p. 126

19. **D**   Find the total distance and total time. The round-trip distance is 12 miles. It takes $\frac{1}{2}$ hour to jog 6 miles at 12 mph, and $\frac{2}{3}$ hour to jog back at 9 mph, for a total of $1\frac{1}{6}$ hours. Do the division, and you get 10.2857 mph.

24. **D**   This one is easier than it looks. Fifty miles in 50 minutes is a mile a minute, or 60 mph. Forty miles in 40 minutes is also 60 mph. The whole trip is made at one speed, 60 mph.

33. **B**   Plug in an easy number for the unknown distance, like 50 miles. It takes 2 hours to travel 50 miles at 25 mph, and 1 hour to return across 50 miles at 50 mph. That's a total distance of 100 miles in 3 hours, for an average speed of $33\frac{1}{3}$ mph. Choices (A) and (E) are trap answers.

Drill 11: Simultaneous Equations, p. 130

26. **C**   Here, you want to make all of the b terms cancel out. Add the two equations, and you get $5a = 20$, so $a = 4$.

31. **D**   Here, you need to get x and y terms with the same coefficient. If you subtract the second equation from the first, you get $10x - 10y = 10$, so $x - y = 1$.

34. **D**   The question is solvable as the example on the previous page was, by multiplication. Multiplying all three equations together gives you $a^2b^2c^2 = 2.25$. Don't pick (B)! Take the positive square root of both sides, and you get $abc = 1.5$.

37. **E**   Here, you need to get rid of the z term and cancel out a y. The way to do it is to divide the first equation by the second one, $\frac{xyz}{y^2z} = \frac{4}{5}$. The z and a y cancel out, and you're left with $\frac{x}{y} = \frac{4}{5}$, or 0.8. Even though there are more variables than equations, ETS questions almost always have a trick to let you solve them the easy way.

Drill 12: FOIL, p. 132

1. $x^2 + 9x - 22$

2. $b^2 + 12b + 35$

3. $x^2 - 12x + 27$

4. $2x^2 - 3x - 5$

5. $n^3 - 3n^2 + 5n - 15$

6. $6a^2 - 11a - 35$

7. $x^2 - 9x + 18$

8. $c^2 + 7c - 18$

9. $d^2 + 4d - 5$

Drill 13: Factoring Quadratics, p. 133

1. $a = \{1, 2\}$ Factor to $(a - 1)(a - 2) = 0$.

2. $d = \{-7, -1\}$ Factor to $(d + 7)(d + 1) = 0$.

3. $x = \{-7, 3\}$ Factor to $(x + 7)(x - 3) = 0$.

4. $x = \{-5, 2\}$ Factor to $3(x^2 + 3x - 10) = 3(x + 5)(x - 2) = 0$.

5. $x = \{-11, -9\}$ Factor to $2(x^2 + 20x + 99) = 2(x + 11)(x + 9) = 0$.

6. $p = \{-13, 3\}$ Factor to $(p + 13)(p - 3) = 0$. Subtract 39 from both sides first.

7. $c = \{-5, -4\}$ Factor to $(c + 5)(c + 4) = 0$.

8. $s = \{-6, 2\}$ Factor to $(s + 6)(s - 2) = 0$.

9. $x = \{-1, 4\}$ Factor to $(x + 1)(x - 4) = 0$.

10.   Factor the expression $(n^2 - 5)(n^2 + 2) = 0$. So $n^2 = 5$ or -2. But n^2 is never negative, so $n = \pm\sqrt{5}$.

Drill 14: Special Quadratic Identities, p. 135

17. **A**   Remember that $n^2 - m^2 = (n - m)(n + m)$. So fill in what you know and solve for what you don't: $24 = (-3)(n + m)$. You don't need to find each variable individually.

19. **B**   Remember that $(x + y)^2 = x^2 + 2xy + y^2$. Again you have all the parts except for what the question is asking for: $3^2 = 8 + 2xy$. So $2xy = 1$ and $xy = 0.5$.

24. **D**   Translate into math. You know that $x + y = 9$ and $x^2 + y^2 = 36$. It's asking for xy. The pieces that the question gives you relate to $(x + y)^2 = x^2 + 2xy + y^2$. So, $9^2 = 36 + 2xy$; $2xy = 45$; and $xy = 22.5$. Notice that (E) is a partial answer.

Drill 15: The Quadratic Formula, p. 137

1.   2 distinct real roots; $x = \{0.81, 6.19\}$

2.   no real roots (2 imaginary roots)

3.   2 distinct real roots; $s = \{0.76, 5.24\}$

4.   2 distinct real roots; $x = \{-1.41, 1.41\}$

5..   1 real root; $n = -2.5$ (2 identical real roots, that is, a "double root")

Comprehensive Algebra Drill, p. 138

3.   **C** $x^2 - y^2$ represents a special quadratic identity and is equivalent to $(x + y)(x - y)$. Therefore, $(4)(2) = 8$.

9.   **D**   Plug In the Answers for x to see which gives 63 as a result. Start with (C). If $x = 1.78$, then $(x + 4)^2 = 33.41$ which is too small; eliminate (A), (B), and (C). Try (D) next. Choice (D) works, so it is the correct answer.

15. **D**   Plug In the Answers to solve for x. When $x = -7$ and $x = -3$, the expression equals 2, so those values of x must the limits of the range of values that work for x. Eliminate answers that don't include both numbers: (B), (C), and (E). To determine if you want values in between -3 and -7, or outside that range on the number line, plug in a value; try $x = 0$. This makes the statement false, so 0 can't be included in the answer. Eliminate (A) and choose (D).

19. **E**   Stack and add the equations to get $3a + 2b + c = 18$.

20. **D**   The expression is undefined when the denominator, in this case $(4x - 2)$, is equal to 0. $4x - 2 = 0$ when $x = \dfrac{1}{2}$, so (D) is the correct response.

23. **C**   When you see variables in the answer choices, Plug In. If $x = 2$, then $(2^{3x})(8^{2x}) = 262{,}144$. Plug in 2 for x in the answer choices. Choice (C) is the correct answer because it is the only one that equals 262,144.

24. **C**   Use the Average Pie to solve for the time it took the train to make the trip. Divide 500 miles by 60 miles per hour. It took the train 8.33 hours to make the trip. If the train decreased its average speed by 25%, the average speed would be 45 miles per hour. Using the Average Pie again, calculate the new amount of time the trip would take. The same trip would now take 11.11 hours, which is approximately 2.78 (or $2\dfrac{3}{4}$) hours longer than the original trip.

25. **C**   If y is directly proportional to x^3, then $\dfrac{y_1}{(x_1)^3} = \dfrac{y_2}{(x_2)^3}$. Plug in the given values to get $\dfrac{1.2}{(4)^3} = \dfrac{y_2}{(12)^3}$. Solve the proportion by cross-multiplying to get $y^2 = 32.4$.

27. C Plug in odd integers for j and k and solve for each answer choice to determine if it is an odd integer. If $j = 3$, and $k = 5$, (A), (B), and (D) aren't odd. Choice (E) is not an integer. Choice (C) equals 3,369, which is an odd integer, so (C) is correct.

30. A Factor the expressions to see which gives you roots that add up to 6 and have a product that equals 8. Choice (A) factors to $(x - 4)(x - 2)$, which gives roots of 4 and 2. The sum of 4 and 2 is 6, and the product is 8. Therefore, (A) is the correct answer.

36. C Plug the values given for a and b into the equation to get $d(t) = 10t + \frac{1}{2}4t^2$. Then, use PITA to find the answer choice that most closely approximates 36. Starting with (C), plugging in 2.4 for t gives 35.52 for $d(t)$, so (C) is the closest approximation and the best answer.

CHAPTER 7: PLANE GEOMETRY DRILL EXPLANATIONS

Drill 1: Basic Rules of Lines and Angles, p. 148

1. $x = 50°$; $y = 130°$; $z = 130°$;

    $a = 50°$; $b = 130°$; $c = 50°$

2. $x = 105°$; $y = 75°$

3. $a = 120°$; $b = 60°$; $c = 120°$;

    $d = 60°$; $e = 120°$; $f = 60°$

8. B When parallel lines are crossed by a third line, any small angle plus any big angle equals 180°.

13. E Plug In! Remember that where the line intersects the parallel sides of the rectangle, any small angle plus any big angle is 180°. Try 80° for the smaller angles s and v, and 100° for the larger angles, t and u. The angles r and w must measure 90° each. Once you've plugged in these values, you'll quickly see that only (E) must be equivalent to angle t.

16. E Because there are two parallel lines transected by a third line, the sum of $\angle DBC$ and $\angle BDE$ is 180°. You don't, however, know anything about the *difference* between them. Plugging in various numbers should soon convince you that the difference cannot be determined. Remember: steer away from such enticing or easy-way-out answers as the question numbers get higher.

Drill 2: Third Side Rules, p. 153

12. E The length of the unknown side, *ST*, must be between the sum and difference of the other two lengths—that is, between 3 and 19. Add the sides and that makes the *perimeter* anywhere between 22 and 38. Notice that (A) answers the wrong question.

17. A Since the triangle is isosceles, the unknown side must be either 5 or 11. But a 5-5-11 triangle violates the Third Side Rule—it's not possible. That leaves only 11 as a possible value of the missing side.

18. E This is just another application of the Third Side Rule. The third distance must be between 2 and 10. Only (E) violates the rule.

Drill 3: The Pythagorean Theorem, p. 154

1. $x = \sqrt{89}$, or 9.4334

2. $n = \sqrt{85}$, or 9.2195

3. $a = \sqrt{15}$, or 3.8730

4. $d = \sqrt{50} = 5\sqrt{2}$, or 7.0710

5. $x = 7$

6. $r = \sqrt{145}$, or 12.0416

Drill 4: Area of Triangles, p. 157

9. E Write out the formula for the area of a triangle, using the lengths the question has given: $\frac{1}{2}ab$. You know that the area is 3*b*, so, $\frac{1}{2}ab = 3b$. Now, solve for *a*: $\frac{1}{2}a = 3$ and $a = 6$.

15. A Both triangles have the same height, and if their areas are equal, they must have the same base as well. Since triangle *OAD* has a base of 8, triangle *ABC* must also have a base of 8.

37. B Notice that the area of *ABC* can be computed two different ways; with $\overline{AC}$ as the base or with $\overline{BC}$ as the base. Either way, the base and height must multiply to the same number, because a triangle can have only one area. That means that 12 times $\overline{BE}$ must equal 9 times 10: $12\overline{BE} = 90$, and $\overline{BE} = 7.5$.

38. C If the perimeter of an equilateral triangle is 24, then each side has a length of 8. Plug that into the formula for the area of an equilateral triangle, and you get 27.71.

44. **D** Just set the formula for the area of an equilateral triangle equal to 12, and solve for *s*. You get 5.26. The perimeter is 3*s*, or 15.79. Choice (A) is a trap answer, one that deliberately places numbers in the answer that are meant to remind you of the question, tempting you to choose something familiar.

Drill 5: Pythagorean Triplets, p. 160

1. $x = 9$

2. $d = 26$

3. $n = 0.5$

Drill 6: The 45°-45°-90° Triangle, p. 162

1. $x = 6\sqrt{2}$, or 8.485

2. $n = 1.5\sqrt{2}$, or 2.121

3. $s\sqrt{2} = 7$, so $s = \dfrac{7}{\sqrt{2}}$. This is equivalent to $s = \dfrac{7\sqrt{2}}{2}$, or 4.950.

Drill 7: The 30°-60°-90° Triangle, p. 163

1. $x = 3\sqrt{3}$, or 5.196

2. $n = \dfrac{5}{\sqrt{3}}$, or 2.887

3. $d = 4\sqrt{3}$, or 6.928

Drill 8: Right Triangles, p. 164

7.   **A** With the Pythagorean Theorem, you could compute the missing length of the longest side. There's only one possible perimeter. Notice that you don't even have to know what it is in order to answer the question correctly. Don't waste time computing! (The hypotenuse turns out to be 11.4, in case you're curious.)

13.   **E** You can't use the Pythagorean Theorem unless you know which side of a right triangle is the hypotenuse. Since you don't know whether 8 or the unknown side is the hypotenuse, it's impossible to know the length of the missing side.

16.   C

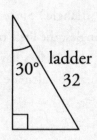

Draw it! You'll find that the floor, wall, and ladder form a 30°-60°-90° triangle. The ladder itself is the hypotenuse, so the hypotenuse is 32. Because the 30° angle is against the wall, the short leg is the ground. So the short leg is 16 and the other leg, or the wall, is $16\sqrt{3}$ or 27.71, which is (C).

19.   B   An isosceles right triangle must be a 45°-45°-90° triangle, with sides x, x, and $x\sqrt{2}$. Since the perimeter equals 23.9, that means $2x + x\sqrt{2} = 23.9$. In order to solve, factor out an x and isolate x. This tells you that $x = 7$, and you can plug this value into the equation for the area of the triangle, or $\frac{1}{2}x^2$. The area of the triangle is 24.5.

Drill 9: Similar Triangles, p. 168

1. $a = 4$; $b = 6.92$; $x = 2$; $y = 1.73$

2. $a = 5$; $s = 15$

3. $c = 11$; $m = 12.25$

37.   A   These triangles are similar because they have identical angles. If one length of triangle ABC is half of a corresponding length of triangle FGH, that means that *all* of the lengths in ABC will be half the corresponding lengths in FGH. The easiest way to solve the problem is by plugging in a base and height for FGH that would yield an area of 0.5; a base of 1 and a height of 1 would be the easiest. Then just plug in the corresponding dimensions of ABC, making sure that they're half of the dimensions in triangle FGH: The base is $\frac{1}{2}$ and the height is $\frac{1}{2}$. The area comes out to $\frac{1}{8}$, or 0.125, which rounds to 0.13.

40.   C   This question is much like question 37, except that you have more freedom to plug in numbers. Once again, the triangles are similar, so you know that they have identical angles. Then just plug in easy numbers. Suppose $AD = 4$; from the problem, $DB = 2$, so $AB = 6$. This shows you that the lengths of the smaller triangle are $\frac{2}{3}$ the lengths of the larger. Suppose $AE = 6$, then $AC = 9$. The area of triangle ADE is then 12, while the area of triangle ABC is 27. $\frac{12}{27}$ reduces to $\frac{4}{9}$.

45.   A   Use the Pythagorean Theorem to complete the dimensions of triangle LMN. It has sides of length 4, $\sqrt{48}$, and 8. If you simplify $\sqrt{48}$, you'll find it's equal to $4\sqrt{3}$. That makes the lengths 4,

$4\sqrt{3}$, and 8, which should look familiar. It's a 30°-60°-90° triangle. (You could still figure it out if you didn't notice that it's a 30°-60°-90° triangle.) Since a right triangle divided by an altitude from its right angle forms three similar triangles, the little triangle *LPN* must also be a 30°-60°-90° triangle. If its hypotenuse has a length of 4, then its legs have lengths of 2 and $2\sqrt{3}$. Those legs are the base and height of triangle *LPN*. Use them to calculate the triangle's area, and you get 3.464.

Drill 10: Quadrilaterals, p. 175

22.   **A**   Use the cool $\dfrac{d^2}{2}$ formula for the area of a square.

34.   **D**   Drawing a height down from *K* gives you a 30°-60°-90° triangle with hypotenuse 6. So the height is $3\sqrt{3}$ or 5.196. Multiplying the base by the height gives you (D). Choice (E) is a trap answer (10 × 6 = 60).

40.   **B**

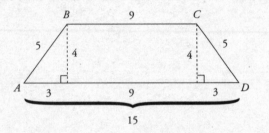

           AD is 9 + 6 = 15. If the perimeter is 34, then *AB* = 5, making this an isosceles trapezoid. If you draw the heights down from *B* and *C*, they will each cut off a right triangle with a base of 3 (half of the 6 you're told about). These are 3-4-5 right triangles, so the height of the trapezoid is 4. Now you can either plug 9, 15, and 4 into the trapezoid area formula, or you can find the sum of the areas of the two right triangles and the rectangle between them. Choice (A) is a trap answer (9 × 5 = 45).

45.   **B**   Each diagonal cuts the rectangle into two 30°-60°-90° triangles, with the diagonal as the hypotenuse. That makes the base and height of the rectangle the x and $x\sqrt{3}$ legs of the triangle. If $x \cdot x\sqrt{3} = 62.35$, then $x = 6.0$, and the hypotenuse of the triangle (2x) has a length of 12.0. The sum of the two diagonals is 24.0.

Drill 11: Circles, p. 181

1. $C = 8\pi; A = 16\pi$

2. $C = 15.85; r = 2.52$ Divide the area (20), which is πr^2, by π and take the square root of the result to solve for r.

3. $A = 5.09; r = 1.27$

Drill 12: More Circles, p. 189

12. **D** Remember that a sector of a circle takes equal portions of angle, circumference, and area. The circle's circumference is 6π or 18.85. Because 4.71 ÷ 18.85 is about 1/4, the sector also takes up one-fourth of 360°, or 90°.

29. **A** Draw a line from B to O to make two shapes. The shaded region is a quarter-circle plus a 45°-45°-90° triangle. The triangle has an area of $\frac{25}{2}$, or 12.5. The quarter-circle has an area of 19.63. They add up to 32.13.

31. **B** As in most shaded-area problems, the trick is to subtract one shape from another to get the shaded region itself. Here, you need to subtract the hexagon's area from that of the circle. To compute the area of the hexagon, divide it into 6 equilateral triangles, each with a side of 4—use the equilateral triangle formula to find their areas. Then subtract the hexagon's area (41.57) from the circle's area (50.27) to get the answer, 8.7.

43. **C** You know that both OA and OC are 2, since they're both radii. The question says that $OA = AC$, which means that AC is also 2. Because triangle OAC is equilateral, all of its angles measure 60°. The radius OA must be perpendicular to line l, making a 90° angle; that makes triangle OAC a 30°-60°-90° triangle. The length of AB is $2\sqrt{3}$, or 3.46.

45. **A** Take one statement at a time. I must be true, since BC is the hypotenuse of a right triangle, and must be longer than the triangle's legs. Because point A could fall anywhere on the left half of the circumference, II *could* be true, but doesn't *have* to be; and III is impossible, since l and m must be parallel.

Comprehensive Plane Geometry Drill, p. 192

3. **A** If $\angle EFB$ and $\angle CGF$ are supplementary, then they add up to 180°. You know that a straight line also equals 180°, so it must be the case that $\angle AFE = \angle CGF$ and $\angle FGD = \angle EFB$. This sort of congruence can only happen if $\overline{AB}$ and $\overline{CD}$ are parallel, so (A) must be true.

5. **C** Because of the right angles shown, $ABCE$ is a rectangle, so if $AE = 7$, then BC also equals 7. Similarly, $AB = 12$. To find CD, note that CDE is a right triangle. You could use the Pythagorean Theorem, but it's easier to note that you have two sides of a 5:12:13 right triangle, so $CD = 5$. To find the perimeter of $ABDE$, add up the sides (don't forget to leave CE out!): 7 + 12 + 7 + 5 + 13 = 44, which is (C).

9. **A** The area of a parallelogram is given by the equation $A = bh$. KJ is a height of the parallelogram. Opposite sides of a parallelogram are equal, so $HJ = 10$. HJK is a right triangle. You could use the Pythagorean Theorem to find KJ, but it's easier to notice that you have two sides of a 6:8:10 right triangle, so $KJ = 6$. The base is 20, so the area is (20)(6) = 120, which is (A).

11.   **D**   Start by drawing the triangle:

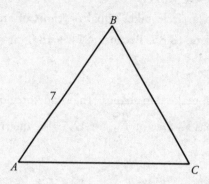

If the triangle is isosceles, you know that two sides must be equal, but you don't know which two sides. Furthermore, what the perimeter could be will be restricted by the Third Side Rule, which states that a third side of a triangle must be greater than the difference of the other two sides but less than their sum.

Take each statement one at a time. For Statement 1, if the perimeter of the triangle was 14, then BC and AC must add up to 7. However, that would make AB equal to the sum of the other two sides; it must be less than the sum, so Statement I is not correct. Eliminate (A), (C), and (E).

Statement II is in the two remaining answer choices, so it must be true. BC and AC must add up to 11. They could be the equal sides, giving you sides 5.5, 5.5, and 7. Or, perhaps one of them is equal to 7, then you would have sides 4, 7, and 7. Either way, the perimeter could be 18, so Statement II is correct.

For Statement III, BC and AC must add up to 21. If they are the equal sides, then BC and AC would both equal 10.5. This fits the Third Side Rule, so Statement III is correct; choose (D).

15.   **D**   The triangles shown are similar triangles because they have the same angle measurements. $\overline{EF}$ is across from the angle that is $x°$, so the corresponding side of the first triangle is $\overline{BC}$. Both $\overline{AB}$ and $\overline{DE}$ are across from the angles that are $z°$, so they are corresponding sides as well. You can then create a proportion using the corresponding sides, fill in the known values, and solve for EF:

$$\frac{BC}{EF} = \frac{AB}{DE}$$

$$\frac{7}{EF} = \frac{6}{4}$$

Cross-multiply then divide:

$$6(EF) = (7)(4)$$
$$6(EF) = 28$$
$$EF = 4.67$$

That matches (D).

24. **D** If the current print is 50 cm², then the bigger print will be 3 × 50 cm² = 150 cm². The area of a square is given by the equation $A = s^2$, so if the area is 150 cm², then the side length will be $\sqrt{150}$ cm, or 12.25 cm, which matches (D).

32. **E** Plug In! Because the triangle is a right triangle, plugging in a Pythagorean triplet works well. Remember that the side opposite the right angle needs to be the hypotenuse. Use a 3:4:5 right triangle and make $x = 3$, $y = 5$, and $z = 4$. Now, you just want to know which answer choice must be true, so plug in these variables and eliminate what isn't true. The only answer that is true with these values is (E).

36. **B** Start by Ballparking. Since the figure is drawn to scale, you know that the value for x is definitely not (E), and probably not (D) either. If minor arc AB is $\dfrac{1}{5}$ the circumference of the circle, then the central angle must be $\dfrac{1}{5}$ of 360°, or 72°. Draw in the central angle:

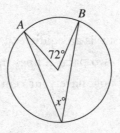

The angle with measurement $x°$ is the inscribed angle of the central angle. An inscribed angle will be half of the central angle, so to find x, divide by 2: 72° ÷ 2 = 36°, which is (B).

45. **D** Draw it! Note that the equation for the circumference of a circle is $C = \pi d$, so if the circumference of the circle is 12π, then the diameter must be 12:

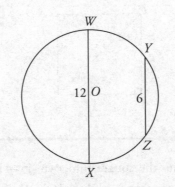

To find the area of sector WOY, use the proportion $\dfrac{\text{central angle}}{360°} = \dfrac{\text{sector area}}{\text{total area}}$. If the diameter is 12, then the radius is 6, so the area is $\pi(6)^2$, or 36π. You still need the central angle, however. You know that all radii are equal to 6, so draw in radii $\overline{OY}$ and $\overline{OZ}$:

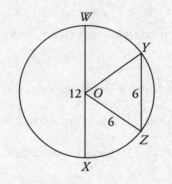

Triangle OYZ has three equal sides; it is an equilateral triangle, so all of its angles are 60°. Because $\overline{WX}$ and $\overline{YZ}$ are parallel, you have two parallel lines transected by a third. Angle WOY is another small angle, so it is also 60°. You now have your central angle, so use the above proportion and solve:

$$\frac{60°}{360°} = \frac{\text{sector area}}{36\pi}$$

$(60°)(36\pi) = (\text{sector area})(360°)$

$$\text{sector area} = \frac{(60°)(36\pi)}{360°} = 6\pi = 18.85$$

That matches (D).

48. **C**   Start by drawing a figure:

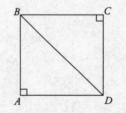

The diagonal of a square splits the square into two 45°-45°-90° right triangles. You could use the $a:a: a\sqrt{2}$ relationship to solve the problem algebraically, but it is easier to Plug In the Answers. The question is asking for the area, so start with (C) and make the area 18 m². The formula for area of a square is $A = s^2$, so the side of the square will be $\sqrt{18}$, or 4.24. You know that the hypotenuse (the diagonal of the square) will be $\sqrt{2}$ times the leg of the triangle: $4.24 \times \sqrt{2} = 6$. The problem indicates that the difference between the diagonal and the side is 1.76 m, so you can test by subtraction. $6 - 4.24 = 1.76$, so (C) is the answer.

You can also test the diagonal directly by using the formula $A = \dfrac{d^2}{2}$, where d is the diagonal of the square. Plugging In the Answers is still the best way to go if you use this formula.

50. **C** First, label what you know. If D is the midpoint of $\overline{CE}$, then $\overline{CD} = \overline{DE}$, and if $\overline{BD} \perp \overline{AC}$, then $\angle ABD$ is a right angle:

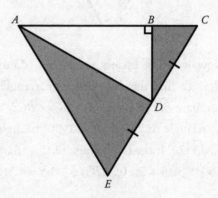

$\overline{AD}$ divides the equilateral triangle in half, so the shaded region is more than half the area. Use this information to Ballpark: $15.59 \div 2 = 7.795$, so (A) and (B) are too small. From here, you could guess or continue to solve it. The next step in solving is to use the formula for area of an equilateral triangle to find the side length: $A = \dfrac{s^2\sqrt{3}}{4}$:

$$15.59 = \frac{s^2\sqrt{3}}{4}$$

$$62.36 = s^2\sqrt{3}$$

$$36.00 = s^2$$

$$6 = s$$

Add this to the diagram:

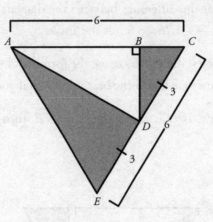

Note that $\overline{CD} = \overline{DE} = 3$. Now, it will be easiest to solve for triangle *ABD* and subtract its area from 15.59 to find the shaded area. To find the dimensions of triangle *ABD*, you can figure out triangle *BCD*, because both triangles share $\overline{BD}$ and $\overline{AB} = 6 - \overline{BC}$. $\angle BCD$ is an angle of the equilateral triangle with a measure of 60°, so triangle *BCD* is a 30°-60°-90° triangle. You know the proportions of the sides of this triangle are a: $a\sqrt{3}$:$2a$. If the hypotenuse of this triangle is 3, then $\overline{BC}$, the side opposite the 30° angle, is 1.5, and $\overline{BD}$ is $1.5\sqrt{3} = 2.60$. $\overline{AB}$ is 6 – 1.5 = 4.5; label all this in the diagram:

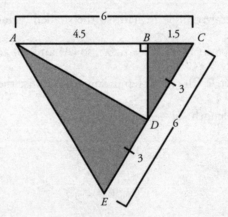

The area of a triangle is $\frac{1}{2}bh$, so triangle *ABD* is $\frac{1}{2}(4.5)(2.60) = 5.85$. The area of the shaded region is the whole equilateral triangle minus triangle *ABD*: 15.59 – 5.85 = 9.74, which is (C).

CHAPTER 8: SOLID GEOMETRY DRILL EXPLANATIONS

Drill 1: Triangles in Rectangular Solids, p. 204

32. **D**   Use the formula for the long diagonal of a cube. Given that the cube's edge is the cube root of 27, or 3, the formula will be $3^2 + 3^2 + 3^2 = d^2$. If you simplify this, you'll see that the cube's long diagonal must be 5.2.

36. **E**   Be careful here; you won't be using the Super Pythagorean Theorem. The sides of this triangle are the diagonals of three of the solid's faces. *BD* is the hypotenuse of a 3-4-5 triangle, and *BE* is the hypotenuse of a 5-12-13 triangle. For *DE*, use the Pythagorean Theorem with $a = 3$ and $b = 12$: $DE = \sqrt{153} = 12.37$. The sum of the three sides is $5 + 13 + 12.37 = 30.37$.

39. **A**   This is a long-diagonal question, with a twist. Each edge of the cube is 1, but you're actually finding the long diagonal of a quarter of the cube. Think of it as finding the long diagonal of a rectangular solid with dimensions $1 \times \dfrac{1}{2} \times \dfrac{1}{2}$. Plug those three numbers into the Super Pythagorean Theorem. You could also solve this by finding the length of *CN* and then using the Pythagorean Theorem on triangle *MCN*.

Drill 2: Volume, p. 214

17. **D**   PITA! Quickly move through the answer choices (starting in this case with the smallest, easiest numbers), calculating the volumes and surface areas of each. The only answer choice that makes these quantities equal is (D).

24. **E**   This one's a pain. The only way to do it is to try out the various possibilities. The edges of the solid must be three factors which multiply to 30, such as 2, 3, and 5. That solid would have a surface area of 62. The solid could also have dimensions of 1, 5, and 6, which would give it a surface area of 82. Keep experimenting, and you find that the solid with the greatest surface area has the dimensions 1, 1, and 30, giving it a surface area of 122.

28. **C**   So you don't know the formula for the area of a pentagon? You don't need to. Just use the formula for the volume of a prism, $V = Bh$.

43. **B**   The sphere has a volume of 4.19. When submerged, it will push up a layer of water having equal volume. The volume of this layer of water is the product of the area of the circular surface (50.27) and the height to which it's lifted—it's like calculating the volume of a very flat cylinder. You get the equation $50.27h = 4.19$. Solve, and you find that $h = 0.083$.

18. **B**   If the cube's surface area is $6x$, then x is the area of one face. Pick an easy number, and Plug In! Suppose x is 4. That means that the length of any edge of the cube is 2 and that the cube's volume

is 8. Just plug $x = 4$ into all of the answer choices to find the one that gives you 8. Choice (B) does the trick. Choice (E) is the formula for the volume of a cube with edge x.

36. C   Plug In! Suppose the sphere's original radius is $r = 2$, which would give it a surface area of 50.3. If that radius is then increased by $b = 1$, the new radius is 3. The sphere would then have a surface area of 113.1. That's an increase of 62.8. Plug $r = 2$ and $b = 1$ into the answer choices; the one that gives you 62.8 is correct. That's (C).

40. B   Just plug in any values for b and h that obey the proportion $b = 2h$. Then plug those values into the formula for the volume of a pyramid.

Drill 3: Inscribed Solids, p. 218

32. B   The long diagonal of the rectangular solid is the diameter of the sphere. Just find the length of the long diagonal and divide it in half.

35. C   Calculate the volume of each shape separately. The cube's volume is 8; the cylinder, with a radius of 1 and a height of 2, has a volume of 6.28. The difference between them is 1.72.

38. B   The cube must have the dimensions 1 by 1 by 1. That means that the cone's base has a radius of 0.5 and that the cone's height is 1. Plug these numbers into the formula for the volume of a cone, and you will get 0.26.

Drill 4: Rotation Solids, p. 222

34. C   This rotation will generate a cylinder with a radius of 2 and a height of 5. Its volume is 62.8.

39. D   This rotation will generate a cone lying on its side, with a height of 5 and a radius of 3. Its volume is 47.12.

46. D   Here's an odd one. The best way to think about this one is as two triangles, base to base, being rotated. The rotation will generate two cones placed base to base, one right-side-up and one upside-down. Each cone has a radius of 3 and a height of 3. The volume of each cone is 28.27. The volume of the two together is 56.55.

Drill 5: Changing Dimensions, p. 225

13. E   Just plug in a value for the radius of sphere A, say 2. So the radius of sphere B is 6. Use the volume formula: A has volume $\frac{4}{3}\pi(2)^3 = \frac{4}{3}\pi(8)$, and B has volume $\frac{4}{3}\pi(6)^3 = \frac{4}{3}\pi(216)$. If you make a ratio, the $\frac{4}{3}\pi$ cancels, and you have $\frac{8}{216} = \frac{1}{27}$.

18. **D** Plug in for the dimensions of the rectangular solid so that the volume is 24. So pick $l = 3$, $w = 4$, and $h = 2$. The volume of the solid which the question asks for will then be $\left(\dfrac{3}{2}\right)\left(\dfrac{4}{2}\right)\left(\dfrac{2}{2}\right) = 3$.

21. **B** Plug in for the length of the edge of the cube—try 2. So the surface area formula gives you $6(2)^2 = 24$, and the volume of the cube is 8. Increasing this by a factor of 2.25 gives you a new surface area of 54. Setting the surface area formula equal to this gives you a length of 3 for the new, increased edge. So the new volume is 27. $27 \div 8$ gives you 3.375 for the increase between the old and new volumes.

Comprehensive Solid Geometry Drill, p. 227

24. **C** Use the volume to calculate the side of the cube: $V = s^3$ so $s = \sqrt[3]{100} = 4.64$. Plug this value into the formula for the long diagonal of a cube: $d = s\sqrt{3} = 4.64\sqrt{3} = 8.04$.

29. **A** $V = l \times w \times h$, so the current rectangular solid has a volume of 72. Once the sides are decreased, it will be smaller, so (D) and (E) are too big. To solve this, calculate the new dimensions of the rectangular solid. 20% of 6 is 4.8, 20% of 3 is 2.4, and 20% of 4 is 3.2. Plug the new dimensions into the volume formula, so $V = 4.8 \times 2.4 \times 3.2 = 36.86$, which is (A).

30. **B** Use PITA to calculate the surface area and the volume of the cube. Start with (C). $SA = 6s^2$, so if the side equals 3, then the surface area equals 54. $V = s^3$, so the volume equals 27. Therefore, the ratio of the surface area to the volume is 2 to 1. It might be hard to determine if you need a bigger or smaller length, so just pick a direction. Try (B). If the side is 2, the surface area equals 24 and the volume equals 8, which is a 3 to 1 ratio of surface area to volume.

34. **D** Calculate the volume of the sphere: $V = \dfrac{4}{3}\pi r^3$. Since the diameter is 8, the radius equals 4. Plug $r = 4$ into the volume formula to get $V = 268.1$. Since the volume of the cube is equal to the volume of the sphere, solve for the side of the cube: $V = s^3 = 268.1$. Therefore, $s = 6.45$. Calculate the surface area of the cube: $SA = 6(s)^2 = 249.5$.

38. **B** The B in the pyramid volume formula is the area of the base, so here $B = 16$. Solve for the volume of the original pyramid: $V = \dfrac{1}{3}Bh = \dfrac{1}{3}(16)(6) = 32$. If the height increases by 50%, the new height is 9. Plug 9 into the volume formula and solve for the area of the base: $V = 32 = \dfrac{1}{3}B(9) = 3B$, so $B = 10.67$ for the new pyramid. Therefore, each side of the new base is equal to $\sqrt{10.67} = 3.27$.

39. **D** Draw in the needed information. Call the midpoint of *HJ* point *X*, and label the side lengths:

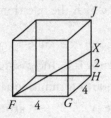

Line *FX* is the same as the long diagonal of a rectangular box with dimensions 4, 4, and 2. Because you want the long diagonal of a rectangular box, you can use the Super Pythagorean Theorem. Make $a = 4$, $b = 4$, $c = 2$, and solve for d:

$$36 = d^2$$
$$6 = d$$

This matches (D).

40. **C** Use Plugging In. Start with c because the vales of both a and b depend on it. If $c = 2$, then $b = 5(2) = 10$ and $a = \dfrac{1}{2}(10) = 5$. Solve for the volume of the rectangular solid: $V = l \times w \times h = 5 \times 10 \times 2 = 100$. Plug in $a = 5$ for each answer choice to see which equals the target value of 100. Choice (C) is the correct answer.

42. **C** The radius and the height of the cylinder are equal to the radius and the height of the cone, so plug the given values into the formula for the volume of a cone to get $V = \dfrac{1}{3}\pi r^2 h = \dfrac{1}{3}\pi(5)^2(4) = 104.72$.

43. **B** Use the Pythagorean Theorem to calculate the height of the triangle. $\left(3\sqrt{3}\right)^2 + b^2 = 6^2$. $b^2 = 9$ so $b = 3$. Because you are rotating around *AB*, the height of the cone that is produced is $3\sqrt{3}$ and the radius is 3. Plug these values into the formula for the volume of a right cone to get $V = \dfrac{1}{3}\pi r^2 h = \dfrac{1}{3}\pi 3^2\left(3\sqrt{3}\right) = 9\pi\sqrt{3}$, which is (B).

47. **B** Start by Ballparking. *BC* is the long diagonal of the rectangular solid, so all the dimensions must be less than 15. Eliminate (D) and (E). To solve this question, you can use the Super Pythagorean Theorem to find the missing side: $a^2 + b^2 + c^2 = d^2$. *BC* is the long diagonal, so it must be d; the known sides 4 and 5 can be a and b, respectively:

$$4^2 + 5^2 + c^2 = 15^2$$
$$41 + c^2 = 225$$
$$c^2 = 184$$
$$c = 13.56$$

That matches (B).

50. **C** First, if the cylinder is inside the sphere, the cylinder must have a smaller volume than the sphere. Eliminate (D) and (E). Next, draw it:

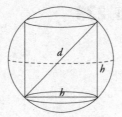

At this point, Ballparking lets you eliminate (A), because the cylinder takes up around half of the sphere. Because the diameter of the cylinder is equal to its height, both have been marked h. In inscribed solids questions, you want to determine the shared dimension; here, the diameter of the sphere is the diagonal of the cylinder; it has been marked d in the diagram. The diagonal, diameter, and height of the cylinder form a 45°-45°-90° triangle. You're given the volume of the sphere, so use the volume of the sphere to find the sphere's diameter and then use that to determine the dimensions of the cylinder.

Use the formula for the volume of a sphere to find the radius:

$$V = \frac{4}{3}\pi r^3$$

$$8000 = \frac{4}{3}\pi r^3$$

$$6000 = \pi r^3$$

$$1909.86 = r^3$$

$$12.41 = r$$

The diameter of the sphere would be double that, or 24.82. As stated above, the diameter of the sphere is the diagonal of the cylinder, which is the hypotenuse of a 45°-45°-90° triangle. The hypotenuse of such a triangle is $\sqrt{2}$ times greater than the legs, so divide the hypotenuse by $\sqrt{2}$ to find the legs: $24.82 \div \sqrt{2} = 17.55$.

To find the volume of the cylinder, use the formula $V = \pi r^2 h$. The height is 17.55, but you need to divide the diameter by 2 to get the radius: $17.55 \div 2 = 8.78$. Now you can solve:

$V = \pi (8.78)^2 (17.55) = 4{,}250.27$

This is closest to (C).

Note: because this explanation rounds throughout, the answer was a bit off. This can happen, especially with a multi-step problem such as this.

CHAPTER 9: COORDINATE GEOMETRY DRILL EXPLANATIONS

Drill 1: The Coordinate Plane, p. 233

1.   Point *E*, Quadrant II

2.   Point *A*, Quadrant I

3.   Point *C*, Quadrant IV

4.   Point *D*, Quadrant III

5.   Point *B*, Quadrant I

Drill 2: The Equation of a Line, p. 235

7.   A   You can plug the line's slope *m* and the given point (*x, y*) into the slope-intercept equation to get $1 = 0.6(3) + b$. Thus, $b = -0.8$, and the equation is $y = 0.6x - 0.8$.

To find the point that is also on this line, go to each answer choice and plug the *x*-coordinate into the formula. You'll have the right answer when the formula produces a *y*-coordinate that matches the given one.

10.   E   Once again, get the line into slope-intercept form, $y = 5x - 4$. Then plug in zero. You get a *y*-value of -4. Notice that this is the *y*-intercept (the value of *y* when $x = 0$).

11.   B   Put the line into the slope-intercept formula by isolating *y*. So $y = -3x + 4$ and the slope is -3.

19.   D   You can figure out the line formula ($y = mx + b$) from the graph. The line has a *y*-intercept (*b*) of -2, and it rises 6 as it runs 2, giving it a slope (*m*) of 3. Use those values of *m* and *b* to test the statements in the answer choices.

Drill 3: Slope, p. 240

4.   C   Use the slope formula on the point (0, 0) and (−3, 2): $\dfrac{2-0}{-3-0} = -\dfrac{2}{3}$.

17.   D   Draw it. Remember that perpendicular lines have slopes that are negative reciprocals of each other. A line containing the origin and the point (2, −1) has a slope of $-\dfrac{1}{2}$. The perpendicular line must then have a slope of 2. Quickly move through the answer choices, determining the slope of a line passing through the given point and the origin. The one that gives a slope of 2 is correct.

23.   A   Once again, the slope-intercept formula is your most powerful tool. Isolate *y*, and you get $y = -3x + 5$. The line must then have a slope of -3 and a *y*-intercept of 5. Only (A) and (D) show

lines with negative slope, and the line in (D) has a slope which is between –1 and 0, because it forms an angle with the x-axis that is less than 45°.

47. **D** Remember that perpendicular lines have slopes that are negative reciprocals of each other. The slopes of x and y are therefore negative reciprocals—you can think of them as x and $-\dfrac{1}{x}$. The difference between them will therefore be the sum of a number and its reciprocal: $x - \left(-\dfrac{1}{x}\right) = x + \dfrac{1}{x}$.

If $x = 1$, then the sum of x and its reciprocal is 2; if $x = 5$, then the sum of x and its reciprocal is 5.2; but no sum of a number and its reciprocal can be less than 2. A sum of 0.8 is impossible.

Drill 4: Line Segments, p. 245

12. **D** Use the distance formula on the points (–5, 9) and (0, 0).

19. **E** Drawing a rough sketch and Ballparking allows you to eliminate (A) and (B). Then, plug the points you know into the midpoint formula and PITA for the coordinates of B. The average of –4 and the x-coordinate of B is 1. The average of 3 and the y-coordinate of B is –1. That makes B the point (6, –5).

27. **D** You'll essentially be using the distance formula on (2, 2) and the points in the answer choices. (–5, –3) is the point at the greatest distance from (2, 2).

Drill 5: Parabola Equations, p. 251

34. **C** This is a quadratic function, which always produces a parabola. If a parabola has a maximum or minimum, then that extreme value is the parabola's vertex. Just find the vertex. The x-coordinate is $-\dfrac{b}{2a}$, which is 3 in this case. The y-coordinate will be $f(3)$, or –1.

37. **B** Use that vertex formula again. The x-coordinate is $-\dfrac{b}{2a}$, which is –1 in this case. That's enough to get you the right answer. (If you needed the y-coordinate as well, you'd just plug in $x = -1$ and solve for y.)

38. **D** At every point on the x-axis, $y = 0$. Plug each of the answer choices in for x, and see which one gives you $y = 0$. You could also put in 0 for y and solve for x; the solutions are 1 and 5.

Drill 6: Circle Equations, p. 254

30. **B** Just plug each point into the equation. The one that does *not* make the equation true is not on the circle.

34.   **E**   If S and T are the endpoints of a diameter, then the distance between them is 8. If they are very close to each other on the circle, then the distance between them approaches zero. The distance between S and T cannot be determined.

50.   **C**   Notice that because the y's equal 0, you can cancel out the y's in all the answer choices. Plug in the points: (2, 0) works in (C), (D), and (E), but (10, 0) works in (A), (B), and (C). It must be (C).

Drill 7: Triaxial Coordinates, p. 257

29.   **C**   This is once again a job for the Super Pythagorean Theorem, which is simply another version of the 3-D distance formula. It's just like finding the long diagonal of a box which is 5 by 6 by 7. Set up the equation, $d^2 = 5^2 + 6^2 + 7^2$, and solve.

34.   **B**   A point will be outside the sphere if the distance between it and the origin is greater than 6. Use the Super Pythagorean Theorem to measure the distance of each point from the origin.

Comprehensive Coordinate Geometry Drill, p. 258

7.   **A**   Choices (C) and (D) have positive slopes, so those can be eliminated. Choice (B) has a slope that is equal to 0 (since it is a flat line), so that leaves only (A) and (E). The graph in (A) crosses the x-axis at a positive value of x, so it is the correct answer choice. Choice (E) crosses the x-axis at a negative x-value, so it doesn't match the graph described in the question.

8.   **B**   Use the slope formula $m = \dfrac{y_2 - y_1}{x_2 - x_1}$ to calculate the slope of the line: $\dfrac{13-7}{4-(-4)} = \dfrac{6}{8} = 0.75$. Choice (B) is the correct answer.

17.   **A**   Draw it! Sketch a coordinate plane, mark the x- and y-intercepts, and draw the line:

The slope of this line is clearly positive; eliminate (C) and (E). The line is more than 45° above the x-axis, so its slope must be greater than 1; eliminate (B). The b in the standard equation of a line $(y = mx + b)$ represents the y-intercept; the y-intercept here is –8, so the answer must be (A).

18. **D** The *y*-intercept is the *y*-coordinate of the point at which a linear equation crosses the *y*-axis (i.e., where the *x*-coordinate equals 0). Therefore, you can Plug In $x = 0$ and solve the equation for *y*:

$$3y - 5(0) - 8 = 0$$
$$3y - 8 = 0$$
$$3y = 8$$
$$y = \frac{8}{3}$$

This matches (D). Another approach would be to get the equation into the slope-intercept form and use the value for *b*, which is the *y*-intercept, as your answer.

25. **D** There are a few ways to approach this question. One approach is to Plug In the Answers; make *x* in the function equal each answer choice and pick the answer with the lowest value of *x*. A quicker way is to remember that if a quadratic is in its general form ($y = ax^2 + bx + c$), the vertex will be the minimum value if $a > 0$. You can find the *x*-coordinate of the vertex using $-\dfrac{b}{2a} : -\dfrac{(-3)}{2(2)} = \dfrac{3}{4}$, which is (D).

29. **D** To find the distance between two points in the *xyz*-coordinate system, use the distance formula:

$$d = \sqrt{(x_2 - x_1)^2 + (y_2 - y_1)^2 + (z_2 - z_1)^2}$$
$$d = \sqrt{(7 - (-3))^2 + (-4 - 8)^2 + (3 - 2)^2}$$
$$d = \sqrt{100 + 144 + 1}$$
$$d = \sqrt{(10)^2 + (-12)^2 + 1^2}$$
$$d = \sqrt{245} = 15.65$$

That matches (D).

30. **C** Rectangle *R* currently has vertices (0, 0), (7, 0), (7, –4), and (0, –4). A rectangle with dimensions ($x + 2, 3y$) would therefore have dimensions (2, 0), (9, 0), (9, –12), and (2, –12). Draw this rectangle:

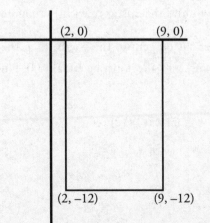

The area of a rectangle is length times width. Here, the x distance is 7, and the y distance is 12, so the area of the new rectangle is $7 \times 12 = 84$, which is (C).

31. **A** Use the distance formula, $d = \sqrt{(x_2 - x_1)^2 + (y_2 - y_1)^2}$, to find the length of each line segment given in the answer choices. You'll find that (A) gives you the greatest length. To save time, you can plot the points and use Ballparking to eliminate (C). Also, there's no need to simplify the square roots to decimal values. Just compare the non-simplified values of each answer choice to determine which line segment has the greatest length.

35. **C** First, you need to figure out the missing x- and y-coordinates. Use the midpoint formula to solve for the missing values.

$$\frac{12 + x_2}{2} = 5$$

$$12 + x_2 = 10$$

$$x_2 = -2$$

$$\frac{y_1 + 7}{2} = 8$$

$$y_1 + 7 = 16$$

$$y_1 = 9$$

Therefore, the endpoints of the line segment are equal to (12, 9) and (–2, 7). Plug these values into the distance formula and solve.

$$d = \sqrt{(x_2 - x_1)^2 + (y_2 - y_1)^2}$$

$$d = \sqrt{(12 - (-2))^2 + (9 - 7)^2}$$

$$d = \sqrt{(14)^2 + (2)^2}$$

$$d = \sqrt{196 + 4} = 14.14$$

Notice that (A) is the distance between each endpoint and the midpoint, so be careful to plug the correct coordinates into the distance formula. You could also plot the points on a coordinate plane and create a right triangle to find this distance with Pythagorean Theorem.

44. **A** If the graph of the quadratic is tangent to the x-axis, then the quadratic has exactly one real root. This means the discriminant, $b^2 - 4ac$, must be equal to 0. Plug in the given values for a and c and solve for b:

$$b^2 - 4(3)(12) = 0$$

$$b^2 - 144 = 0$$

$$b^2 = 144$$

$$b = \pm 12$$

Note in the last step, when you take the square root of 144, there are positive and negative roots of *b*. The answer which matches one of these roots is (A).

47.　**B**　Start by drawing the figure:

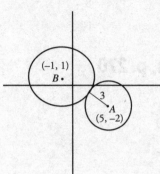

The radius of circle *B* will be the distance between the centers of circles *A* and *B* minus the radius of circle *A*. Therefore, you need to find the distance between the centers and then subtract 3.

To find the distance, you can use the distance formula, or you can draw a right triangle. If you draw a right triangle, the *x* distance is 6 and the *y* distance is 3. Use the Pythagorean Theorem to find the distance between the centers:

$$a^2 + b^2 = c^2$$

$$6^2 + 3^3 = c^2$$

$$45 = c^2$$

$$6.71 = c$$

This is the distance between the centers, NOT the radius of circle *B*; eliminate (D) as a trap answer. You need to subtract the radius of circle *A* to find the radius of circle *B*: 6.71 − 3 = 3.71, which is (B).

CHAPTER 10: TRIGONOMETRY DRILL EXPLANATIONS

Drill 1: Trig Functions in Right Triangles, p. 265

1.　$\sin\theta = \dfrac{3}{5} = 0.6$; $\cos\theta = \dfrac{4}{5} = 0.8$; $\tan\theta = \dfrac{3}{4} = 0.75$

2.　$\sin\theta = \dfrac{5}{13} = 0.385$; $\cos\theta = \dfrac{12}{13} = 0.923$; $\tan\theta = \dfrac{5}{12} = 0.417$

3. $\sin\theta = \dfrac{24}{25} = 0.96$; $\cos\theta = \dfrac{7}{25} = 0.28$; $\tan\theta = \dfrac{24}{7} = 3.429$

4. $\sin\theta = \dfrac{6}{10} = 0.6$; $\cos\theta = \dfrac{8}{10} = 0.8$; $\tan\theta = \dfrac{6}{8} = 0.75$

Drill 2: Completing Triangles, p. 270

1. $AB = 3.38$; $CA = 7.25$; $\angle B = 65°$

2. $EF = 2.52$; $FD = 3.92$; $\angle D = 40°$

3. $HJ = 41.41$; $JK = 10.72$; $\angle J = 75°$

4. $LM = 5.74$; $MN = 8.19$; $\angle N = 35°$

5. $TR = 4.0$; $\angle S = 53.13°$; $\angle T = 36.87°$

6. $YW = 13$; $\angle W = 22.62°$; $\angle Y = 67.38°$

Drill 3: Trigonometric Identities, p. 275

25.   **D**   Use FOIL on these binomials, and you get $1 - \sin^2 x$. Because $\sin^2 x + \cos^2 x = 1$, you know that $1 - \sin^2 x = \cos^2 x$.

31.   **C**   Express $\tan x$ as $\dfrac{\sin x}{\cos x}$. The cosine then cancels out on the top of the fraction, and you're left with $\dfrac{\sin x}{\sin x}$, or 1.

39.   **A**   The term $(\sin x)(\tan x)$ can be expressed as $(\sin x)\left(\dfrac{\sin x}{\cos x}\right)$ or $\dfrac{\sin^2 x}{\cos x}$. The first and second terms can then be combined: $\dfrac{1}{\cos x} - \dfrac{\sin^2 x}{\cos x} = \dfrac{1 - \sin^2 x}{\cos x}$. Because $1 - \sin^2 x = \cos^2 x$, this expression simplifies to $\cos x$.

42.   **E**   Break the fraction into two terms, as follows: $\dfrac{\tan x}{\tan x} - \dfrac{\sin x \cos x}{\tan x}$. The first term simplifies to 1, and the second term becomes easier to work with when you express the tangent in terms of the sine and cosine: $\dfrac{\sin x \cos x}{\tan x} = \dfrac{\sin x \cos x}{\dfrac{\sin x}{\cos x}} = \cos^2 x$.

The whole expression then equals $1 - \cos^2 x$, or $\sin^2 x$.

50.   E   Plug In! Make $\theta = 20°$:

$$\frac{\sin 20° \tan 20° - \sin^2 20° \cos 20°}{\sin^2 20° \cos 20°} = \frac{(0.342)(0.364) - (0.342)^2 (0.940)}{(0.342)^2 (0.940)} = 0.132$$

This is your target. Plug in $\theta = 20°$ and look for what equals 0.132. The only choice that is close is

(E).

Drill 4: Degrees and Radians, p. 278

Degrees	Radians
30°	$\frac{\pi}{6}$
45°	$\frac{\pi}{4}$
60°	$\frac{\pi}{3}$
90°	$\frac{\pi}{2}$
120°	$\frac{2\pi}{3}$
135°	$\frac{3\pi}{4}$
150°	$\frac{5\pi}{6}$
180°	π
225°	$\frac{5\pi}{4}$
240°	$\frac{4\pi}{3}$
270°	$\frac{3\pi}{2}$
300°	$\frac{5\pi}{3}$
315°	$\frac{7\pi}{4}$
330°	$\frac{11\pi}{6}$
360°	2π

Comprehensive Trigonometry Drill, p. 279

14.   A   First, cosine is always between −1 and 1, inclusive, so you can eliminate (D) and (E).

SOHCAHTOA tells you that $\cos = \dfrac{\text{adjacent}}{\text{hypotenuse}}$. You know that the hypotenuse is 7, but you need

to find the adjacent side. You need to use the Pythagorean Theorem: $a^2 + b^2 = c^2$, remembering that

c must be your hypotenuse. So, if the unknown side is b, then $6^2 + b^2 = 7^2$, $36 + b^2 = 49$, $b^2 = 13$,

$b = \sqrt{13}$. Therefore, the value of $\cos \theta$ is $\dfrac{\sqrt{13}}{7}$, (A).

19.   E   You are given the measurements of the sides opposite and adjacent to θ. Therefore, according to

SOHCAHTOA, you want to use tangent. Set up the problem: $\tan\theta = \dfrac{11}{6}$. To isolate θ, take $\tan^{-1}$

of both sides:

$$\tan^{-1}\left(\tan\theta\right) = \tan^{-1}\left(\frac{11}{6}\right)$$

$$\theta = \tan^{-1}\left(\frac{11}{6}\right) = 61.39$$

This is (E).

23.   E   Start by solving for θ. First, take the square root of both sides of the equation:

$$\sqrt{\tan^2 \theta} = \sqrt{4.60}$$

$$\tan \theta = 2.145$$

Next, take $\tan^{-1}$ of both sides to solve for θ:

$$\tan^{-1}(\tan \theta) = \tan^{-1} 2.145$$

$$\theta = 65$$

Finally, put this value of θ into the second expression and solve:

$$\cos\frac{65}{5} = 0.974$$

24.   C AB is opposite of the angle with degree measure x, and AC is adjacent to that angle. There-

fore, you want to use tangent. SOHCAHTOA tells you that $\tan = \dfrac{\text{opposite}}{\text{adjacent}}$. Putting in

what you know, you find that $\tan 19° = \dfrac{AB}{10}$. Multiply both sides by 10 to solve for AB:

$10 \tan 19° = AB$, so $AB = 3.44$, (C).

29. A

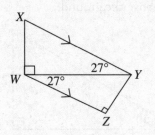

If *XY* is parallel to *WZ*, then *WY* is a third line transecting two parallel lines. ∠*YWZ* is therefore equal to ∠*WYX*, or 27°. *WY* is the hypotenuse of triangle *WYZ* and is equal to 8. *YZ* is opposite ∠*YWZ*, so you can use sine to solve for *YZ*. Remember that $\sin = \dfrac{\text{opposite}}{\text{hypotenuse}}$, so here $\sin 27° = \dfrac{YZ}{8}$. Solving for *YZ*, you find that $8 \sin 27° = 3.63$, (A).

38. B   First, the value of sine must be between −1 and 1, inclusive, so you can immediately eliminate (D) and (E). Even though the information is given to you in radians, on the SAT Subject Test in Math 1 you should deal with the expression in degrees instead. First, use $\cos^{-1}$ on both sides of the equation to find θ:

$$\cos^{-1}(\cos \theta) = \cos^{-1} 0.173$$

$$\theta = 80.04°$$

Put that value of θ in to the expression to find $\sin \dfrac{\theta}{4}$:

$$\sin \dfrac{80.04}{4} = 0.342$$

This matches (B).

40. C   First, cosine can only be between −1 and 1, inclusive, so eliminate (D). These two triangles have equal angles where they intersect. Both triangles also have a right angle. Therefore, the other angles must also be equal, so $x = y$ and $\cos y = \cos x$. Because $\sin x = \dfrac{3}{5}$, you can use SOHCAHTOA and plug in the sides of the bottom triangle. Make the side opposite the angle with degree measure $x = 3$ and the hypotenuse = 5. You have a 3:4:5 right triangle, so the side adjacent to the angle with degree measure x is 4. Cosine is $\dfrac{\text{adjacent}}{\text{hypotenuse}}$, so $\cos y = \cos x = \dfrac{4}{5}$, which is (C).

42.   **B**   Draw the triangle you will need. The side opposite the 50° angle will be 225, not 250, because the pillar raises that point 25 feet above the ground:

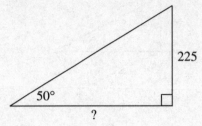

To find the side you want, use tangent. Make the unknown side x and set up the problem using SOHCAHTOA:

$$\tan 50° = \frac{225}{x}$$

Multiply both sides by x and divide both sides by tan 50° to isolate x:

$$x \tan 50° = 225$$

$$x = \frac{225}{\tan 50°}$$

Use your calculator and you find that $x = 188$, which is (B).

46.   **A**   When asked for a specific value and given numbers in the answer choices, Plug In the Answers! Starting with (C), make each answer the value of θ. Remember that to find $\cos^2 \theta$ on your calculator you need to first find $\cos \theta$ and then square the result. The value you get with (C) is too small, but it may not be clear which direction to go from there. Keep trying until one choice gives a value close to 1. The only choice which works is (A).

To solve this problem algebraically, first isolate $\cos^2 \theta$ by multiplying both sides by $\frac{3}{4}$:

$$\left(\frac{3}{4}\right)\left(\frac{4\cos^2 \theta}{3}\right) = \left(\frac{3}{4}\right)(1)$$

$$\cos^2 \theta = \frac{3}{4}$$

Next, take the square root of both sides:

$$\sqrt{\cos^2 \theta} = \sqrt{\frac{3}{4}}$$

$$\cos \theta = 0.866$$

Finally, take $\cos^{-1}$ of both sides to isolate θ:

$$\cos^{-1}(\cos \theta) = \cos^{-1} 0.866$$

$$\theta = 30.002$$

This is closest to (A).

47. **B** Plug In! Make $x = 20$. This would make $\sin 20° = 0.342$ and $\cos 20° = 0.940$. Substitute these values into the expression:

$$\frac{0.342^2 - 0.940^2}{0.342^4 - 0.940^4} = 0.9994$$

The only answer which is even close to 0.9994 when $x = 20$ is (B).

To solve this algebraically, you need to factor the denominator. The denominator is a difference of squares: $a^2 - b^2 = (a + b)(a - b)$. Therefore, you can factor as follows:

$$\frac{\sin^2 x - \cos^2 x}{\sin^4 x - \cos^4 x} = \frac{\sin^2 x - \cos^2 x}{\left(\sin^2 x + \cos^2 x\right)\left(\sin^2 x - \cos^2 x\right)}$$

You can then cancel the $(\sin^2 x - \cos^2 x)$ term from the numerator and denominator, and you are left with $\dfrac{1}{\sin^2 x + \cos^2 x}$. You know from the section on trigonometric identities that $\sin^2 x + \cos^2 x = 1$, so you're left with $\dfrac{1}{1} = 1$, which is (B).

50. **C** Plug In! Make $x = 40$. If that's the case, then $y = 50$. Next, try Statement I. $\sin 40° = 0.642$ and $\cos 50° = 0.642$. If you want to be sure, you can try a different set of numbers, but Statement I will always be true; eliminate (B) and (D). For Statement II, $\tan 40° = 0.839$, whereas $\tan 50° = 1.191$. You know that Statement II isn't always true, so you can eliminate (E). For Statement III, $\sin 40° = 0.642$ and $\sin 50° = 0.766$, so $\sin^2 x + \sin^2 y = (0.642)^2 + (0.766)^2 = 0.999$, which is basically 1 (given that you rounded). Statement III is true, so choose (C).

Another approach is to consider the trigonometric relationships. In Statement I, the side opposite angle x is the same as the side adjacent to y, and the hypotenuse never changes. Therefore, $\sin x = \cos y$ always.

In Statement II, remember that $\tan = \dfrac{\text{opposite}}{\text{adjacent}}$. The side opposite x is the side adjacent y, whereas the side opposite y is the side adjacent x. Therefore, the relationship between $\tan x$ and $\tan y$ will depend on the lengths of those two sides (if the side opposite x is greater than the side opposite y, then $\tan x > \tan y$). However, you do not know the relative lengths of the sides, so you cannot know whether Statement II is true.

For Statement III, think back to Statement I. $\sin^2 y = \cos^2 x$, because the side opposite y is the same side as the side adjacent to x. Therefore, you can substitute in, and you get $\sin^2 x + \cos^2 x = 1$. That's one of the trigonometric identities that you've learned, so you know that Statement III is always true.

CHAPTER 11: FUNCTIONS DRILL EXPLANATIONS

Drill 1: General Functions, p. 287

14.   E $f(-1) = (-1)^2 - (-1)^3 = 1 - (-1) = 1 + 1 = 2$

17.   B $f(7) = 10.247$. $f(8) = 11.314$. That's a difference of 1.067.

26.   B $g(3) = 3^3 + 3^2 - 9(3) - 9 = 0$

29.   D $f(3, -6) = \dfrac{3(-6)}{3 + (-6)} = \dfrac{-18}{-3} = 6$

30.   A   PITA for n, plug each answer choice into $h(x)$, and see which one spits out 10. Alternately, you could solve $10 = n^2 + n - 2$ by setting n equal to 0 and factoring; the solutions are -4 and 3.

33.   E   The greatest factor of 75 not equal to 75 is 25. Therefore, $f(75) = 75 \cdot 25 = 1,875$.

34.   E   If $y = 3$, then $g(-y) = g(-3)$. Because $-3 < 0$, $g(-3) = 2|-3| = 2(3) = 6$.

Drill 2: Weird Functions, p. 289

34.   B   Just follow instructions on this one, and you get $-64 - (-27)$, or $-64 + 27$, which is -37. Choice (C) is a trap answer.

35.   A   You've just got to plow through this one. The original expression ¥5 + ¥6 becomes $5(3)^2 + 5(4)^2$, which equals 125. Work through the answer choices from the top to find the one that gives you 125. Choice (E) is a trap answer.

36.   B   The function §a leaves even numbers alone and flips the signs of odd numbers. That means that the series §1 + §2 + §3…§100 + §101 will become $(-1) + 2 + (-3) + 4 + (-5) \ldots + 100 + (-101)$. Rather than adding up all those numbers, find the pattern: -1 and 2 add up to 1; -3 and 4 add up to 1; and so on, all the way up to -99 and 100. That means 50 pairs that add up to 1, plus the -101 left over: $50 + -101 = -51$.

Drill 3: Compound Functions, p. 292

17.   D   Plug in a number for x. Try 3. $f(g(3)) = f(7) = 21$, and $g(f(3)) = g(9) = 13$, so the difference is 8.

24.   E   To evaluate $f(g(-2))$, first find the value of $g(-2)$, which equals $(-2)^3 - 5$, or -13. Then put that result into $f(x)$: $f(-13) = |-13| - 5 = 13 - 5 = 8$.

25. **B** PITA. Plug in 3 for $g(x)$: $f(3) = 5 + 3(3) = 14$. Nope—eliminate (A). Now plug in 4 for $g(x)$: $f(4) = 5 + 3(4) = 17$. Any of the other choices would leave a variable in the compound function, so (B) is the answer.

32. **D** Just plug in a nice little number, perhaps $x = 3$. You get $g(f(3)) = g(64) = 12$. Now just plug 3 into the answers for x, to see which one hits your target number, 12.

36. **C** $f(g(3)) = 5$. $g(f(3)) = 3.196$. The difference between them is 1.804.

Drill 4: Inverse Functions, p. 295

22. **B** Plug a number into $f(x)$. For example, $f(2) = 1.5$. Since $g(1.5) = 2$, the correct answer is the function that turns 1.5 back into 2. Choice (B) does the trick.

33. **B** PITA, starting with (C). Take each answer choice, plug it in for x in $f(x)$, and see which one spits out 9.

35. **E** The fact that $f(3) = 9$ doesn't tell you what $f(x)$ is. It's possible that $f(x) = x^2$, or that $f(x) = 3x$, or that $f(x) = 2x + 3$, and so on. Each of these functions would have a different inverse function. The definition of the inverse function cannot be determined.

Drill 5: Domains and Ranges, p. 301

24. **A** This function factors to $f(x) = \dfrac{1}{x(x-3)(x+2)}$. Three values of x will make this fraction undefined: -2, 0, and 3. The function's domain must exclude these values. You could also plug in values for x and use POE.

27. **E** This function factors to $g(x) = \sqrt{(x+2)(x-6)}$. The product of these binomials must be nonnegative (that means positive or zero), since a square root of a negative number is not a real number. The product will be nonnegative when both binomials are negative ($x \leq -2$) or when both are nonnegative ($x \geq 6$). The function's domain is $\{x: x \leq -2$ or $x \geq 6\}$. You could also plug in values for x and use POE.

30. **D** Take this one step at a time. Because a number raised to an even power can't be negative, the range of a^2 is the set of nonnegative numbers—that is, $\{y: y \geq 0\}$. The range of $a^2 + 5$ is found by simply adding 5 to the range of a^2, $\{y: y \geq 5\}$. Finally, to find the range of $\dfrac{a^2 + 5}{3}$, divide the range of $a^2 + 5$ by 3, $\left\{y: y \geq \dfrac{5}{3}\right\}$, or $\{y: y \geq 1.67\}$. The correct answer is (D). You could also plug in values for a to determine the possible values for $t(a)$.

34. **D** Because this is a linear function (without exponents), you can find its range over the given interval by plugging in the bounds of the domain: $f(-1) = -1$, and $f(4) = 19$. Therefore, the range of f is $\{y: -1 \leq y \leq 19\}$.

Drill 6: Graphs of Functions, p. 305

9. **D** It's possible to intersect the graph shown in (D) twice with a vertical line, where the floating point duplicates an x-value on the curve.

15. **B** It's possible to intersect the graph shown in (B) more than once with a vertical line, namely at each point where the graph becomes vertical.

Drill 7: Range and Domain in Graphs, p. 309

17. **A** The graph has a vertical asymptote at $x = 0$, so 0 must be excluded from the domain of f.

24. **D** Only two x-values are absent from the graph, $x = 2$ and $x = -2$. The domain must exclude these values. This can be written as $\{x: x \neq -2, 2\}$ or $\{x: |x| \neq 2\}$.

28. **C** The graph extends upward forever, but it never goes lower than -3. Its range is therefore $\{y: y \geq -3\}$.

37. **C** Plug in a big number, such as $x = 1,000$. It looks like y approaches 5.

48. **E** Plug the numbers you are given into the equation to see what happens to the graph. In I, if $x = 2$, then $y = -\dfrac{1}{0}$, which does not exist. Therefore, I is definitely an asymptote, and you should eliminate answer choices without I in them, that is, (B) and (C). Now, try plugging in a big number for x, like $x = 1,000$. y heads toward -1, which means $y = -1$ is also an asymptote, and III is correct. Cross off answer choices without III in them, in other words, (A) and (D). The correct answer is (E).

Drill 8: Roots of Functions, p. 312

16. **D** PITA! Plug In each choice for x into $f(x)$ to see which one spits out 0.

19. **C** The function $g(x)$ can be factored as $g(x) = x(x + 3)(x - 2)$. Set this function equal to zero and solve for x. You'll find the function has three distinct roots, -3, 0, and 2.

25. **D** The roots of a function are the x-values at which $f(x) = 0$. In short, the roots are the x-intercepts—in this case, -4, -1, and 2.

Drill 9: Symmetry in Functions, p. 315

6. **D** "Symmetrical with respect to the *x*-axis" means reflected as though the *x*-axis were a mirror. That is, the values of the function above the *x*-axis should match corresponding values below the *x*-axis.

17. **E** An even function is one for which $f(x) = f(-x)$. This is true by definition of an absolute value. Confirm by plugging in numbers.

Comprehensive Functions Drill, p. 319

1. **C** Make $x = -4$ everywhere within the function:

    $-(-4)^2 - 3(-4) + 5 =$

    $-16 + 12 + 5 = 1$

    That matches (C).

8. **D** Plug In! Make $x = 2$. If $h(x) = x^2 - 3$, then $h(2 + 2) = h(4) = 4^2 - 3 = 13$. This is your target; circle it. Then plug $x = 2$ into each answer choice. Only (D) equals 13 when $x = 2$.

10. **B** Plug In the Answers! Make each answer choice equal to a and plug it into the function in place of x. Starting with (C), if $a = 0$, then $f(0) = \dfrac{0^2 - 2(0)}{3} = 0$. Eliminate (C). Because the function has an even exponent, it can be hard to determine which direction to go, so just pick one. When you try (B), you find that $f(-3) = \dfrac{(-3)^2 - 2(-3)}{3} = 5$, so (B) is the answer.

12. **C** Start with the innermost set of parentheses. The weird symbol is simply a function, and the function tells you that $\sqcap\, x$ is the "greatest integer less than or equal to *x*." Therefore, $\sqcap\, 0.5$ is the greatest integer less than or equal to 0.5, which would be 0. Now, the problem is $\sqcap\, (\sqcap\, (0))$, so do the innermost function again. This time, 0 is the greatest integer less than or equal to 0, so $\sqcap\, 0 = 0$. When you apply the function the third time, you're still stuck with 0, so the answer is (C).

15. **B** Because the problem asks for the range of a linear function, you only need to plug in the extremes of the domain. When $x = -8$, the function equals $0.7(-8) - 2.5 = -8.1$. This is the minimum, so you can eliminate (C), (D), and (E). When $x = 3$, the function equals $0.7(3) - 2.5 = -0.4$. Eliminate (A) and choose (B).

16. **C** Start with the innermost parenthesis. Make $x = 3$ in $f(x)$: $f(3) = \dfrac{3^2 + 3}{2} = 6$, so $g(f(3)) = g(6)$. Next, make $x = 6$ in $g(x)$: $g(6) = 5(6) - 4 = 26$. That matches (C).

22. **E** Because $f(g(x)) = x$, $g(x)$ is the inverse function of $f(x)$. Plug in to the $f(x)$ function, then take the result and plug it into the $g(x)$ functions in the answers to see what gives you your original

number. Make $x = 7$ to avoid repeating numbers in the question and dealing with negative numbers:

$f(7) = \dfrac{(7-3)^3}{5} = \dfrac{64}{5}$. Now, plug $x = \dfrac{64}{5}$ into the answers and look for the one which gives you 7; that answer will be the inverse of $f(x)$. Only (E) works.

36. **A** The function $g(x)$ is shifted to the right 5 units and down 3 units. To shift a function to the right 5 units, you must subtract 5 within the parenthesis; eliminate (B), (C), and (D). To shift a function down 3 units, you must subtract 3 outside the parenthesis; eliminate (E) and choose (A).

40. **E** Plug In! Make $x = 2$. To find $f(g(2))$, start by finding $g(2)$: $g(2) = 3(2) - 1 = 5$. Therefore, $f(g(2)) = f(5)$. Next, find $f(5)$: $f(5) = 2(5)^2 + 5 = 55$. So $f(g(2)) = 55$; this is your target, so circle it. Lastly, make $x = 2$ in each answer choice and eliminate each choice that doesn't equal 55. Only (E) works.

42. **E** Plug In for x. Because so many of the answer choices are about 0, start with $x = 0$. You may not even know what "ln" means, but your calculator does. Your calculator will give you an error for ln 0, which means that $x = 0$ must NOT be in the domain; eliminate (B), (C), and (D). The difference between (A) and (E) is that (A) includes negative numbers, whereas (E) does not, so try a negative number. Make $x = -2$. Once again, your calculator will give you an error message, so eliminate (A) and choose (E). For more information on natural logs, see Chapter 12.

48. **E** Plug In the Answers! Make each answer choice $= x$, and eliminate the choices which do not make $f(x) = 0$, because they are roots. Only (E) does not make $f(x) = 0$.

CHAPTER 12: MISCELLANEOUS DRILL EXPLANATIONS

Drill 1: Statistics, p. 327

25. **B** If the sum of a list's elements is zero, then the mean must also be zero. It's impossible to know what the median is; the list could be {0, 0, 0, 0, 0, 0, 0, 0, 0, 0} or {−9, 1, 1, 1, 1, 1, 1, 1, 1, 1}. Both lists add up to zero, but have different medians. The mode is not necessarily zero for the same reasons.

38 **C** The answer choices all talk about mean and median. Use the Average Pie when you want to solve questions about mean:

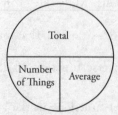

You know that the seven starting employees have an average annual salary of $42,000:

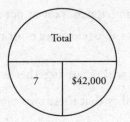

The Average Pie tells you to multiply to find the total: 7 × 42,000 = 294,000. When the eighth employee is added to the company, that changes both the number of things and the total. There are now 8 employees, and the new total is 294,000 + 38,000 = 332,000. These numbers can go back into the Average Pie:

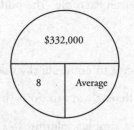

The Average Pie tells you to divide to find the new average (mean): 332,000 ÷ 8 = 41,500. The mean is definitely less than $42,000; eliminate (D) and (E).

To find the median of the annual salaries of all eight employees, start with what you know from the first seven. If you lined up the first seven employees consecutively by annual salary, $42,000 would be in the middle:

The other salaries must add up to 294,000 − 42,000 = 252,000. The easiest set to try out is when every salary is 42,000:

When you add the eighth employee's salary, the set becomes the following:

Because there is an even number of elements, you take the average of the middle two elements. Here, both middle elements are 42,000, so the median is 42,000. Eliminate (A).

Try a new starting set. Make the three salaries below the median salary 40,000, and the three salaries above the median salary 44,000. The mean and median will still be 42,000:

Then add the eighth employee:

Now, the middle two values are 40,000 and 42,000, which makes the median the average of those two values, or 41,000. The median of the eight annual salaries doesn't have to be 42,000, so eliminate (B) and choose (C).

Drill 2: Probability, p. 337

13. **A** There are only two things that can happen, rain or not rain. If 5 out of 12 possible outcomes mean rain, then the other 7 of the 12 possible outcomes must mean no rain.

16. **A** The probability that two events will occur together is the product of the chances that each will happen individually. The probability that these two events will happen together is $\frac{2}{5} \cdot \frac{1}{3}$, or $\frac{2}{15}$.

20. **B** Out of a total of 741 cookies, 114 are burned. The probability of getting a burned cookie is therefore $\frac{114}{741}$. That reduces to $\frac{1}{6.5}$, which is equivalent to $\frac{2}{13}$.

24. **B** For the product of the numbers to be odd, both numbers must be odd themselves. There's a $\frac{3}{6}$ chance of getting an odd number on each die. The odds of getting odd numbers on both dice are $\frac{3}{6} \cdot \frac{3}{6} = \frac{9}{36} = \frac{1}{4}$.

44. **C** This one's pretty tricky. It's difficult to compute the odds of getting "at least one basket" in three tries, since there are so many different ways to do it (basket-basket-basket, miss-miss-basket, basket-basket-miss, and so on). It's a simpler solution to calculate the odds of Heather's missing all three times. If the probability of her making a basket on any given try is $\frac{4}{5}$, then the probability of her missing is $\frac{1}{5}$. The probability of her missing three times in a row is $\frac{1}{5} \cdot \frac{1}{5} \cdot \frac{1}{5}$, or $\frac{1}{125}$. That means that Heather makes no baskets in 1 out of 125 possible outcomes. The other 124 possible outcomes must involve her making at least 1 basket.

Drill 3: Permutations, Combinations, and Factorials, p. 344

27. **B** All committee questions are combination questions, because different arrangements of the same people don't count as different committees. The number of permutations of 12 items in 4 spaces is $12 \times 11 \times 10 \times 9$, or 11,880. To find the number of combinations, divide this number by $4 \times 3 \times 2 \times 1$, or 24. You get 495.

32. **D** The number of permutations of 6 items in 6 spaces is $6 \times 5 \times 4 \times 3 \times 2 \times 1$, or 720.

45. **A** Compute the number of combinations of females and males separately. The number of combinations of 17 females in 4 spaces is $\frac{17 \cdot 16 \cdot 15 \cdot 14}{4 \cdot 3 \cdot 2 \cdot 1}$, or 2,380. The number of combinations of 12 males in 3 spaces is $\frac{12 \cdot 11 \cdot 10}{3 \cdot 2 \cdot 1}$, or 220. The total number of combinations is the product of these two numbers, $220 \times 2,380$, or 523,600.

Drill 4: Group Questions, p. 346

25. **A**   Remember the group problem formula: Total = Group 1 + Group 2 + Neither − Both. Then Plug in the numbers from the question, so $530 = 253 + 112 + N - 23$, and $N = 188$.

28. **C**   Remember the group-problem formula: Total = Group 1 + Group 2 + Neither − Both. Then Plug in the numbers from the question, so $T = 14 + 12 + 37 - 9 = 54$.

42. **B**   Plug in a number of tourists that you can easily take $\frac{1}{3}$, $\frac{2}{5}$, and $\frac{1}{2}$ of—like 30. If the total number of tourists is 30, then 10 speak Spanish, 12 speak French, and 15 speak neither language. Once again, plug these numbers into the group formula to get $30 = 10 + 12 + 15 - B$. This simplifies to $30 = 37 - B$, so $B = 7$. Seven tourists speak both Spanish and French. That's $\frac{7}{30}$ of the whole group.

Drill 5: Logarithms, p. 349

1. $2^5 = 32$, so $\log_2 32 = 5$

2. $3^4 = 81$, so $x = 81$

3. $10^3 = 1{,}000$, so $\log 1{,}000 = 3$

4. $4^3 = 64$, so $b = 4$

5.   Exponents and logs undo each other, so $x^{\log_x y} = y$

6. $7^0 = 1$, so $\log_7 1 = 0$

7.   The sidebar tells you that $\log_x x = 1$

8. x to what power is x^{12}? The 12th power, of course! $\log_x x^{12} = 12$

9.   1.5682—use your calculator

10.   0.6990—use your calculator

Drill 6: Visual Perception, p. 352

27.   **A**

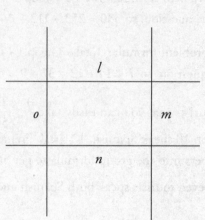

Drawing the described set of lines results in something looking like the above. As you can see, line *l* is parallel to line *n*, but neither of the other two statements is true.

42.   **D**   Whenever a circle intersects with a face of cube and pokes through (as opposed to touching at just one point), it creates a circle.

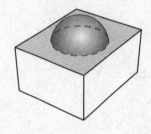

It's probably easiest to get six intersections by having the sphere intersect with all six faces of the cube.

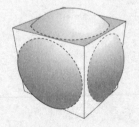

It's also possible to get five by having nearly the same picture but moving the sphere up a little so as not to intersect with the base of the cube. Seven is too complicated, though; there are only six faces of the cube, so how are there going to be seven circles?

Drill 7: Arithmetic and Geometric Sequences, p. 355

14. **E** An arithmetic sequence is formed by adding a value again and again to an original term. From the second term to a sixth term is 4 steps. Going from 4 to 32 is a change of 28 in four steps, making each step an increase of 7. The fifth term must then be 7 less than the sixth term, or 25.

19. **E** Going from the first to the seventh term of a sequence is 6 steps, and going from 2 to 16 is a difference of 14. That makes each step an increase of $\frac{14}{6}$, or 2.33. To find the 33rd term, plug these numbers into the formula for the nth term of an arithmetic sequence: $a_{33} = 2 + (33 - 1)\frac{7}{3} = 2 + 74\frac{2}{3} = 76.67$.

Drill 8: Logic, p. 358

28. **D** The basic statement here is: sophomore $\rightarrow$ not failing. The contrapositive of this statement would be: failing $\rightarrow$ not sophomore. Choice (D) is the contrapositive.

33. **B** The basic statement here is: arson $\rightarrow$ building burns. The contrapositive would be: no building burns $\rightarrow$ no arson. Choice (B) directly contradicts the contrapositive.

35. **C** The basic statement here is: not genuine $\rightarrow$ ruby. The contrapositive would be: not ruby $\rightarrow$ genuine. Choice (C) paraphrases the contrapositive.

Drill 9: Imaginary Numbers, p. 361

25. **C** Remember that the powers of i repeat in a cycle of four. Divide 51 by 4, and you'll find that the remainder is 3. i^{51} will be equal to i^3, which is $-i$.

36. **D** Only (D) contains two values that do not cancel each other out. $i^{11} = i^3(i^8) = i^3(1) = i^3 = -i$, and $i^9 = i(i^8) = i(1) = i$. So $-i - i = -2i$, not 0.

40. **B** Use FOIL on the top of the fraction, and you get $\frac{4 - 16i^2}{5}$, or $\frac{4 + 16}{5} = \frac{20}{5} = 4$.

Drill 10: Matrices p. 365

30. **D** In matrix multiplication, the two inner dimensions (the number of columns in the first matrix and the number of rows in the second matrix) must be equal; the resulting matrix will have as many rows as the first matrix and as many columns as the second matrix.

Comprehensive Miscellaneous Drill, p. 366

6. **C** This set has 14 elements. The median in a set with an even number of elements will be the average of the two middle elements. The two middle elements are 32 and 52. To find the average, add and divide by 2: $\frac{32+52}{2} = 42$, which is (C).

15. **A** With every "if...then" statement, the contrapositive is always true. In other words, if the statement "If A then B" is true, then "If not B then not A" is also true. Here, the contrapositive of the statement "If you complete the marathon in under 5 hours, then you must have prepared adequately for the marathon" would be "If you do not prepare adequately for the marathon, you will not complete the marathon in under 5 hours," which matches (A).

    Choice (B) is not necessarily true; there may be other reasons besides lack of preparation which would lead to not completing the marathon in under 5 hours. Choice (C) assumes that adequate preparation is all that is required to guarantee a finish in under 5 hours. Choice (D) talks about "poor marathon performance," which isn't included in the original statement. Choice (E) talks about both failing to finish the marathon and not preparing at all; neither concept is included in the original statement.

18. **A** Use the definition of log to convert this problem into an exponent problem: $\log_b n = x \Leftrightarrow b^x = n$, so $\log_x 256 = 8 \Leftrightarrow x^8 = 256$. You can then either solve by taking the 8th root of both sides (on the TI-84, you would press 8, then MATH-> $\sqrt[x]{}$, then 256), or you can Plug In the Answers for x. Either way, you find that $x = 2$, which is (A).

25. **B** First, determine the number of employees who have weekly salaries of more than $800. Because you want more than $800, add up the last two columns (remember that the y-axis is in hundreds of employees): 150 + 300 = 450. Next, determine the total number of employees by adding up all the columns: 100 + 50 + 400 + 300 + 150 + 300 = 1,300. Finally, divide the number of employees with salaries of more than $800 by the total number of employees and multiply by 100 to find the percentage: 450 ÷ 1300 = 0.346; 0.346 × 100 = 34.6%, which is closest to (B).

26. **D** The median is the middle data point of the set. First, determine the total number of employees by adding up all the columns (remember that the y-axis is in hundreds of employees): 100 + 50 + 400 + 300 + 150 + 300 = 1,300 employees. Because there are an even number of employees, the median of the set will be the average of the two employees in the middle. The middle will be at 1,300 ÷ 2 = 650, so you need the weekly salary of the 650th and 651st employees.

    To find these employees, start at the leftmost column and start counting. There are 100 employees making $500 a week, and 50 more making $600 a week. The "last" employee making $600 a week is the 150th employee, as ranked by weekly salary. There are 400 employees making $700 a week, so those employees are the 151st through 550th employees. There are 300 employees making $800 a week, so those employees are the 551st through 850th employees. This means that the 650th and 651st employees are both in this group making $800 a week, so the median of the set must be $800, (D).

34. **C** Draw it! Start by drawing the piece of paper with the squares in the four corners:

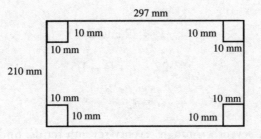

To find the volume of the resulting box, remember the formula of a rectangular box: $V = l \times w \times h$. If Sandra is going to fold up the sides of the box, the height will be the side of the squares cut out of the corners, or 10 mm. To find the length and the width, draw in where Sandra will fold the box and find the resulting rectangle:

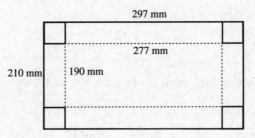

Note you have to reduce each side by 20 mm, because there are two squares of side length 10 mm which are cut from each side.

You now know that the length of the box is 277 mm and the width is 190 mm. Use your volume formula to solve: $V = 277 \text{ mm} \times 190 \text{ mm} \times 10 \text{ mm} = 526{,}300 \text{ mm}^3$, which is (C).

35. **B** To find the probability of two events both happening, find the probability of each event individually and multiply. Nathalie has a total of 26 bottles of nail polish, so the probability that the first bottle is mauve is $\dfrac{5}{26}$. Because she doesn't replace the bottle, there are now 25 bottles in the collection, so the probability that the second bottle is blue is $\dfrac{4}{25}$. To find the probability of mauve followed by blue, multiply the two fractions: $\dfrac{5}{26} \times \dfrac{4}{25} = \dfrac{20}{650} = \dfrac{2}{65}$, which is (B).

38. **E** Start by determining what the arithmetic sequence is. If the fourth term is 22 and the sixth term is 32, then going up two terms resulted in an increase of 10. This means that the difference between terms must be half of 10, or 5. Because you know the difference, you can now use the equation of an arithmetic sequence to find the initial value. This equation is $a_n = a_1 + (n - 1)d$, where a_n is the nth term of the sequence and d is the common difference between terms. In this case, $n = 4$ and $d = 5$:

$$a_4 = 22 \text{ and } d = 5$$

$$22 = a_1 + (4 - 1)5$$

$$7 = a_1$$

To find the sum of the seventh through seventy-seventh terms, find the sum of the first seventy-seven terms and then subtract the sum of the first six terms. To do so, use the formula for the sum of an arithmetic sequence: $n\left(\dfrac{a_1 + a_n}{2}\right)$.

Using the equation for the sequence as determined above, the seventy-seventh term can be found as follows:

$$a_{77} = 7 + (77 - 1)5 = 387$$

The sum of the first 77 terms is therefore:

$$77\left(\frac{7 + 387}{2}\right) = 15,169$$

You already know that the sixth term of the sequence is 32, so you can determine the sum of the first six terms:

$$6\left(\frac{7 + 32}{2}\right) = 117$$

Finally, subtract the sum of the first 6 terms from the sum of the first 77 terms to be left with the sum of the seventh through seventy-seventh term:

$$15,169 - 117 = 15,052$$

This is (E).

42. **B** Use the Group Equation: Total = Group 1 + Group 2 + Neither − Both. Make the Sine Wave Spectacular Group 1 and the Matrix Mixer Group 2. Note that there is no one who does neither ride, so that value will be zero:

55 = 37 + Matrix Mixer + 0 − 23

Combine the constants on the right hand side:

55 = 14 + Matrix Mixer

Subtract 14 from both sides:

41 = Matrix Mixer

But wait! The question wants to know how many people ride the Matrix Mixer but do NOT rider the Sine Wave Spectacular as well. So you need to subtract the number of people who rode both rides to be left with the number of students who rode just the Matrix Mixer:

Just Matrix Mixer = 41 − 23 = 18

This is (B).

You can also get close to the answer by using Process of Elimination and some common sense. There are only 55 students, so there's no way that 64 students could be riding the Matrix Mixer; eliminate (E). If you want the number of students who ride only the Matrix Mixer, you can't include anyone who rode the Sine Wave Spectacular. So, if you subtract the number of students who rode the Sine Wave Spectacular from the total class, you get 55 − 37 = 18, which is the HIGHEST possible value for number of students who rode just the Matrix Mixer, so you can eliminate (C) and (D), which leaves you with two to guess between.

47. C This is a combination question because you want the total number of possible groups available (order doesn't matter). You want to determine how many groups of machinists are available and multiply that number by the number of groups of laborers. You want to multiply because each possible group of machinists could be matched with any possible group of laborers; multiplying will give you the total number of overall groups.

To find the number of possible groups of machinists, start by finding the permutation. You are choosing 3 machinists, so make three spots:

Next, fill in the number of machinists available for each spot and then multiply. Because each machinist can only fill one spot, you need to count down as you go:

7 6 5 = 210

Because order doesn't matter, you need to divide by the factorial of the number of spots: 3! = 3 × 2 × 1 = 6:

210 ÷ 6 = 35

Now, repeat the process for the laborers. Make 4 spots this time, fill in the numbers, and multiply:

 = 360

Once again, order doesn't matter, so divide by the factorial of the number of spots: $4! = 4 \times 3 \times 2 \times 1 = 24$:

$360 \div 24 = 15$

Finally, multiply the number of groups of machinists by the number of groups of laborers:

$35 \times 15 = 525$

This is (C).

50. **D** One approach is to Plug In and use your calculator. Because you want a product matrix of $\begin{bmatrix} 0 & 0 \\ 0 & 0 \end{bmatrix}$, the easiest place to start is by making $x = 0$, $y = 0$, and $z = 0$. Your calculator will tell you that $\begin{bmatrix} 0 & 0 \\ 0 & 0 \end{bmatrix} \times \begin{bmatrix} 1 & 0 \\ 1 & 0 \end{bmatrix} = \begin{bmatrix} 0 & 0 \\ 0 & 0 \end{bmatrix}$. Choice (E) does not have to be true, as $xyz = 0$ in this case; eliminate it. The remaining answer choices talk about x and y, so focus your attention on these variables. Try making $x = 2$ and $y = -2$, while leaving $z = 0$. Your calculator will tell you that $\begin{bmatrix} 2 & -2 \\ 0 & 0 \end{bmatrix} \times \begin{bmatrix} 1 & 0 \\ 1 & 0 \end{bmatrix} = \begin{bmatrix} 0 & 0 \\ 0 & 0 \end{bmatrix}$. This lets you eliminate (A), (B), and (C), so you're left with (D).

The other approach is to remember your matrix multiplication rules. The first row, first column of the product matrix will be the dot product of the first row of the first matrix by the first column of the second matrix. Because the first row, first column of the product matrix is 0, it must be true that $(x)(1) + (y)(1) = 0$, or $x + y = 0$. If you solve this for x, you find that $x = -y$, which is (D).

Part V
Final Practice Test

Chapter 13
Practice Test 2

MATHEMATICS LEVEL 1

For each of the following problems, decide which is the BEST of the choices given. If the exact numerical value is not one of the choices, select the choice that best approximates this value. Then fill in the corresponding oval on the answer sheet.

Notes: (1) A scientific or graphing calculator will be necessary for answering some (but not all) of the questions on this test. For each question, you will have to decide whether or not you should use a calculator.

(2) The only angle measure used on this test is degree measure. Make sure that your calculator is in degree mode.

(3) Figures that accompany problems on this test are intended to provide information useful in solving the problems. They are drawn as accurately as possible EXCEPT when it is stated in a specific problem that its figure is not drawn to scale. All figures lie in a plane unless otherwise indicated.

(4) Unless otherwise specified, the domain of any function f is assumed to be the set of all real numbers x for which $f(x)$ is a real number. The range of f is assumed to be the set of all real numbers $f(x)$, where x is in the domain of f.

(5) Reference information that may be useful in answering the questions on this test can be found below.

THE FOLLOWING INFORMATION IS FOR YOUR REFERENCE IN ANSWERING SOME OF THE QUESTIONS ON THIS TEST.

Volume of a right circular cone with radius r and height h:
$$V = \frac{1}{3}\pi r^2 h$$

Volume of a sphere with radius r: $V = \frac{4}{3}\pi r^3$

Surface area of a sphere with radius r: $S = 4\pi r^2$

Volume of a pyramid with base area B and height h:
$$V = \frac{1}{3}Bh$$

USE THIS SPACE FOR SCRATCHWORK.

1. Rob and Sherry together weigh 300 pounds. Sherry and Heather together weigh 240 pounds. If all three people together weigh 410 pounds, then what is Sherry's weight, in pounds?

    (A) 110
    (B) 115
    (C) 120
    (D) 130
    (E) 145

2. If the point (5, 2) is reflected across the x-axis, then what are the coordinates of the resulting point?

    (A) (5, 0)
    (B) (0, 2)
    (C) (5, –2)
    (D) (–5, 2)
    (E) (2, 5)

GO ON TO THE NEXT PAGE

3. If $r = \dfrac{2}{3}$ and $s = 6$, then $\dfrac{s}{r} + \dfrac{4}{r^2} =$

USE THIS SPACE FOR SCRATCHWORK.

(A) 4
(B) 6
(C) 9
(D) 12
(E) 18

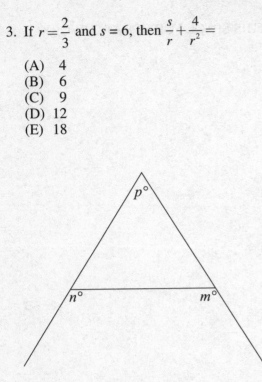

Figure 1

4. In Figure 1, what is the value of p in terms of m and n ?

(A) $m + n - 180$
(B) $m + n + 180$
(C) $m - n + 360$
(D) $360 - (m - n)$
(E) $360 - (m + n)$

5. After 8:00 p.m., a ride in a taxi costs $2.50 plus $0.30 for every fifth of a mile traveled. If a passenger travels b miles, then what is the cost of the trip, in dollars, in terms of b ?

(A) $2.5 + 0.3b$
(B) $2.5 + 1.5b$
(C) $2.8b$
(D) $30 + 250b$
(E) $250 + 30b$

GO ON TO THE NEXT PAGE

6. If $|y - 3| = 4y - 7$, then which of the following could be the value of y?

USE THIS SPACE FOR SCRATCHWORK.

   (A) $\dfrac{3}{4}$

   (B) 1

   (C) $\dfrac{5}{4}$

   (D) 2

   (E) 5

7. What is the slope of the line given by the equation $y + 3 = \dfrac{5}{4}(x - 7)$?

   (A) $-\dfrac{4}{5}$

   (B) $-\dfrac{2}{3}$

   (C) $\dfrac{3}{7}$

   (D) $\dfrac{2}{3}$

   (E) $\dfrac{5}{4}$

8. If $a = \cos\theta$ and $b = \sin\theta$, then for all θ, $a^2 + b^2 =$

   (A) 0
   (B) 1
   (C) 2
   (D) $(\cos\theta + \sin\theta)^2$
   (E) $(\cos\theta \cdot \sin\theta)^2$

GO ON TO THE NEXT PAGE

USE THIS SPACE FOR SCRATCHWORK.

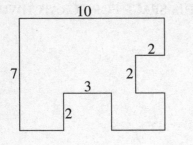

Figure 2

9. In Figure 2, if every angle in the polygon is a right angle, then what is the perimeter of the polygon?

(A) 34
(B) 42
(C) 47
(D) 52
(E) 60

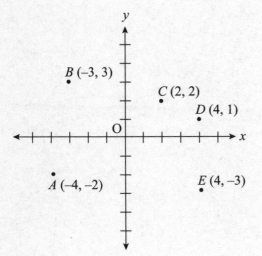

Figure 3

10. For which of the points shown in Figure 3 is $|x + y| > 5$?

(A) A
(B) B
(C) C
(D) D
(E) E

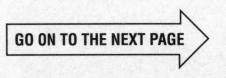

GO ON TO THE NEXT PAGE

Questions 11-12 refer to the chart below, which shows the monthly sales made by a salesperson in 1996.

USE THIS SPACE FOR SCRATCHWORK.

Keri s Monthly Sales for 1996

◯ =100 units

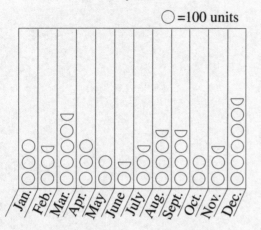

11. As a saleswoman, Keri receives a $10.00 commission for each unit she sells. In any month in which she sells more than 300 units, she receives an additional bonus of $1,000.00. What was the total amount Keri received in bonuses in 1996 ?

(A) $3,000.00
(B) $4,000.00
(C) $5,000.00
(D) $6,000.00
(E) $8,000.00

12. In 1996, Keri had the greatest total income from commissions and bonuses in what three-month period?

(A) January, February, March
(B) February, March, April
(C) March, April, May
(D) July, August, September
(E) October, November, December

GO ON TO THE NEXT PAGE

13. If a varies directly as b^2, and $a = 14$ when $b = 2$, then what is the value of a when $b = 5$?

    (A) 3.6
    (B) 14
    (C) 35
    (D) 70
    (E) 87.5

USE THIS SPACE FOR SCRATCHWORK.

14. If $\dfrac{1}{x} = \dfrac{4}{5}$, then $\dfrac{x}{3} =$

    (A) 0.27
    (B) 0.33
    (C) 0.42
    (D) 0.66
    (E) 1.25

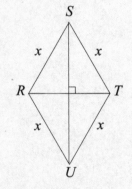

Figure 4

15. In Figure 4, sin ∠*RSU* must be equal to which of the following?

    (A) cos ∠*RTU*
    (B) cos ∠*TSU*
    (C) sin ∠*SRT*
    (D) sin ∠*STR*
    (E) sin ∠*TRU*

GO ON TO THE NEXT PAGE

16. If $y = \sqrt{x} + \dfrac{1}{x-3}$, then which of the following

    statements must be true?

    I. $x > 1$
    II. $x \neq 3$
    III. $x \neq -3$

    (A) I only
    (B) II only
    (C) I and III only
    (D) II and III only
    (E) I, II, and III

USE THIS SPACE FOR SCRATCHWORK.

17. Sphere O is inscribed in cube A, and cube B is inscribed in sphere O. Which of the following quantities must be equal?

    (A) An edge of A and the radius of O
    (B) The diameter of O and the longest
        diagonal in A
    (C) An edge of B and the diameter of O
    (D) An edge of B and the radius of O
    (E) An edge of A and the longest diagonal in B

18. If $a - x = 12$, $b - y = 7$, $c - z = 15$, and $a + b + c = 50$, then $x + y + z =$

    (A) 16   (B) 18   (C) 34   (D) 66   (E) 84

GO ON TO THE NEXT PAGE

MATHEMATICS LEVEL 1—*Continued*

19. A jeep has four seats, including one driver's seat and three passenger seats. If Amber, Bunny, Cassie, and Donna are going for a drive in the jeep, and only Cassie can drive, then how many different seating arrangements are possible?

    (A) 3
    (B) 6
    (C) 12
    (D) 16
    (E) 24

USE THIS SPACE FOR SCRATCHWORK.

20. If $\dfrac{1}{2}x - 3 = 2\left(\dfrac{x-1}{5}\right)$, then $x =$

    (A) 9   (B) 11   (C) 13   (D) 22   (E) 26

21. Line l passes through the origin and point (a, b). If $ab \neq 0$ and line l has a slope greater than 1, then which of the following must be true?

    (A) $a = b$
    (B) $a > b$
    (C) $a^2 < b^2$
    (D) $b - a < 0$
    (E) $a + b > 0$

GO ON TO THE NEXT PAGE

USE THIS SPACE FOR SCRATCHWORK.

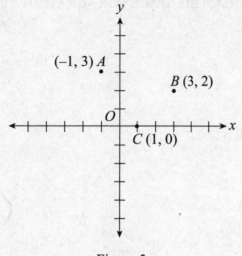

Figure 5

22. In Figure 5, points *A, B,* and *C* are three vertices of a parallelogram, and point *D* (not shown) is the fourth vertex. How many points could be *D* ?

    (A) 1
    (B) 2
    (C) 3
    (D) 4
    (E) 5

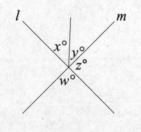

Figure 6

Note: Figure not drawn to scale.

23. In Figure 6, lines *l* and *m* intersect as shown. If $y = \frac{2}{3}x$ and $w = 2z$, then $x =$

    (A) 30   (B) 40   (C) 48   (D) 60 (E)   72

GO ON TO THE NEXT PAGE

24. Circle O has a radius of r. If this radius is increased by t, then which of the following correctly expresses the new area of circle O ?

    (A) πt^2

    (B) $2\pi(r + t)$

    (C) $\pi(t^2 + r^2)$

    (D) $\pi(r^2 + 2rt + t^2)$

    (E) $4\pi(r^2 + 2rt + t^2)$

USE THIS SPACE FOR SCRATCHWORK.

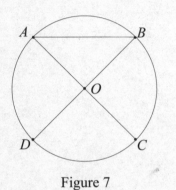

Figure 7

25. In Figure 7, AC and BD are perpendicular diameters of the circle with center O. If the circle has an area of 9π, what is the length of AB ?

    (A) 2.12
    (B) 3.36
    (C) 4.24
    (D) 6.36
    (E) 8.48

26. If $x < |x|$ and $x^2 + 2x - 3 = 0$, then $2x + 4 =$

    (A) –2   (B) 2   (C) 6   (D) 8   (E) 10

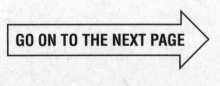

GO ON TO THE NEXT PAGE

USE THIS SPACE FOR SCRATCHWORK.

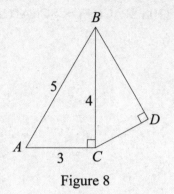

Figure 8

27. In Figure 8, triangles ABC and CBD are similar.
    What is the area of triangle CBD ?

    (A) 3.07
    (B) 3.84
    (C) 5.24
    (D) 7.68
    (E) 9.60

28. If $i = \sqrt{-1}$, then $(5 - 3i)(4 + 2i) =$

    (A) $14 - 2i$
    (B) 16
    (C) 24
    (D) $26 - 2i$
    (E) 28

29. If $f(x) = x^2 - 5x$ and $f(n) = -4$, then which of the
    following could be the value of n ?

    (A) -5
    (B) -4
    (C) -1
    (D) 1
    (E) 5

GO ON TO THE NEXT PAGE

30. Two identical rectangular solids, each of dimensions $3 \times 4 \times 5$, are joined face to face to form a single rectangular solid with a length of 8. What is the length of the longest line segment that can be drawn within this new solid?

(A) 8.60
(B) 9.90
(C) 10.95
(D) 11.40
(E) 12.25

USE THIS SPACE FOR SCRATCHWORK.

31. Which of the following most closely approximates $\left(5.5 \times 10^4\right)^2$?

(A) 3.0×10^5
(B) 3.0×10^6
(C) 3.0×10^7
(D) 3.0×10^8
(E) 3.0×10^9

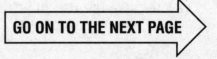

GO ON TO THE NEXT PAGE

x	$P(x)$
0	$\dfrac{1}{16}$
1	$\dfrac{1}{4}$
2	n
3	$\dfrac{1}{4}$
4	$\dfrac{1}{16}$

32. If a fair coin is flipped four times, the probability of the coin landing heads-side-up x times is shown in the table above. What is the value of n ?

   (A) $\dfrac{1}{8}$

   (B) $\dfrac{3}{16}$

   (C) $\dfrac{5}{16}$

   (D) $\dfrac{3}{8}$

   (E) $\dfrac{1}{2}$

33. A sample of metal is heated to 698°C and then allowed to cool. The temperature of the metal over time is given by the formula $n = 698 - 2t - 0.5t^2$, where t is the time in seconds after the start of the cooling process, and n is the temperature of the sample in degrees Celsius. After how many seconds will the temperature of the sample be 500°C ?

   (A) 16 (B) 18 (C) 20 (D) 22 (E) 24

GO ON TO THE NEXT PAGE

34. Perpendicular lines *l* and *m* intersect at (4, 5). If line *m* has a slope of $-\dfrac{1}{2}$, which of the following is an equation for line *l* ?

USE THIS SPACE FOR SCRATCHWORK.

(A) $y = \dfrac{1}{2}x - 1$

(B) $y = \dfrac{1}{2}x + 3$

(C) $y = \dfrac{1}{2}x + 5$

(D) $y = 2x - 1$

(E) $y = 2x - 3$

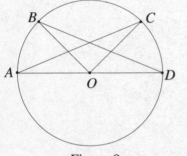

Figure 9

35. In Figure 9, points *A*, *B*, *C*, and *D* are all on the circle with center *O*. If $\angle BDA$ measures 25°, and $\angle CAD$ measures 32°, what is the measure of $\angle BOC$ in degrees?

(A) 33
(B) 66
(C) 123
(D) 147
(E) 303

36. If $4^{x+2} = 48$, then $4^x =$

(A) 3.0
(B) 6.4
(C) 6.9
(D) 12.0
(E) 24.0

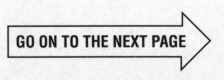

GO ON TO THE NEXT PAGE

37. If $r(x) = 6x + 5$ and $s(r(x)) = 2x - 1$, then $s(x) =$

    USE THIS SPACE FOR SCRATCHWORK.

    (A) $-4x - 6$

    (B) $\dfrac{x - 2}{3}$

    (C) $\dfrac{x - 8}{3}$

    (D) $3x - 6$

    (E) $4x + 4$

38. Of the 850 stores in Noel-Bentley County, 250 have alarm systems and 450 have guard dogs. If 350 stores have neither alarm systems nor guard dogs, then how many stores have both alarm systems and guard dogs?

    (A) 100
    (B) 150
    (C) 200
    (D) 500
    (E) 700

39. If $\log_9 27 = n$, then $n =$

    (A) $\dfrac{1}{3}$

    (B) 1

    (C) $\dfrac{3}{2}$

    (D) $\sqrt{3}$

    (E) 3

GO ON TO THE NEXT PAGE

MATHEMATICS LEVEL 1—*Continued*

40. A cylindrical cup has a height of 3 inches and a radius of 2 inches. How many such cups may be completely filled from a full rectangular tank whose dimensions are $6 \times 7 \times 8$ inches?

   (A) 8
   (B) 9
   (C) 12
   (D) 17
   (E) 28

USE THIS SPACE FOR SCRATCHWORK.

41. Line segments AC and BD intersect at point O, such that each segment is the perpendicular bisector of the other. If $AC = 7$ and $BD = 6$, then $\sin \angle ADO =$

   (A) 0.16
   (B) 0.24
   (C) 0.39
   (D) 0.76
   (E) 0.85

42. Which of the following boxplots represents the data set with the greatest interquartile range?

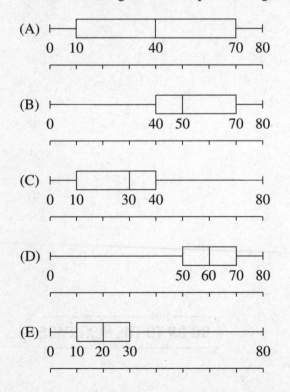

GO ON TO THE NEXT PAGE

43. If $f(x) = kx$, where k is a nonzero constant, and $g(x) = x + k$, then which of the following statements must be true?

    I. $f(2x) = 2f(x)$
    II. $f(x + 2) = f(x) + 2$
    III. $f(g(x)) = g(f(x))$

  (A) I only
  (B) II only
  (C) I and II only
  (D) I and III only
  (E) I, II, and III

USE THIS SPACE FOR SCRATCHWORK.

44. A rectangular room has walls facing due north, south, east, and west. On the southern wall, a tack is located 85 inches from the floor and 38 inches from the western wall, and a nail is located 48 inches from the floor and 54 inches from the western wall. What is the distance in inches between the tack and the nail?

  (A) 21.0
  (B) 26.4
  (C) 32.6
  (D) 37.0
  (E) 40.3

45. If $f(x) = \sqrt{12 - x^2}$, then which of the following is the domain of f?

  (A) $\{x: \ x \neq \sqrt{12}\}$

  (B) $\{x: \ x \geq 0\}$

  (C) $\{x: \ -\sqrt{12} \leq x \leq \sqrt{12}\}$

  (D) $\{x: \ 0 < x < \sqrt{12}\}$

  (E) $\{x: \ 0 \leq x \leq 144\}$

GO ON TO THE NEXT PAGE

"If a tree falls in the forest,
a sound is heard."

USE THIS SPACE FOR SCRATCHWORK.

46. If the statement above is true, then which of the following CANNOT be true?

(A) No tree falls in the forest, but a sound is heard.
(B) No sound is heard as a tree falls in the forest.
(C) A sound is heard as a tree falls in the forest.
(D) No tree falls in the forest, and no sound is made.
(E) A sound is heard in the forest as no tree falls.

47. At a dance competition, each of six couples must compete against the other five couples in a dance-off three times before the winning couple can be declared. How many such dance-offs will occur?

(A) 12
(B) 33
(C) 45
(D) 60
(E) 63

USE THIS SPACE FOR SCRATCHWORK.

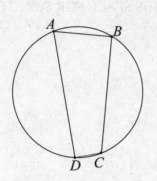

Figure 10

Note: Figure not drawn to scale.

48. In Figure 10, $AB = 4$, $BC = 7$, and $CD = 1$. If AC is a diameter of the circle, then what is the length of AD ?

(A)　　3
(B)　　6
(C)　　8
(D)　$\sqrt{65}$
(E)　　10

49. $(0, 0)$ and $(-2, 2)$ are the coordinates of two vertices of an equilateral triangle. Which of the following could be the coordinates of the third vertex?

(A)　$(-2.0, 0)$
(B)　$(-0.73, 2.73)$
(C)　$(-0.73, 0.73)$
(D)　$(0, 2.0)$
(E)　$(0.73, 2.73)$

50. What is the distance between the two x-intercepts of the graph of $y = x^2 - 9x + 19.25$?

(A)　2.0
(B)　3.5
(C)　5.5
(D)　10.25
(E)　28.25

STOP

IF YOU FINISH BEFORE TIME IS CALLED, YOU MAY CHECK YOUR WORK ON THIS TEST ONLY.
DO NOT WORK ON ANY OTHER TEST IN THIS BOOK.

Chapter 14
Practice Test 2:
Answers and
Explanations

PRACTICE TEST 2 ANSWER KEY

Question Number	Correct Answer	Right	Wrong	Question Number	Correct Answer	Right	Wrong
1	D	___	___	26	A	___	___
2	C	___	___	27	B	___	___
3	E	___	___	28	D	___	___
4	A	___	___	29	D	___	___
5	B	___	___	30	B	___	___
6	D	___	___	31	E	___	___
7	E	___	___	32	D	___	___
8	B	___	___	33	B	___	___
9	B	___	___	34	E	___	___
10	A	___	___	35	B	___	___
11	B	___	___	36	A	___	___
12	D	___	___	37	C	___	___
13	E	___	___	38	C	___	___
14	C	___	___	39	C	___	___
15	A	___	___	40	A	___	___
16	D	___	___	41	D	___	___
17	E	___	___	42	A	___	___
18	A	___	___	43	A	___	___
19	B	___	___	44	E	___	___
20	E	___	___	45	C	___	___
21	C	___	___	46	B	___	___
22	C	___	___	47	C	___	___
23	E	___	___	48	C	___	___
24	D	___	___	49	E	___	___
25	C	___	___	50	A	___	___

PRACTICE TEST 2 EXPLANATIONS

1. **D** All three people weigh 410 pounds, but Rob and Sherry weigh 300 pounds; therefore, Heather must weigh 410 − 300 = 110 pounds. Because Sherry and Heather weigh 240 pounds, Sherry must weigh 240 − 110 = 130 pounds. If you don't want to handle the question this way, you can simply PITA. That means starting with (C) and using the answer choices as Sherry's weight. For example, if Sherry's weight is 120 pounds, that makes Rob's weight 180 pounds and Heather's weight 120 pounds. Those three weights don't add up to 410 pounds, so move on and try the next answer choice. Choice (D) works.

2. **C** Draw a rough sketch:

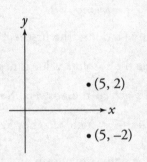

   The point (5, 2) is 2 units above the *x*-axis, so its reflection will be 2 units below the *x*-axis. Reflecting the point across the *x*-axis keeps the *x*-coordinate the same but changes the sign of the *y*-coordinate.

3. **E** This is just Plugging In. Plug the values given for *r* and *s* into the equation.

$$\frac{s}{r} + \frac{4}{r^2} =$$

$$\frac{6}{\frac{2}{3}} + \frac{4}{\left(\frac{2}{3}\right)^2} =$$

$$\frac{6}{\frac{2}{3}} + \frac{4}{\frac{4}{9}} =$$

$$\left(6 \times \frac{3}{2}\right) + \left(4 \times \frac{9}{4}\right) =$$

$$\frac{18}{2} + \frac{36}{4} = 9 + 9 = 18$$

4.   A   You're given variables and no numbers, so Plug In. Suppose $p = 60$. The other two interior angles of the triangle must then add up to 120°. For now, Plug In 50 and 70, making the angle above n a 50° angle, and the angle above m a 70° angle. Then, because there are 180° in a straight line, you know that $n = 130$ and $m = 110$. Now that you have values for each of the variables, you can go to the answer choices and see which one works. You're looking for the answer choice that is equal to p, or 60. Only (A) works, and that's the correct answer.

5.   B   You've got variables in the question and the answer choices, so Plug In. Suppose that you're traveling 5 miles ($b = 5$). That means that your fare will include an original $2.50 plus five $0.30 charges ($1.50) for each of the 5 miles traveled (which is $7.50), for a total of $10.00. To find the correct answer, plug $b = 5$ into the answer choices and see which one gives you a value of 10. Only (B) does the trick.

6.   D   You have to set up two different equations. The first is if what's in the absolute value is nonnegative, and the other if what's inside the absolute value is negative. The first equation is $y - 3 = 4y - 7$, which simplifies to $y = \dfrac{4}{3}$. That's not in the answers. So set up the second equation: $-(y - 3) = 4y - 7$. This simplifies to $3 - y = 4y - 7$, which becomes $5y = 10$ and $y = 2$.

7.   E   You may recognize that this is the point-slope form and that the slope is $\dfrac{5}{4}$. If you don't see that, rewrite the equation into slope-intercept form.

8.   B   Substitute for a and b. So $a^2 + b^2 = \cos^2\theta + \sin^2\theta$. You know the identity $\cos^2\theta + \sin^2\theta = 1$, so the answer is (B).

9.   B   A friendly reminder—the perimeter is what you get when you add up all a polygon's sides. The most common careless mistake on perimeter questions is to calculate the area instead, as in (E).

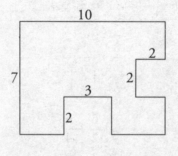

Figure 2

In the end, this is a simple addition question. The polygon can be seen as a 7 × 10 rectangle with two notches cut into it. The notches add to the polygon's perimeter, but figuring out how much they add is the tricky part. A plain 7 × 10 rectangle has a perimeter of 34. The notch cut into the bottom of this rectangle adds 4 units to this perimeter, not 7. The three horizontal segments on the bottom of the figure must still add up to 10, the length of the rectangle; only the vertical segments add length. In the same way, the notch cut into the right side of the rectangle adds 4 units of length, not 6, because the vertical sides must still add up to 7, the rectangle's height; only the horizontal segments add length. The total perimeter is 34 + 4 + 4, or 42.

10. **A** The thing to be careful about here is taking the absolute value at the right time. To find $|x + y|$, you have to add x and y together first, and then take the absolute value. If you take the absolute value of each quantity before adding, you're likely to get a wrong answer. The only pair of coordinates whose sum has an absolute value greater than 5 is (A), because $-4 + -2 = -6$, and $|-6| = 6$.

11. **B** Keri sold more than 300 units in only four months in 1996: March, August, September, and December. That means four bonuses, for a total of $4,000.00.

12. **D** The trick here is to remember the bonuses. In the 3-month periods shown in (A), (B), and (E), Keri sold 1,000 units, earning $10,000 in commissions. Each 3-month period also includes one bonus, raising her income for that period to $11,000.00. In the 3-month period shown in (D), however, Keri earns more. She sells 950 units, earning $9,500.00 in commissions, and also receives two bonuses, for a total of $11,500.00.

13. **E** Set up a proportion: $\dfrac{14}{2^2} = \dfrac{a}{5^2}$. Simplify: $4a = 350$, and $a = 87.5$. You can also approximate. When b goes up, a goes up. So you can eliminate (A) and (B).

14. **C** It's algebra time. Whenever two fractions are equal, you can cross-multiply.

$$\frac{1}{x} = \frac{4}{5}$$

$$4x = 5$$

$$x = \frac{5}{4}$$

You're not done when you've solved for x, though. The question asks not for x, but for $\dfrac{x}{3}$. To produce the right answer, you have to divide by 3.

$$x = \frac{5}{4}$$

$$\frac{x}{3} = \frac{5}{12} = 0.41666\ldots$$

15. **A** The four right triangles inside the quadrilateral are congruent; they have legs and hypotenuses of equal length. The exact lengths of the segments don't matter. For convenience's sake, you can plug in values for the lengths. Suppose that the right triangles are all 3-4-5 triangles. That makes the hypotenuses 5.

The value of $\sin \angle RSU$, according to SOHCAHTOA, will now be $\dfrac{3}{5}$. The correct answer choice will be the one that also equals $\dfrac{3}{5}$. Choice (A) is correct.

16. **D** There are two common sorts of nonreal numbers that are important on the SAT Subject Test in Math 1. These are the square roots of negative numbers (imaginary numbers) and numbers divided by zero (undefined). The expression $\sqrt{x} + \dfrac{1}{x-3}$ will therefore be real only if x is zero or greater (so that the quantity under the radical isn't negative) and only if x doesn't equal 3 (so that the fraction's denominator isn't zero). You can see that x doesn't have to be greater than 1 ($x = 0$ is allowed, for example), so Statement I is out. This allows you to eliminate (A), (C), and (E). Statement II is definitely true because it is in both remaining answer choices. Statement III must also be true, since x must be greater than or equal to zero. The correct answer is (D).

17. **E** Always sketch situations that are described but not shown. Here's the situation described in the question:

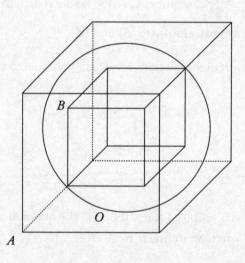

Cube A is the outermost shape. Sphere O is inscribed inside it, and cube B is then inscribed within the sphere. You can use this simple sketch to check your answer choices. As you can see from your sketch, one edge of A is equal in length to the diameter of O, which in turn is equal to the diagonal of B. The correct answer is (E).

18.   **A**   This is a fancy simultaneous-equations question. It's impossible to solve for the value of x, y, or z, but you can find the value of their sum. It's done by adding the equations, like

$$a - x = 12$$
$$b - y = 7$$
$$c - z = 15$$
$$\overline{a + b + c - x - y - z = 34}$$

This equation can be written as $(a + b + c) - (x + y + z) = 34$. And since the question tells you that $a + b + c = 50$, you can simplify the equation even further:

$$50 - (x + y + z) = 34$$

$$-(x + y + z) = -16$$

$$x + y + z = 16$$

19.   **B**   Since Cassie's stuck in the driver's seat, the number of permutations of the people in the car is simply determined by the possible arrangements of passengers in the 3 passengers' seats. The number of permutations of 3 items in 3 spaces is given by 3!, which equals $3 \times 2 \times 1$, or 6.

20.   **E**   PITA. See which value of x in the answer choices makes the equation true. It's (E).

21.   **C**   Remember that slope is equal to "rise" over "run." A line that has a slope greater than 1 is changing vertically (along the y-axis) faster than it's changing horizontally (along the x-axis). Line l might look like

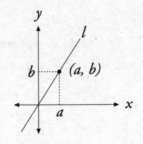

As you can see, a and b don't have to be equal—in fact, they can't be. You can also see that a doesn't have to be less than b—a will be less than b when they're both positive, but b will be less than a when they're negative. Of all the statements in the answer choices, only (C) must be true. Since b is always farther from zero than a, its square will always be greater than the square of a.

22.   C

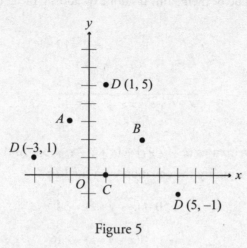

Figure 5

This one is a little tricky. The best way to approach it is by experimenting with sketches. If you examine the possibilities carefully, you'll see that there are three possible locations of the missing vertex.

23.   E   PITA works well on this one. Just take the values of x from the answer choices and fill in the values for the other angles using the formulas $y = \dfrac{2}{3}x$ and $w = 2z$. You'll know you've got the right answer when the values produced obey the Rule of 180°. If $x = 72$, then $y = \dfrac{2}{3}(72)$, or 48. The sum of x and y is then 120, which means that $w = 120$, since it's a vertical angle. The equation $w = 2z$ gives you $z = 60$. If you check all those numbers against the Rule of 180°, you'll see that (E) is the correct answer.

24.   D   The new radius of circle O is $(r + t)$. To find the circle's area, just plug this quantity into the formula for the area of a circle, $A = \pi r^2$. To do this, you'll need to use FOIL.

$$A = \pi(r + t)^2$$

$$A = \pi(r^2 + rt + rt + t^2)$$

$$A = \pi(r^2 + 2rt + t^2)$$

Alternately, you could plug in something like $r = 5$ and $t = 3$. The new radius is 8, making your target answer $\pi(8)^2$ or 64π. Only (D) works.

25. **C** You can find the radius of the circle from the area you're given, just by plugging the area into the formula and solving.

$$A = \pi r^2$$

$$\pi r^2 = 9\pi$$

$$r^2 = 9$$

$$r = 3$$

Because OA and OB are both radii, each must have a length of 3. And because they're perpendicular, they must be legs of an isosceles right triangle. That means that $\triangle ABO$ has angles measuring $45°$, $45°$, and $90°$, and must therefore have sides in the ratio $1{:}1{:}\sqrt{2}$. The length of the hypotenuse, AB, is simply $3\sqrt{2}$, or 4.24.

26. **A** Solving $x^2 + 2x - 3 = 0$ is just a matter of factoring.

$$x^2 + 2x - 3 = 0$$

$$(x - 1)(x + 3) = 0$$

$$x = -3, 1$$

The funny looking equation $x < |x|$, however, tells you that x is negative. That means that x can only equal -3. To find the answer, just plug $x = -3$ into the expression $2x + 4$.

$$2(-3) + 4 = -6 + 4 = -2$$

27. **B** The corresponding parts of similar triangles are proportional. To figure out a value in one triangle from the corresponding value in the other, you need to know what the proportion is. Luckily, this question gives you the hypotenuse of both triangles—5 and 4, respectively. This allows you to set up this proportion.

$$\frac{\text{any part of } \triangle ABC}{\text{the matching part of } \triangle CBD} = \frac{5}{4}$$

To find the area of $\triangle CBD$, you'll need to know the lengths of both of its legs. Use the proportion to find these lengths from the legs of the larger triangle. First, find the longer leg, BD:

$$\frac{4}{BD} = \frac{5}{4}$$

$$5BD = 16$$

$$BD = \frac{16}{5} = 3.2$$

Then, find CD:

$$\frac{3}{CD} = \frac{5}{4}$$

$$5CD = 12$$

$$CD = \frac{12}{5} = 2.4$$

Once you know that $\triangle CBD$ is a right triangle with legs 2.4 and 3.2, all you have to do is plug these lengths into the area formula for triangles.

$$A = \frac{1}{2}bh$$

$$A = \frac{1}{2}(2.4)(3.2)$$

$$A = 3.84$$

28. **D** For this question, you need to remember how FOIL works, and that i^2 can be replaced by −1.

$$(5 - 3i)(4 + 2i) =$$

$$20 + 10i - 12i - 6i^2 =$$

$$20 - 2i - 6i^2 =$$

$$20 - 2i - 6(-1) =$$

$$20 + 6 - 2i =$$

$$26 - 2i$$

29. **D** PITA. Plug each answer choice into the function for x, to see which one spits out −4. Choice (D) works, because $f(1) = (1)^2 - 5(1) = 1 - 5 = -4$.

30. **B** It's a good idea to sketch the situation that's described in this question:

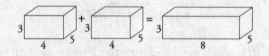

As you can see, only one dimension of this solid is doubled. It's now a rectangular solid of dimensions $3 \times 5 \times 8$. The longest segment that can be drawn within this solid is the long diagonal, which can be found using the Super Pythagorean Theorem.

$$d^2 = a^2 + b^2 + c^2$$

$$d^2 = 3^2 + 5^2 + 8^2$$

$$d^2 = 9 + 25 + 64$$

$$d^2 = 98$$

$$d = \sqrt{98} = 9.899$$

The correct answer is (B).

31. **E** Type this into your calculator, being careful to use parentheses. You should get either 3025000000 or something like 3.025e9. To get 3025000000 into scientific notation, you need to move the decimal point 9 places to the left, which means your power of 10 will be 9; pick (E).

32. **D** The probabilities must add up to 1; the probabilities shown in the table add up to $\frac{5}{8}$, so n must be $\frac{3}{8}$.

33. **B** Don't let all the scientific talk scare you. All you're being asked to do is find the value of t for which $n = 500$. To do that, just PITA. Plug each answer choice in for t, to see which one makes $n = 500$. Choice (B) works.

34. **E** Perpendicular lines have opposite reciprocal slopes. That means that if line m has a slope of $-\frac{1}{2}$, line l, which is perpendicular to it, must have a slope of 2. That alone lets you eliminate the equations in (A), (B), and (C), all of which have the wrong slope. So the answer must be (D) or (E). Since the point (4, 5) is on the line you're looking for, you can plug that point in for (x, y) in the equation of a line to see whether it makes the equation true. If you plug (4, 5) into (D), you get $5 = 2(4) - 1$, which is wrong. Cross off (D) and choose (E).

35. **B** For this question, it's important to remember the difference between central angles and inscribed angles. Central angles, like $\angle AOB$ and $\angle BOC$, are like pie slices that start at the circle's center. The arcs they intercept are equal in measure to the angles themselves. Inscribed angles, on the other hand, start on the edge of the circle, like $\angle BDA$ and $\angle CAD$. The arcs they intercept are twice as great in measure as the angles themselves.

Since $\angle BDA$ is an inscribed angle measuring 25°, the arc it intercepts, AB, must measure 50°. For the same reason, the arc intercepted by $\angle BDA$ must measure 64°. That's a total of 114° out of the semicircle $ABCD$, which leaves 66° out of the 180° half-circle. That's the measure of arc BC. Since arc BC measures 66°, the central angle BOC must also measure 66°. The correct answer is (B).

36. **A** This question tests your understanding of exponent rules. You're told that $4^{x+2} = 48$, but how do you solve for 4^x? Remember that when you multiply exponential terms that have a common base, you add the exponents. In the same way, you can express addition in an exponent as multiplication.

$$4^{x+2} = 48$$

$$4^x \times 4^2 = 48$$

Once you've taken this step, solving is easy.

$$4^x \times 16 = 48$$

$$4^x = 3$$

37.　**C**　Just plug in a number for x. If $x = 2$, the problem reads $r(2) = 17$ and $s(r(2)) = 3$. But that means you can substitute 17 for $r(2)$ in the second equation, so you know that $s(17) = 3$. Since the problem is asking for $s(17)$, and 3 is your target number, plug in 17 for x in the answer choices, to see which answer choice hits 3. Only (C) works.

38.　**C**　Use the Group Problem Formula, Total = Group 1 + Group 2 + Neither − Both. Here, you've got 850 = 250 + 450 + 350 − Both. So Both = 200. Pick (C). You need to memorize this formula!

39.　**C**　Rearrange the equation to read $9^n = 27$, then change each base to 3: $(3^2)^n = 3^3$. So $3^{2n} = 3^3$, which means that the exponents are equal: $2n = 3$. Therefore, $n = \dfrac{3}{2}$.

40.　**A**　The cylindrical cup has a radius of 2 and a height of 3. Its volume, given by $V = \pi r^2 h$, is $\pi(2)^2(3)$, or 12π. The volume of the rectangular tank, given by $V = lwh$, is $6 \times 7 \times 8$, or 336. To find out how many times the cup can be filled completely from the tank, just divide 336 by 12π using your calculator:

$$\frac{336}{12\pi} = 8.913$$

As you can see, the cup can be filled almost 9 times, but can be filled *completely* only 8 times. The correct answer is (A).

41.　**D**　Always sketch situations that are described but not shown. The situation described in this question would look something like this:

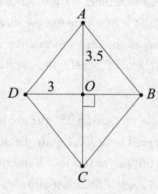

Segments AC and BD form right angles, and each cuts the other exactly in half. Segments BO and DO have lengths of 3, and segments AO and CO have lengths of 3.5. If you sketch segments AB, BC, CD, and DA, then you have four identical right triangles. You can use the Pythagorean Theorem to find the length of each hypotenuse.

$$a^2 + b^2 = c^2$$

$$3^2 + 3.5^2 = c^2$$

$$9 + 12.25 = c^2$$

$$21.25 = c^2$$

$$c = 4.61$$

When you know the lengths of each side, you can use SOHCAHTOA to figure out the value of $\sin \angle ADO$. The side opposite $\angle ADO$ is AO, and the hypotenuse is AD. You can use the lengths of these segments to find the value of the trig function.

$$\text{sine} = \frac{\text{opposite}}{\text{hypotenuse}}$$

$$\sin \angle ADO = \frac{AO}{AD}$$

$$\sin \angle ADO = \frac{3.5}{4.61} = 0.76$$

42. **A** The interquartile range is the difference between the third quartile and the first quartile; put simply, it's the width of the entire box in the middle of the boxplot. Choice (A) has an interquartile range of $70 - 10 = 60$; no other choice comes close.

43. **A** Plugging In can work wonders for you on this one. The constant k can be anything. Let's say it equals 3. If that's the case, $f(x) = 3x$, and $g(x) = x + 3$. Using these values makes it easy to plug into the function to test each of the three statements.

Suppose $x = 2$, take a look at Statement I. Using your values, you can plug into the statement to see whether it must be true.

$$f(2x) = 2f(x)$$

$$f(4) = 2f(2)$$

$$3 \times 4 = 2(3 \times 2)$$

$$12 = 12$$

Statement I works so far, so keep it and move on. Here's how Statement II looks with the values plugged into it.

$$f(x + 2) = f(x) + 2$$

$$f(4) = f(2) + 2$$

$$3 \times 4 = (3 \times 2) + 2$$

$$12 = 8$$

Statement II is definitely NOT true, so you can eliminate it. That gets rid of (B), (C), and (E), leaving only (A) and (D). Since Statement I is present in both answers, you can forget about it. To pick the right answer, you need to check out Statement III.

$$f(g(x)) = g(f(x))$$

$$f(g(2)) = g(f(2))$$

$$f(2 + 3) = g(3 \times 2)$$

$$f(5) = g(6)$$

$$3 \times 5 = 6 + 3$$

$$15 = 9$$

Statement III definitely isn't true either, so you can get rid of it. That eliminates (D), leaving only (A).

44. **E**   This is a Pythagorean Theorem question disguised by a complicated physical description. Making a sketch of the southern wall can help clear this up.

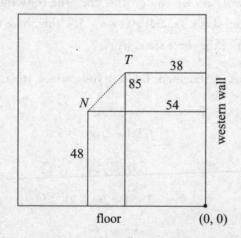

As you can see, the nail and tack can be viewed as points on a coordinate plane. The coordinates of the points are given by their distances from the floor and the western wall. The coordinates of the tack are (–38, 85), and the coordinates of the nail are (–54, 48). These are larger coordinates than you're used to working with, but you can work with them normally. To find the distance between the tack and nail, use the distance formula.

$$d = \sqrt{\left(y_2 - y_1\right)^2 + \left(x_2 - x_1\right)^2}$$

$$d = \sqrt{\left(48 - 85\right)^2 + \left(-54 - \left(-38\right)\right)^2}$$

$$d = \sqrt{\left(-37\right)^2 + \left(-16\right)^2}$$

$$d = \sqrt{1369 + 256}$$

$$d = \sqrt{1625}$$

$$d = 40.31$$

45. **C** The domain of the function $f(x)$ is the set of values that you're allowed to plug into the function in the x position. The only numbers not in a function's domain are those that make the function produce nonreal numbers—that is, fractions with zero in the denominator and even roots of negative numbers. There are no fractions in this function, so any values not in the domain of f will be those that make the square root negative.

For $\sqrt{12 - x^2}$ to be a real number, the quantity under the radical, $12 - x^2$, must be zero or positive. To find the values of x that make $f(x)$ real, just write that as an inequality, and solve.

$$12 - x^2 \geq 0$$

$$-x^2 \geq -12$$

$$x^2 \leq 12$$

$$-\sqrt{12} \leq x \leq \sqrt{12}$$

This is the domain of $f(x)$. The correct answer is (C). You could also PITA. Just pick numbers that are in some of the ranges in the answer choices, but not others, and plug them into the function to see if they work.

46. **B** The basic rule of logic most commonly tested on the SAT Subject Test in Math 1 is the contrapositive. When you see any statement in the form "If A, then B," then you automatically know that the statement "If not B, then not A" is also true. That's the contrapositive statement. In this case, you're given the statement "If a tree falls in the forest, a sound is heard." The contrapositive of this statement is, "If no sound is heard, a tree doesn't fall in the forest."

The question asks you to pick the logically impossible answer choice. That will be a statement that contradicts either the original statement or the contrapositive of the original statement. Choice (B) is directly opposed to the contrapositive.

47.   **C**   The first couple must compete against 5 couples. The second couple has already faced the first couple, so they have to compete against only four new couples. The third couple has to compete against three new couples, and so on. This means that to make sure everyone competes in a dance-off with everyone else, there have to be 5 + 4 + 3 + 2 + 1 = 15 dance-offs. Multiply 15 by the 3 times this must happen, and you get 45.

48.   **C**

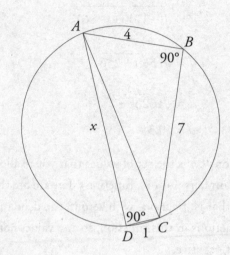

Figure 10

If you draw diameter *AC*, you divide the quadrilateral *ABCD* into two triangles. Both $\angle ADC$ and $\angle ABC$ are inscribed angles that intercept a half-circle, or an arc of 180°. Since inscribed angles intercept arcs that have twice the measure of the angles themselves, that means that both $\angle ADC$ and $\angle ABC$ are 90° angles and that, therefore, $\triangle ADC$ and $\triangle ABC$ are right triangles that share a hypotenuse. This hypotenuse is the key to finding the length of segment *AD*.

Because you know the lengths of the legs of right triangle *ABC* (*AB* = 4 and *BC* = 7), you can use the Pythagorean Theorem to find the hypotenuse's length: $4^2 + 7^2 = c^2$. So $c = \sqrt{65}$. Once you know that the hypotenuse of both triangles has a length of $\sqrt{65}$, you can use the Pythagorean Theorem again to find the length of the missing leg of the other right triangle.

$$1^2 + x^2 = \left(\sqrt{65}\right)^2$$

$$1 + x^2 = 65$$

$$x^2 = 64$$

$$x = 8$$

The segment *AD* must therefore have a length of 8. The correct answer is (C).

49. **E** The segment from (0, 0) to (–2, 2) has a length of $2\sqrt{2}$, or 2.83 (you can think of it as the diagonal of a square with sides 2 units long, or the hypotenuse of a 45°-45°-90° triangle). If you sketch this line segment, you'll see that there are two possible locations for the third vertex of an equilateral triangle constructed from that segment.

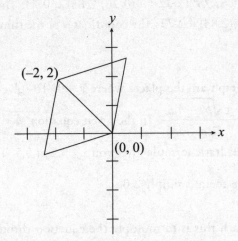

Before you start doing more complicated calculations, make the best sketch you can of the situation that's described. You may find that you can eliminate a few answer choices just by looking at your sketch and guesstimating. On this question, if you can draw the figure accurately, the answer is obviously (E).

If not, there are a couple of ways to find the coordinates of these vertices, but the simplest way is to use trigonometry. Start with the upper vertex. Draw an altitude from this point to the x-axis to produce a right triangle.

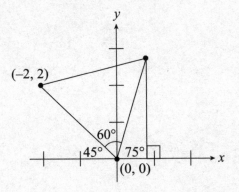

Since the hypotenuse of this triangle is one side of the equilateral triangle, you know it has a length of $2\sqrt{2}$, or 2.83. The Rule of 180° also lets you figure out the measure of the lower acute angle in this right triangle. It must measure 75°, since it forms a straight line with the 45° and 60° angles. All you need to find the coordinates of the third vertex are the legs of this right triangle. Trigonometry is the easiest way to find them. The length of the horizontal leg, adjacent to the 75° angle, will be $(\cos 75°)(2\sqrt{2}) = (0.26)(2.83) = 0.73$. The length of the vertical leg will be $(\sin 75°)(2\sqrt{2}) = (0.97)(2.83) = 2.73$. The coordinates of the third vertex in this position will therefore be (0.73, 2.73).

50. **A** The x-intercepts of a graph are the places where $y = 0$. To solve $0 = x^2 - 9x + 19.25$, use the quadratic formula, $x = \dfrac{-b \pm \sqrt{b^2 - 4ac}}{2a}$. In the given equation, $a = 1$, $b = -9$, and $c = 19.25$. Plugging these values into the quadratic formula gives you $x = 3.5$ or 5.5. These points are both on the x-axis, so the distance between them is simply 2.0.

Another way to approach this is to multiply the equation through by 4 to clear out the decimal, and then factor. You get $0 = 4x^2 - 36x + 77$, which factors to $0 = (2x - 7)(2x - 11)$. This makes the x-intercepts $\dfrac{7}{2}$ and $\dfrac{11}{2}$; their difference is 2. Perhaps the quickest method would be to graph $y = x^2 - 9x + 19.25$ on your calculator and see where the graph crosses the x-axis.

HOW TO SCORE
PRACTICE TEST 2

When you take the real exam, the proctors will collect your test booklet and bubble sheet and send your bubble sheet to a processing center where a computer looks at the pattern of filled-in ovals on your bubble sheet and gives you a score. We couldn't include even a small computer with this book, so we are providing this more primitive way of scoring your exam. (For a printable bubble sheet, check your online student tools.)

Determining Your Score

STEP 1   Using the answer key, determine how many questions you got right and how many you got wrong on the test. Remember: Questions that you do not answer don't count as either right answers or wrong answers.

STEP 2   List the number of right answers here.

(A) _____

STEP 3   List the number of wrong answers here. Now divide that number by 4. (Use a calculator if you're feeling particularly lazy.)

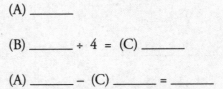

(B) _____ ÷ 4 = (C) _____

(A) _____ − (C) _____ = _____

STEP 4   Subtract the number of wrong answers divided by 4 from the number of correct answers. Round this score to the nearest whole number. This is your raw score.

STEP 5   To determine your real score, take the number from Step 4 and look it up in the left column of the Score Conversion Table on the next page; the corresponding score on the right is your score on the exam.

PRACTICE TEST 2
SCORE CONVERSION TABLE

Raw Score	Scaled Score	Raw Score	Scaled Score	Raw Score	Scaled Score
50	800	25	530	0	330
49	780	24	520	−1	320
48	770	23	510	−2	310
47	760	22	510	−3	300
46	740	21	500	−4	300
45	730	20	490	−5	290
44	720	19	480	−6	280
43	710	18	480	−7	270
42	700	17	470	−8	260
41	690	16	460	−9	260
40	680	15	450	−10	250
39	670	14	440	−11	240
38	660	13	430	−12	230
37	650	12	430		
36	640	11	420		
35	630	10	410		
34	610	9	400		
33	600	8	390		
32	590	7	380		
31	580	6	370		
30	570	5	370		
29	560	4	360		
28	550	3	350		
27	550	2	340		
26	540	1	340		